W9-AUT-769

NOBODY SPE

*Self-Portraits of
American Working Class Women*

AKS FOR ME!

NANCY SEIFER

SIMON AND SCHUSTER • NEW YORK

Copyright © 1976 by Nancy Seifer
All rights reserved
including the right of reproduction
in whole or in part in any form
Published by Simon and Schuster
A Gulf+Western Company
Rockefeller Center, 630 Fifth Avenue
New York, New York 10020
Designed by Edith Fowler
Manufactured in the United States of America
1 2 3 4 5 6 7 8 9 10

Library of Congress Cataloging in Publication Data

Seifer, Nancy.
   Nobody speaks for me!

   1. Women—United States—Biography.   2. Labor and
laboring classes—United States.   I. Title.
HQ1412.S44   301.41'2'0973   76-11836
ISBN 0-671-22308-9

Acknowledgments

For helping me to meet and learn about most of the women in this book I especially want to thank: Armando Canava, Mary Jean Collins-Robson, Kay Eisenhower, Linda Garcia Gutiérrez, Betty Heiss, Valentine Hertz, Chris Hintz, Judy Jager, Maxine Jenkins, Happy Lee, Ann Lewis and Jerry Marcinowski.

Thanks to my friends and family for all of their encouragement, enthusiasm and support, and especially for their understanding of my preoccupation with "my project" during most free hours over the past year and a half.

Most of all, I want to express my gratitude to Richard Robertiello, Alice Kossoff, Irving Levine, Wendy Weil, Suzanne Schmill, Barbara Peters and Lucy Komisar, each of whom—in a very special way—helped make it possible for this book to come into being.

To the women in this book
and to others like them

Contents

Preface   11
Introduction   27

TAKING CARE OF THE NEIGHBORHOOD   39

Mary Sansone   40

Unusual Origins on Brooklyn's Henry Street · The Most
Difficult Change: Marriage and Motherhood · Up from
the Basement: The Congress of Italian-American Organizations · A Lifetime of Fighting Pays Off · Postscript

Janice Bernstein   88

The Splendors of Boston's Blue Hill Avenue · Redlining
and Blockbusting · Everyone Loses Except the Banks ·
If the Book Sells . . . . · Postscript

WOMEN HELPING WOMEN   135

Dorothy Bolden   136

Forty-two Years a Maid, Starting at Nine in Atlanta ·
Early Stirrings of the Civil Rights Movement · National
Domestic Workers, Inc. · Politics, Poverty, and Too
Little Love · Postscript

Betty Gagne   178

Iowa's Farmlands to Washington, D.C. · Chicago's
Southwest Side—Before and After the Civil Rights
Marches · Back to Work, Seven Children and Twenty-
eight Years Later · Women's Health in a Working Class
Neighborhood · Postscript

JOINING THE RANKS: UNIONISM AND FEMINISM   219

Cathy Tuley   220

Missouri to Married Life in California · Organizing Clerks in Alameda County · Tom Tuley on His Wife's Changing Role · Struggling for Equality · Postscript

Bonnie Halascsak   258

Never at Home in Small Town Indiana · U.S. Steel's First Woman Security Guard · Steelworkers NOW · A Commitment to Change · Postscript

PRACTICAL POLITICS   297

Rosalinda Rodriguez   298

A Family of Migrant Workers · Marriage and Chicano Politics · Roy Rodriguez Talks about the Raza Unida Party · Frustrations and Challenges of a City Councilwoman · Postscript

Anita Cupps   344

Rural Alabaman Roots · Anita and Johnny Cupps on Coal Mining Politics · Anita and Chris Hintz on Alabama Women for Human Rights · New Perspectives · Postscript

LISTENING TO EACH OTHER ACROSS CLASS LINES   387

Ann Winans   388

Ghetto to Ghetto in Minneapolis · Married Woman, Working Mother · A Cycle of Misery On and Off the Job · A University Environment, the Women's Movement: New Options · Postscript

Terry Dezso   438

Growing Up French and Catholic in Woonsocket, Rhode Island · Marriage, Nine Children, Divorce · Help from the Mothers' Group: Reminiscing with Nancy Chance · A Whole New Life: Teacher, College Student, New Marriage · Postscript

Preface

I do have more hope now. I've seen that there are others concerned and I think this is the problem of the Silent Majority today. They feel they're alone. And yet when we get together, we can do a lot.

Bonnie Halascsak

When you compare with other women, things that they went through and things they had done, you realize that you're not fighting a losing battle by yourself. You start feeling that it can be won, so it gives you a lot of hope.

Anita Cupps

The phantom of the Silent Majority appeared suddenly on the American scene in the wake of the turbulent din of the mid-1960's. After years of strident protest movements, unrelenting attacks on "the System," and sweeping demands for change, it seemed welcome in many quarters as a portent of a new, more pacific reality. The more tangible reality—that of a nation convulsed by social upheaval—was, perhaps, a mass media exaggeration or a jarring moment in our history that would now fade into oblivion.

The legitimacy that this new illusion quickly gained was, in retrospect, one of the shrewder Nixonian coups. The President and his public relations team managed to convince a significant portion of the electorate that the "silence" of the majority was in direct proportion to its approval of him and of his leadership. Only the "radical fringe," the "professional protestors," were unhappy with his policies. Hadn't he quelled the mass protests that drove Lyndon Johnson from office? Hadn't he been reelected by an overwhelming majority in 1972?

At the same time as the label "Silent Majority" gained currency, another chimeric population was discovered—the Middle Americans. Amorphous and undefinable, Middle Americans and the Silent Majority became virtually undistinguishable. What they shared, it seemed, was support of Richard Nixon and of the status quo. Nixon thoroughly identified with his illusory creations. He saw in them the backbone of the nation—hard-working, patriotic, responsible, God-fearing, law-abiding people. They lived the life that he had been born into.

Like the Silent Majority, Middle Americans were for law and order, free enterprise and a reduction of government spending and of "big" government in general, with the exception of the military. The phrase conjured up images of farmers sweating out in the sweeping plains of the Midwest and factory workers grinding out an honest day's labor, the first asking only to be left alone to get their crops off to market, the second to get their automobiles off the assembly line—both striving to provide for their families and lead clean, decent, church-going lives.

These legends dominated the conservative politics of the early 1970's, until Watergate, our belated and ignominious departure from Vietnam and the disastrous impact of the economic downturn spelled sudden death for the latest American myths. Horatio Alger, fair play and two cars in every garage finally bit the dust. As our national self-image was shattered, those who had been dubbed the Silent Majority and the Middle Americans were asking questions and looking for answers along with everybody else.

The myth of the Silent Majority died hard. It had been manufactured and packaged for marketing so skillfully that few of us had stopped to question its legitimacy. Surely, silence can be as much a sign of disapproval as of approval. It can denote passive acceptance. Or it can quite simply represent the absence of a voice, or of a means of making one's voice heard. From where I was sitting in the late 1960's, I began to perceive that the Silent Majority was voiceless but not out of choice.

There were growing signs of frustration from working class people, who numerically comprise the majority of Americans, as defined by income, level of education and type of job (although the term "working class" has also at times been used interchangeably with Middle America and the Silent Majority). The anger seemed to stem from two sources, conflicting at times: an inability of most working class people to make their voices heard publicly on major issues and an uneasy feeling that they were not well-informed enough to do so.

In New York City, that kind of frustration climaxed dramatically in an outburst of violence on May 12, 1970, when thousands of construction workers walked off their jobs to "knock heads" with largely young anti-war protestors on Wall Street. As they lined up ten or twelve abreast in the side streets adjoining City Hall, wearing orange hard hats and carrying clusters of American flags, they chanted angrily and carried placards which read "All the way, U.S.A.–love it or leave it." It was a chilling spectacle. On one level it looked as though the question of the legitimacy of the United States' presence in Vietnam was about to be fought out on Wall Street by young kids and grown men. But on another level, it was a battle that had to do with the guts of our changing society.

Many of us can point to a moment in our lives when long-held values and beliefs are shattered in a flash of new insight. Suddenly, the world is seen from a different perspective. One loses the capacity to think in simple black and white terms and becomes immersed in a sea of varying shades of gray. Good and evil give way to the complexities inherent in all moral problems. That May day in 1970 was such a moment for me.

I was twenty-six years old, an employee of Mayor John Lindsay's administration. Like most of my colleagues, I was a classic middle class liberal. We were working for a man who was the essence of the 1960's political liberal–an advocate of the poor, the black, the disadvantaged. There was an air of righteousness around City Hall in those days. We, those who were sympathetic to our conception of social progress and the disadvantaged constituencies were the "good guys." The hard hats, symbolic of those whom we regarded as obstacles to achieving our goals, were the "bad guys."

I had arrived at that stage logically enough. Like many Jewish middle class kids of my generation, I grew up in relative affluence, first in a Long Island suburb and then in Chicago. Since on the whole I lived much as those around me did, I didn't feel particularly privileged. Still, there were reminders from parents of how fortunate we were compared to the rest of

the country, and to the rest of the world. Underlying those reminders was the unspoken fear that our good fortune might
well be tenuous.

In spite of the tangible success of many Jews who came to
this country at the turn of the century, there was the memory,
even in my young unformed consciousness, that millions of
people had been exterminated not very long before because
they were Jewish. Well before I understood the meaning of
the word prejudice, I was aware that some Americans did not
like Jews. I still have a vivid recollection of my friends and I
being chased home from school one day by a group of girls
we'd never seen before who bellowed at us, "You dirty kikes,"
a word I'd never heard.

So there was affluence but there was also latent insecurity.
If there is a formula for producing a middle class Jewish liberal, perhaps that is it. Out of that somewhat contradictory
state, there often grows both a strong identification with the
underdog and the means, or access to the means, to help. Un-
burdened of a daily struggle to provide for basic necessities,
one can afford to be an "idealist."

One of my first memories of the University of Michigan is
of John F. Kennedy, then a candidate for the presidency, an-
nouncing his proposal for a Peace Corps on the steps of the
Student Union. It was a warm September evening in 1960; I
had just begun my freshman year. Most of what Kennedy had
to say got lost in the crunch of the crowd, but that idea sparked
my imagination and I tucked it away.

Those were the years when our country still innocently
thought in terms of an affluence that seemed to know no
bounds. Michael Harrington had discovered the "other America," the America of the poverty-stricken, but the extent of
destitution, illiteracy, malnutrition and despair that existed in
our midst was still a fairly well-kept secret from those among
us who did not live in or near it. We were still "America the
bountiful," and we owed others at least some portion of our
abundance.

When I left the University of Michigan I was formally prepared for but unenthusiastic about the prospect of teaching
high school French. By a stroke of luck, I landed a job at the
Labor Department in Washington in the summer of 1964, as a

secretary-translator for a special economics seminar. Participants came from "underdeveloped" countries in Asia, Africa and Latin America. As I translated the Africans' papers from French to English, I became increasingly fascinated.

That was Lyndon Johnson's first summer in office and, as the foundation for the Great Society was being laid, summer interns in Washington were invited to a series of conferences called White House Seminars. Every two weeks about three thousand college students gathered in a hotel ballroom to listen to Vice President Hubert H. Humphrey, cabinet members, senators or congressmen and ask them some questions. Sargent Shriver was a super-salesman of the Peace Corps. I bought it.

In the fall of 1965 I was on my way to the Ivory Coast, West Africa, along with eleven other volunteers. We had been trained to teach women who had never had any formal schooling in a special program set up by the Ivory Coast government. As "B.A. generalists," the most common species of Peace Corps volunteers at that time, we were experts at little, but we had emerged from a three-month training program with varying degrees of proficiency at teaching subjects ranging from basic French literacy (French had become the Ivory Coast's national language), elementary math and geography to sewing, health care and nutrition.

Those two years were in many ways among the most personally gratifying of my life. And it was an enlightening experience to see my own culture from the perspective of one so vastly different, yet one in which I had grown to feel so much at home. But like tens of thousands of other returned volunteers, I came home feeling that I hadn't quite lived up to my end of the bargain. As trainees, we had come to believe so naively, with an almost religious fervor, that our contributions were in some measurable way going to "help" Africa. The help, of course, was negligible. Our government was exporting youthful American idealism instead of expertise of significant value to developing countries. We were the last to find out.

Though somewhat seasoned, my idealism was largely intact, and my attachment to Africa led me to a job with the African-American Institute in New York City. My responsibility was to organize and administer a leadership training program in community development for a group of African women who had coincidentally been selected from the Ivory Coast that year. They spent two months studying and traveling in the United States. When the program ended, I left the Institute and found a job in city government.

I'd been in New York for a year and a half and I was impressed by what John Lindsay seemed to be trying to accomplish. He was providing a voice for minority groups and he was attracting national attention to the needs of the growing numbers of urban poor. I was enthusiastic about being part of an administration that was working to bring about what I considered to be progressive social change.

After Lindsay's reelection in 1969, I was hired to set up and direct what became the City Hall Neighborhood Press Office. Since the mayor's press secretary was riveted on the three city dailies and the three major networks, there was a communications void with the 150 or so community, ethnic and foreign language weeklies and monthlies. It was the readers of those papers and their neighbors who had come close to defeating Lindsay's bid for reelection. They were largely working class and of white ethnic backgrounds and they perceived him as "the mayor of the blacks and Puerto Ricans" and "the pawn of the limousine liberals." They felt certain he had little, if any interest in them.

We developed a fairly effective communications system with the community weeklies. We read the papers, identified local problems and brought them to the attention of appropriate agencies. We also had a small reportorial staff who addressed press releases to the interests of specific communities. Much of it was clearly a matter of public relations, but it represented a new responsiveness from City Hall and established a greater two-way flow of information.

When it came to the papers that were addressed to specific nationality groups, we were unsure who the readers were, apart from non-English-speaking residents. The papers that were printed in English—like the Irish press, one Greek paper, parts of Armenian, Polish, and other papers—seemed to indicate a great deal of interest in news from the "old country" as well as in local events and individuals who came from the same background. But many had nationwide circulations and it was not clear how the publishers and readers perceived their relationship to the city they lived in.

We went out to interview the editors. One reaction was mild shock. None of them could remember when the city government had shown any interest. As a consequence, there was some suspicion of our motives when we asked about the problems and concerns of their readers in relation to the city. But one response left me dumbfounded. When the editor of a Hungarian paper on the Upper East Side was asked about his readers' local concerns, he replied that they really had none. All around him, the walls of the old neighborhood were tumbling down to make room for new luxury high rises, which the displaced Hungarian residents could never afford to live in. A once-flourishing parish was withering away. The editor commented politely that some extra trashcans would be useful.

It was clear that we were not getting through and that, in all likelihood, the city government and ethnic communities had never communicated in that way. In more prosperous and stable times, ethnic neighborhoods were better able to function as self-contained little islands. The local political machine may have been called upon for an occasional special favor or service, but the community as a whole asked nothing of government.

> I think in general the plight of the working class community is virtually unexplored. . . . They are hard-working people and taxpayers, . . . and it always seems that they have too much to get help from the government and yet they have too little for a lot of the better things. So it's a constant struggle.
>
> *Betty Gagne*

By 1970, urban life was changing dramatically and working class people caught much of the fallout. A pattern of neighborhood devastation at the hands of government and big business was evident in New York and other industrial cities across the country. Appearing older and weather-beaten, stable and viable ethnic neighborhoods were chosen regularly for demolition to make way for cross-town expressways, utilities, industrial parks—"urban renewal."

Banks began the practice of redlining—refusing to make mortgage or home improvement loans in areas they deemed "high risk"—and real estate agents followed with blockbusting, swooping into those areas like vultures, threatening their residents to sell their homes or lose their life savings. City services were declining. Crime and air pollution were rising. Industry was leaving the city, taking thousands of jobs with it. The depressed economy threatened the lives of increasing numbers of families.

At the same time new services and programs were being developed for black and Puerto Rican communities through funds from the War on Poverty. There were community health centers, day care centers, job training programs, small business loans, preschool programs, home repair loans, drug prevention programs, legal aid, scholarships—programs that many working class people needed but were not eligible for. Their incomes were above the official "poverty line."

The need for those kinds of programs and services grew in working class communities. So did their anger that their tax dollars were providing welfare recipients with programs they themselves could not benefit from. With deep pride in their self-sufficiency, many working class men were moonlighting or working overtime and their wives were working as well, just to make ends meet.

In addition to economic and neighborhood issues, there were broader cultural issues. Student demonstrations and campus take-overs seemed to express contempt for what many first- and second-generation working class families wanted most for their children but often could not afford: higher education. Longhairs and flower children with their apparent scorn for material wealth and conventional sexual mores were insulting to their values.

Slogans such as "Black Power" and "Black is Beautiful" threatened their security in the ethnic group pecking order. It hadn't been long since they were the "wops" and "polacks"—close to the bottom but not quite there. Now, in the process of becoming Americanized, they had been turned into the new pariahs—"hard hats," "racists," "pigs."

Every new movement is revolutionized but I think the feminist movement came off too strong. It made a lot of housewives feel so inadequate for staying home and being mothers. Then it began to come off like they were man-haters and anti-family. I think it should have stuck to equal rights and equal pay.

Mary Sansone

Then came the Women's Movement—still another polarizing force, yet another threat to the values and stability of working class people's life-styles. It may have been relatively easy to tune out in the early years, as bizarre as some of the rhetoric may have sounded and the demonstrations may have appeared. But as women began to talk about new options and fulfilling their potential, the movement became increasingly difficult to ignore. And as the economy forced an increasing number of women into the labor force, the movement's implications became even more unsettling to the male breadwinner whose self-esteem derived mainly from that role, and to the woman whose life's commitment was to husband, children and home.

And then there was the Vietnam war. The protest against it came largely from the middle class, whose sons were far less likely to serve in the armed forces than working class boys. Working class people, especially those who were relatively "new" Americans, were often proud to have their sons fight for their country, but their patriotism was linked to another factor, which was poorly understood. The fear of "Commies" was not just reactionary paranoia, as it appeared to some middle class liberals. Many had come to this country, or their parents or grandparents had, to escape Communist rule of what had been their homelands. They were more familiar with the terrors of life behind the Iron Curtain than the kids waving Viet Cong flags, and they knew it.

What happened around City Hall and on Wall Street in May of 1970 came first as a shock. Why would such vast numbers of New York City construction workers take such pains to plan a counterdemonstration against a bunch of kids? What was it that incited men to hurl bricks and rocks at youngsters and even at the police? Why were the attacks against Lindsay so vicious?

My responses to the issues of our times had been as predictable as the sunrise until that day. But after about six months of experience with the ethnic and community press, I was able to see things from a new vantage point. I was jolted out of my complacence, out of a kind of parochial isolation many of us find ourselves in when we surround ourselves with people of like mind.

By that time I had learned something of the alienation of the white working class and of their feelings toward the Lindsay administration. I had some sense of the separateness of the ethnic enclaves in the city and of the whole structure of subcultures that most of us at City Hall had been fairly ignorant of. I had learned something of the values and cultures of people who identified as Italians, Poles, Ukrainians, Irish, Norwegians, Lithuanians, Greeks, Hungarians, Germans and others, at the same time as they identified as American.

New York wasn't just black, Puerto Rican and Jewish ghettos on the one hand and affluent Manhattan on the other. But at City Hall our horizons hadn't yet stretched much farther than that. It was those narrow horizons that almost defeated Lindsay. And it was that coalition of the rich and the poor, the upper middle class liberals and the minority groups, that was at least in part responsible for the Wall Street rage.

The construction workers picked the war as a target, but their feelings of frustration and alienation from the "mainstream" were just as strong, if not stronger, when it came to welfare, special programs for minority groups, the youth culture, the Women's Movement. I began to see that it was a protest against the "counterculture," and a kind of generalized letting off of steam. And, as the picket signs graphically indicated, it was also a protest against the Lindsay administration, which seemed to have sympathy for everyone's problems except the "working man's."

I began to build a case to convince the mayor and his staff that something had to be done to deal with the polarization between groups and to respond to the legitimate needs of working class people. I attended conferences in Washington and New York, where people around the country concerned with these issues had begun to gather to share experiences and plan strategies for change. I spoke with community leaders and a variety of "experts," few as there were at the time, and I read everything I could lay my hands on.

By 1970 the Silent Majority was being alternately labeled by certain writers as the "forgotten majority." Middle Americans were also being called the "Angry Americans," the newest and potentially largest group of protestors. Now, in place of silence, there were wildcat strikes, street demonstrations, and new claims on government and industry to pay attention to their concerns.

Despite the animosity that existed, I believed it was possible for John Lindsay to establish a dialogue with what amounted to the city's largest constituency and that it was the administration's responsibility to reach out to working class communities. A combination of pride in their self-sufficiency and a general distrust of government had tended to block them from seeking help from government. Yet it seemed to be so clearly in everyone's best interest for these communities to develop new organizations able to take advantage of programs like day care and senior citizens' centers, which they generally did not even know they were entitled to, and to be assured of having a voice in decisions regarding the fate of their neighborhoods.

> We get too professional, always dealing with this here paper. Common sense ought to be in print too, but we don't do that.
>
> *Dorothy Bolden*

I continued a memo-writing campaign—our mode of communication at City Hall—for close to a year before I got a skeptical go-ahead. During that time, my consciousness was raised on two fronts. First, I became aware of the extent to which negative stereotypes blinded many middle class professionals to the real needs of working class people and virtually precluded the possibility of any real sympathetic understanding.

I began to see how destructive our own set of prejudices was. There was a feeling among many liberals at that time, and I'm sure there still is, that being white, in and of itself, makes for upward mobility in America. It's only the blacks and other minority groups that really need the help of government and other institutions. If you're born white and you don't "make it," the fault must lie somewhere within you. And it's no easy task convincing dyed-in-the-wool New York City liberals otherwise.

But there were also moments of grave doubt about what I was trying to do. At one of the first community meetings I attended, in a church basement in Brooklyn, I had accurately anticipated some negative reaction. There was some growling and grumbling when I was introduced as a member of the mayor's staff. But there I stood, talking about the possibility of bringing a senior citizens' center into that neighborhood, something that the residents apparently needed and wanted, when a woman shouted from the back of the room, "I don't want those monkeys coming near this community."

I understood that the connection in her mind was between government-sponsored programs and blacks coming into her neighborhood, and I panicked. I thought I must have made a terrible mistake. Perhaps some of my dubious City Hall colleagues were right after all. Maybe I really was trying to help "the wrong side."

> Probably the fact that there were racial problems in this area has turned off some of the people who might have given us an ear earlier. [Now we're] being labeled white ethnics, the bad guys. I think they blame the people for their insecurities.
>
> *Betty Gagne*

All the negative stereotypes I used to have flooded my mind once again. I looked for a quick exit but couldn't leave. As I sat there, I tried to see the world from the vantage point of the people in it. I began to see that they themselves were hardly "the problem," but they were saddled with an unbelievable array of problems.

Some of the elderly could no longer afford to pay their rent and could scarcely afford food. Young couples were leaving the neighborhood for lack of adequate housing. The police precinct was moving to newer quarters elsewhere. The kids were getting into dope. Vandalism and all sorts of crime were on the rise. The fire station had recently closed, the school was

a hundred years old, a factory had been trying to convince the
city to raze several blocks of homes so it could expand its facilities, the sanitation department showed up infrequently,
health care was inaccessible. The only time-worn access to help
—local vestiges of the old political machine—could not cope
with that array of problems and didn't seem interested in
trying.

A community organization grew out of that meeting. It eventually developed some leverage vis-à-vis city government and
served as a vehicle for change. But one of the most significant
changes was the way in which the people began to relate to
neighboring minority communities. Instead of focusing only
inward, they began to look outward and recognize the similarity of problems and needs. The differences lay only in the
severity of problems. New coalitions became possible.

I heard a similar litany of problems in Italian, Polish, Irish,
Greek and other ethnic working class neighborhoods around
the city. It became apparent that being part of an organized
group that could make itself heard and felt helped to reduce
the almost overwhelming feeling of powerlessness. Once the
pressure was relieved, prejudices began to diminish. The poor
and minority groups were no longer the prime target of their
frustrations. I began to feel relieved and reassured about my
instincts.

> I told him how I felt, that I was doing the same job as
> the men, and he laughed at me. He told me this was a
> man's job and I said, "Yeah, but I'm doing the job. I just
> don't have the money or the title and I don't think it's
> fair." But he just kept making fun of me. It was terrible.
>
> *Ann Winans*

My consciousness as a feminist also developed during those
years. It became apparent that it was not only liberal biases
that made it so difficult for me to get strong support for what
by then seemed like such a logical course of action to take.
There was also some bias against me. I did not have a law
degree or any other special credentials as most of the mayor's
senior staff members did. I was also young and had the least
seniority. And I was a woman.

Before the message struck home, I was unabashedly honored to be part of the mayor's staff. I felt privileged, as women did in that time, to work in "male domains." I accepted the fact that I had to shout to be heard and that only rarely would my opinions have an impact. I had no regrets about working long hours and on week ends for something I believed in.

Gradually, I began to understand the meaning of sexism as I gained a new sense of the worth of what I was doing. It merited more than a patronizing pat on the head and a begrudging acceptance. Things were changing for the better in a number of communities, the level of hostility toward the mayor had even decreased, and I felt the program should be expanded. At that time, my immediate superior began to sense the political value in it, wanted to take over and turn the effort into a form of old-style machine politics. New programs and jobs developed by new community organizations would become part of the patronage bailiwick of old bosses. In June of 1972 I resigned.

Armed with my new feminist consciousness, I went to work for the National Project on Ethnic America, which was sponsored by the American Jewish Committee. My first major assignment was a study of the relationship of working class women to the Women's Movement. I had very mixed feelings about it. On the one hand, I felt the report was badly needed. I had gotten to know many working class women in the city and I knew that the tactics of some feminists were needlessly alienating them. I also sensed that many middle class feminists mistakenly perceived working class women as a major obstacle to achieving their goals, much as civil rights, anti-war and student movement leaders in the 1960's viewed working class people as "the problem."

While I felt it was important to create a sympathetic understanding of the concerns of working class women and to begin to outline some possible coalition strategies, I also felt rather "illegitimate." I was not a working class woman and felt I should leave the task to someone of that background. I was afraid that I might misrepresent these women or do them less than justice. And I had very little information to go on apart from my own experiences.

There were a few recent public opinion surveys and studies

on women in general from which I could extract some relevant information. But the major research done on a group that represented over half the women in America was over a decade old, which meant that it predated the new Women's Movement. It portrayed working class women as passive, dependent and uninvolved in the outside world. I had firsthand evidence to the contrary. I had seen hundreds of women emerging from traditional roles to bring about change in their communities. They were, in fact, the backbone of the new community organizations. So, in spite of my qualms and a dearth of documentation, I got to work on an eighty-page pamphlet, *Absent from the Majority: Working Class Women in America.*

The pamphlet apparently struck a sympathetic chord and began to fill a vacuum in women's literature. I was being invited to speak at conferences, on radio and TV and in college classrooms *about* working class women. I felt ill at ease. It was one thing to advocate the needs of a group and to advocate coalition-building and quite another to assume the role of spokesperson for a group one is not a part of. Still, there was a great void. In the rush of new literature inspired by the feminist movement, there was hardly a mention of working class women.

People who write books, articles or poetry are almost without exception highly educated. Much of the new work quite naturally reflected middle class lives. After *Absent from the Majority,* friends began to ask me when I was going to write a "real" book. As I considered the prospect, it occurred to me that a book of oral histories of the lives of working class women would not only help fill the void in women's literature, but it could provide an opportunity for women who would never write about themselves to be heard. They could talk about their lives.

—NANCY SEIFER

Introduction

When I first started going to organizing meetings, for the first time I felt maybe I could really do something to change things somehow.

Cathy Tuley

My reason for doing this book was not only to provide a voice for women who are not normally heard. I wanted to learn more about the ways in which working class women around the country were changing and why. I wanted to understand what had brought about change in their lives, what had given them a new sense of themselves or a new feeling of power in relation to the world around them.

The husband of one of the women asked me bluntly when I first met him, "What do these women have in common besides you?" I was a bit hard-pressed to answer him precisely, since they are all so different. But there was one common denominator: each of their lives had changed rather significantly over the course of the last six to eight years and illustrated the transition from fairly traditional housewife to activist.

Obviously, an activist is not created overnight. A few of the women had been involved in community affairs in one form or another during much of their lives. All of them have firm convictions and see themselves as strong-willed. Many were surprised at themselves and the way they responded to challenges. They did not have the self-image of a leader or an activist, and many still do not, in spite of their successes. But in all cases, they had the makings of an activist. What was needed was the circumstances to evoke those qualities.

These ten women are not "typical." People who have the courage to confront the status quo and transcend the boundaries of their lives are not "average." But I feel strongly that they are in many ways representative of millions of women in their attitudes, their values, their perceptions of the world, and their life-styles. They reveal a great deal about the enormous potential of American women as we emerge from conventional roles and about further change that might be anticipated in family and community life, in religion, politics, the economy, and in society as a whole. Their stories also reveal a great deal about America in the mid-1970's.

The women in this book are a portrait of American diversity. Their ethnic and religious backgrounds include: Irish, Italian, Jewish, black, Chicana, English, white Southern Baptist, French, Norwegian and German. They live in the East, the West, the Midwest and the South; in cities, suburbs, small towns, and rural areas. One has a blue-collar job, six have white-collar jobs and three, immersed as they are in community activities, consider themselves "basically housewives." As of the summer of 1974, when I met them, their ages ranged from twenty-four to fifty-eight. One common denominator, which had no bearing on their selection, is that all are married and all are mothers.

Their experiences illustrate a wide range of issues that concern working class women and their families, and the kinds of events and problems that spark their activism. The spectrum is broad. It covers Chicano politics and coal-mining politics; sexism in the workplace and union organizing; blockbusting and neighborhood social welfare problems; the Civil Rights Movement and the Women's Movement.

The criteria I used for selecting the ten women to interview were less hard-and-fast rules than loose guidelines. While they all fit what has become a commonly used definition of "working class" in some ways, most of them do not fit it in all ways. The term "working class" is still a somewhat awkward one in this country, perhaps in part because of lingering Marxist overtones and in part because we are supposedly a "classless society." One talks about "working people" rather than working class people. And yet there are three significant factors that distinguish the lives of the working class from those of the middle class: level of education, type of job and income.

In general, working class people have had a high school

education or less. They hold blue-collar or lower level white-collar jobs. And their level of income hovers in a range somewhat above the official poverty level and below what might be considered a "comfortable" standard of living. Experts estimate that 60 percent of the American population belongs to the working class.

In the mid-1960's, the income range was generally considered to be between $5,000 and $10,000 a year for a family of four in an urban area. By the early 1970's, the range was approximately between $9,000 and $14,000. With the current level of inflation, it's now anybody's guess. But most working class people tend to use the phrase "just getting by" to describe their economic situation.

The income level itself is perhaps the least important of the three factors when it comes to understanding working class life-styles. There are crane operators who earn far more than college professors, and plumbers and electricians who earn more than engineers. In my own view, a college degree—as both a symbol of "higher" learning and a certificate leading to wider options—is the most significant factor separating the working class from the middle class.

> I always welcomed the Women's Movement, right from the start. It was something I was waiting for.
>
> *Ann Winans*

One factor which had absolutely no bearing on the selection of the ten women was their attitude toward the Women's Movement. From what I knew at that point, I would have expected to find more negative than positive feelings on the subject. I had heard the phrase "I'm no women's libber but . . ." from countless working class women I knew. The rest of the phrase usually went, ". . . if being a women's libber means speaking out for what is fair, wanting equal pay for equal work, and wanting more out of life than just housework, well I guess I've always been one."

The disclaimer seems to have had as much to do with media images of burning bras and storming into men's bars as with the notion that men are responsible for women's oppression. Most of the women I had gotten to know did not view men in general, or their husbands in particular, as the source of their problems. They generally sympathized with their husbands, with the kinds of jobs they had to endure, with the strain of constant financial pressures they lived with. As opposed to many middle and upper middle class women, they saw few advantages in leading "men's lives."

It seemed evident that the Women's Movement was not likely to be the prime moving force for change, as it was in the lives of many middle class women who had their consciousnesses raised by joining a women's group or devouring the new literature—women who suddenly gained a new perspective on their place in the world, didn't like what they saw and decided to try to change it.

By 1974 there was more than a hint of feminism in the atmosphere that seemed to affect most American women, at least to the degree that slightly more "aggressive" behavior was somewhat more acceptable. But I knew that working class women were much more likely to change in response to a problem that affected them directly, in their neighborhood, in their family, or in the workplace. They reacted less to abstract ideas about equality than to concrete problems related to their daily existence.

The women also seemed much more likely to become activists on behalf of others facing similar problems than feminists seeking their own personal fulfillment in life. For the most part, they seemed to shy away from the feminist label and from any association with the movement.

With that set of preconceptions, I was somewhat surprised to find that the response of the women I interviewed was, on the whole, more positive than negative. A few of the women now consider themselves ardent feminists; a few feel no involvement with the movement at all; the rest fall somewhere in the middle, with considerable ambivalence. Their reactions echoed recent national public opinion surveys, which reveal a greater public acceptance of the movement's goals than of its methods in achieving them.

Over the course of the year and a half that I worked on this book, one question that was asked of me repeatedly was: "How did you find the women to interview?" Since I followed my instinct more than any particular "system," my responses were rather evasive. But I feel that I should offer a brief explanation. Through my work at the Institute on Pluralism and Group Identity (which grew out of the National Project on Ethnic America), through publications I received, meetings I attended and people I met, I had a fairly good sense of new developments concerning working class women around the country. Then, once *Absent from the Majority* was published, my office became a small clearinghouse.

I learned, for example, that a group called Steelworkers NOW (National Organization for Women) had formed in Gary, Indiana, and through some women I knew in Chicago NOW, who had supported the effort, I discovered Bonnie Halascsak, the first woman plant security guard at U.S. Steel. I had been interested in the organizing efforts of domestic workers and, by chance, met someone from the Southern Regional Council in Atlanta who told me about Dorothy Bolden.

In a publication called *Union WAGE* (Women's Alliance to Gain Equality) I had read about a campaign to unionize clerks in the San Francisco Bay Area, and through an organizer for the Service Employees International Union, I met Cathy Tuley. At a conference in Washington, I met a woman who had set up a new organization called Alabama Women for Human Rights, who told me about the new political involvement of coal miners' wives and, in particular, about Anita Cupps.

I knew a few of the women, to varying degrees, before I contemplated the idea of the book. I've known Mary Sansone for what seems like forever, as if she were a part of my family. I met her when I was at City Hall and when CIAO (the Congress of Italian American Organizations) was still in her Brooklyn basement. I met Terry Dezso through a friend in Connecticut who wanted help on an article she was writing about the mothers' group that Terry had been part of. Ann Winans wrote a moving letter to me after she saw a write-up of my pamphlet in the *Ladies' Home Journal,* and we started a long correspondence.

In other cases I was interested in a particular group or community. I was aware of new organizing activities among Chicana women in southwest Texas, and through a chain of contacts in Washington and a lot of help from the Texas Institute for Educational Development in San Antonio, I found Rosalinda Rodriguez. Through the Southwest YWCA in Chicago, which had initiated a number of new programs with working class women in a multiethnic area, I met Betty Gagne. And through the Mayor's Office in Boston, I learned about Janice Bernstein, who had helped to lead a battle to save her Jewish neighborhood.

> I've never had anybody interview me or sit listening and taping whatever I say before. I'm not one to talk that much, and when I heard about your coming I thought, why me? I felt real honored, but at the same time I guess I was a little cautious.
>
> *Rosalinda Rodriguez*

> Nancy, of all the women in Boston, why in the world did you choose me? There are so many others who have done things. Are you sure you did the right thing?
>
> *Janice Bernstein*

> Really I thought it would be kind of boring, not only to you but to the readers. I didn't know what I had to offer and I still don't.
>
> *Anita Cupps*

Identifying candidates for the book, according to the loose criteria I had established, was relatively easy. There must be thousands of working class women throughout the country whose lives would have been equally interesting. But once I identified them, convincing some of them to talk about their lives was another story. Anita Cupps gave me the most difficult time, resolutely insisting that she had absolutely nothing of interest to say, until I showed up at her house in Sumiton, Alabama, and verbally twisted her arm. But many of the other women expressed similar misgivings.

The contrast between these women and those who were pouring out their souls in the pages of new books and magazines was dramatic. All of them had faced challenges in their lives and responded to them with what I considered to be an extraordinary amount of courage and strength. Many had endured more than their fair share of hardships. Yet, almost invariably, they seemed to feel that their lives had relatively little significance to anyone but themselves, their families and perhaps a few close friends.

It was not only a lack of writing skills and speaking platforms that made for the silence. I began to see how a society that values material wealth and status symbols devalues those who lack them and how that societal devaluation turns inward into low self-esteem. Even though a four-year college degree has relatively little worth in the job market these days, it seems to represent a chasm between those who feel they have something worthwhile to say and to contribute to the larger society and those who don't.

> I think one problem with the Women's Movement is that some groups of women do have definite advantages, because of their positions and education and bringing up. That might always be the way it is, that some people will have an easier way to go. It'd be nice to see women accepted as equals, regardless of what type of training they've had.
>
> *Cathy Tuley*

One of the most discouraging aspects of what I learned from the interviews was the level of communications barriers between working class and middle class women. Just as some middle class feminists continue to perceive working class women as a hindrance to the kind of change they are working for, many working class women—both feminists and nonfeminists—feel that movement leaders are insensitive to their needs and values.

Stereotypes and labels persist in blurring the commonality of needs and making interaction difficult. But a deeper, more underlying problem, which defies clear-cut solution, is the inadequacy that many working class women feel in relationship to the college-educated middle class. In exploring this dilemma, which to me is one of the most serious problems we face as a nation struggling to become a more viable democracy, I found a fairly consistent and dismaying confirmation of what I had observed in some of my relationships with women in New York City.

I know a woman from Queens who was a tiger in her own neighborhood. She had no reservations about making her presence felt and her voice heard. Then we attended a meeting in Washington, D.C., together, with about twenty-five other women from different cities. About half were neighborhood leaders, and half were college-educated "professionals" of various stripes. It was her first trip to Washington and the first meeting she had attended outside her community. In that environment, she fell silent. For two days, she sat back and listened. She felt intimidated by the "professional" people and was unable to share her opinions.

> I've met a lot of people who've gone to college and . . . sometimes I feel what I say doesn't interest them because they know so much more and have been so many more places.
>
> *Rosalinda Rodriguez*

During the interviews, I probed this issue in the hope of finding some formula for reducing class barriers to communication. What I found was a general feeling among the women that there was no one factor—a college degree, a greater facility with words, a style of dress, an appearance of wealth, broader experience in the wider world, travel, or any number of other advantages—that in itself was a problem. Rather, it was a combination of those factors that often made them feel self-conscious about their speech, insecure about the value of their opinions and sometimes unsure about trusting their instincts.

Totally apart from the ten women in this book, each of whom is perceptive, expressive and has carefully thought out views and opinions, the feeling of "not knowing enough," so often experienced by working class people, is what played right into the hands of the perpetrators of the Silent Majority hoax.

Traveling around the country right before Richard Nixon released the tapes that led to his departure from the White House, I asked a variety of people how they felt about his innocence or guilt in regard to Watergate. While my survey was hardly scientific, there seemed to be a kind of correlation between the level of education and a willingness to give the President the benefit of the doubt. The less the education, the greater the willingness. Over and over again I heard answers like, "He knows more than we do. Maybe he was involved, but maybe it was for some good reasons that we don't know about yet."

> Sometimes at the end of the week that refrigerator is pretty empty and I just don't have the money to go out and replenish it as fast. These are damned trying times for the housewife. I don't know what's going to happen to the economy, but I think it's going to get a lot worse before it gets better. I think this country has made too damn many mistakes. First of all the grain bit. Imagine selling it and then having to buy it back! Then the milk thing, where they dumped all that milk. Then look at this oil business. Do you know that they made 300 percent profit? Can you believe it? And you know there's never been a real oil crisis.

> *Janice Bernstein*

Like many people, I feel that Watergate was a fortuitous and healthy purge for this country. But in addition to bringing down a government that was apparently scheming tyranny, it seems to have served as a kind of leveler. Finding out about what often lies behind positions of power and status, people seem much more likely to trust their own instincts and fight for what they believe to be rightfully theirs. There is a sense that the public is questioning, perhaps more than ever before, institutions and institutional leaders that were once held sacrosanct.

And more than ever before, individuals are taking responsibility for change into their own hands and forming new organizations to make institutions more responsive. As devastating as the summer of 1974 was in political and economic terms—Watergate, Ford's pardon of Nixon, the energy crisis and a rate of inflation that had millions of Americans worried about how to feed their families—my own experiences left me with renewed faith in people; in the women in this book and many others I met along the way.

Getting to know each of the women was a personally enriching experience for me. After some initial hesitation about speaking freely to a total stranger (which I was in most cases) and some uneasiness about the presence of a tape recorder, they shared their lives with an openness, a trust and a generosity that I could never have anticipated. In several instances, their husbands did too.

It was emotionally difficult and at times bewildering for me and, I think, for many of the women. After spending the good part of several days delving deeply into their lives, it was time for me to pack up and leave. Each time I experienced the kind of wrenching feeling one has when one leaves a good friend. But in this instance I had known most of them for only a matter of several days, and I was not entirely sure when and if I would see them again.

It has been over a year now since the interviews were completed and I feel as though each of the women has somehow become a part of me. In the process of transcribing close to one hundred hours of tapes, piecing their lives together in the form in which they appear in this book, corresponding with them and talking with them on occasion, I feel as though I know them better than many people whose paths I've crossed on a daily basis for years.

> Maybe sometimes you have to endure a lot. It makes you think more and try to find things out. And if it's bad enough, then you have the guts to change it.
>
> *Terry Dezso*

Although the material circumstances of my life are different from theirs, each of them evoked in me a set of memories of experiences through which I could identify. Listening to them, I gained new insights into the significance of certain events in my own childhood, my own ethnic background, my own insecurities, my own search for identity and all the personal challenges, traumas, exhilaration and pain one encounters on the road to self-discovery.

For one reason or another having to do with each of their separate personal histories, all of the women seemed to share that instinctive identification with the underdog—an empathy for those less fortunate. Perhaps that was why I felt an almost immediate rapport with them. And while it hadn't occurred to me until I read through the transcripts, each of them seemed to truly enjoy differences in people. They are all natural "coalition-builders," my favorite kind of person.

A deep involvement in helping others with similar problems is another common trait among them. In some cases, their original motivation was personal—the illness of a child, a life's savings invested in a neighborhood, discrimination in a job, a decision about getting a divorce and starting a new life. But even in those cases, the personal motivation led to a commitment to bringing about change that would benefit others in like circumstances. In other cases, the motivation stemmed from a sense of rootedness in a community and a long history of involvement with the people in it.

Whatever the motivation, there is a spirit of communalism that exists among working class women that one finds far less frequently among the middle class. They seem not to be infected by that college-bred disease of competition, survival of the fittest. Perhaps it is because middle class people do have more options in life and have less need to depend on one another in exercising them that we tend to be more individualistic and self-interested than communal. I, for one, feel that that is our loss, and a great loss to a nation increasingly afflicted by alienation.

In that spirit of communalism lies an important message in terms of the future of the Women's Movement in America. Its potential success as the most significant movement for social change in our history will depend to a great extent upon the involvement of working class women and upon our ability to relate communalism to feminist goals. The potential is there. It will grow to the extent that the goals that the movement espouses become increasingly relevant to the lives of working class women and to the extent that we can find new ways to overcome superficial barriers that divide us.

The women in this book left me with a new sense of optimism about both our country as a whole and our future as women. It is not only a matter of their own personal struggles and success stories. For many, there are no ultimate successes, just ongoing struggles. But each has emerged a fighter, in many cases a recognized leader, committed in some way to improving the quality of her own life and the lives of others around her. That, in my book, is cause for celebration.

Two final notes. Since over a year elapsed between the time I completed the interviews and the time that all of the pieces of the book finally came together, I asked each of the women to bring me up to date on the major changes that have taken place in her life in the course of the year. A brief postscript follows the text of each oral history.

Each of the women has read and approved the contents attributed to her. Many had some qualms about publicly revealing certain portions of their interviews. They feared they might in some way jeopardize their relationships with family members, employers or members of the community. But almost without exception—in spite of their hesitations—they decided to let their statements stand as told to me in the hope that other women who read this book might derive some benefit from the experiences that they have lived through.

December 1975

Taking Care
of the Neighborhood

Mary Sansone

Janice Bernstein

Mary Sansone in her office in lower Manhattan.

At CIAO's first press conference, February 5, 1975, where the results of the first demographic study on Italian-Americans in New York City were released. *Left to right:* Gladys Harrington, Commissioner of the Human Resources Administration; Harrison Goldin, Comptroller of the City of New York; Josephine Casalena, CIAO staff member; Mary Sansone; Bayard Rustin, Director of the A. Philip Randolph Institute; Nancy Seifer; Robert Steingut, City Councilman.

BOTH PHOTOS BY JOAN ROTH

Mary Sansone

UNUSUAL ORIGINS ON BROOKLYN'S HENRY STREET

I was born in 1916 on Henry Street in South Brooklyn. At that time, we were very, very poor. We were living with my mother's mother. Grandma lived in the basement and we lived upstairs. And my father was busy doing his thing with the International Workers of the World.

In those days, most of them did volunteer work. They didn't have hired organizers like they do now. This is why we were so poor. He used to work in a factory sometimes, doing some operating work on men's clothing, but it never lasted too long. He'd pull the shop out on strike and that was the end of his job. From the day I remember my father, that was the only thing he ever did. His aim in life was to get everybody organized and get everybody to live together.

My father left Italy and came to the United States when he was twenty-seven. He was ready to be ordained. He only had six months to go. If he'd stayed there he'd have had to be a priest, and something happened that made him give up the priesthood. Nobody knows what. Before he died, he was in a coma for three days and friends of his stayed with him constantly in the hope that he would divulge why he left the Church, but he never did. All he talked about was Dante and *The Divine Comedy*.

He died at fifty-seven, when I was about twenty-one. When I went to Italy fifteen years ago, I went to see my uncle there. I knew that these two brothers were very close. They both had the same philosophy. So I asked him. I said, "Gee, Uncle Paul, maybe you could tell me why Papa left the Church." He said, "If your father wanted you to know, he would have told you."

He said, "He didn't believe in influencing anybody. He believed in working with people and helping people."

My father had a very interesting family. There were three sisters and three brothers. My uncle in Italy was a socialist. He was also a very brilliant man. He had graduated as a navy captain, but he didn't like it. He came to the United States for a while, and then he went back to Italy and worked with Mussolini with the liberal newspapers. That was before fascism. When Mussolini became Il Duce, he went to my uncle and insisted that my uncle join him, but he refused so he was put in jail.

My uncle was in jail for a number of years and he had a few children. So my father's other brother, who was a member of the syndicate here, was a good-natured guy, and he supported the kids in Italy. While my uncle was in jail, he was writing books and sending them underground to my father, and my father would have them published here. They were about socialism and fascism, that kind of thing. He died when he was quite old, long after my father. But he was released from prison right after World War II.

Up until the time that I was fourteen, my father never did anything other than organizing work. He would go to Union Square and deliver speeches on behalf of the Socialist Party. And he used to write for the *Italian Proletariat,* which was a very liberal paper. He made a little money from that but not too much. And they used to have a little garage near the *Proletariat* where he would help the illiterate Italians who came over to read and write. When he came here, he spoke French fluently, and Latin, of course. He didn't know English, but he picked it up. Every morning he would go and buy *The New York Times* and about five or six other newspapers, and you couldn't disturb him until he finished his newspapers.

My mother's family is interesting too. My grandfather, like most immigrants, came to America and left a wife and three children in Italy. When he came here, he lived with some people as a boarder and he was working as a longshoreman, carrying coal or something like that. He was also having a lot of fun with some other women here while my poor grandma was working in the fields in Calabria.

The next thing my grandfather knows is my grandma finds herself in America with three kids. He had never sent for her. Those women were really very strong. She just came and presented herself to her husband and found out that he was fooling around. But they got along, because they both lived to be eighty-two! And from three children they wound up with eight.

Grandma bought the house in South Brooklyn. What used to be a one-family house turned out to be a four-family house and we all lived together. Grandma had boarders who she took care of, so there was some money. And Grandpa had to forget about his girlfriends, because she made sure he did. But that was the trend in those days. The man would come here for economic reasons and forget about his wife over there.

I used to work on the ships doing volunteer work for the Italian Welfare League, and I used to see the men meeting their wives. I'll never forget one night. It was a very sad case. This man hadn't seen his wife for twenty-five years, and he looked like a real Dapper Dan, you know? He was very well-dressed with a cane and all. Then he saw this woman and he ran. We couldn't find him anywhere. So we had to keep his wife until we could locate him.

My mother was only eighteen when she married. She was related to my father. When he came from Italy, he went to look for the other Crisallis. There's ten years' difference between them. The funny thing is, there's no proof of their marriage. When us kids get together we still laugh about that. We knew my father did not go to church. And from what we heard from my mother, she didn't marry in Brooklyn, but she didn't know where she married. If I know my father, he was clever enough to convince her somehow that they were married. He was so worldly and she was a very timid woman.

When my mother came here she was three years old. She attended Mother Cabrini's school, but I think she only went for four or five years. Then she stayed home and helped her mother raise all the other kids. She was a beautiful woman and she loved my father very much. She didn't know too much about what he was doing. The only thing she knew was he must be doing the right thing because he loved people. All my mother really knew was being at home and taking care of the children—first her mother's children and then us.

There are five kids in our family. First came my sister Josie, then me, and then my brother Joey. The last two kids were much younger. My brother Jimmy was born when I was about fourteen, and then my sister Millie was born two years later. My brother Joey is just like my father. And when I was growing up, my mother would tell me, "You're just like your father." As a matter of fact, something happened that made me feel very sad. When my father died, my mother said, "I bet you wish it was me instead." She lived for about fourteen more years. It was sad, because my father and I were so close to each other and I seemed to do everything that he was doing.

My father was like the town schoolteacher. We lived on the parlor floor and at that time we were just three kids. Then there was my mother's brother upstairs who had two kids. And my other aunt had two kids. And so we were all together. My father would sit down at night and we'd all sit around him and he'd tell us stories. Then somebody donated a piano and my sister used to take piano lessons next door for twenty-five cents a week. My cousin upstairs used to play the guitar and my brother used to play the violin and my father would organize plays. We were always doing something.

We had a very happy life. We don't even remember the starvation, you know? Grandma always fed us. She'd make macaroni and beans and send it upstairs. My father was a thin guy. He ate very little. But he was always there. At night we'd be sitting on the stoop and he'd come from Union Square and if he had ten cents in his pocket you'd see him coming home with ice cream cones for all the kids. He lived for his work and his kids.

Everyone remembered my father. He was so interested in books. When he died, we didn't have any furniture. All we had was books. I got a call from a doctor way out in Indiana telling me that he'd found the newspapers that my father wrote and he wanted to know if I had any of his books and things. But my father died in a hurry and my brother was in the Army. I was too young and I got too sick to know what was going on. So everybody kept his books. The only thing they left us was the Encyclopaedia Britannica he bought us when we were kids.

When I was about fourteen, my uncle who was in the syndicate needed a shop to front for him—a business, something for taxes, you know? So he decided to put up a pastry shop and he asked my father to run it. Nothing would go on with my father there, but they had this shop. My father was some businessman! He used to leave early in the morning, buy his six newspapers and go to the store which was on Henry Street and Union Street. He'd lock the door, put the box of milk outside and, when the customers came, they'd pick up their own milk. He couldn't be bothered until he finished his newspapers. Then as soon as somebody else came, he would leave the store and go to Union Square.

The only thing he used the business for was to make speeches. At night he'd go back there and he'd be talking to everybody. He was quite an orator. People enjoyed listening to him. He always spoke about his principles and beliefs. He talked about organizing and the need for reforms. And he knew what was going to happen in the future. What's happening today, Papa was talking about thirty years ago. Like he didn't believe in wearing mourning and people aren't doing that now. And he also believed in free love. He had no problem with two people living together if they loved each other. He used to say, "Who needs a piece of paper? If I love somebody, do I need a paper with a stamp on it?"

I hated the store. I was never there. I couldn't weigh a pound of cookies. I just didn't like it. My sister Millie used to help my mother with the store after my father died. She was always a very sick little girl and it was very difficult for her. My sister Josie helped my mother sometimes and my brother Jimmy used to like it. But Joey hated it, like me. My mother loved it. She died when she was sixty-one, on her way home from the store. To her it was a diversion, going there, talking to people, meeting new people. She was very kind, but she was an excellent businesswoman with the very little education that she had.

The strange thing is, while my father was organizing, my uncle's group was actually fighting him. Yet they liked each other as brothers. When my father tried organizing the longshoremen, some young man was killed. He was thirty-three years old and buried alive, and I guess everybody knew it. I think the only reason why my father was not touched was because my uncle was a member of that group. Otherwise, I think he would have been dead at a young age.

I used to see the racketeers wiped out in front of me on Henry Street. Everything used to happen in front of my house. It was a tough neighborhood, very rough. All the shooting used to take place across the street from the pastry shop. I'd see them die right in front of me, but I guess it became a part of everyday living. It's just like when you see the cowboy pictures. As a child, we didn't understand the reason why. Nobody talked about it.

I didn't ever know about my uncle until long after my father died. My father never spoke about it. They were brothers, and with Italians there's a strong family tie. At least there was. You could be miles and miles apart, but you're still brothers or sisters. My father and his brother lived in two different worlds and yet they never interfered with each other's world.

My uncle would never tell my father, "What you're doing is wrong." He always respected my father. But he had gotten himself involved in something that perhaps he didn't know what the hell he was getting into. It was one of those things. And once you get in there, there's no getting out. But I know one thing—he never bragged about it or even talked about it.

We were always taught to dislike that caliber of people from the time we were children. It's not like a lot of Italian families that would look at the racketeer and call him "a man of respect." We were brought up not to respect them. But my father would never speak of his brother and he would never associate his brother with the others.

The funny thing is, my uncle was the pacifist in his syndicate. He wasn't the killer. After he died, a lot of people said, "Oh, now that he's gone, everybody'll get killed." But still, I refused to take anything from him. When I married, he wanted to give me a wedding. But at that time I knew what it was all about, so I never took anything from him.

I think there are probably very few Italians who don't have a relative somewhere involved in the syndicate. It's true for a lot of reasons. One reason is that when the Italians first came to this country they were so abused that they had to do something. They did what some of them knew best, and that was to shoot. I think the shooting was done for survival, to protect themselves.

They were being abused by the Irish a lot. They couldn't get jobs and when they did, they were second-class jobs. And when they went to church, in the Irish church, the Italians would have to sit at the back. The Italians weren't even permitted to pray at the same altar. Then, also, from what I've heard, a lot of the children went to school with their little sandwich, you know, with peppers and eggs and broccoli or something like that, and the teachers would poke fun at them. So the kids didn't want to go to school.

So these were the problems that caused the mafia. They had to do something, so they started breaking heads. And the next thing you know, it was used to exploit people rather than for the purpose for which it started. Most things happen that way. They start for one reason and they wind up totally different. It's like the union movement. The unions started for very good reasons. But today, as far as I'm concerned, you find some of the biggest racketeers running the unions. I think people like Sacco and Vanzetti and my father must be turning over in their graves, because that isn't at all what they intended. In those days, the union leaders weren't even getting paid. Today some of them make more than the President of the United States. It's sad how a good thing can be turned into such a bad thing.

South Brooklyn, where I lived, was the Italian ghetto. I only had contact with other ethnic groups through my father when I started going around to meetings with him at the age of ten or twelve. There was the Jew, the black, but to me it was no different. They were all Italian because my father never said, "He's Jewish or he's black or he's Puerto Rican." He would just take them home. My father took everybody home.

At school, all the kids were Italian and the teachers were all Irish. In those days, the teachers always made you feel inferior. I remember them being very rough, even though I don't remember ever being spanked myself. I remember teachers referring to us as "guinea kids" and using the word "wop." But in our home, I don't remember my father making any distinctions between one ethnic group and another.

The things that stand out most in my mind about the neighborhood I grew up in were the racketeers and the shooting. But, you know, I lived in that neighborhood all my life and I was always protected. I used to come home any hour of the night and there was always somebody following me to make sure that I got home safe. They were my uncle's friends. You see, racketeers would only shoot each other. It's the same today. Of course, they exploit people terribly and if you don't accept them they might get violent.

The nicest memories I have are just of my own family, and especially my father. All he believed in was that we should go to school. From the time I was very young he would say, "I don't care if we have bread and onions. My kids have to go to school." And it seems we were the only kids on Henry Street that went to school. Most of the kids on the block just went to grade school. A few had maybe one year of high school. We were the only ones that continued, because my father had such a great influence on us.

You've got to realize that most of the Italians that came to this country came to make money with the hope that they would go back to their own country. Nobody wanted to stay here. So their only concern was making money and going back. But, of course, most of them never did go back. They stayed here and their kids never went to school. Though quite a few did go back after their Social Security started coming. They retired and took it back with them and they could live very well there before inflation, which is worse there than it is here.

When I was twelve years old, my father got me involved in the Junior Wobblies. I think it was because he realized that I had a problem and he was the only one who realized it. He used to hate anybody that came into the house and said Josie was prettier than I was. I remember relatives who would come in and say, "Look at Josie's pretty curly blond hair," and then say something unkind about my straight black hair. I remember it all, how everyone praised Josie.

But, you see, there are two things in life, when you're suffering an inferiority complex. Either you hate yourself and you put yourself down, or you try to fight and put yourself up. Because of my father, I fought to better myself. My mother didn't have any idea what the hell was going on. If it wasn't for my father, Lord knows what would have happened to me. In fact, I think every good thing in my life has happened because of him.

So he was with the IWW and then I was with the Junior Wobblies, and he pushed me and the next thing I knew, I was the president of this group in Brooklyn at twelve years old. When I delivered my first speech, he was crying in the back of the room. I was talking about the kids joining me and some day becoming organizers like our fathers were, you know? And then we had a little play and I sang the "Indian Love Call" and I recited the poem "Laugh Clown Laugh," which I still remember. And then he introduced me to people at the IWW. That's how later I became involved in doing organizing for the union and in the Rand School.

I went to Textile High School because I wanted to get a high school diploma and my mother wanted me to be a designer, and that was the only school that would give me both. It was on Eighteenth Street in Manhattan, and I had to trot all the way there from Brooklyn, but I said, "All right. I'll please her but I'll also please myself because when I get out of there I'll have a diploma and can do whatever I want." But I hated sewing. So to convince my mother that I couldn't sew, in one of my elective subjects they told me to sew a suit and I put the sleeves in upside down. That ended my career as a dress designer!

I graduated high school at eighteen. That was in 1934 and my father took quite sick so I went to work in a factory doing sewing. I hated the routine and the surroundings and I just hated sewing, but I wanted to go into a factory because I liked what my father was doing, organizing. I didn't go with the intention of staying there. The way the employers abused the girls was awful. The only way a girl could get a promotion was to go to bed with the employer. And he would pass by while they were working and feel her here or touch her there. It was really disgusting. These were nonunion shops and that's what the union was for, to protect the girls.

In the summertime, the heat would kill those poor people. No fans, no nothing. It was horrible. You had ten minutes for lunch in some shops, maybe a half hour in others. You could only talk during the break and the only break they had was lunch. They used to have one bathroom for men and women. Today they call it the new movement. In those days, that was the only one they had, so it was a necessity. All the abuses they had to take were terrible.

By the time I went to work, a lot of the shops were organized. Those that weren't organized were afraid of the union. This is what I tell people when they say they're against unions. Even like the people who work on Wall Street and say they're doing fine. What I say is, "It's only because of the fear of being unionized. If there were no unions at all, they'd treat you like slaves."

Anyway, by then the Rand School knew of my father's activities and I had been active too. After a year in the factory, they asked me to be an assistant organizer at the ILGWU—the International Ladies Garment Workers Union. My job was to go into the factory, pretend I was working and then pull the shop out on strike. I'd usually stay a couple of weeks. How many times they wanted to kill me, once they'd find out what I was there for! But that was my life. I'm still doing scary things. Of course, in those days, girls didn't do such things, you know? Sometimes I'd get in a truck and shoot upstate to organize shops there. Naturally my mother wasn't too happy with what I was doing.

I would work during the day and go to the Rand School at night. I did that for four or five years. Now it's called the New School for Social Research. In those days, the Rand School was attached to the union movement, and for twenty years I was afraid to tell people that I had attended the Rand School for fear they would think I was a Communist. The only people who attended the Rand School in those days were the ultra-radicals. But all of my education was paid for by the union.

I graduated from there and then I went to the New York School of Social Work, which is now Columbia. I went there at night, too, and whatever money I made during the day would help support my mother. My father died shortly after I started the Rand School. I remember working and going to school for thirty-five cents a day. I remember many a time I walked to the Brooklyn Bridge from the school, which was on

Twelfth Street, across the bridge and all the way to my house. In those days I had a good figure. You ate little and walked a lot.

While I was still going to school the war broke out. I applied for a job at the Social Service Department of the Brooklyn Red Cross and they needed someone there. So what I was doing was, I used to go to work during the day and go to school at night. Then I had to take some courses during the day, so I would work at night and go to school days. I did that for six years. This is why when I look at the kids today, I think they have it easy. My husband would not think of our son Ralphie working while he's going to school. That's because Zack was fortunate to come from a family where he didn't have to do both. But I'm glad I had to. I think it did a lot for me.

Most of my friends never joined me in what I was doing. A lot of their parents thought I was nuts anyway. Going to night school and campaigning and striking and demonstrating. A lot of people would say, "Oh, she's crazy like her father," you know? Crazy like my father. When my father died, he had so many people visit him that the funeral parlor was mobbed for three days. So that means there were an awful lot of people that respected what he did.

But the girls' families didn't understand why I should be going to school. I remember when my sister Josie was going to St. John's University, my own relatives—and we were so poor as I mentioned—they would tell my father, "I don't know why you let your daughter go to school. If you'd keep her home and send her to work, at least she'd support you." That's what happened in my neighborhood. As I said, I don't know of anyone on my block that finished high school except us.

After the war I kept working for the Brooklyn Red Cross. In the Social Service Department there, we were concerned with things like trying to get emergency furloughs and trying to get guys out of the Army for hardship reasons. Then we tried to help the wives and families out with their problems and made sure they got their allotment checks on time. We had a lot of emotional problems and we had to do a lot of investigation work. Some of the soldiers claimed they weren't well and would fake being crazy just to get out of the Army, you know? Some of the things they did were unbelievable.

Then in 1949 a man named Skouras* who was president of
Fox studios called me. They were starting a campaign to raise
funds after the war to help the orphans of the different countries. It was called the United Nations Appeal for Children. As
a matter of fact, this is what started a big story with my uncle.
He almost wanted to have me killed.

What happened was, every ambassador here at the United
Nations sent for a representative from his country to come to
New York with two children so their country would be represented in the campaign and they would get a sum when the
money was divided. But when it came to Italy, the ambassador
was afraid to send for someone because they feared the Com-
munists would be elected and then they wouldn't be able to
take part. The campaign was supposed to start the day after
the elections were to take place in Italy.

Well, as it turned out, Italy turned Christian Democrat. At
the last minute they needed somebody, so they called me. They
knew about me from my work with the Italian Welfare League
and also I did some interpreting work for the consul general.
They needed someone who spoke English well and someone
that was active and young and interested in running around.
Somehow I seemed to fit the picture. Then since I was going
on the ships as a volunteer anyhow, they asked me to pick two
little kids to represent Italy in the United Nations.

So I picked up a brother and a sister whose house had been
bombed in Sicily. The mother was an American citizen, so she
came here and then little by little, when she could save enough
money, she was calling in the rest of the family. I met this family because my sister Josie lived nearby. And remember I told
you my uncle with the syndicate was a very good-natured guy?
He loaned this family seven thousand dollars to call in the rest
of the family.

So I got acquainted with the two little kids and I represented
Italy in the U.N. Appeal for Children. When the other representatives came over, we stayed in New York for a few days
and then we went to Washington. I still have the pen and pictures from our visit with Truman, where Margaret Truman

* Spyros P. Skouras, major motion picture executive, president of Twen-
tieth Century–Fox from 1942 to 1962; died 1971.

played for the kids. Then the others had to leave after ten days when their visas ended, but I proceeded to travel and I visited twenty-three states with those kids.

The poor kids came with nothing, but they went from rags to riches. The Italian Welfare League dressed them up like a little queen and king. The people in the different cities would meet me and I would speak about the two kids and their family and how their house was bombed. So here I am, traveling all over the country with them for about a month. I got a $25,000 donation from Ford.* Altogether I collected close to $200,000 for the United Nations Appeal. That was quite an experience.

Even before that, while I was working at the Red Cross, I was becoming recognized as special. Everybody seemed to know me. There weren't too many Italian-American social workers then and women just didn't do that kind of work. The only thing women were permitted to do was be a teacher. So there was myself and two or three others, but I just happened to be the youngest of the group and I was very active. And I wasn't just a social worker, I was involved in everything, like I am today.

So what happened was I met a doctor and a judge who started an organization called American Relief to Italy and they asked me to work with them in organizing it. They wanted a young Italian-American girl who was a social worker and who would know how to contact people. Most of my work there was making contact with people and raising funds, which is what I had done for the United Nations campaign. And I'll tell you something, there aren't too many generous Italian-Americans. Most of the contributions were from Jews.

Well I became executive secretary of the medical department of American Relief to Italy, and we had letterheads printed up. Now Italians don't believe in putting down too many names, and they have a very good reason for it. People will look down the list and if they don't like a name that appears there they automatically don't give. But since we had to

---

* Henry Ford II, grandson of founder of the Ford Motor Company; chairman and chief executive officer of the Ford Motor Company since 1960, appointed president of the Ford Foundation in 1945; currently trustee.

collect money, we sent out letters with my name, Mary Crisalli, as executive secretary.

Evidently, the syndicate thought my uncle was involved. Here the letters are going all over the piers and everyplace and they must be going, "Hmmm, Mary Crisalli, Jimmy Crisalli's niece." Immediately they associate it with my uncle and they think it's a front, you know, that he was getting money from it and he wasn't dividing it with the others. I didn't know any of this, so I'm just doing my thing.

Well at this point, my uncle gets ahold of my poor mother, who was very meek, and he tells her, "I have to talk to your daughter." So my poor mother says, "What's going on?" She never even knew I traveled twenty-three states. She thought I was going to my sister's house. I was afraid to tell her I was flying. It came out in the newspapers and somebody said, "Oh, I see your daughter went to Washington." She said, "My daughter? She's over at her sister's house." I didn't have to do that with my father, but for her peace of mind I had to do it.

So my mother's scared stiff. She calls me and says, "Your uncle wants to talk to you." And I said, "About what?" By this time, I was pretty smart to what he was doing. I mean as a child, nobody had talked about it so he was just a nice uncle. But he'd told my mother, "I'm gonna kill her." So I says, "Good. Tell him to come home." Then my brother Joey decided that he would come home that night too and we'd all sit down and talk.

So my uncle says to me, "I want you to quit what you're doing." So I said, "My father would never tell me that. He would say, 'I'd like you to quit because . . .' Now you give me two reasons why you'd like me to quit. If I'm doing something illegal or immoral I'll quit. If not, the hell with you." Well nobody answered to the king in that manner. The head of the syndicate is referred to as the king. My brother Joey said, "She's right. Why do you want her to quit?" He says, "Because I said so." So I said, "Well, I'm sorry. As far as I'm concerned, you can drop dead."

With that, he takes his hat, bangs it on the table and he runs off. And that was the end of that. I never saw him again until a few months before I got married. He was so furious. I said to him, "You just tell whoever your hoodlum friends are that we're not even related." I don't even know what he finally told them. All I know is we used to avoid each other.

But then we got very close before my marriage. Later he realized that he was wrong for doing what he did and then he used to come to the house and he was very nice. One day he said to me, "You know, I respect you for what you're doing. You're just like your father, and I always respected your father." He was very nice then. In many ways he was very sad. Doing the things he was doing made him sad. He didn't want to be what he was, but he just got involved.

THE MOST DIFFICULT CHANGE: MARRIAGE AND MOTHERHOOD

I didn't marry Zack until I was thirty-two and my mother was having a rough time with me. Every night I was coming home with somebody else and she couldn't understand it. And all the time I'd hear, "Why aren't you married?" from my relatives and everyone. My mother was really going crazy. But let me tell you something. My mother wouldn't live with anybody but me and I know she enjoyed what I was doing. It was just that she was so afraid of public opinion, you know? Because after I got married and stayed home with the kids she says, "I can't understand how you gave up your whole life for a man!"

I was just too involved in what I was doing to get married. I just wasn't ready. I enjoyed what I was doing so much, with American Relief to Italy, the United Nations, with the Red Cross during World War II. Then I did immigration work and a lot of different things. I was helping people and it was very good for me.

I did a little campaign work too, like I do today, but only for people I knew. It started when I worked at American Relief to Italy and I got a call from Joe Corso, the one who was recently elected one of the ten worst judges in New York! He says, "You don't know me but I've heard a lot about you. I'm running for the State Assembly in a predominantly German neighborhood and I'm the only Italian," he said, "and I know I can't make it unless you help me." So I said, "But I don't know anything about politics." He says, "Do me a favor, run my campaign like you ran American Relief to Italy's medical aid."

So what I did was I organized this campaign with a couple of friends of mine. It was in Bushwick and they were all German then. The nice clean streets, you know? Spotless. They were always cleaning their sidewalks. And it was easy going into their homes. We were social workers and they were interested in help. We ran such a campaign for Joe Corso. He came in two to one. From then on, he wouldn't run unless I did his campaign.

But I was never really involved in politics. I mean I was never a party person and never went into the clubhouses. I never worked as a committeewoman. Never worked for a leader. I never wanted to. They wanted me to run for Congress in South Brooklyn many years ago. I wouldn't do it because I loved the work I was doing. Zack always laughs because he says, "You don't know anything about politics and people look at you like a big politician." And I say, "That's true!"

Well, as I told you, I did some work with the Italian consul general. Every time a group would come in from Italy, he would ask me to take them around the city and interpret for them. So one year, a group of doctors came in with the International Congress of Pediatrics, and one of the doctors was Zack's brother. He was looking for me because he had a letter from my cousin, Mary Crisalli, who was also a doctor in Genoa. So we became very well acquainted. Some of the doctors went back, but he stayed on because he became rather interested in me.

Then his visa expired and he had to go back. I didn't want to go to Italy and he said that he didn't think he wanted to stay here. But we used to correspond with each other and one day he wrote me, about six months after that, and he said his brother was coming to the United States. He wanted me to show him around and help him if I could, because he thought his brother wanted to stay in America.

When I met Zack it wasn't romantic or anything at first. In fact I think that was the furthest thing from my mind because I was still interested in his brother. They were different types, you know? But after being with Zack . . . well, he came here in January. It wasn't until the end of April that we decided we liked each other and in June we were married. So it was a very short courtship.

Zack was born in the United States and he always had a desire to come back. When he was in Italy, since one brother was a doctor and the other was an engineer, the father thought he should be a lawyer. But he never really liked law. Then the father had a big farm and thought that maybe Zack would manage the farm, but Zack didn't like the farm. He did practice law in Italy for about six years, in Naples, and he passed the exam to be a judge. He was mayor of Castellammare, a town near Naples, for about three years. He must have been about twenty-nine when he was mayor, because he came to America when he was thirty-two.

Somehow or another that life didn't attract him. He didn't like law or politics and he wanted to leave Italy and come to America. He didn't know whether or not he wanted to stay here, but he knew that as long as he was in Italy he would have to be a lawyer. It's not like the United States, where you can change easily. There, if you decided not to practice law anymore, you'd have to get into another profession or people would look down on you.

So he came to America and then we married, so he had no choice but to stay here. When he first came we had an agency, a little office on Court Street. I used to do immigration work and Zack used to do Italian law work. We didn't make too much money, but it was something. I figured he'd get started in something like this and it would be good for him. But then I took sick after Carmella was born, a year after we were married. I had a pulmonary embolism that settled in the left leg. Zack couldn't run the office by himself because he didn't speak English well enough, so he had to give it up. It was difficult for him and for me too, to stay home.

It was very difficult for Zack when he came from Italy, because he hadn't mastered the language. After our agency closed, he decided to take a job. All he would have needed was another year of school before he could sit at the bar, but he didn't want to be a lawyer. He had done some teaching in Italy and that didn't attract him either. So finally he chose to go to the piers. He was doing office work and he was doing

FOR YOUR INFORMATION

To **M. Seaman**

From **J. d'Aurelio**

Date **12-2-76**

☐ PLEASE RETURN   ☐ MAY BE RETAINED OR DISCARDED

COMMENTS:

The books were delivered to me in the library. I called 4 to Madison Ave. bookstore & they informed me you had ordered the books.

McKINSEY & COMPANY, INC.
Library — NYO

914 8/71

checking, and then he became a shop steward with the ILU—
the International Longshoremen's Union.

You know, I think today, after fifty years, he finally found
what he was looking for. It's strange but for many years, he
told me, he never knew what he really wanted. But he's done
some magnificent work with the senior citizens in Little Italy
and he just loves it. Zack always loved the old folks. As a matter of fact, my mother was crazy about him. I think that was
one of the things that attracted me to him. He's very good-
natured and he loved my mother so much and she felt very
comfortable with him.

Being married was very difficult for me to get used to. I'm
going to be very honest. When I think back to all the nights
that I cried . . . And I would never say anything to anybody.
I always looked like I was happy and gay. It was very difficult
for me because I was so outgoing, you know, and all of a sudden I found myself confined to a house, a husband, and then
children. I had Carmella after a year, because when you're
thirty-two you don't want to wait too long, and then I was sick.
So it was kind of rough.

Then I was really in quite a situation. A couple of months
after I got well, my mother took sick with a heart condition, so
I was caring for her. Then we all moved into this house, and
then . . . well my whole life changed. My mother couldn't
understand me. My friends would look at me and could never
understand the change. I think one of the reasons why I stayed
home was because my friends would look at Zack and say,
"Oh, if I had a wife like yours I'd be president of this or that
group." And that would hurt me. I didn't want anybody to put
him down. I didn't want to feel superior to him, and I didn't
want him to feel inferior to me. But I was already in the newspapers and if I had continued, Lord knows, I probably would
have been very prominent these days.

Also, I believed in staying home when I had kids. There was
no day care then, and I wasn't going to leave my kids with anybody. My mother was always at the pastry shop, so there I
was. I had this big house and we needed financial help and I
really do like children. So, rather than go out to work, I decided to do some foster care work. We came to this house

when Carmella was close to six and Ralphie was almost two, and we got three foster kids less than a year after we moved in, in 1954.

I did foster care work for about ten years. Altogether I had twelve foster kids, usually about four or five at the same time. We have three large bedrooms upstairs, and the den on the first floor also used to be a bedroom. But it was very rough. They would give me kids to get them ready for adoption or get them ready to go back to their own home. Most of them had parents who had problems and they would go back after the problem was resolved. Some stayed for six months and some stayed a couple of years. I found it interesting because I kept busy with them. I used to do what my father used to do. I would write plays and the kids would act them out. And I'd give cocktail parties. I still have movies of some of the things we did.

The kids were from different backgrounds. Some were Italian, I had a Puerto Rican kid, I had a German kid. And I thought this kind of bringing up would be good for my own children, because they come from such a segregated community here with just Italians and Jews. It's always been that way since we moved here. So I thought bringing some other kids in would be good, because I know when I was a child it was a help to me. But apparently Carmella didn't feel that way.

You never know if what you're doing as a parent is right or wrong. I was always under the impression that it would help her learn to live with other children and get along with them. She tells me now that when they were very young it did, but then she thought it invaded her privacy. Carmella was the first child and I think we kept her on a pedestal and maybe I spoiled her because I had the other children and because within myself I felt guilty that I may have been taking some things away from her. What I tried to do was make her feel that she was mine and I would take her out by herself, like to the movies or away for a weekend. When she was nine, we went to Italy for ten weeks and we always gave her the best bedroom all to herself. Ralphie was younger, but he never seemed to have a problem with it.

Even from a very young age, I think Carmella was always trying to develop her own personality, her own independence.

She was always fighting me but she always told me that she wanted to do things like I did. One day I detected something and I sat down with her and I told her, "Look, when I was your age I was not like me today." I said, "This came with many years of experience and you're a lot more fortunate than I was at your age. At least your parents can do the best for you, and you don't have to worry about tomorrow." Then, she just wouldn't listen. But it's really strange. Now she's turning out to be just like me.

I think the biggest problem I had with both my kids was due to the Catholic religion. When we first came here, I didn't know too much about the neighborhood. Carmella was five and there was this brand new parochial school that had a kindergarten. The public school didn't have one. And everybody said that parochial education is much better than the public schools. I didn't know anything about it, never having gone, and I figured, well, maybe I missed something, you know?

Well Carmella started kindergarten, and from that time on they started injecting a lot of fear in her. They taught her about the devil and for about ten years she had that fear of the devil at night, and we didn't know about it. She always seemed happy and gay. With Ralphie, if he was disturbed, I would always know about it. They started telling Ralphie that if his mother and father don't go to communion that when we die we'd go to hell. And my kid was very impressed by this. I was really having problems.

I finally went to receive confirmation when Ralphie was in about the eighth grade, for his sake. My father's sister had baptized us behind my father's back. Her name was on the baptismal papers. She always thought my father was crazy. But we never received communion or confirmation and, when I was getting married, they were saying I shouldn't marry with the Church because I never really entered the Church. But the pastor of the church here said, "I'm going to marry you myself, anyway."

Now, neither one of my kids go to church. I went for a while after I received confirmation but, never having gone as a child, I was struck by the hypocrisy of some of the priests. I do believe in religion, though. I think everyone should believe in something. I'm not really an atheist and even though my father claimed he was, I don't think he was. He would tell us that what divides people is the Church, and he would speak unkindly of it sometimes, but he never spoke unkindly of the religion itself. He believed there was one God and we were all his children, regardless of color, creed or race.

Anyway, the first few years of married life we were so poor I couldn't even buy a dress. But I was so used to poverty, I guess it didn't bother me anymore. Even before that, I made enough to live, but I never had any money. I used to give more than I made. Like when I was working for the Red Cross and we used to deal with some of the wives whose husbands were in the Army, I'd bring the allotment check and I'd feel so sorry for the kids that I'd go to my mother's store and pick up some cake and cookies for them. It was always that kind of thing. I think the only time I was able to save some money was when I did foster care work.

During those ten years I was at home all the time. I never left. But I always maintained my contacts with the people I had met prior to my marriage. At election time I would do political campaign work from my basement and all the kids would help, stuffing envelopes for the mailings. Then I would invite people to my home for dinner—people connected to the agencies, political figures that I had met and liked, contacts that I made and didn't want to lose. See, behind my mind, I always had the idea of going back to the kind of work I was doing prior to my marriage.

Even Lyndon Johnson came to my house for dinner when he was vice president. I was doing campaign work for Congressman Amfuso at the time. What happened was, his district was broken up and it became a choice between him and Rooney, who was also congressman at the time. One of them would lose their seat, and Johnson was rooting for Amfuso. They couldn't use any of the party offices to do campaign work, because it wouldn't be right for the party to be working for one and not the other. So they said, "Gee, how about using Mary's house?" So one Sunday they came here to discuss strategy for Amfuso's campaign and in walked Johnson. I liked Johnson. My son Ralphie and I did a lot of work in his Young Citizens for Johnson.

Oh boy, the work that was done in my basement was really

something. We sent out 65,000 pieces of literature for Frank Sedita when he ran for attorney general, before he was mayor of Buffalo. As a matter of fact, when we were working for Sedita, Carmella was seventeen and she went to the party headquarters to find someone to get her license notarized. There was nobody there and she turned around and said to the guy, "You know, my house looks more like headquarters." All the work was really being done downstairs here. But the kids enjoyed it. They met all the celebrities, you know?

It was funny but from the time I lived here, since I always had foster children, I always looked like a dirty housewife. I wasn't at all concerned with how I looked because I was just in the house! And I can get very sloppy. Nobody knew too much about me. I felt, well, if I tell these people about the people I knew prior to my marriage and traveling twenty-three states for the United Nations and meeting the President of the United States, they would think I was making up a story. So I never spoke to anybody about anything, other than how the children were doing.

Then all of a sudden, every once in a while, I would have these parties in my house and you'd see all these limousines with the chauffeurs and people would wonder. As a matter of fact, it aroused the curiosity of so many people in the neighborhood that they actually asked me what the hell was going on. So I said, "Well, they're just some people I know." I wouldn't dare tell them. We have nice neighbors, but I've always been too busy to get involved with them, like visiting for coffee, other than if something is needed.

Well, one day my neighbor was telling a friend of hers, she says, "You should see my neighbor next door. She has Judge so-and-so and Congressman so-and-so coming over." So this lady says, "Who're you kidding? Everytime you see her, she looks like a dirty housewife." So about six months later this woman needed a favor and she went to my neighbor. She still didn't quite believe her, so she was a little reluctant to come here, but she came and sure enough, I was able to help her. It was to help get her son into Annapolis and naturally, this was a big thing. The family was so proud.

As I said, it was strange. For many years I never said anything. Just a few months ago I met a woman who lives across the street who I never met in my life. She says to me, "I've been dying to meet you." She says, "When you moved here I'd say to myself, well, who's the celebrity on the block?" She says, "Somehow or other it never seemed like it was you." Half of the things I did in my life always sounded like I was bragging anyway and who would believe it, you know? I mean at times I didn't believe it myself.

UP FROM THE BASEMENT: THE CONGRESS OF ITALIAN-AMERICAN ORGANIZATIONS

Those ten years when I was at home being a foster mother, I always did social work. Even the priest at the church on the corner would send me anybody who went there looking for help. So I kept myself busy between my own children and the foster kids and helping everybody that needed help in the community. And I was footing my own bills. By 1971, when we first got some money from the city for CIAO, I was in debt to the First National City Bank for forty thousand dollars.

I first met the people at the bank in 1964, when I started with CIAO. I think they were interested in me because of some of my political contacts. They knew I could be helpful to them, and let me tell you what I did for them. When Abe Beame was elected controller in 1965, the guy who was first executive vice president really wanted to meet him badly. One day, before Beame was in office, he called and said he and two other bank officers wanted to meet him.

I had Beame's number at his old job at the bank, so I called him up and he says, "Fine, Mary. Right after I get into office, you come with the three gentlemen and have breakfast with me." So I arranged the appointment, and from that day on they had an open door to the controller's office. To me, that was worth a lot more than the miserable forty thousand that I've been paying interest on all these years. At one point I hoped they'd forget it, but they never did.

I was borrowing money from the bank over a period of about seven years, up until the time CIAO got money from the Lindsay administration, which was only three years ago. So you figure from 1964 to 1971, all the contacts that I made for

CIAO and all the work that I did prior to getting a nickel. Trips to Washington, trips to Albany, meeting people, getting things started. When I finally met Lindsay, I had already been working on the first two day care centers.

We started CIAO in 1964 from my basement. Zack kept saying he thought it was about time the Italians got together. He was always after me about doing something for the Italians. I had been working for everybody else, so he said, "How about doing something for the Italians?" A number of people felt this way too. And, of course, I knew there were plenty of poor Italians because of the work I had been doing prior to my marriage. And then, even while I was at home, a lot of poor people used to come over to me for help, so I was aware of the great need in the Italian community.

There were a lot of people who needed to get on welfare who I was able to help. Then there were problems with housing and people were being kicked out of their homes because they couldn't afford to pay. I'm going to tell you something. When I got married in South Brooklyn, the gifts I received from the poor people . . . Not luxurious gifts. Like one woman brought me one cup and saucer because I helped her with welfare. And there were hundreds like that. So I knew there was a need in the Italian community. This bullshit that the Italians don't want programs is just not true. The reason why it looks that way is that they were told there is no handout for them.

So I had known a number of people I had met in my various walks of life and I sought them out and invited them to get together and talk about the possibility of developing something. We got together with about six or seven groups. It took us a while to get a name together, but then when we figured out the Congress of Italian American Organizations, which spells CIAO, well we liked that name a lot. No politicians were involved, just people that had their own organizations and were interested.

We had Angela Carlozzi of the Italian Welfare League, and we had the professional and businessmen's association. Then we had the real estate association, and the U.S. Customs Association, and the war veterans. Then we got a New York State charter and we started formally as an organization. But for a long time, the members of CIAO didn't know what the hell I was doing and I didn't even bother talking about it because they wouldn't have understood it then. They were just happy that I was doing something and we were getting more members in.

What I had in mind was developing programs for the Italians but I didn't want to say that right away because Italians didn't know anything about programs. What they had in mind was uniting. They felt where there's unity, there's strength, and the reason Italians don't have any political strength in the city or the state is because they're not united. Just the idea of having an Italian governor, for example, was important to them. Not that the Italian governor's going to do anything for the Italians, because as many times as I went to an Italian in political office to get help for the Italians, I never got it.

At the beginning I went along with it, because I knew I needed a group behind me or I would not be recognized by the city. But while they were talking about uniting, I was thinking about doing something for the poor people. It took me a while, but then all of a sudden I started working in the communities myself. None of them had too much time to form the organization, so I was doing it all by myself.

For a long time, even in my own CIAO, I couldn't talk about the Italians having problems. We had the same problems as any other group. The only thing is, they didn't want to recognize it. They were ashamed. It's just like what happened many years ago when a kid was born retarded. The kid was kept at home so nobody would see the retarded child. They kept hiding their problems under the rug.

I think a lot of that was due to the fact that they were told that there was nobody that could do anything for them anyway. So what could they do but just forget it? I mean if they went to one of our district leaders and said, "Say look, I don't have any money, where do I go?" he'd send them a bag of coal rather than saying, "We have somebody who can help you get some welfare." So naturally that person would feel, well, it's a shame that I'm poor and there's nobody to help me.

But as soon as we offered them help, they accepted it graciously. As soon as we opened the first day care center, 95 percent of the kids that registered were from Italian families— some broken families, children born out of wedlock. So how different are we from other groups? I think it's in the mind. This is what the Italians would like to believe, that we're different. But I don't think we are. We have the same problems everybody else does, only the other people are smarter than we are. They know where to go to solve their problems and our poor people never did.

Then also things were changing all over the place. There was the Civil Rights Movement. My brother Joey went down south to help the blacks come up north and my cousin did too. So we knew that the whole world was changing and unless we changed with it, we weren't going to get anywhere. The Italians still had nobody to help them and everybody was still telling them there was nothing for them. Even before the Civil Rights movement there was welfare, but then it was for the poor Jews. The leaders told the Italians it wasn't for them.

See the Jewish people would help their people but the Italian people never did. The Italians will only give provided people know and they can play Mr. Bigshot. If they were contributors, we could run groups such as CIAO and we could build our own centers without government money, with all the wealthy people we have. Some of the richest people in this country are Italians, but many of them are still of the old theory that every Italian has made it, so they don't give.

I remember going to some of the rich ones once with a proposal for CIAO. These are some of the same people I went to for American Relief to Italy. The reason they didn't give anything then was because they wanted to be the originators. They wanted to know why they should give me a contribution when they could send it directly, but you knew damn well they weren't going to do it. I went back to this one guy for CIAO. He sat me down and told me it was a very good idea and that's how far I got. Then another time I went to visit a judge in his chambers. We sat down and he said, "You're doing a beautiful job." And that was the extent of that. Well, that's the typical Italian. Even in Italy they're not contributors.

So then I started with the city because programs meant working with the city and I just felt the city has to do something for us. So what happens, I start going to the city and even to the state and it was the same thing all over the place. Even the Italians in government would say, "Oh, come on, you must be crazy. The Italians don't need anything. They take care of their own families." Well, we're doing such an excellent job of it that we have the second highest school dropout rate in the city. And we have a very high drug addiction rate.

So for a group that's doing such a fine job of taking care of ourselves, we're failing somewhere down the line. And my feeling is that the first failure is the language barrier. We have between twenty and twenty-five thousand Italians coming into this country every year. And the second thing is, the Italians, like everybody else, want to live like the Joneses. And since there was no day care for them, they would leave their kids with anybody and half their kids were left out in the street, getting involved. I think that was one of the biggest failures.

Well, we started in South Brooklyn. Buddy Scotto,* who is very community-minded, has always been active in his area so we talked about doing something. He started in Carroll Gardens. Then we knew that in South Brooklyn there was a very bad narcotic problem. What do we do? We fight to develop a rehabilitation center. It almost took our lives, but we did that and now we have a program, a storefront center.

Then we were talking about a day care and senior citizens' center and Buddy thought we ought to do it in South Brooklyn. I thought it would be a very good idea, but I knew that at one time there had been a big fight in the community because the city wanted to put up a day care center and after spending almost a hundred thousand dollars it flopped. I learned after that the reason it flopped was because the people in the neighborhood didn't know what the hell the city was putting up. Nobody bothered to organize the community first. So I said, "Okay, let's try it." There was the old theater which was vacant and we spoke to the landlord.

The next step was to go to the community and meet with them and find out what their needs were. And that's what we did. We met with every group, with the exception of the politicians. See, the Italian politicians . . . I can't speak about all the politicians, but it seems some of the Italians don't want the people to emerge. Because if the people in their community

* Salvatore Scotto, community leader and political maverick with strong family ties in South Brooklyn.

emerge, they fear they might lose their power. So, as long as they have the people down, they can do whatever they want with them.

Now the young generation is emerging and all that's beginning to change. One of these guys that's been a district leader for about five hundred years just almost lost his own seat and his candidates for the State Senate and the Assembly lost the election. You see the young people are not taking the garbage that the old folks did. The old folks worked hard and this guy would send them a little basket of fruit around Thanksgiving and that kept them quiet and loyal to the leader. But that was all he ever did for them, except maybe for some little favors.

The jobs were usually given to the members of the political club. Outsiders didn't get the jobs. The outsiders only got the basket and a lot of promises. These guys are about fifty years behind times in the way they operate. They can't cope with the young generation that really wants to change things, although some of them are still doing well with the old generation. They always made them feel obligated for that basket, or many years ago it was a bag of coal. That was how they bought their loyalty.

Well, I kept fighting. I wanted to prove that the Italians have the same problems that everybody else has and, with a little help, they can do the same things that everybody else can. They can be taught to accept programs, and welfare if they're in need, and other things that other groups have. And the main thing was not to be ashamed of it. For quite a while it looked like it was going to be a lost battle. I was getting opposition from the members of CIAO and nobody was listening in the city. Then fortunately I met two people in the city who helped me: that was Gladys Harrington and you.

The first one was Gladys Harrington in the Human Resources Administration. Somebody in South Brooklyn had given me her name and I went to meet her. She had heard about me getting involved and she told me, "Mary, you're barking up the wrong tree." And she taught me how to deal with the city. And then I met you and you introduced me to Mayor Lindsay. But what really did it was when you got involved with the ethnic groups and you got the mayor interested in becoming involved with the white ethnics. Well, then we began to get some help, contrary to what the Italians have always said.

See the Italians have a beautiful way of gossiping and speaking unkind of the city and the state, not realizing that they never asked for anything or fought for anything. So how the hell does anyone know that they need anything? So I wanted to change that too. First they kept saying that the Jews get everything. Then it was the blacks get everything. So I said, "How about the Italians getting something? How the hell do you expect to get anything if all you do is organize and play cards? Why don't you get out there and fight?"

It took me a long time to convince them that when the city started giving out the ethnic grants, CIAO was the first white group to get a grant. I think there are still doubts. And I told them that we were the first white group that got day care and seniors' programs without any help from an organization. The Jews got it with matching money at the beginning, but we got 100 percent funding from the city, the state and the federal. So I say to them, "I can't gossip anybody because I know what we've gotten, and I don't see where we've been discriminated against. We discriminate against ourselves."

Another problem is there's always been a tremendous amount of jealousy among the Italians. They're always fighting with each other or running against each other in elections instead of working together. That's what happened with the storefront we have now, the community service agency in the Bensonhurst section of Brooklyn. Before we found this store, Roberta, the director, had found a much nicer store, right in the middle of all the Italians and we thought it would be ideal. So one day I get a call from the owner of the building and he says, "I want to know what kind of work you'll be doing because we got calls that said you'll be bringing blacks and Puerto Ricans in." I said, "That's not true. However, if there are blacks and Puerto Ricans in the community, they have a right to the services."

What happened was the district leader did not want us there because his clubhouse was two doors away. So when we figured that out, what else could the landlord say but, "Okay, you can have the store." So we left a deposit of two hundred dollars and then I get a call from the district leader. He said, "You know, Mary, my club is there, and I'm doing the same thing you're doing," which is bullshit, because he's never done anything for anybody. He says, "Maybe you could move a little ways from here."

Well, I fight all the time and I said who needs it right now? So I said, "Okay, provided you get me my two hundred dollars back." He says, "Don't worry about it Mary, I'll make sure you get it back." Well we moved and we never got the two hundred back. And this is typical. If he had an ounce of brains, he would have permitted us to stay there and worked together with us and we could have been a great help to him. He could have sent his own people in to us. But he was jealous and afraid we would be doing more business than him.

The new storefront is mobbed with people. The biggest problem that Roberta has now is housing. A lot of the seniors are being kicked out of their houses because the landlords want higher rents. And then she has a lot of welfare cases. Now that guy's a district leader. Why the hell doesn't he take care of these things? Well, they never did do anything for the people. But now there's a store that reads "The Congress of Italian American Organizations" so all the Italians feel free to come there. And if they don't speak the language, there's someone there that does, someone they can relate to.

I guess in some ways I'm a threat to some of the Italian leaders and the organizations, because I got rid of this myth about not taking anything from the government. Then I even became a threat to Joe Colombo.* People would say, "But all he has to do is pull out a gun and shoot you!" But I was a threat

---

* Joseph Colombo, Sr., named by U.S. Senate as head of one of New York City's five major organized crime families. Formed the Italian-American Civil Rights League in 1970; started by picketing the FBI in Manhattan for alleged harassment of his son, broadened protest to attacks on government and the press for creating a "conspiracy" against Italian-Americans and for use of the word "mafia"; rapidly developed sizable grass roots base with a program of anti-defamation and social services. Shot in the head in June 1971 at a Unity Day rally at Columbus Circle and never regained full command of his faculties. The loss of its leader, as well as indictments for fraudulent financial dealings, led to precipitous decline of the IACRL.

to Colombo because he wanted to be *the* organization, the only one, that could help the Italians. So what he tried to do was buy me. If I became part of him, then he would still be the only one. And when he didn't get that, well . . . I guess I'm lucky I'm still walking the streets.

I feel the only reason why I am alive is because Colombo knows that two of my good friends are Ralph Salerno* and Nick Pileggi.† Ralph has spent his life fighting the racketeers and Nick writes about them. But still the neighborhood cops and the cops around my office downtown tell me never to walk alone at night and always make sure I know who's coming in.

The first time I met Colombo was around election time in 1970. This woman I knew also knew him quite well and she called my house one day and she said he wanted to talk to me. So I called Ralph Salerno and he said, "Go ahead and see what he wants." So we set a time and the woman came to pick me up and she was all dressed up with a mink, because she was going to see the king, you know? I walked out with a dirty housedress and dirty shoes and she looked at me and said, "Aren't you dressing up?"

So I said, "This is exactly what I think of him."

We went there and we sat down and he said, "You know, Mrs. Sansone, you and I are doing the same work. Why can't we do it together?"

So I said, "Look, the day I start working with you I'm going to lose my respectability and that's something you don't buy."

And he said, "Well, you know, I'm not such a bad guy."

I said, "Well, there's a little good in everybody and I guess there's some good in you."

So then he said, "What is it you want? What are you fighting for?"

"Well," I said, "maybe one day we can have a building for the Italians like everybody else has. You know, the blacks have

---

* Ralph Salerno, retired New York City Police Department sergeant, considered an expert in its organized-crime unit. Since retirement has written a number of books and served as a consultant in the criminal justice field. Testified before McClellan Committee hearings (Select Committee on Investigation of Improper Activities in the Labor or Management Field, 1957–1961) on labor racketeering.

† Nicholas Pileggi, New York journalist noted for incisive coverage of state and local politics and organized crime.

the Urban League and the NAACP. The Jews have the American Jewish Committee and the American Jewish Congress. So maybe one day we can have a building for the Congress of Italian American Organizations, a place where the Italians can go when they need help."

He says to me, "What does it cost, a million bucks? A million and a half?"

So I said, "Perhaps. I don't know too much about real estate, but it could be."

He says, "Good. You have it."

I says, "No I don't. All I have right now is money that I owe the bank." Then I looked at the time and I said, "I'm going now."

He said, "Oh, before you go I'd like to invite you to my festival that the Italian-American Civil Rights League is having."

So I said, "No thank you, I can't afford it." The tickets were two hundred dollars each.

He says, "Oh no, I want you and your husband to come as my guests."

I said, "No thank you."

He says, "What are you afraid of? The governor is coming, the mayor is coming."

I said, "And Mary Sansone isn't coming." So with that I left.

Then right before the festival he called me to find out if I was coming or not, but of course I stuck to my guns. I wasn't going. Then a couple of months after that he called and he said he would like me to go to a meeting of his and speak on behalf of what CIAO is doing. Zack was very much against it, but me being adventurous . . . and also I thought it would be a good idea if I went. I wanted to show him that not every Italian is frightened by a Joe Colombo. So again I spoke with Ralph and Nick and they said, "Oh, go ahead. What have you got to lose?" Of course I realized the day after that I almost lost my life. They sounded pretty sure, but when I got home I found Ralph waiting for me and Nick was on the phone. So they couldn't have been that sure I wasn't going to be shot or something!

Nevertheless, I went and Carmella came with me. I was sitting on the dais and when I got up to deliver my speech, someone from the audience gets up and says, "Mrs. Sansone, before you deliver your speech we've got a few questions to ask you."

So I said, "I wasn't aware that I was to be interrogated."

He says, "Well, you ain't gonna be interrogated. We's jus' gonna ask yous a coupla questions." He says, "Are you associated or affiliated with Ralph Salerno?"

I said, "I don't have to answer that, but I will." I said, "I'm not associated or affiliated with him, we just happen to be very good friends. I like what he does and I admire him."

Well, apparently those were all the wrong words. But I said, "Now can I deliver my speech?" So I spoke and I was very careful not to use the word crime. I just spoke of the problems of the Italian community. Then one guy who is now serving seven years in jail looked at me and said, "Mrs. Sansone, I neva hoid of CIAO and I live in Bensonhurst." So I looked at him and I said, "Well, from the looks of you, you don't need CIAO."

Then Joe Colombo got up to the mike and he says, "Mrs. Sansone, you know I admire you and I respect you but if you really respected us," he said, "you would join us to work for the Italians against Ralph Salerno and Nick Pileggi."

So I said, "Look, I did not come here to discuss them. However, if you want to discuss them I will give you their phone numbers and you can call them up and invite them." So naturally, the king became very indignant. He dropped the mike and with that all the women got up and started yelling, "Kill her, kill her." Those were the wives and the girlfriends. The women start and then the men chime in. My poor daughter was scared stiff. She had diarrhea for a week.

Then Colombo's son got on the mike and he said . . . he called me "You."

I said, "Please address me as Mrs. Sansone." Of course by this time I was getting a little nervous.

He says, "We have proof that you testified before the crime commission."

So I said, "Look, I don't know where you got your phony proof from. I never testified before the crime commission, because I don't happen to be an authority on crime."

Well this created chaos. The son gets on the mike again and he says, "Mrs. Sansone, you insulted us and we didn't insult you."

I said, "What did I say?"

He says, "You said you're not an authority on crime, meaning that we are."

So I said, "That's not true. I said that I, Mary Crisalli Sansone, am not an authority on crime. I didn't mention anybody else." So that kept them quiet.

Then they started with CIAO. "You can't become a member of CIAO unless you got a Ph.D.," you know? Some guy says, "What's a Ph.D.? It's a degree. A degree is a degree. Anybody can have a degree. Even a thermometer has a degree and you know what you can do with that!" Well that ended that.

I was there until one o'clock in the morning, and when I'm ready to leave I get on the mike. I had to have the last word. And I said, "Dear friends, I came here to talk to you about CIAO, but apparently you're not interested in the welfare of the poor." So then I just said "Thank you" and I walked down. Then Joe Colombo came over and he wanted to give me the Civil Rights League pin. I just took his hand and cast it aside and ran out of there.

After that I started getting phone calls in the middle of the night, all kinds of calls. But I was very glad I went because there were a lot of people there that were good and innocent that realized for the first time what was really going on. One night at a meeting in Queens some time after that a man came over to me and he said, "Mary Sansone, you were eight feet tall that night."

I'll tell you, I was pretty damn scared. And then there was poor Carmella in the audience. But I said to myself that they're not going to touch me. First, because I'm a woman. Then because there were about a thousand people there. Also, they knew of my association with Ralph Salerno and Nick Pileggi. And then don't forget that Joe Colombo was in trouble himself with the big guy, Gambino.* As a matter of fact, after that night I got lots of calls from the people that hated Colombo telling me that I would get revenge. I said I wasn't interested in revenge. I just wanted to go there and prove to Mr. Colombo that not everybody is afraid of him, you know?

---

* Carlo Gambino, named by U.S. Senate as head of one of New York City's five organized crime families; known as "boss of all bosses." Now in his seventies, with a heart condition that has foiled government attempts to deport him.

A LIFETIME OF FIGHTING PAYS OFF

Do you know that after ten years of staying home with little children, when I started out again, I couldn't speak English? It was very, very difficult for me. After ten years, I couldn't face a crowd anymore. Standing up in front of a mike really frightened me for a while. It took me about two or three years before I was able to speak. I was scared stiff. Because even when I had parties at home it was just a small group, and we didn't talk about too much, you know? Then here I am going out and becoming an orator.

But Zack was always my best critic. We used to sit down and he would write my speeches for me. And he would insist that I practice them in his presence, so he could check me out. Thank God I overcame that. Now I don't have to write speeches anymore. I can get up and say exactly what I want to say, and that's it.

At the beginning with CIAO, I really had no problem. It was when I became successful that the problems started, because then they all wanted to claim CIAO. Prior to that, nobody could be found. They would come to the meetings religiously, but they weren't even paying dues. Nobody contributed a nickel toward any of the expenses.

A few of the people on the board, nice people, thought what I was doing was a wonderful thing if I could succeed in doing it. The only thing was, they didn't have faith that I would succeed. And I don't blame them, because I was being kicked out of everybody's office, and a lot of the people kicking me out were Italians. But I was determined to succeed, no matter how much debt I went into. There were times I was really worried about my debt and I thought I might have to sell my house or something to pay it back.

But I was so determined and I think that within myself I was sure that I was going to meet somebody that would help me. Also, because of my background, I was pretty well convinced that I had the right experience. I had done organization work from the time I was very young with my father, so I had a knowledge of organizing. And putting programs together is just having good sense and knowing how to organize. I knew that was one of my best features—getting people together.

Well, when we got approval for the first day care center, that did it. I knew I had succeeded. When I started, I didn't know too much about day care. I got smart about it after I met Lou Favre and Bob Davis at the Agency for Child Development. They sat down and they educated me. The only thing I knew before that was that a day care center was a good place for mothers to leave their kids if they had to go to work. And that was the only thing that was important to me at the time, to help these poor women who had been separated from their husbands, and the poor girls who were unfortunate enough to have a baby without a husband, to find a place to leave their children so they could live a dignified life.

Of course there's a lot to day care that I've learned, such as the beautiful education that the kids get and the psychological effect it has on them. We had a four-year-old kid that couldn't say a word, he was so panic-stricken because of the constant argument between the mother and the grandmother over having this kid. He was born out of wedlock. But after a while, the child was able to speak. It helped him a lot to get away from the environment at home where there was constant hostility and come to the center where everybody loves him and he gets lots of attention.

Also, it helps prepare kids to accept going to school. You get a lot of kids who start crying when they first go to school because of the traumatic change from the house to the school, whereas with day care they start going at three and by the time they're ready to go to grade school they accept it with no problems. We were told by the principals of some of the schools that our kids are attending now that they're so far advanced that many of them are ready for the second year.

And look at the mother and the psychological effect it has on her. She's so much at ease and she feels so secure knowing that the child is well taken care of and eats well. They're given breakfast, they're given a snack, then they're given a hot lunch and then another snack. So even if the mother doesn't have time to cook at night, the child has eaten well all day. And we have a lot of fathers that don't have wives. The child is happy to see the father at six o'clock when he picks him up and the father is ready to accept the child.

At the Fifty-ninth Street Center we have ninety-six children in day care and forty in the after-school program for kids from six to twelve. And then we have family care, which is for little babies from the age of three months. You get some children who find it very difficult to be in a classroom with fifteen or twenty other kids and they're better off with a mother and a father in a home. So we place them in a home for the day, and it's very good for the child. There are seventy-five children in family care. At the Court Street Center we have eighty children in day care and forty after school.

Then think of all the people we've put to work. We have five classrooms on Fifty-ninth and there are three teachers in each classroom. And unlike what people think, every teacher's got to be certified. The assistant teacher has to have at least sixty college credits and then the teacher's aide, well, I always say a good mother will make a good teacher's aide. So there are three qualified people in the classroom working with fifteen to twenty kids.

It really makes me feel very good when I walk in and I see all those kids, you know. They're beautiful. We had a graduation ceremony last June that was really something. But even better than day care is the seniors. They are really something else. They're beautiful and they are so grateful. Here were all these women and men in the neighborhood that had no place to go. The children are married and the husband's dead, or the wife. They're completely alone. Where can they go, to church? Now they have a place and they just love it.

This is another myth, that the Italian woman would not accept senior centers. We've got five thousand people registered on Fifty-ninth Street and at least 80 percent of them are Italian. They're at an age now where they don't have a care in the world and they couldn't care less about what they do or what they say or how they behave. They're beautiful because they're so completely uninhibited. They're having a marvelous time. It makes me feel very good when I go there and I see these women doing the same thing that they gossiped every young girl for doing. Like they're living with men because their Social Security will be taken away from them if they marry. And they think nothing of it, you know? It really amuses me.

And then you should see Zack's seniors in Little Italy who are so different from these. They used to wear the black handkerchiefs around their heads, you know? Now some of them are wearing wigs! They went to Washington, they went to the horse races the other day, and I think they're planning to go to Florida. And when the people from Little Italy do that, that's really something. These used to be the real stereotyped Italians. The homebodies, who would never think of going into a center. And now he's gotten close to five hundred people registered. He had to do a lot of outreach work, going into their homes to get them out. But he just loves it and they all love him. Zack has done a magnificent job.

At the Fifty-ninth Street Center we had no problem. Here we have the first- and second-generation Italians who are more modern. They dress well, they went out to work and they're used to going out. In Little Italy you find the seniors that never left their homes, never went out to work. They were the typical mothers who stayed home and took care of their children. And the men would never think of going into a center either. They would play cards, you know, with a group of men at a society, one of those little storefronts they have, or play bocci. But they would never think of mixing with women!

They had a fashion show last June that was something, all these shapes and sizes. And the guts these women had to go on the stage and model! There was this one woman, and I think the whole community came out that night just to see her. She's about my height, which is about four foot six inches, and she weighs about two hundred pounds. A big fat belly, you know? They just wanted to see if she had the nerve to model a gown, and sure enough she did. But this is what makes it so beautiful, the fact that they don't care. Now they're relaxed. They have a little security, maybe they have a little pension, and they don't have to worry about their children because most of them are settled. So they don't have a worry in the world.

We also have other programs in addition to day care and senior citizens. We have English as a second language, which is brought into our centers in the evening, and we have over a hundred people in both centers that are registered for that.

And we have a high school equivalency program, which is packed. That's for all ages. Then we have an adult education program for the seniors, which is doing very well. As a matter of fact, the seniors graduated last June. They got their diplomas and they were thrilled. They took regular school courses—some English, a little history, social studies.

Last summer we had a very good summer youth program. They had photography, they took the kids on trips. Carmella did a fantastic job with that. We got fifteen Neighborhood Youth Corps kids to assist her and she had over two hundred children registered. From the Youth Corps kids we found somebody that had taken dancing lessons, so she was in charge of the dancing group. Somebody else that played the piano was in charge of the music group. Then we had the photography group and a dramatic group. And she put all these groups together and at the end of the season they performed. What a beautiful thing. The drama group did *Snow White and the Seven Dwarfs*. They were little kids from five to twelve. They were just fantastic.

Well, when all these programs finally started it made me feel, well, I've accomplished my mission. I'm able to prove now to the Italians that it's not just the blacks and the Jews and the Puerto Ricans that get things. You can get things if you fight hard enough and don't give up. Another fault that the Italians have is that they're very impatient. They'll ask you for something and if they don't get it instantaneously, well then you're no good, you're not going to do anything for them. But you know as well as I do that you're not going to get anything unless you fight for it.

As I said, it took six or seven years before we got a response from the city, so for all that time, before my office opened in 1971, I worked out of the basement. Besides the debt I went into with the bank, there was also the money I spent that I was making with the foster children. So I would venture to say that the whole six years must have cost me close to a hundred thousand dollars. You figure that I was doing the same work practically that we're doing in the office, only I did it alone. I had two telephones and my telephone bill alone was over a hundred and fifty dollars a month.

You know, not one member of CIAO ever asked me, "Mary,

where are you getting your money from?" Never. And still, when we succeeded, they all claimed CIAO. But I never let them forget that it's mine. It's gotten to a point now where the members will say, "Well, let's not forget that CIAO belongs to Mary. It's her baby." But you see, I even had to fight them. But I guess fighting is easy for me because I had to fight all my life. I had plenty of experience.

Years ago, when I was a young girl, I didn't even realize that I was a girl. I always worked with men and to me, well, I was just one of them. But later on, when I got involved with politics, I realized that every time a politician got up to make a speech and thank everybody that did something for him, my name was never mentioned. At the beginning it didn't bother me too much, but then I realized there must be a reason why he's not talking about me. Then I used to get very angry and I would tell them off. First I didn't realize it had anything to do with being a woman. To me, I was just one of the group doing the work. It's just that I was the only one wearing a skirt. But later on with CIAO, by then I was pretty smart. This is why none of them ever got to be executive director.

Even though I have an office and everything now, I'm still doing the same things I've always done, only I'm doing them outside my house rather than in the basement. Things haven't changed that much. These are the things I did in a way prior to my marriage. Even being on television doesn't overexcite me. I'm glad that I'm able to bring the message across and I can tell people exactly how I feel. But I think the biggest change in my life was getting married and staying home with the children. That was a complete change for me.

I really enjoy my work very, very much. Even the fighting. It aggravates me, but I enjoy my work. And I enjoy hearing about Zack's seniors, that's part of it too. And I enjoy my kids. I like listening to Carmella and her problems, and Ralphie's ambition. I think Ralph wants to go into politics. First I was hoping he would become a doctor, but he chose to take law. He won't be ready to become a politician for about ten more years, so maybe within that time we can get rid of some of the trash that we have in Washington and Albany. The young generation is much less inhibited and much more sincere, so maybe there's a chance that they can change things.

The way things are now, I don't like politics. As far as I'm concerned, you can't be yourself when you're a politician. You're always someone else and you're never telling the truth. You go into a community and you tell people what they'd like to hear and it's not really what you want to say. And that's not me. Also I feel I'd like to help people and once you become a politician you're generally helping the wrong people. You find yourself working only for the people that work for you. It has to happen. Let's assume I run for Congress and a group of people get together to pay for my campaign. My first obligation would have to be to the people who worked for my campaign, whether they merited a job or not.

Then, say you go to Washington and you're a liberal congressman who wants to vote for some programs. But if your constituents don't want you to vote for some bill, and your constituents are usually the people that supported you financially, you're going to find that very liberal person not voting for that bill. Every politician is controlled. Every one. You can't help it. To me, politics is another syndicate. Somebody pulls the strings and then you're obligated. Unless you're rich, like a Rockefeller, and then you can buy people off so it's the same thing. It's a vicious cycle.

Even today people come up to me and want to know why I don't run for the Senate or something, but I won't. I like being myself. I like to express myself the way I want to. If I feel like telling a politician to drop dead, I want to be in a position where I can. If I become a politician, I can't anymore. But maybe by the time Ralphie is old enough things will be different. He's only nineteen now.

Carmella's turning out to be very much like me. It's funny, because I told you how she felt about me when she was a child. Now I hear her telling her friends about her mother. She was really happy when they saw my picture in the newspapers and they went out and bought about twenty copies. I think as they're growing up my kids are beginning to appreciate what I'm doing.

Carmella's teaching now and she's working toward her master's in guidance. Then she says she'd like to go to Italy for her Ph.D. in educational administration. She's getting divorced now, but with all of these plans she certainly shouldn't have gotten married. From the day she married I always said, "Carmella, don't have children for at least ten years." And she said, "You think I'm crazy?" Because if two people separate, the person that suffers is the child. But Carmella loves children and I think her whole life will be revolving around working with children.

Ten years ago I never imagined I'd end up where I am today. It never occurred to me. I knew I was going to do something, but I didn't know in what capacity. At one time I thought maybe I'd take a job with the city, but then I got involved with CIAO. A couple of years ago the President of the United States offered me a job with the Interstate Commerce Commission and I felt flattered, but I turned it down. I don't ever want the Italian people to feel that I'm using CIAO to get a job, but also I was discussing it with Zack and he said, "What would CIAO do if you left?" And I do feel that—I may sound presumptuous—but I know that if I leave CIAO, it will never get further than it is.

Then in addition to CIAO I'm on so many boards that I can't keep them straight. I'm on the National Council of Senior Citizens. I'm on the advisory board for the SEEK Program* with the City University. I'm on the advisory board for the citywide group for the Bicentennial. I'm with the Mayor's Task Force. And it seems that I'm the token white in the black community and the token Italian in the Puerto Rican community.

Then there's the coalition of blacks and Italians that Bayard Rustin† and I started. We had a symposium on affirmative ac-

---

* SEEK (Search for Education, Elevation and Knowledge) Program provides special coaching and counseling for underprivileged students at the City University of New York. Started in 1966, originally designed for minority students, began to include low-income white students in early seventies.

† Bayard Rustin, executive director of the A. Philip Randolph Institute in New York since 1966. A civil rights activist since the 1940's, he helped establish the Congress of Racial Equality (CORE) and the Southern Christian Leadership Conference (SCLC), which Martin Luther King, Jr., headed. Was instrumental in organizing the historic August 1963 March on Washington for Jobs and Freedom, where over 200,000 people converged to dramatize black demands. Once seen as a radical, later viewed as too moderate by some blacks for criticizing black separatism, maintaining alliances with white groups and speaking to the need for coalitions in labor and other fields.

tion and coalitions last spring and the steering committee still meets. I think it's very important to show a little unity between Italians and blacks, that they do get together like the Italians and the Jews. I think it would be helpful to both groups to know that there are some Italian groups that accept the blacks and that there are some blacks that accept Italians.

Then I'm on a couple of committees for Hugh Carey for governor. I have the Alliance for a Safer New York. We're also with the Educational Forum. Then I'm on the board of the New York State Congress of Senior Citizens. And I'm on Senator Fred Harris's tax reform committee. Oh glory, I don't know how many committees I'm on. I can't attend all the meetings. I'm constantly on the go, but it's lovely, though. You keep busy, and you're always doing something for someone.

Now my ambition is to see the development of programs in every Italian community. Because when I develop programs in an Italian community, we're getting the Italians to work with other ethnic groups too. That would be something my father always wished for and if I could succeed in doing just that I would be happy. And I think if I had the opportunity to accomplish that, I could do it. You see, if the problems of Italians are responded to, it's much more likely that they'll work with other groups. There's no question about it.

That's what we did in South Brooklyn and we did it over here in Bensonhurst and we're even starting to do that in Little Italy and that's not easy. Then about three months ago I went to Rosebank on Staten Island, but I was thrown out of there. They're all Colombo's people and they said to me, "You said you would help any Italian group. Would you help the Civil Rights League or the Italian American Coalition?" So I said, "I didn't say every group, I said most every group."

The next thing I know, they sent me a letter. They said they didn't need me. Then right before my grant for the center in Little Italy was to go before the Board of Estimate, I got a call from the borough president of Staten Island telling me that he will not approve my grant unless I give him a commitment that I will not go into Staten Island without consulting him first. When I asked him why, he said the Italian people wanted it that way. So I said to him, "Not only will I give you a verbal commitment, but I'll send you a written commitment."

I did and I made two copies—one for Nick Pileggi and one for myself. So as you notice I'm still having problems with the mafia. But I'm determined to go back and develop programs on Staten Island.

I'd like to see the different ethnic groups working together as much as I want to help the Italians, and I think the best way to do that is to have people work around issues together. And this is why it's so important that programs be given to the ethnics—blacks and whites, equally. What causes a lot of the hostility is the fact that you're getting more than I am, or vice versa. I may hate you only because the city is being nicer to you than it is to me, and we both have the same problem.

Being a poor person all my life, I feel that if all the poor people are given enough to exist, at least there won't be all that hostility between them. As far as the rich are concerned, well they're always fighting each other anyway about who has more. Human nature is very funny and people are all jealous of one another. But I think that I would be extremely happy if I could see everybody work together and be happy together before I died, rather than a lot of hostility.

● POSTSCRIPT

Mary Sansone's determination to go into Staten Island—a New York City borough with a large Italian-American population—won out over her political opposition. By late 1975, Staten Island had two new CIAO chapters. One already has committees on education, political action and human relations and is working to establish a senior citizens' center. The other ran a voter registration drive and is developing a Bicentennial project to depict the contributions of Americans of Italian descent through photography displays, slide presentations and brochures.

The February 1975 release of a demographic study, "A Portrait of the Italian-American Community in New York City," was a major factor contributing to CIAO's increased political muscle and to its growth. The first such study done by an Italian-American group, it exposed the extent of poverty and illiteracy among first- and second-generation Italians. In presenting the dramatic statistics at CIAO's first press conference, Mary served notice on the government that she expects responsiveness. "Italian-Americans do have needs," she concluded. "We want our rightful share and we want it now."

Newspapers from New York to Honolulu carried the story, with headlines that read: "Study Adds Italians to New York's Disadvantaged Minorities"; "A Survey on Italian-Americans Finds Government Is Ignoring Their Needs"; "City's Italian Poor Suffer in Silence." The word quickly reached Washington, and through a bizarre and bumbling bureaucratic route, the federal government did respond.

Senator Hubert Humphrey received the study and directly contacted the Community Service Agency (formerly OEO) to see why CIAO wasn't receiving funding. The New York regional office responded that an Italian group *was* being funded. But when a Washington delegation from CSA came to New York, they were taken to see CIAO's programs instead of those of the funded group, which apparently had little to show for the federal grant it had received.

At the end of the visit, when the director told Mary that she should contact her senators in Washington if she wanted *continued* funding, she said she "smelled a rat" and called up the regional office in a rage. "By mistake," as she put it, "they took them to CIAO because CIAO is the only group that really helps poor Italians and somebody in the government didn't want to be embarrassed." The upshot was a grant of $110,000 to CIAO. According to Mary, the agency was extremely impressed by CIAO. It was probably equally embarrassed by the foul-up.

The grant was a stroke of luck, since it came at a time when CIAO's programs were suffering from New York City's fiscal crisis. But once the funds arrived from Washington, Mary became embroiled in a long and complicated bureaucratic-political struggle to have the money released by the city. "I have to get involved in straightening out the city," she said, "because the mayor's budget department doesn't speak to the controller's office."

"While the city is going down, CIAO keeps going up," Mary noted with irony, largely because it is depending less on the city and more on the federal government—and most recently on private foundations—for its survival. In addition to the CSA grant, CIAO now has two Italian-speaking staff members paid for by ACTION. They are supervising a corps of fifteen VISTA volunteers, also assigned to CIAO, who provide a variety of community services to Brooklyn residents. Paradoxically, though, CIAO headquarters had just moved into a suite of offices twice as large as the first one when a few staff members had to be laid off because of the city's budget crisis.

Mary is still fighting, but the combat zones are getting closer to home and some of the battles have been personally devastating. Recently, when the city took a large slice out of the budget of one of CIAO's day care centers, she sat down with the staff to devise a plan to protect all of their jobs. Her proposal was that each staff member take one hour a day less in pay. The staff voted it down, forcing her to fire six people.

The fighting goes on in the Italian community as well. When the demographic study was released, Mary received angry phone calls from several wealthy individuals and representatives of organizations who told her she had "disgraced the Italians by putting them on the same level with poor minority groups." Some felt sure the statistics were incorrect and threatened to take CIAO to court. She responded, "They came from the city, so sue them."

What hurt her the most is that letters of congratulations on the landmark study came pouring in from Jewish, black, Puerto Rican, Irish, Polish, American Indian and other groups, but there was not one from an Italian organization. In part, Mary thinks, that may have had to do with envy about CIAO's accomplishments. But she also suspects that "Italians are the worst chauvinists in the world. They would never have treated a man the same way."

At home, there is good news. Carmella has completed her second master's degree in guidance and counseling and hopes to go to Italy to get her Ph.D. in child psychology. Ralph scored well on the law boards and plans to enter law school next year. Zack is still extremely satisfied as director of CIAO's senior citizens' program in Little Italy, which plans to move to a new building early next spring. And Mary, despite unending problems, continues to thrive on boundless energy and determination.

Janice Bernstein on the Mattapan street where she used to live.

Janice Bernstein (*second from left, front row*) at a meeting of the Ledgewood Senior Citizens' Center in the Mattapan section of Boston.

Janice Bernstein

THE SPLENDORS
OF BOSTON'S BLUE HILL AVENUE

I was born in Dorchester on May 1, 1931. I lived in Dorchester-Mattapan all my life. Born there, bred there and lived there till only four years ago.

My mother was divorced when I was fourteen months old. She had to go out to work, so I was raised by my grandparents. I was an only child and they spoiled me rotten. They didn't want anything to happen to the little baby, you know? I wasn't even allowed to go out in the street without an escort until I was in my early teens.

My grandmother and her sister came here from Russia. They had lost their parents from what they used to call consumption in those days. They were two lonely creatures, but their parents had put away some money for them. They decided to come to America and they were the talk of the shtetl there—their village—just like in *Fiddler on the Roof*.

My grandfather came from Russia too. His father and mother were very well off. He fell in love with my grandmother and he followed her here, but his father disowned him so he came here penniless. He married my grandmother when she was about nineteen and they came to Boston, to the West End. There were a lot of Jews in the West End then, just like New York had its Jewish ghetto, with a lot of Russian Jews. Then there were the German Jews and those two hated each other. But you know as far as I'm concerned, a Jew's a Jew. Who gives a damn if he's Russian or English or Chinese!

My grandfather was a jack of all trades. He opened up a grocery business. He could paper and paint. Whatever he touched he could fix. But he was a very sick man. Whatever venture he went into, he got sick and had to drop whatever he was in at the time. It was a real tough struggle for them. My mother told me about days when she didn't even have a penny for an ice cream and her mouth would just sink right down into her shoes. They had a bed and a chair and that was it. Then of course, as time went by, things got a little better.

I was the love of my grandfather's life. I could do no wrong. Whatever I wanted, he gave me. Even up to my teens, he was walking me to school every day. I was the only one being walked to school, so finally I said, "Look, Zaydeh, you're embarrassing me. Enough's enough already." I was pudgy as heck and ridiculed by the kids no end.

My grandparents had four children who worked and helped support them. My grandfather became a big wheeler-dealer in the synagogue and that was his whole life. He was Orthodox, not to the extreme of not answering the telephone on Saturday, but he wouldn't handle money and he wouldn't ride on Saturday for any reason. Then he was sort of semi-retired and he became secretary of the synagogue. He got paid for handling the books and he was like the sexton too. People remember him. He was really something. He took that shul from nothing and built it up to triple its membership.

His one ambition in life was to be rich. He only wanted to give to the shul. Nothing could please him more than to say that Mr. Alpert pledged a thousand dollars. But he just never had the money to do that. He used to collect funds for the Combined Jewish Philanthropies too. I was only a little tot at the time and I would go with him from door to door. No one would say no to my grandfather. He just wouldn't take no for an answer.

We had this potato sack to collect the money in and then we'd go to the captain, Sadie Goulson. Her house was like a beehive with people coming in and out all day, bringing the money they collected. She'd fill barrels with it. My grandfather would so proudly empty his sack into that barrel. You can't imagine the thousands of dollars they collected from Roxbury, Mattapan and Dorchester. And God bless Sadie. She still collects for them.

There was a warmth we had in those days, a very protective warmth. We moved three times into apartments, until the last time when we bought a three-family house on Harvard Street in Dorchester in 1941. My grandfather took such pride in that house. My aunt moved in downstairs with her husband and two children and we had a very fine neighbor upstairs. We were like one whole family in that building.

When my mother and father got divorced, my father left, and my mother had to support us. She worked for twenty-two years as a salesgirl. She got married again twenty-two years later to a cousin of my husband's. The year after I got married, my husband and I fixed them up. He was a very kind, wonderful man whose wife had passed away. My mother lived nine years of delirious happiness with this man who when they made him they threw away the mold. He was the only father I ever knew.

Funny thing is, about ten years ago I got a very strange note in the mail with forty dollars in it from Denver, Colorado. No name on it, but I knew it was from my father. So I wrote him a letter and I said, "For God's sake, you could at least sign your name. I know who it's from." After that we started corresponding.

When I was a kid, every once in a while my father's mother would send me a gift. I knew her name but I had never seen her. I had heard that she was the head salesgirl in the fur department at Chandler's. So one day when I was about thirteen, I went into town with my girlfriend for the first time and we happened to go right by Chandler's. I said to myself, I want to go see what my grandmother looks like.

I was a little nervous, but I was curious and something sort of pulled me up there. I asked somebody who she was and then I went over to her and I asked her if she knew who I was. She said, "No." So I said, "I'm your granddaughter." Well, she was so thunderstruck I thought she was going to have a heart attack. We got very close after that and I saw her quite a bit. She could never explain her son.

My dad, my stepfather really, died a terrible agonizing death from cancer in 1963. That was December, and the following February my grandfather died. He was over eighty then. My grandfather, God bless him, was the kind of person who was always crying wolf. Whenever he wanted his own way he would say in Yiddish, "I'm dying, I'm dying." We got to a point after a while where I suppose we just didn't believe him anymore. But one morning he told my aunt he wasn't feeling well and by the time my mother came into the room he was dead.

My mother's been living with me for twelve years now, since my dad got sick. We were always more like girlfriends than mother and daughter, but we're complete opposites. She's an introvert and I must take after my father, there's no doubt about it. Now we're as close as two peas in a pod. We love garage sales and we go to them every Saturday morning. I like to take her out because she has no diversion. Every day of the week she goes to take care of her mother, who's eighty-six years old. My grandmother's got a clear mind like a bell and not a wrinkle on her face, just like my mother, but she's almost a total invalid now.

When I was a kid, my mother had one day off a week plus Sunday and she'd spend that whole day cleaning house. My grandmother did the cooking and we always wondered how she learned to cook. I mean she came here as a very young girl. Where'd she learn to make all those things? Every Friday morning you could wake up to the smell of challah at the table. She must have been up since three o'clock in the morning baking. Gee, I tell you, those were the days.

Years ago when kids got married, they went on their honeymoon and came right back. They just never moved out of the neighborhood. They'd live with the mother for a while and then they'd move into a house across the street or around the corner. Come Sunday, there weren't too many cars on the road. Family would visit family. Our table was always filled with fruit and nuts and people would come for tea. Uncles, aunts, cousins. Then they had friends from the same shtetl that lived around the corner, and they would come over too.

As a youngster, I used to look forward to the Jewish holidays. We'd walk Franklin Field, which you wouldn't dare walk now, and you'd see all your old friends sitting there on the wall. And of course we'd be wearing new shoes and our feet hurt like hell, but we didn't care. We'd walk with our blisters and all, hoping the boys would look at us. And we looked forward to the preparation and the smell of the food. As a young girl, those were my happiest days.

It was a way of life that I really loved. The political rallies,

how they met at the G & G. That was like a landmark on Blue
Hill Avenue. It was a kosher-style restaurant and this was
where everybody congregated. The old people would sit there
for hours over a cup of tea. All the politicians would come
there. Kennedy, Adlai Stevenson. They'd put up a platform
with loudspeakers and they'd have the lights up in the sky.
You could hear it for miles around and we'd come from all over
to see it.

Even President Roosevelt drove down famous Blue Hill
Avenue when he was running in the late 1930's. I remember
my grandfather putting me on a box so I could see the President when he rode by. He'd turn over in his grave if he ever
knew how Roosevelt really felt about the Jews. That's the sad
part of it. There were Jewish worshipers all over the country
who revered this man. But my grandfather would say to me,
"Wave, wave, it's President Roosevelt." And everybody would
shout out.

Blue Hill Avenue was a beehive of activity. Everything re-
volved off of it. You didn't have to go anywhere else to get
anything. You could get born there and die there. Doctors to
funeral parlors. You could have your hair done, have a mas-
sage. There was the post office, library, banks. If you weren't
happy with one bank, you went to another. On the warmest
days you'd find people so massed on the sidewalk, you'd have
to walk in the street.

You could never walk down Blue Hill Avenue and not meet
somebody you knew. It was either a relative or an old school
chum, or somebody you met at a wedding or a bar mitzvah.
Ordinarily it would take maybe twenty minutes to walk down
the avenue from where I lived, but you'd always meet somebody at the baker or the butcher and it would end up taking
two hours. Everybody knew everybody and there was a closeness. I never had any fear. We never locked our doors.

Every neighborhood has its problems, but there was a feeling of warmth and contentment there. You'd feel like somebody
took a robe and put it over you to comfort you and said, "Don't
worry my child. Everything's going to be fine." I really miss
that. I get along beautifully with my neighbors now, but it's
different. I'm in a foreign country. It's a mixed block—a few

Jewish families, Italian, French-Canadian, Anglo-Saxon, all kinds—which I think is good. The way trends are now, you've got to learn to live with other people. But that closeness is not there that you have in an ethnic neighborhood.

When we first moved to Morton Street it was a very mixed area. At school it was about 40 percent Jewish and 60 percent non-Jewish. And there were fights. When the kids came out of Hebrew School they were beaten up by the Irish. Way back there was an Irish builder who bought a lot of property in Mattapan and brought in the first Irish families. They were looked down on by the Protestants something terrible because of the umpteen children.

Then the Protestants and the Catholics looked down on the Jews when they moved in after the Chelsea fire in 1907. They had no place to go so they started to migrate slowly into Dorchester and Mattapan. Then as time went by, it got predominantly Jewish. Little by little most of the others moved out and you got what you call "the line." Like the line in South Boston now that says blacks shouldn't go beyond a certain point. I think what it all boils down to is they just didn't like the idea of the Jews moving in.

My best school year was the last one! My marks were good, but I was just lazy. I would do my homework five minutes before I had to go to bed. It was boring. And their ways of teaching were boring, boring, boring. They went through the same ritual with every kid in school. In those days, teachers weren't able to get married so they were the real old maid types.

There were very few Jewish teachers then. They were Catholic or Protestant and a lot of them were very anti-Semitic. A few were wonderful, but some were really rough. If you stayed out on the Jewish holidays they made remarks to you. A lot of the Jewish children really went through the mill in those days. There were always ethnic slurs and the swastika on buildings, and then there were anti-Semitic remarks in chalk or paint on the front of the synagogue.

It still goes on. Synagogues have been burned and vandalized here in the past couple of years. My children know that it's a part of life, but they're smarter than I was. I led a much more sheltered life and it took me a while to learn. They know what to answer. And of course nowadays on the Jewish holidays notices are sent out and the schools are asked not to give any tests on those days.

I've always kept my kids out on all the holidays because we observe them. We're Conservative, not Orthodox, but I really feel that there should be some tradition in every family. I cook all the traditional foods on the holidays. Even though I've broken away from a lot of my beliefs in the past, I feel that you have to have something.

I guess I kind of dreaded school. I had my share of teasing from the kids and on many an occasion my grandfather came running up to school to find out what was going on with some of those teachers. But then I learned to fight my own battles and had a few skirmishes where I actually beat up some of the kids who made life so miserable for me. But as the years went by, I had lots of friends. As kids get older and a little wiser you don't have those problems, really. But children can be cruel.

In my younger days, my ambition was to be an artist. I wanted to go to college and I had an opportunity to go to the Vesper George School. My art teacher taught me privately too and I had won some contests as a kid. But as far as that was concerned, when I was sixteen my mother got me a job in Filene's, where she was working. I worked in the stock room two nights a week after school and on Saturday. Then I was transferred to the big house, they called it, which was a big stock room.

The money coming in was good and I just had no money to go to college. My mother said to me, "Janice, I can't send you. I haven't the means." She said, "Wouldn't it be better to work and make some money?" Well, I worked my way up there in no time. I got up to the merchandise adjustment office and I had a darn good job up there. So that was it, as far as my schooling was concerned.

I had wanted to go to college very much, but I don't think it would have added anything really or changed my life in any way. I still paint and I make my own designs for needlepoint, but it's just become a hobby to me. I read a lot and find out whatever I want through reading. If I had known I was interested in writing, maybe I would have taken up a writing course. But I got a job that I had no training for and I did well at it, so how would college have helped?

The merchandise adjustment office was like a complaint department. I worked there for ten years and that gave me really good communication with people. I used to write letters to customers and I could just about turn down any illegitimate complaint, but very nicely. They taught me how to get the word across but to be a little diplomatic too. It was really interesting. You got to know the crooks from the authentic people, you know? And we had a lot of laughs in that place. Before I left I was offered the job of assistant director there. I was sorry to leave, but I was pregnant and my husband wanted me to quit work already.

The way I met my husband was a funny situation. I was working at Filene's and going out with a lot of the fellows there, but in groups. We never dated singly, we were all just friends. There was a bunch of about seven or eight guys and girls who met at work, Jews and Gentiles, and we'd go out to lunch together or for cocktails, and we celebrated everything together.

Then Bob Brennan, a very dear friend of mine, was going into the service. We gave him a farewell party and he asked if I would write and let him know the news of the day and I said I'd be happy to. One day, after he was away for maybe three months in training, he wrote me a letter saying that there was a nice Jewish boy who lived just around the corner from me and nobody writes to him except his family. Bob let him read my letters and he thought they were great, so would I mind writing to this boy.

So I figured, well, I'm already writing to two other guys in the service, one more wasn't going to hurt. So I said, "What the heck. Sure I will." We exchanged pictures and we liked each other's pictures. Then he said he was coming home in April on leave, before going overseas, and he would like to see me. So I said, "Fine." He looked like a nice boy in the picture and his letters were very nice.

Well, he came in and surprised me. I didn't expect him that day and he came right up to see me at Filene's. I looked at him and I said, "It's you!" He says, "It's you!" We went out that night to different night clubs and it was a very exciting night.

He wined and dined me for three weeks and I had the most marvelous time that I've ever remembered in my life. And I had a beautiful figure then. I was very thin.

Before he left for Korea he told me that he would be gone for eighteen months and he asked me to wait for him. I really liked him, but I was at my peak then. I was having a ball and I thought, gee, eighteen months is an awful long time to wait. I said, "I'll let you know." But believe it or not, I waited for him and I did not go out with anyone outside of my group.

So Sumner and I corresponded and I used to draw pictures for the boys—pin-up girls and stuff which they loved. Then the night he came home after eighteen months he proposed to me. We got engaged and he gave me a hope chest and two years later we got married. We waited two years because Sumner didn't know what he was going to do yet.

I said I could work and save up money for us, so I stayed at Filene's until two and a half years after we were married, when I was pregnant with my son. Then we waited four years before I got pregnant with my daughter. I wanted two kids and we were just lucky it worked out that way.

Sumner had wanted to be a doctor at first. He was in pre-med, but he just couldn't master the chemistry part of it so he turned to business. After the service he went to night school to train to be an insurance salesman, but he just wasn't happy with that kind of work. He's a nice, quiet, honest, clean-cut, handsome guy. But you know not everyone can be a salesman. You've got to be a conniver and my husband's not a conniver.

Since his insurance business was at night, he decided he'd go and help my stepfather out at his cleaning and tailoring store. My stepfather was quite an important guy. He was called the Mayor of Beacon Street. When he was young, he went from door to door and all the wealthy people became his customers. He served only the elite.

So Sumner would pick up and deliver and work in the store and do his insurance at night. Then my stepfather passed away, and my mother left him the store, lock, stock and barrel. But there was one flaw there. The overhead was tremendous and my husband was not a tailor, where my stepfather was. My husband had to hire three tailors to do the work and they were taking home more pay than he was. Then the landlord kept raising the rent, and eventually my husband had to sell the whole business for practically nothing. My stepfather had a gold mine there, but he was the whole business.

In those years, I would do odd jobs from the house. For years after I left Filene's, when they got bogged down at Christmastime I would help them write the letters. Then I was doing statistical typing for an accountant, which I hated. I typed themes for college students and stuff like that. I did all kinds of work I could do at home for some extra money, which we always needed. I really don't believe in leaving children when they're young. They fly away from you fast enough.

My husband's a very devoted father. He loves kids and he would have liked to have a dozen. I had a miscarriage after Karen, so then I said that's it for me. But he took over from the time I came home from the hospital. He never had any qualms about picking up the children like some fathers have, or feeding them at night. Once a week I'd go out with my card group or Mah-Jongg group and he'd think nothing of feeding the baby and putting it to sleep.

My husband is the kindest most easy-going person. We made a vow not to argue in front of the children and if he sees I'm upset he knows just what to do. He walks out of the room! I get over it, because who am I going to argue with? He gets along with everybody. He always sees the good side. I used to be hard on people and hold grudges like my mother, and my grandfather was like that too, but my husband's influence really changed me.

I was absolutely happy just being a housewife. I loved it. The only thing I hate to do is shop for food, but I love to bake and I love to cook. I love to take care of my family and have company over. I was never dissatisfied with my life.

REDLINING AND BLOCKBUSTING

When I first got married, we lived with my in-laws for two and a half years on Fessendon Street in Mattapan, right next to a big synagogue. I got pregnant two years later and we took a four-room apartment on Esmond Street across Franklin Park, right around the corner from my grandparents on Harvard

Street, so I was a constant visitor there. They were crazy about the grandchildren.

Even after we got married, it would be unthinkable not to spend Rosh Hashanah walking down Blue Hill Avenue with the baby carriage and proudly parading your children in front of your friends and neighbors. Who could do that now? You see black faces peering out at you wondering what you're doing in their neighborhood. It's not the same. But it could have stayed relatively the same because it was a neighborhood that really asked very little out of life. Only to be left alone, to live in peace.

In the 1950's, it wasn't the 50,000 Jews that we once had. There were maybe 15,000 or 16,000 Jews. But these were people who were going to stay in the neighborhood until they died. And young couples like us were buying houses in the area. In other words, we'd never have 50,000 Jewish families again, but Jew would replace Jew, and they were there to stay. They weren't going anywhere.

It was an old community. Young people were moving out to the suburbs, and you can't blame them. You can't accuse them of abandoning their people really. Hey listen, the immigrants that came here, their children moved to Newton and Brookline years ago to try to improve themselves. I'll say one thing about a Jew. If they can improve themselves through education or any other way they'll do it. And their families weren't having problems in Dorchester and Mattapan before the banks came into it.

But the apathy that surrounded the community helped kill it too. You know this old philosophy of Jew helping Jew was at the beginning. When they first came here to the United States their hand was always out to help the next person. Now it's not so. When a Jew becomes prosperous, and this is the way it is unfortunately, a good many of them forget their own past. They live in their own little affluent world and couldn't give one damn about what happens as long as it doesn't affect their own community. This third generation of Jews is a selfish lot, unfortunately. If it isn't going to benefit them, they're not going to reach out their hand. Though there are some who aren't that way.

When our second child was born the four rooms were just

not enough for us and we decided to look for a house. By then, several black families had taken over property there. They bought conventional. They worked very hard for their money and they were fine people. On Esmond Street next door to us was Judge Godene and his children, and there was a professional dancer and her husband. We would walk into Roxbury and go into the bagel place and there were blacks around all the time. There was no fear then at all.

There was no problem because they were the northern blacks then. There's a big difference between the southern blacks who were very oppressed and the northern blacks. Even though there was job discrimination and everything else in the North, they were not oppressed in the same way. When the southern blacks started to get bused up here at night in the thousands of buses that came in, and Roxbury started to burst at the seams, they had to go somewhere. But they didn't go to the left and they didn't go to the right, which was Irish and Italian mostly. They went right down Blue Hill Avenue, where the Jews lived.

We bought our house on Ormond Street in Mattapan in 1963. It was a two-family house and my in-laws lived downstairs, and then after my stepfather died my mother moved in with us. Living on the hill in Mattapan was my one-time ambition in my younger days. That was where the classy Jews lived. And I always loved that street. You could sit up there and look out all over Mattapan from my top-floor window. There was an excitement about watching Blue Hill Avenue. The hustle and bustle was just constant. Even at two o'clock in the morning there were people riding down the avenue.

The first four years of our life up on Ormond Street was happiness all over again. It was mostly Jewish, but we had Catholic families on that street and Protestant, and one black family that moved in a couple of years after I did. The Youngers. He was a policeman. There were 140 white families and one black family and there was all harmony on that street. We'd sit out there every day in front of my house, because I had the biggest driveway on the street, and we'd talk together. And you could walk anywhere very peacefully.

One day I was hanging out clothes on the line, and I happened to hear a neighbor in the back asking another neighbor to come to a meeting at his house. It struck me kind of funny, so I kept listening, but I could only get dribs and drabs about people getting frightened, rumors. So then I yelled over to him and I said, "Jack, I didn't mean to overhear, but are you having some sort of a neighborhood meeting?" Of course, you know, I have to know everything that's going on in my neighborhood. I was just that type of person. Even to this day people call me up and ask me if I heard this or that story.

He told me that there was something going on, there were some rumors, and they're going to check it out. They were having the first neighborhood meeting and somebody from the Jewish Community Council was going to come to help see what was wrong. So he says, "Bring as many friends as you want." A couple of days later I brought some friends and we went to the meeting.

What had happened was, they had heard rumors that the crime rate had gone up 33 percent in one year in Dorchester and that the neighborhood was turning black. People were panicking so, that they were underselling their houses to get out. I said, "Something's wrong. Why are people panicking so? If they hold on to their property, nothing can happen." But you see, it wasn't that simple. We still didn't really know what was happening in Dorchester until one day, we started getting calls that real estate agents were blockbusting. They started calling up on the phone, asking if we wanted to sell our homes.

In the meantime, we had meeting upon meeting and we decided to form an organization. Dorchester had the bulk of the Jews and Mattapan was more of an integrated community religious-wise, but we decided to call it the Mattapan Organization. By the time we got the organization off the ground, we realized that there was nothing we could do to save Dorchester, but we could save Mattapan. Not by keeping blacks out, but to make sure that it was truly integrated. Because we all wanted to live there till we died. I thought we'd marry our kids out of there. My in-laws thought they'd be carried out in coffins from there.

The organization started in 1967 and we came across an article very unexpectedly about a rabbi in Laurelton, New York, where the community seemed to be having the same problems that we were. The rabbi was coming home from services and noticed four "for sale" signs on one street. He went to the next street and he noticed some more "for sale" signs. Then he decided to investigate it on his own and this intrigued us.

What happened was they were having racial tensions and fights in a community where they never had those problems before. When they found it was the speculators coming in and blockbusting, they decided to open up their own real estate agency, for no profit. You could get a license to sell a house if you weren't taking a commission, and it worked successfully. We thought we'd try the same thing. We thought we could put these real estate agents that were blockbusting out of business. But by the time we got started, we were already six months too late.

When we first got our real estate committee together, we still didn't really understand what was happening. Then my friend Harry Sklar went into a bank and there on the wall was a map of Dorchester and Mattapan, and on that map one certain area was outlined in blue. Then and there he knew what was happening. They made a line on a map designating certain streets, and it was within this line only that low-income families, preferably black, could get mortgage money insured by the federal government.

You see it was right after the Martin Luther King murder and after the rioting that went on in Roxbury, and something had to be done to help that community. It was bursting at the seams and needed help to get into housing, and the only ones that could help would be the banks. Mayor White asked them for help, but he did not ask for the line or for blockbusting. Personally, I thought the mayor had a great idea. It's as simple as this: if you own your home, you don't burn it. Those bankers could have turned out to be such heroes. You could have pinned medals on them for what they were doing. But it backfired.

What they did was they set up the BBURG (Boston Bankers Urban Renewal Group) with twenty-four banks, and they got twenty-nine million dollars from Washington, from HUD (Department of Housing and Urban Development), for mortgage money. Then they drew this line and even though the black community leaders questioned the line, and the people too, they were so desperate to move that they just shut their mouths. The banks turned around and simply told them, and I have testimony on this where it says it in plain English, "If you don't like it, we won't give you any mortgages." So it's like you give a person a piece of bread who hasn't eaten for a week and, God, they'll gobble that bread up and that's it.

The line just happened to be in the middle of the biggest Jewish community in Boston. It wasn't in South Boston, where the Irish are. It wasn't in East Boston, where the Italians are. It was right in the middle of Dorchester-Mattapan. There was no opposition from the Jewish people per se, but by the time they knew what hit them it was too late. It started in 1967, and by 1968 it had saturated Dorchester and was halfway into Mattapan.

Nine new real estate agents opened up within a tiny radius in one year, all around the area. They started with the hill where I lived and they surrounded us. They took one house at a time and then one street at a time until the whole hill was saturated with black families. What we tried to do was to keep the people from moving. We had an awful lot of people that were interested in what was going on and didn't want to move out of the area, so we formed block meetings.

When the first two black families after the Youngers moved in, we invited them to our meetings because we wanted them to know what we were doing. And they were thrilled. They said they didn't want the street to become all black. They said, "We moved here because we want it to stay mostly white. We know city services will stop otherwise and the neighborhood will go downhill." They were northern blacks and they came to our meetings and they didn't want the poor riffraff coming in either.

If there's one way for an exodus to begin, there's ten different ways. You had like a puzzle, and each piece of that puzzle fit in very conveniently. The Lewenberg School was a middle school, a junior high school. Many great people came out of that school and it was the number one school in the Boston area, outside of Boston Latin School. In two years it changed racially from 40 percent black to 99 percent black.

When it began to tip the scales by over 50 percent, the School Department according to law had the right to stop open enrollment then and there. But no matter how many meetings we had with them, they just wouldn't do it. They said they couldn't turn anybody away if there was a seat available, but that wasn't true. In fact, the Department of Health, Education and Welfare admitted that the School Department and the School Committee were very wrong in what they did. I guess the School Department figured our area was pinpointed anyhow. It was going to die.

Also, they didn't take the disciplinary measures which they had every right to do. For instance, if a child was caught stealing or hurting another child or extorting, they had a right to suspend that child and call up the parents. But instead, they'd transfer the child to another school. You see, you can't hide a problem. You've got to face it. I don't have the solutions, but I'm much wiser because of what happened.

All they had to do was get together with community leaders, black and white, and discuss it. You know the best way to solve a problem is by sitting around in a circle and getting it out of your system. You might end up beating each other up, but if people are concerned it will work out. Sometimes the simplest way seems the hardest. If they called the NAACP, if they called white and black community leaders, if they had meetings with troubled youngsters and found out the reason for the hostility in them, I'm sure they would have . . . well it's working now. They have what they call a cluster method where certain problem children are handled in a small group and it seems to be working out beautifully.

The school was the reason for part of the exodus. Some parents were so afraid to tattle on a kid for fear of repercussion that they just simply got up and took their kids out of school and moved. But a lot of us were determined to stay. We had only been in our house four years when all this started to happen, and we put five thousand dollars into it, which was a heck of a lot of money to put into a house in those days, and we got a 5½ percent mortgage.

Not only that, but I know I got involved because, damn it, I think I care a little. I saw what was happening to my neighbors who were happy walking down Blue Hill Avenue and couldn't do it anymore. On crutches, with canes, they'd be knocked down. I said to myself, "Hey, you're going to be old some day. Are you going to be ignored like they're being ignored?" So I made up my mind then and there. Because you can't abandon them. You just can't. They came to this country with nothing but the clothes on their back. And their children and their children's children don't seem to give a damn. You go to these nursing homes I go to now and you see these people who are forgotten, people that I remember who were active in the community, some of them in my grandfather's shul. And they tell me, "Janice, nobody comes to see me." And I don't know what to say to them.

Anyway, at one point we got up to between five or six hundred members in the Mattapan Organization. There was the beautification committee, which they put me on, then there was the real estate committee, which was one of the biggest. Then there was police, schools and recreation. My committee was trying to bring improvements into the area. I had about forty-five or fifty members. Then we combined it with the recreation committee, so I inherited those members too.

You know Mattapan had always asked for very little. They were content with their playgrounds, with the trash collection. It was peaceful and quiet. But I thought that if we bettered things that people would have an incentive to want to stay. I knew that in the new communities that go up they bring in all these things, so that's what we did.

I became very good friends with two people at the Parks Department and they really bent over backward to do whatever they could within their limits. I asked for recreation equipment for playgrounds and they told me how to go about getting it. I asked for new lighting, I got that. It's who you know, not what you know, unfortunately. I really have to give them credit for understanding the situation and trying to do what they could to help, but it didn't keep the people from moving.

When all this began my husband was on the real estate committee and he would come to meetings on the days when he wasn't working. But he had three jobs then. He worked on Saturday selling at our friend Harry Sklar's stationery store to make a few extra dollars, and he still does. Then he was working at Jordan Marsh at night, selling. His main job was at the Mattapan Little City Hall at that time, so he would leave work, go right uptown, and come home at ten or eleven at night. And one day he got sick. I said to him, "Sumner, you've got to give up a job. You just can't keep up this pace and the hell with the damn money. I want you around for a hundred years." So he quit the Jordan's job.

Before that, he would sleep most of the time he had off because he'd be so tired. But after he quit Jordan's he got active and joined the police committee too. We were both active and we both attended all the meetings. The beautification meetings were at my house, until it got so big that we just couldn't and we had to meet at the school. But I had meetings at my house most of the time. I believe in people sitting around informally. Sometimes you get more with a little honey.

My kids came to some of the meetings, but I think they were too young to understand a lot of things and they resented my not being at home at night. My mother was a permanent baby-sitter. And when my mother would come to the meetings, my in-laws who lived downstairs would sit, or vice versa. I always made sure that the kids had their supper and were ready to go to bed before I left, but they resented it, especially if we had a meeting every night of the week.

Anyway, during this time racial tensions were high, and understandably so. Here you have a quiet community where nobody bothered anybody, and all of a sudden you get hand-bag snatchings and the robberies go up and it's an unsafe neighborhood. So to keep things cool, the city's Office of Cultural Affairs was setting up a summer entertainment and recreation program that they called Summerthing later on. It was a great idea. A certain amount of money was allotted, so much from the city and the rest was contributions from people.

Cathy Kane from the Mayor's Office was going into all the Boston neighborhoods to interview people. I guess she knew about me because of all the letters and calls I made for the beautification committee. She appointed me coordinator for Mattapan. I thought it was a great idea because where tensions were so high and people were so suspicious of each other, maybe, just maybe, there would be a chance for neighbor to meet neighbor and get to know each other.

Also, that first summer in 1968, Sumner was home and could take care of the kids while I worked. After he sold his business he thought he could go to school and take up computer, but then he found out that the G.I. Bill didn't cover him any longer. So he walked the streets for months and we exhausted just about every penny we had in our banking account. But that summer I made a little money and he was collecting unemployment so, between the two of us, we were able to make do with what we had.

The summer of 1968 I ran the program in Mattapan with a limited budget. I got paid very little but I was just happy to try to keep the neighborhood together. It was really such a terrific summer that I thought maybe things might turn back a little bit. You know, that people would begin to trust each other again.

I ran classes for the children, arts and crafts, and guitar lessons and dancing lessons and photography. And they opened the school for me so the kids could have classes there. Then we had nighttime programing so the adults could come too. The Boston Ballet came down to the playground and rock 'n' roll bands. Then there was all kinds of ethnic dancing, I had square dancing, we showed first-rate movies outdoors. It was really a terrific year. And it was really a mixed group. A good number of blacks participated too.

The second year was even better than the first, because I had more money to work with so I was able to bring in more entertainment, and I could have workshops for some of the older people as well as the youngsters. The third year was devastating. Nineteen-seventy was worse than I could have imagined. By then, a great many black people had moved in and it was already tipping the scales. And some of them would do anything in their power, unfortunately, to disrupt the performances. And we couldn't leave anything in the playground without a guard anymore. It was always stolen.

We started to get kids in there that were just out to get whitey, no matter what. We never had this before that summer, but every other word out of their mouths was "mother fucker," "honky," "white trash." They just hated the whites and that was it. It was a group of real southern blacks. You could tell from their accent.

We really tried. I brought in soul singing and the Graham rock 'n' roll gospel singers to try to bring about a compatibility, for people to learn about other cultures. But then our equipment from the photography workshop was stolen. I used to have so much equipment left over that I would save it for the following year. Then I had things stolen out of my garage. It was incredible. Something we never anticipated before.

I had worked so hard to make it a good program. The long hours. I was at every performance and every workshop to make sure that things went well. I hired teachers who I thought could really handle all kinds of kids and we had no problems the first two years. But that third year, I never experienced things like that in my life. And that's what I think happened to the Jewish community that caused this huge exodus. They had never experienced the problems that they had then. Some with their children in school, some with their homes, and then the businessmen.

People couldn't stay in business anymore. I remember going up to one couple who were robbed at least a dozen times. It was a shop where they sold fabrics and items for sewing, like a five and ten. They had been in that block for forty years. My family did business with them and over the years they had increased it. But they couldn't keep up with the thievery so they decided to close it.

The husband said, "You know, we knew everybody on this block at one time. Now they're all strangers to us." They always dealt with black people and he says, "What did we ever do to them that would cause them to act this way?" His insurance was canceled. He couldn't get any more, so he boarded up the store. Blue Hill Avenue has become plywood city. If it wasn't burned out, it was rock-infested. Windows were smashed. It was just unbelievable.

It was a tough neighborhood. Here we had a drugstore on the corner of our street and my son could not walk to that drugstore anymore. I often wondered what would happen if I ever saw my kid or somebody else's kid being attacked. Would I run for the police? Would I not get involved? What would I do? And then it happened.

My kid was only twelve years old and at the corner of our street there was a place where you could get hamburgers and soft drinks. By that time we had a car pool because we couldn't let our kids come home by bus anymore. Children were constantly being attacked up and down the street. No child was safe, black or white. So it was my day for the car pool and when we got to the corner of our street, my son said he wanted a milkshake. So I said, "Okay, I'll drop you off here."

I kept a baseball bat in my car. To this day, I'm still referred to as the lady with the bat. It's a lousy reputation to have, but it really got to the point where you could not go out in the street without some sort of a weapon, and I felt that was the safest for me to carry. You couldn't even stop at a traffic light, that's how bad it was.

He went in to get his milkshake and he came out wedged between two black kids, pushing him from both sides. The kids were huge compared to his size and there was a third one in back, kicking him in the behind. My kid was shaking so that the milkshake was spilling all over and he looked like he was in shock. All I could think of was three against one, and I just took that baseball bat out of my car and started chasing those kids.

It's more than likely that a group of them could have gotten together and beaten me up, but I never thought of that. I just ran after them with that bat and I could feel my heart pounding. I almost lost all my equilibrium, but I was swinging that bat and my face must have showed rage because they ran like hell. Everybody was standing around watching, but nobody did anything. Well finally I put my son in the car and a policeman came by.

Of course, after that we had to have the place patrolled with police inside and out. It became a police school and we had to have buses take those kids from Roxbury directly home, with a police car following to make sure that the kids did not get off at any other bus stop. Then businesses were closed from 2:30 to 3:30 every day. There was so much pilferage they refused to stay open until the kids went home. And a police car was stationed at the bottom of that hill, every single day.

I used to really feel bad for my neighbors who were black. They were the nicest people. They were good friends and they really wanted to live in harmony with us. And they could have very easily. All of this is such a tragic thing. In fact right after that incident, the niece of my neighbor next door who was black called me on the phone and she said, "Mrs. Bernstein, I saw what happened and I know those three kids." And she said, "If you promise not to tell my name, I'll give you their names so you can go up to the school and report them." I said to her, "I won't say a word."

She gave me their names and the next day I went traipsing up to the school. We happened to get a new principal up at the Lewenberg School that wasn't going to stand for any nonsense, so he was delighted to see me. He said, "If more parents would just come up, we could get rid of these trouble-makers, but they're afraid." He says, "These three kids that you named are some of the worst troublemakers in school, but I have no evidence."

Then he said, "You sit out in that front office and I'm going to call them in. You just nod and tell me if it's them." Well they saw me sitting there, they recognized me, and they turned pale. The principal suspended them for three days, until the parents came. Then they were transferred to another school. I refused to prosecute them because actually my kid wasn't hurt, but let that be a lesson to them. The NAACP came running up there with a lawyer, but the principal said, "Now, look, I have a witness and I don't want to keep troublemakers at this school." You wouldn't believe the vandalism in that school. You walk in there now and there's a policeman with a walkie-talkie at the door.

I'll tell you something. Kids reflect what their parents are. As I said, it wasn't the northern blacks. Here we had a bunch of low-class people and there's low-class in every religion and race and every ethnic group, I don't care who you are. But some of these people are really emotionally disturbed. They come from parents who hate. They don't teach those kids re-spect for people—their teachers or people who live on their street. Or respect for property. You don't piss out the window. And don't throw garbage in the backyard. Because I've seen that. I don't understand. It's emotionally disturbed people and I don't know what can be done to help them.

You have a group of people that were persecuted for four hundred years. Now I'm so sick of hearing about that that I feel like throwing up. Say listen, there isn't one religion or ethnic group that hasn't gone through persecution at one time or another. Especially the Jews, who were supposed to be the "chosen people." I don't know what the hell they were chosen for except to suffer all their lives. But you talk about the potato famine with the Irish, and what went on with the Crusaders, and the Protestants hated everybody, and then you've got the Ku Klux Klan. So I mean there hasn't been one group that hasn't gone through it. So all right.

In my family, we had many relatives that were killed in the concentration camps. If I spent the rest of my life hating every German and telling them they're no goddamned good and I don't trust any of them, and I keep looking back to the past, then I have no future. I have to look toward the future and try to better things so that something like this will never happen again. So I'm sick and tired of being blamed by the blacks. First of all, my grandparents weren't even born here and they had nothing to do with their persecution!

I really had respect for Martin Luther King because he spoke out and he really got his people aroused. The only thing I regretted was that, as peaceful a man as he was supposed to be, no matter where he went violence followed him. But his was a very untimely death and a useless death, as was Bobby Kennedy's and Jack Kennedy's. I think he really led his people the right way. It's just what happened afterward. There is such a movement of hatred against white people and I don't know where it's going to end.

At meetings I go to, people have just come out and said, "Well you being white would feel that way." Why can't you have an intelligent conversation with a person without being called a racist, a bigot or a honky? And one day I brought that up. I said, "If I say 'black' and you say 'white,' does this mean I'm a racist? If we have a difference of opinion, am I going to call you a Jew hater?" There's still so much hatred.

I just don't know what happened. When I went to high school, we had some black kids but there were never any problems. We worked on projects together and if you look at the pictures in the yearbook of the different clubs that we had, they were all mixed. We never had this. I used to be very liberal. I used to truly believe, those poor people, what they went through. I was so damn liberal I didn't mind living in an integrated community. And I was happy that blacks were getting decent housing.

When my new neighbors first moved on the street, I went all

out to make them feel welcome because I knew they worked hard and they wanted the same things I wanted for my kids. And we became such good friends—the Sinclairs, the Latimeres, the Youngers. Our kids went to school together. Mine were always over at the Sinclairs' house. Everything was great.

Even when the BBURG started, I was all for it. I thought it was a great thing to help low-income families, until we saw what was happening. Blacks were heading down our way, there was no doubt about it, but it probably would have taken fifteen or twenty years before it became all black, like Roxbury. And if the low-income people were allowed to buy housing in other areas of the city too, it might not have happened altogether. There would have been some black families in Mattapan and some in other communities. That's the way it should be and that's the way it was when we first bought our house, before BBURG.

Another piece of the puzzle was the Association for Better Housing. It was run by the Reverend Harold Ross, who, by the way, according to the newspapers now has tax problems and other financial problems. Governor Sargent's wife was the president. This was the one social agency that could accept somebody applying for a mortgage through BBURG or decline them. Now isn't freedom and liberty taken away from a person if they can't go to any bank they want to get a mortgage? They had to go through BBURG, which all the savings banks were part of, and this one social service agency which BBURG selected.

The association was supposed to do counseling. Some counseling they did! If people went to the banks, they'd send them directly to the Association for Better Housing. Can you imagine one agency having the power to tell a person whether or not he can get a mortgage? I mean if a black man came in and said, "I want to live in Stoughton," they'd say, "Well it's not within the line so you can't get a mortgage through BBURG." What happened to the freedom in this world? They were supposed to see to it that the FHA (Federal Housing Authority) inspectors inspected the property right, to see that the people wouldn't get bilked. Well, in the end, everybody got bilked.

Anyway, we had block meeting after block meeting. Some of my friends were really very upset, especially if they had children at the Lewenberg School. And of course other people were upset because they put everything they had into their homes, like we did. And when people said they weren't going to move, I really believed them. I thought we had that street nipped in the bud.

While we were trying to open up the real estate office, I paid little attention to my street. Then all of a sudden I noticed three moving trucks in one day and I said to myself, there's something wrong here. I found out that one of the neighbor's children was beaten up in front of the house and her bike was thrown down the hill. My neighbor was scared out of her wits, so she put her house up for sale and she moved out. I don't blame her.

You know there's beating up and there's beating up. Every kid I think in their life has had an instance of it. But here there's a fear of black people, a fear of people who do not fear you, and that's different. My husband says, "There's always somebody bigger than the next guy. Somebody's afraid of somebody. And it's up to their own community," he says, "to get these kids in tow." They know who the troublemakers are.

Do you know what they did about the recent busing situation? They warned those black kids and said to them, "Don't you throw any rocks at the white kids and stay cool, man, because South Boston is waiting for the black community to start something so they can say to Judge Garrity,* 'See, we told you it's an unsafe area to go into.'" Now if they can do that, then why couldn't they keep those bums under control?

The crime didn't come slowly, it came fast and it hit this neighborhood like a ton of bricks. The people didn't expect it and they couldn't understand it and they still can't get over it. No person is safe in that area. My friend Dave Brothers has one of the three remaining drugstores in the area out of twenty that once existed. The people begged him not to leave. Now he has a guard that he has to pay for by himself and he wears a bullet-proof vest because he was robbed too many times. His own wife was robbed coming out of the drugstore by two black kids.

I don't think there's one white resident living there now who hasn't had a house robbed or been attacked, or had something

* Judge W. Arthur Garrity, Jr., federal district judge charged with overseeing implementation of the Boston school desegregation plan.

happen which left its mark. And you know, throughout the years, black people have gotten more from Jewish people than any other ethnic group. In the center where I work now these old Jewish people have such stories to tell. One is more devastating than the rest.

Well, we continued to have block meetings and committee meetings. It got to the point where my kids would say to me, "Mommy, aren't you ever going to stay home anymore?" We would eat supper and run and sometimes we had supper meetings. If there was a panic in the street we had to call an emergency block meeting and get the people together. I went from being a housewife and just knowing my neighbors on the street to constant activity. It was three years like that.

Sometimes it became so discouraging. We had so many deaf ears turned on us. I can't tell you the frustration. The phone calls, the letters, the meetings. And all those people who said they would not get up and move, moved. And I could understand it—the pressure, fear. It's not a nice thing when someone calls you up on the phone and says, "Blacks are moving in on your street. Get out now while you can get the price."

Toward the end, I'd say more than 60 percent of the white people left in Mattapan were fifty years old and over. You know, to uproot a person who has lived in an area seventy or eighty years, I think it's the worst thing you can do. After believing they were going to stay there till they died, it really had a traumatic effect on them. Many of them just died. Their hearts just gave out. They came out of big, spacious homes and had to go into two and three rooms in a project, sometimes one room, and it killed some of them. Less than a thousand are left now.

Do you know that out of 141 families, there were only seven white families left on my street in two years? My neighbors were all gone and my friends would say to me, "Janice, give up. You're fighting a losing battle. You're fighting powers-that-be that you're not powerful enough to fight." But I just was not a giver-upper. The Mattapan Organization had finally opened up an office on Blue Hill Avenue and there were only twelve of us left, and my husband and I were two of them. We fought to the very end.

In fact, the day we closed our office in June 1970, I was in shock. I couldn't believe this had happened. By that time, more than half of Mattapan was already black. I knew it was hopeless. But you know it's a funny thing. You'd think that I would have given up, wouldn't you?

EVERYONE LOSES EXCEPT THE BANKS

Within six months Ormond Street cleared out. I never saw so many moving trucks in all my life on one street like mine. I guess the final straw that made us move was when my in-laws were driving up the street one day and the kids from the Lewenberg School jumped on their car and tried to open the door. My mother-in-law said, "That's it. We've got to get out of here." We owned the house together, so we decided to sell. It took nine months to get a buyer approved by the Association for Better Housing and we lost our shirts.

If we'd sold our house in normal times, we would have gotten twice as much back on it as we paid. We had put five thousand dollars in modernizing it when we moved in and we had to sell it for less than we bought it for. We lost our life savings in Mattapan. When we came into this house we had nothing. But nothing! Not even a pot to piss in, pardon the expression.

Let me explain something else about BBURG. They picked an area where they could make a quick profit when they picked our neighborhood. Most of the people had either paid up their homes or they had a low mortgage interest. Where ours was 5½ percent, the people coming in were paying 8 and 9 percent interest. It was a quick turnover and they made themselves an awful lot of money.

You know what the result of all this is? Out of the two thousand homes that were sold in the Mattapan area through BBURG, somewhere between a thousand and fifteen hundred have been abandoned or foreclosed. The banks didn't lose anything. The only ones who lost out were the people. The blacks were bilked and so were the whites. It was a deliberate scheme to make a lot of money. But the banks wouldn't have lost one red cent if the black families were able to choose where to live, and we still would have had a nice, mixed neighborhood.

Well, we had been looking for months in every suburb area

we could find, but we've always loved the city of Boston and there isn't much left in Boston that you can really call home anymore. At least we couldn't. Finally we decided to look at West Roxbury, just as a lark. It's actually the only part of the city that's like country, and it has the lowest crime rate. Mostly city workers—policemen, firemen, politicians—responsible people. We hit upon this house completely by accident. The minute we saw it, we said, "Okay, that's it!" That was in 1971.

About a month after I moved in, I got a call from the Jewish Community Council. They were always passing the buck to me. Whenever somebody would come in to talk about the Dorchester-Mattapan situation, they'd send them to Janice. I wished I had made a tape recording so I wouldn't have to go through it again. I was dry in the mouth from it. And I had so many college kids writing their themes. I had nothing against the kids doing it for their homework, but nothing ever came out of it except they got their credits. Nobody ever looked at them and I mean some of those kids had damn good ideas, good solutions. So look at them!

Anyway that March I got a call from Bob Segal, who was director of the Council at the time. He said to me, "Janice, I got two guys in from Washington, from the Senate Anti-Trust Committee under Senator Hart, and they're investigating the Mattapan-Dorchester situation. They're going to have hearings here." So I got very excited, but I said, "What do you want from me?" He said, "Will you talk to them?"

So Jack Blum got on the phone and he said, "We understand that you're quite up on what went on from the beginning and we'd appreciate your help." So I said, "Well you're five years too late, but all right." Within the hour, they came to the house. We were still living out of boxes, but fortunately I had marked every box that I took with me, just in case, and there was the box out in the sun porch. Nothing in order, just all the papers, posters, newspaper articles, documents, letters, everything I had collected from 1967. I had kept it all.

So they looked through the box and shoved some stuff in a folder to have it photostated and then they said, "We would appreciate it if you would get a group of Mattapan residents together. We'd like to hear what you have to say." So we got the group together here and we had meeting upon meeting.

We had all belonged to the Mattapan Organization and each one of us had a different tale to tell of what happened that was sadder than the next one. I guess they really felt sorry for us.

Then they told us there were absolute anti-trust violations and they asked us if we would testify at the hearings. So I said, "I'd like to know if it's going to do any good. I got other things to worry about." Then Jack Blum says to me, "You know, Janice, with all the material that you've got, you ought to write a book someday." Of course I thought he was joking. Me write a book? Are you kidding?

The hearings took place in September 1971 and I testified. Reverend Ross was there, the bankers were there, FHA officials, HUD. And then it came out what they did to the area. Afterward, Jack Blum called me up and he said, "Janice, I've got to tell you something before I leave. You have enough evidence in your files, plus all the evidence from the hearings, to start a class action suit against BBURG." So I said, "What will it accomplish?" He says, "Not only will you perhaps get back what you lost, but you'll get satisfaction."

We finally got a lawyer who was very interested and said he felt we had an excellent chance of winning. But the problem was we had no money to get the suit off the ground. None of us had any money to lay out, because we had lost it all on the sale of our homes. What we went through, I wouldn't wish on my worst enemy. Again the meeting upon meeting, going through it all over again. Finally we went to the Jewish organizations for money because we felt it was their obligation to stand behind us.

By this time I was in with some of the Jewish organizations. I had to find out what was going on there and the only way I was going to find out was by joining them. Also, by then I was involved with Ledgewood, a center for the Jewish elderly, so I automatically got onto some of the boards. So I was no stranger to them. I presented our case at a meeting and I really let them have it. I said they had an obligation to us because they let that community die. They didn't stand behind their own people, the people that pay their salaries. Do you know that Mattapan, Dorchester and Roxbury at one time were the largest contributors to their organizations?

Well, they realized their mistake, so they were going to start us off with three thousand dollars, just to get the suit off the ground. They have this legal council made up of lawyers, rabbis and members of these organizations that make the decisions and the day I presented my case and I said that it might possibly go up to ten thousand dollars, not one man on that council flinched an eyebrow.

The thing is, they would have lost nothing. We were so positive the case was going to be won and, if it was, the banks would have to put up a pool of money and anybody involved in the suit would be paid, including expenses for the lawyer and treble damages or whatever.

The day it was all set, we were 99 percent sure that we were going to get the money to back us. Our lawyer was ready to start the suit the next day. But in the meantime, what happened was three men came up to this legal council. All three were lawyers who had bankers as clients and they were on the boards of the organizations and big contributors. They came to show just cause why the Jewish organizations should not get involved in a class action suit.

They said, "What was so horrible about what happened in Mattapan? Look at all the wonderful things the banks did. Look at all the people they helped." Then one of them said, "Besides, gentlemen, let me inform you that our image and relations with the black community could possibly be severed." They were so damn afraid that black people would think that Jewish agencies did not want blacks to live in a Jewish community. Their own people got burned, but Jews are so worried about their image, and yet through the years no matter what they've accomplished their image is still the same.

Anyway, they decided against backing us. There was no place to turn after that. You want to hear what I did? I even contacted Edward Bennett Williams, this big lawyer from Washington who took care of Hoffa and was involved in the Watergate. He wrote me a very nice letter back, that he really sympathized with the situation, but he said we're better off to keep it with some lawyer in Boston and he gave me a little advice.

In my mind there was no doubt that we would have won it, but we had no money to get us off the ground. So I decided

as a last desperate attempt to write to the newspapers. If I believe in something, until there is absolutely no place else to
turn, I will try everything. Somehow I always feel that that
one little extra thing might help.

So I wrote to the *Jewish Advocate* and the local newspapers
telling them about the class action suit and hoping against
hope that some philanthropic person who lived in the community or had relatives here—maybe some Rockefeller or some
Kennedy fellow—would suddenly appear and say, "Oh, I got
the money and I'll lend it to you." But nobody came through.

I got about thirty-three calls in response, mostly from college kids who were so sympathetic and angry and wanted to
help us. They didn't even live in the area but they wanted to
hold rallies, give out circulars, approach the rabbis for money.
I told them to forget about it. The other people who called
had got stung and had no money but wanted to contribute a
few hundred dollars to help us get started. But we needed at
least three thousand dollars and what had been offered between all of us didn't even come up to a thousand, so we
couldn't risk it.

That was when I contacted Jack Blum again, in Washington.
He said to me, "Why don't you get it all down on paper?" I
said, "Jack, I don't know if I can do it. There's so much to tell
and I think it would just break me up if I had to go through
it all over again." He says, "Look, relax a while, get all your
notes together, and then when you have it all categorized,
think about it and put things down on paper." And that's what
I did.

One day, it was a lousy, rainy, miserable day and I saw
something on television that reminded me of Mattapan. I took
out all my papers and folders and started to sort everything
out. It took me about three weeks. I never realized all the
letters I had kept, all the documents and articles. Some of them
were real bombs—letters that never should have reached my
hands but friends got copies to me. And I have it all recorded
in the book, signatures and everything. I was so careful not to
be sued that I documented everything, even to the page
number.

I got a book on how to do it, *Writer's Market*. How to start
a manuscript, how to write, how to bring out the best points

in a story. I went through that book with a fine-tooth comb. And I took out other books from the library on how to write, too. Then I wrote the preface and rewrote it, and rewrote it again, and then a fourth time. Once I got through with that, I said, "I think I can do it and I'm going to try." I worked day and night. Getting it on paper took me about a year, and then the typing took about six months. And I did everything like the book said.

I really feel that what I wanted to express came out in the book and maybe now that it's out I won't feel so bitter. I really have been awfully bitter about the whole thing. It just wasn't fair that this should happen to our community that was so viable and happy for so many years, and that people like those bankers should have so much power. Really, it's incredible and something has to be done to stop it.

Like I said in the last chapter, no one person or federal agency should be trusted. You can see what happened. There has to be the involvement of the people. If somebody comes over and wants to change the zoning in a one-family residential area to a business area, you better watch out, because that can change your whole community. People have to really be very careful.

Sometimes I still can't believe it happened. I wouldn't give up right down to the end. Even my mother kept saying to me, "Give up already! There's no place you can go." We probably should have bombed a few real estate offices or something. I'll tell you something. I'm really not a violent person, but we should have gone to every real estate office in the area and told them, "You better watch your step." And we should have marched up those streets and had rallies on Blue Hill Avenue and bombarded all the politicians in the area—Senator Kennedy, Governor Sargent, Mayor White. If we had done all that, and if we had the Jewish organizations behind us, maybe we would have gotten somewhere.

The truth is, you have to know people and you have to raise your voice. But with all the people I knew, I guess I didn't know the right ones. Even one of the mayor's assistants, who I think really did the best he could, admitted that they didn't come in when they should have. How can you be any more truthful than that? He says that if he knew then what he knows now, he would certainly have put a stop to it. Everybody's entitled to a mistake, but sitting up there in City Hall they should have made sure they knew more about it and did something to stop it.

While I was working on the book this February, an article appeared in the newspaper that said the indictments against people involved with BBURG would be coming out before summer. The U.S. Attorney's Office here in Boston was investigating the situation along with the FBI. There's maybe eighty people involved—FHA, HUD, bankers, real estate agents. So I wrote but they wouldn't tell me who, even though I know who some of them were.

So I waited. Summer came, summer went and nothing happened. So I called up the Attorney's Office again and spoke to the lawyer investigating the indictments. The only answer he could give me was there absolutely will be indictments eventually, but he didn't know when. The hearings were in 1971. It was going into the fourth year already!

I was so mad about what happened, I had to tell the world. I had great grandeurs of telling people what a terrible thing happened in Dorchester and Mattapan and that if they learned a lesson from it and guarded themselves, maybe it would never happen again any place else. That's what I first wanted.

But also, there's another important message to be learned here: the conspiracy of how things were done. The more I got into it, as each chapter was formulated, it became clear. When I first started on the book I wasn't that clear as to what really happened. But when I did more investigating and had more interviews, it was as if the whole sky suddenly opened up. And I said, "Sumner, I know what happened. I know what they all did." He said, "Well where have you been?"

IF THE BOOK SELLS . . .

This whole experience was a big turning point in my life. It changed my outlook on life an awful lot. I learned that you can't trust people like I used to. I was very . . . maybe naive, let's put it that way. I always believed in telling the truth. I believed if you said yes, it meant yes. If you said no, it meant no. But I found out that people who said yes meant no. And if they said maybe it meant no. And certainly no was emphatic.

You just couldn't believe these people. They represented us, supposedly, because we voted them into office. But nobody represents me anymore, nobody. I represent myself. And no one's going to speak for me and tell me what's in my mind. No more. No Jewish organization, nobody.

I think I've become much wiser and more aware of things and I've found that if you don't fight for what you want, you're not going to get anywhere. You're constantly going to be stepped on. I haven't found a rabbi that I like and that's why I no longer belong to a shul. Their philosophy is: turn the other cheek and it will go away. Well, it isn't going to go away. If you're happy in your home and you want to keep that home, you have to fight for it. But you can't fight alone. I discovered that you've got to join groups and be involved in your community.

Before all this, I was a housewife. That's all I was. And I never in a thousand years ever thought anything like what happened would come about. Outside of belonging to the Hadassah for a few years and the Ladies' Auxiliary of the Knights of Pythias, which is a Jewish fraternal organization, I wasn't really involved in anything. The Mattapan Organization was an experience I never had before. We had blacks and whites, Jews, Catholics and Protestants. Only about 5 percent were Protestant and I think it was about 55 percent Jewish, but it was still a very mixed group.

I got to know people that I didn't know lived in my community. People like Father Hurley who was on the real estate committee and became my dear friend. I used to call him Rabbi Hurley because I found so much in him that was lacking in the rabbis in the area. In fact when he was being transferred to another church, I wrote to Cardinal Cushing, whom I adored beyond words. There's another man that they threw away the mold when they made him.

I wrote asking if there was something they could do to keep Father Hurley in our area. Cardinal Cushing said he couldn't give special attention to one, and Father Hurley had already been there for ten years where usually you're transferred after five years, but he knew about what Father Hurley had done in the community and he wished me well. Father Hurley couldn't believe I really wrote to the cardinal. I told him, "Yeah, I did because I love you and I felt you were important to the community." But it didn't help.

Anyway, the Mattapan Organization brought us together with a lot of wonderful people we might never have known. Then I learned I could do things I'd never done before. The first time I had to make a speech I was so nervous I think I almost wet my pants. It was a report on the beautification committee at the first Lewenberg School meeting, and my legs were shaking the whole way up to the stage. I got up there and I saw all these people staring at me, maybe two hundred of them, some I knew and some I didn't. The first couple of paragraphs I know I babbled because I was so flustered. Finally I just got so nervous I put the paper aside and tried to say it from memory and it turned out better. Then as time went by I got more confidence in myself.

I don't really think I have leadership. I think I just have some people that like me, and that's not really leadership. I like people and I just got to know a lot of them and I guess the feeling became mutual. I have a strong mind of my own and I'm not afraid to say what I want to say. In fact, there was a time when I didn't mince any words. I was open and frank when I really shouldn't have been. My husband used to say, "A little finesse helps," and his advice was always good. Now I can be outspoken and disagree with someone without hurting their feelings.

Direct contact with people is very important to me. The first day I moved in here I was knocking on doors and introducing myself to people. I like to be alone in solitude when I'm thinking or working on something, but there are certain hours of the day when I love my family around me. And I take my neighbor across the street shopping once a week. I love people around me and I love to be in on things. I'm planning to organize a Worley Street Block Association one day, pull people out and have them get to know each other.

As I mentioned, it wasn't until after we started the Mattapan Organization that I got involved with the big Jewish organizations. They came to us much too late, when the only thing they could do was help the elderly who were left in the neighborhood. Most of the younger people were already gone. Well, I just felt that as far as the elderly were concerned, I was going to do all I could to help them. So I helped get the Ledgewood Center established and since the Jewish agencies are sponsoring it, one thing led to another so now I'm on a couple of boards.

I'm vice president of the board at Ledgewood now and I'm also chairlady of the senior adult committee. All the presidents of the different groups at the center report to me and I relay their messages to the bigshots at the Associated Jewish Community Centers, where I'm on the senior adult committee. I represent Ledgewood there and we get together with people who are from all the different centers, and also I'm on the board of the AJCC. Then I'm on the urban affairs committee of the Jewish Community Council. It doesn't mean a damn thing, titles. And see, they're all intertwined when you come down to it. They're all under the Combined Jewish Philanthropies where the real bigwigs are. Also, I'm on the board of the Anti-Defamation League.

We service over seven hundred people now at Ledgewood and we have everything—legal counsel, free examinations, eye tests, and a hot lunch program five days a week. And of course a drop-in place to come in. You know we don't have the G & G anymore. It's gone. So they've got to have a place to come in and meet with their friends.

I bring all their complaints to the board and I'm a tough cookie. Of course some of them don't have legitimate complaints and they complain for the sake of complaining, but they've got to be heard. You can't turn a deaf ear on them. So I say, "Yes, Mrs. Siegel," and "Yes, Mrs. Kaplan, you're so right. I'll see what I can do about it." And then Mrs. Siegel will forget what she told me the day before and come up with another complaint. When I'm home I get calls all the time about what's going on—the card players shouldn't be playing in with the meetings, there shouldn't be smoking. So now we have a room for smokers and a room for card players and everybody's happy.

Many of them do have legitimate complaints that we help with, about the maintenance of their buildings, or they're having stones thrown at their windows, or the landlord won't fix a lock. We see to it that that lock is fixed, but whether the complaints are legitimate or not, a lot of these people are people I grew up with in my neighborhood. You've got to have compassion for them. You can't ignore them and let them die out with the wind. They're going to be around a lot longer than we anticipated and we have to accommodate them to the very end.

The Combined Jewish Philanthropies came out with a statement that was really something. They said at one of the board meetings that they realized they were tragically late in coming into the situation, but they would do all they could to make sure that every Jew was taken care of. They knew what was going on, but they were so afraid of being called a bigot and a racist. This is the whole problem. They can organize rallies for Soviet Jewry or Israel, but they couldn't do it to protest block-busting in the largest Jewish community.

Finally, through pressure, they decided to do something and I'll tell you how it happened. A man came over to me at a meeting several years ago and he had a stack of index cards four inches thick. I don't know where he got it, but it showed names, addresses and phone numbers of regular donors from Dorchester-Mattapan to the Combined Jewish Philanthropies, the over-all agency that feeds the money to about seventy-one agencies under them.

So this man with the cards says to me, "Hey, Janice, I want to show you something." He said, "Look, we support these agencies. Without us, they can't survive. We're going to call these people up and we're going to tell them that when they come campaigning for the money this year not to give to the CJP, but to give to the Israel Relief Fund." I said, "Go ahead," even though I didn't participate in it.

Each person got about twenty cards to call and then each one that got called, called a friend, and the friend called a friend. And when the CJP started their campaign, they were told by these people that they were going to contribute directly to the Israel Relief Fund and they got a little panicky. It started in 1969 and for two years their funds went way down and they had to cut their budget. The people simply said unless you help Dorchester and Mattapan they won't contribute to the CJP anymore.

So I would admit to the fact that pressure had a great deal to do with them getting off their behinds. Plus the fact that some of them really just didn't realize what was going on until they were taken on a tour down Blue Hill Avenue. Of course they were devastated with what they saw. They quickly had an emergency meeting and they decided they had to help whoever's left.

Some of the ones still left are moving out because they're scared, but some can't afford to. And some of them are still living on streets where they're being robbed and beaten and they can't get out. I cannot believe that they don't have somebody—family or someone—but some don't. We felt we had to locate the ones who couldn't get out somehow, so we formed an outreach program and we got some money and hired some students to do an over-all research of the area. This was in '73 and we found out there were less than a thousand Jews left. So we got most of their names and addresses and we contacted the families of those who had families, and then we wrote to all of them and made personal calls asking them to contact us if they needed help. Most of them responded.

Besides Ledgewood, I've gotten involved with the nursing homes in my area too. The year I moved here Cathy Kane called me and asked me if I would still continue with Summerthing, where I had such good relations with elderly people. She wanted me to make up a list of all the elderly groups in Boston so that through Summerthing they could reach them. So I called every church and synagogue and every neighborhood group. It's really fantastic how many elderly groups exist of every race, religion and nationality.

Then Cathy asked me if I would bring entertainment into the nursing homes in my area. So for three years I took over the nursing homes in Roslindale and West Roxbury here, plus my center in Mattapan. I brought in things like a jewelry workshop for those that could work with their hands. We had grandparents' days. And they want entertainment so badly they eat up anything—especially clap-alongs and old-time singing and my son and I are good at that. But then I decided to write the book so I didn't work on it anymore, after the summer of '73.

It was right after I first started with Summerthing in 1968

that my husband got his job with the city. After he sold the cleaning business he walked the streets for seven months. Then later that year they were opening up Little City Halls and I got a call from a friend of mine who told me they were looking for workers and they wanted me to work there in Mattapan. So I told them my husband needed a job and since he was so familiar with the area he would be well suited for it.

I didn't think it was a good idea for a wife and husband to work together in the same place anyway, and he was feeling pretty low. I mean here's a guy with a college education and smart, but not a pusher. Just a nice guy. I guess there's no room for nice guys. Well, finally they hired him and now he's coordinator in the Allston Little City Hall. The only thing wrong with all this is it's a city job where there's no tenure. It's an appointive job, so when a new mayor comes in, my husband is out.

He really is an A-1 worker. He loves the job he's doing there, servicing the people. He speaks fluent Yiddish and he took up Spanish, so he's able to accommodate all of the people. I think the Little City Halls will never be abolished because they've gotten to be an absolute necessity now. They deal with all kinds of city problems. People pay their bills there. When the street light doesn't go on, or the street needs paving, snow removal, things like that, they'll come there. And they tell the people where to go with complaints they can't handle there.

Sumner is so well known there now that they only ask for him. He's really quite a guy. He always liked working with people. In his quiet way he wins their confidence and they just constantly come back to him. We get calls here at night sometimes from people that need help. But it's a disappointment when you work so hard and hardly get paid a decent wage for it. It really is sad how low their salary is.

My husband and my daughter have a love affair going like you never saw in your life. She loves her father like he was the only thing on earth. My son and I have always been very close. He'll come to me first. My daughter will go to her father first for advice, and then she'll come to me. I think that's good that they can go to the person they have the most confidence in. My daughter and I sit and have long talks all the time about what goes on. Intimate things, like she's starting to ask me about petting, what's it all about. She's fourteen now and I figure it's up to me to tell her.

She made a remark to me recently that made me laugh. She said, "Why is it that boys can do anything they want and they don't get a bad reputation, but if it's the girls that do something they're the ones that get the bad reputation?" And I really couldn't answer that question. I said to her, "With all the women's lib and everything else, it's still really a man's world."

My daughter was raised very differently than I was. She has a father around. And I led a very sheltered life and I want her to experience things that it took me years to experience. She's starting to go out with groups now, which is something I could not do until I was sixteen. And she already knows more about life than I ever did at that age. I used to think if you kissed somebody you got pregnant, you know? That's how it was in those days. But I think life for her is going to be very different. She's independent and I think opportunities will be far more open for her.

I would love to be a grandma but I want her to do whatever she wants to do. It's her decision to make. She hopes to get married someday and even now she tells me how she'll raise her children. She tells me she wants to go to college and she wants to work and be able to save a little money, have a little something in the bank before she gets married. She's only fourteen but she has these ideas and I think she'll probably stick to them.

My son is eighteen now and he started college at Bentley's this year. He wanted to go into computer technology and science, and study how to build the machines. He's at that machine constantly, figuring out things. He also wants to be a CPA. He's got an amazing mind, and he's also an accomplished artist. He's been assigned to do printing for the school.

I think I've done a pretty good job with my kids. They're good kids, they really are. I don't think they'd ever try to deliberately hurt somebody or cause them to feel bad. Maybe I coddled them a little when they were younger, but when they get older I think they have to have responsibility. And they have to be responsible to themselves. I always told them not to be ashamed to say what's on your mind if you know you're right. And try to help people as much as you can, but don't get walked on.

Despite all that's happened, I really enjoy life. I'm awfully glad I'm up here and not six feet under. I'm a free woman. I can go where I want, do whatever I want, within reason, of course. I like living and I love to be with people. I enjoy gardening, my vegetable garden and flowers. And I don't really have to account to anyone. My husband and I have a terrific relationship and the communication is great. Don't think we're a perfect couple. We have our ups and downs, but I think it's a damn good marriage. If I had it to do over again, I think I'd marry the same guy, have the same kids and do the same things mostly that I did before. So I really can't complain.

I would just like money-wise for it to be a little better. That's the biggest problem. I worry about my bills. My husband can't stand it if he owes a penny. I pay all the bills and many a night I don't sleep, worrying about it. With the economy the way it is, my gas bill's gone up, my electric bill's gone up, and my husband's salary just isn't enough. And I've got such a good husband. He's really worked so hard to make a dollar.

While my kids were young I stayed home all these years and I worked in the summer, only because I could work out of the house and make my own time. And I dabbled in other things that I got a few dollars for. But the bills have become devastating now. We just can't get by. It's impossible. The outside of the house really needs to be painted but we can't afford that. We've given up an awful lot of luxuries. We don't go out to eat often. We go to a local movie when it's dollar night. If we're going out with our couples club, who are all well-off with the exception of us, we'll try to put a few dollars aside if we know in advance.

It's a tough way to live, but I suppose we're happy and tomorrow could be a better day. Look, I won two hundred dollars at Bean-O the other night. I never in my life expected the sun to shine like that on me. But it upsets me when my kids come to me and ask for something, and they very rarely do because they know the circumstances, but sometimes they'll say, "Oh, I wish I had this." And I would like to turn around and say to them, "If you want it, go ahead and pick it out."

I'd like to go into a store and not look at the price sometime, and buy it because I want it. I've been without so much that it's become an everyday thing with me, but I think before I go off this earth I would like a little something out of life.

I don't want to be rich, I just want to have a little money in the bank for a rainy day, and enough to pay my bills. I'd like to pay cash for something once in a while. If I need a new TV set, not to charge it or have to say, "Send me three payments." No creditors at my door, thank God, although sometimes I get a warning letter if I don't pay it for two months. But you know it could always be a heck of a lot worse. Instead of being here, I could be in some two-by-four apartment collecting a welfare check. So I say, "Accept what you have, hope that it might be better, and thank God it's not worse."

My husband and I have talked about my going out to work now. When the economy was better, I thought I could get almost any job I wanted. At one time they would have taken me back at Filene's at a moment's notice. And I type eighty words a minute, so that helps. But if that book is published, and if I'm lucky enough and it sells, maybe some of our troubles will be over for a while. Maybe we could travel. I would love to see the United States and then go to Israel and Hawaii.

I've spent many a sleepless night trying to visualize the good part of it. What would happen if it does sell? Would I go and look for a job eventually, or would I write again? I think now that I've got the bug, I think I would spend my life writing if it sells. I've had ideas of what I would do. Like I'm already thinking of a title called "The Mayor of Beacon Street," which is about my stepfather, because he was really an unusual man. I have other ideas too, but this is only thoughts.

If the book is successful that means I have capabilities I never realized I had before. And I've always believed that if you have a talent, you should try to push it any way you can. I don't know if I'm talented enough that it will be accepted, but if I am, then that has proven something to me. I always told my husband, I think you've got to take a chance in life. This was something I wanted to do and I made up my mind that I was going to do it. So I think if you make up your mind that you want to try something, do it! If it doesn't work, at least you can say you tried.

● POSTSCRIPT

Janice Bernstein spent much of the last year looking for a publisher for her book, with discouraging results. "After five rejections from publishers," she wrote, "I have come to realize the difficulties a 'first time' author has." Just recently, however, a new magazine on contemporary Jewish affairs agreed to print one chapter of the book—on the Lewenberg School. A Boston journalist will be helping Janice to rewrite it. She hopes this will lead to publication of the entire book one day.

In late October 1975, Janice began working two days a week at a new needlepoint store at a shopping mall a few minutes away from her home. She is helping to manage the store, selling and instructing, as well as designing and making needlepoint canvases commissioned by customers. She is now working on a huge canvas of the Wailing Wall in Jerusalem. "I love the job and I love the people," she said. "It's right up my alley. And I can't tell you how good it feels to have that extra spending money in my pocket. It wasn't fun having to leave the house many days with maybe just a quarter in my bag."

Because of her job, Janice has had to miss several meetings of the many boards she is a member of and had been thinking of resigning. "If I can't give my all," she said, "I feel guilty. But they talked me out of quitting." She always manages to spend time with the elderly in Mattapan, however. There are fewer than five hundred in the area now, and almost none of those who remain are able to move, due to the lack of adequate and affordable housing elsewhere.

For a while, it appeared that the class action suit was very much alive again. A Jewish philanthropist, who discovered that it had never really gotten off the ground because of a lack of funds, offered to pay an attorney to take it on. Janice again went out to obtain statements from former residents of Mattapan-Dorchester in a last attempt "to get some restitution for the victims of the powers that be." But again, "The case just fizzed out." The attorney moved to California, and it was difficult to find another one, due in large part to the enormity of the case. Devastated, Janice decided to give up on the suit once and for all.

"HUD continues to be the largest landlord in the country," she wrote. "Each day one can look in the newspapers and see all the abandonments and foreclosures which are increasing at an incredible rate. Many of the homes have been destroyed by fire and vandalism. On streets where homes used to be so well-kept there are now vacant lots. At a time where housing is so important the area is well on its way to becoming a desert. What a sad reminder of a once beautiful and viable community. I become ill every time I drive through the area."

Until the fall semester of 1975, Janice was emotionally caught up in the busing situation. Her daughter Karen attended the ninth grade in a school that experienced so much disruption and disorganization that the year was virtually wasted. The school was forced to close quite often and the advanced class that Karen had been in for the previous two years was eliminated. In addition, there was constant fear of going into certain lavatories alone, walking in certain corridors and riding up certain escalators. Karen and her friends felt safe in the school only when they were in groups.

Many white students moved out of the city and others began to attend private schools, for which their parents are "using their last pennies." Janice wrote, "I firmly believe that Boston (as Detroit) will shortly have more black students than white. When this happens, busing will have been to no avail. The situation caused havoc, violence and hatred, and quality education has not been achieved. To force a child to be bused several miles away to integrate schools when a school exists right across the street is, in my estimation, ridiculous. Socially it is better to mix, but people feel safer going to school in their own neighborhood."

By the fall term of 1975, Karen's school situation had improved noticeably. Janice believes that magnet schools are part of the answer. The students have a wide array of electives which she described as "fantastic," and there is new equipment for photography, arts and crafts, court stenography and other courses which Janice herself would like to be able to take.

Another part of the answer, she feels, is that the principal "got tough" this year. Now when kids set off fire alarms for the sake of disruption—which happened frequently the year before—their photographs are automatically taken on the spot. As a result, that form of disruption has virtually ceased. "But unfortunately," Janice said, "there is still no togetherness. On school trips and on the school's premises, black and white and Puerto Rican students travel in separate groups. Schooling is much better now, but integration is not working."

Women Helping Women

Dorothy Bolden

Betty Gagne

Dorothy Bolden (*left*) at a special meeting of the Atlanta City Council on the CETA (Comprehensive Employment Training Act) program.

Dorothy Bolden and her husband at home in Vine City, Atlanta.

BOTH PHOTOS BY JOAN ROTH

Dorothy Bolden

FORTY-TWO YEARS A MAID, STARTING AT NINE IN ATLANTA

I was born here in Atlanta, over in Vine City. I've been there in and out practically all my life. My mother was a maid. First she was a schoolteacher for the first grade in the rural areas. My grandfather was a minister and he taught her how to teach. Since she didn't get any degree at any school, she couldn't teach when she came here to Atlanta. So she was a maid and I assume it just went through my family.

After a while we moved across the city to Summerhill, from Vine City. That was all black too. We never did have a whole house to ourselves—my mother and father and brother and I. We always roomed with someone. My mother had friends and they would go in together and get a house. Wherever my mother thought work was closer, she would move. When we moved from Summerhill we moved to Fourth Ward, up near Auburn Avenue, and that was all black too.

When I was about three I lost my sight. I fell on my head and they thought maybe I broke my neck, but I didn't. It affected my eye nerve. I went to Grady's Hospital and stayed there for a while. They treated it but it didn't do any good. My father brought me from Grady's one day and he was crying, and this man was selling peanuts on the corner and he asked him what was the matter, and he said, "Well, my daughter, seems she's going to be blind the rest of her life."

So this man gave him a little card to go see an eye specialist. But back in those days, in the heart of the twenties, you didn't have money to go see a specialist. You didn't even know what a specialist was. My daddy was a chauffeur and he was only making seven dollars a week. But the people he was working for helped him to pay for this doctor.

The doctor said he couldn't guarantee that I would see. All he could do was give me the most painful shots that anyone could receive—a shot at the back of my neck and another one between the eyes—to strengthen my nerves. He kept my eyes bandaged up for a length of time, and my sight did come back. I was cross-eyed at first, but it came back. I was five or six then. He kept giving me shots and then bandaging my eyes.

It's a thing I don't like to talk about really, because people today don't believe in the miracles that God performs on living creatures. This is a modern time, and you know, you just don't talk about these things because people don't believe it. But all the records are at Grady's.

I started school late and I loved school. I didn't get a chance to go until I think it was in 1932. I was about twelve years old when my eyes began to act up on me again. They began to run, just like I was crying. I had a beautiful handwriting and I always would sit up and write because I wanted to go to school so bad. But Georgia had a law that said that anything affecting a child in school, she couldn't attend school.

They sent these doctors around to visit the schools and they told my mother then that my eyes were going to get worse and worse. They carried me to Grady's and the doctors said they had to operate on them, but my mother was fearful of an operation on my eyes, that I would lose my sight and never regain it again. She preferred me having my sight than my education, so she withdrew me out of school then. It was either school or the operation, and then she wasn't able to buy the glasses I needed, so I had to give it up.

But you know, when God takes something from you, he gives you back something double. You know, people don't realize that being blind is a blessing. Because your eyes are in your heart. If you lose a hand, your next hand is much stronger. And so my mind was much stronger and my heart was much stronger. And when I got my sight I thought it was such a beautiful thing to see everything and everybody. Doing things for other people, well I think that was given to me from birth up. Even when I was real small and I couldn't see quite right yet, if I had some pennies and I passed some child on the street, I always had to give him something.

I was working when I was nine. I was baby-sitting, and washing baby diapers and learning how to clean. My mother was taking in the washing and ironing at that particular time, and I would baby-sit for the people she was working for. I was a bright little girl and I was always eager to do things and I could clean house very good. My grandmother taught me and my mother taught me and it always gave me pride. I liked to see things neat and pretty. By the time I was fourteen I was working strong. I had a regular job for a family.

My grandmother was a farmer out in Covington. During the Depression we didn't have nothing and I lived through my grandmother and grandfather. The pressure didn't hit the farmers because they could raise what they wanted. They had chickens, they had turkeys, they had ducks, they had cows. They had fresh vegetables and they had a smokehouse that they cured all this meat in. They raised the meal, the flour and they got the lard from the hogs. They weren't hungry and they'd furnish you food. They were your best bet to survive if you were anywhere near.

My grandfather was commuting up here and he would come up on Decatur Street and come on over and get us and carry us children back down there. I have an extra-large family—aunts and uncles and cousins. Those were the happy days. You were taught to appreciate life and I'm sorry that young people from this generation won't know what the country life is like.

Country life is a mellow life. It's a life that you live to enjoy. Running over the hills, kicking in the clay dirt, going down in the gullies and coming back up. Eating the wild berries and grapes like the muscadines. Going through the woods searching for different things to eat on, the maypop and a lot of those things that children wouldn't dare touch today. The sweetness of the peaches and the plums and the honeydew melons.

My grandfather always said I was a very smart child. Nobody ever had to tell me what to do. I always knew what my duty was. If I was in the country, I was up in the morning washing the dishes. Or if it was in the summer, I'd go get the whitewash to wash the fireplaces. My job was to sweep the front yard with brushbrooms, to keep it pretty and clean. And that was a dear job to me because it was a responsibility and I appreciated responsibility.

My mother said I was a very strange child. I always wanted to be a missionary worker. That was my desire from a child up. I think that was instilled in me. I always have been very religious. My mother was a Baptist and my father too. But I built my own thinking about this. I didn't think like other children. I always respected the elders. They've always been my closest friends. And I loved children, babies most of all.

Black people at that time weren't resentful. It was just the way things were. We came into this life like that and respected it as that. There wasn't anything that we thought should have been any different. Of course eventually we began to think different, but when we were young and we were courting-girls, we made the best out of the life we lived. We were locked into one area and we didn't have any place to go except one, Auburn Avenue, but we all had a good time.

We would get off from work, dress up, put on our best and just walk from one side of Auburn Avenue to the other. That was *the* street—sweet Auburn Avenue. It was like Basin Street. In Atlanta, it was black people's street, where everybody assembled to have a good time. You'd go down there looking good, and you'd meet your boyfriend there and go to the night spots.

That's where I met my first husband, at the Savoy Hotel, where the big bands would come. I was eighteen then, when we married. He was young and I was young. He volunteered for service, but the war hadn't broke out yet, so he wasn't getting but about twenty-one dollars a month. And that wasn't enough to take care of me and nobody else on. I had one child then. We only stayed married about a year.

My job then was mostly nursing babies. I worked all over the city of Atlanta. About that time you were always looking for a little more money, so if you heard of a job making more, you'd quit and go get another one. So I worked domestic a lot, but I worked public jobs some too. I've been an elevator operator, I've been a waitress, a trucker. At Sears Roebuck I was the first chute girl they hired, to keep other girls supplied with work.

I did a lot of public work like that. I worked at a linen supply laundry, I washed and dried Greyhound buses, I did a little of everything, just to experience something else. But I always ended up in domestic. Before the year went out, I'd be somebody's maid. And I loved the job. But being in a low-income area like that, you didn't have a lot of choice. You'd get out of one bag into another bag.

I know I was always very talkative and I always spoke my opinion. I was arrested once for talking back to a lady that I worked for, and I was sent to jail. It was one of my employers out on Peachtree Street. She had told me to do something and she had said it in such a nasty tone, till I dressed and left. I was in my twenties then and I hadn't ever had anybody talk that nasty to me.

So I left and I was walking home and the police drew me aside and picked me up. They carried me first to my mother and they said I was sick in the head because I talked back to my employer. So they put me up in the big Rock jail—the county jail—and they said I was mental. This was the way they did you then.

It happened I had an uncle that ran a place of business and he had a little money, and he hired two psychiatrists to examine me. So, they let me out, had to turn me loose. I imagine I'd be up there today or died up there, if it wasn't for my uncle. Because at that time, blacks were locked in. We were locked completely out of our great society, as they say today. We didn't have anything, and whatever they said at that particular time went.

I was there for five days and four nights and, oh, it did so much for me. I saw the filthy surroundings there. I didn't sleep because the bed was so dirty. And that gave me a sense of direction for what I wanted to do in life. That taught me to appreciate all my mother had taught me. I knew I didn't want to live behind bars! I couldn't even eat the food. My uncle and my boyfriend and my mother's husband would come up and bring me food and let me smoke. After I got out, they sent me to Grady's to be examined to make sure I didn't catch any sickness in there.

You know God puts us in different situations to mold us into things. And maybe He was molding me. A lot of people thought I should have a resentment against whites for this. And it happened at a time when we didn't know anything about integration. But I think that's stupid, just because she did that to me. Why prosecute the whole white race because of some one person? And you know, whites do the same thing. They'll prosecute the whole black race for some one thing the blacks do. That's just stupid. It's ignorant to a whole phase of life.

If they said the girl stole something, she was just going to be prosecuted. No one would even discuss it. They used to say you stole butter, you stole eggs, then they'd say you stole my best so-and-so. Then they'd tell their friend, when the girl quit, that they fired her. They have ways of doing things like that. But I never had any bitterness in my heart against this woman. I don't even know that lady's name now. That erased completely out of my mind.

I used to travel a lot, doing domestics. I'd stay sometimes sixty days or ninety days, then I'd get lonesome and come home. I went all over; places like Chicago, Alabama. They'd advertise the jobs here and I'd take the chance of going. In the different cities, I'd go around to the different communities and watch the people. But I wouldn't go anywhere unless I could work and live in.

I was always a smart girl to save a little money. My mother always taught me, never ask the man for a cigarette, a cold drink, nothing. White or black, she didn't care who it was. Because if you take something, you leave yourself wide open to questions you wouldn't want to reply to. So I'd always put a little money away in the post office or the bank.

The first time I went up north I went to Chicago. I got the job out of the paper and they sent for me. I knew it was a Jewish family by the name. Most of what I was working with were Jews, because I had been around Jews all my life. We were surrounded with Jews when we lived over in Summerhill. Jews lived on one end and the blacks lived on the other end. Jews and black folks mix together and mostly that's the way it always has been.

They were Jews that came from overseas. Some of them were Russian Jews and they had a language that you wouldn't understand and their accents were different from yours, but we didn't pay it any attention. They couldn't understand English too good and we couldn't understand the Hebrew and the Yiddish and all this. And they were fasting Jews. You know, they'd fast when the holidays came up. They were no put-on Jews, they were the real thing. And you really were taught to do things by them—how to keep house and what they wanted done. They were really people I loved to be around. You got a chance to think and to feel the movement of them and what and who they were.

They didn't have a whole lot of luxury, even the rich ones. They saved what they had. And then some poor Jews were mixed with them too and they looked after each other. Jews have always been this way. They have a good pattern. I think that Gentiles and black people, if they should happen to look at it and look at how they made their progress, you could learn something.

This surely wasn't their country, and they knew how to survive in it. They got to be some of the richest people over here, by sacrificing. Plenty of times they ate just bread and butter. You could take a piece of their bread and chew on it for hours, and it was just delicious. It was that hard and tough and healthy bread.

I got to know both races of people, Gentiles and Jews, by living with them in their house. This is why I think a lot of blacks can understand whites better than whites can understand blacks. They kept us apart otherwise, so you don't know about my culture too much, but I know a lot about your culture and the way you live.

Well this family in Chicago was very lovely to me because I was from out of town, down south, and sure to God they weren't going to let anything happen to me. I was a very young girl and she was proud of me, how I conducted myself. I would go out, and they never questioned me, they'd just tell me to be careful. The first weeks I didn't go any place, then, when I first went, her daughter took me. Then I learned how to guide myself downtown and I would catch the El and go anywhere I wanted to go.

I was treated with the most respect, better than I was down here. Being from the South, it was like you were a different person. I think that had a lot to do with it. And they don't want you to jump up and leave, because they sent for you, and in some ways they're responsible for you. Also I think my personality is different from a lot of people. I didn't go there, you know, wild-hearted. My eyes were just on the city alone. I was just glad to get away from home, but I was strictly a worker. I didn't come there to play.

They left me in their house just like it was my own house. I was just a rank stranger and they didn't know if I was going to cart off everything while I was there or not. But she didn't have to worry about that. And if they went to the movies they would ask me would I like to go. And I said no, because I hadn't been treated that way here in the South and I wasn't going to try to pretend that I was. I told them thank you, but I was going out by myself. But this is the way it operated.

I learned so much in the North. I would not have been able to organize these women without it, if I didn't have some kind of experience with the human elements of life. In my time off, I'd go to the cabarets. This is like a restaurant or a night spot, but in the North they always called them cabarets. I would order some food and that would give me my chance to sit there and look. And that's how I learned the movement of people, how people react to things. And on a socializing level, it makes different people act differently where they go in and drink alcohol and eat.

It even helped me in the community, to know how to get people to accept you, how to get them to believe you and trust you. And this is why they'll always tell you education is out on the streets, mixing and mingling with people. I accepted this as my institution of learning.

There's several ways you can be a missionary worker. You can do it on a community basis along with your Christianity. I told my grandfather, "I'll never be able to go to school to learn to be a missionary worker." He said, "Well, if God believes that you can be one, you don't have to go to school to learn this. It's out there in the wilderness and you have to go out there and accept it." And this is where I learned mine.

My foresight began to get real good. Even if I was washing dishes, I was concentrating on what I'd seen. And I was talking within myself and I'd let it respond back to me. And the response was beautiful. So I said, "Well, I haven't lost too much. If I had gone to school, I don't think I'd be able to foresee what I foresee now." My mother used to laugh. She said, "The more you go, the wiser you get." She said, "Next time you come back, I think you're going to be a fortune teller!"

When I work in the daytime now, my time is to God whether I hit a time clock or not. And I'm hitting one, and He's the timekeeper. But I've tried to tell people my time is valuable, because whatever the day has closed out, tomorrow has not promised to me. I may be closed out too with the day. And I do worry about things I ought to be able to accomplish in a day's time. My daily prayer is: "Just let me live to help someone this day, as I move on, doing my daily duty as you have chosen me to do it." It hurts a great deal when you can't help a person that you really want to get over and help. That person just stays within the back of your mind if you really care.

Well, things have changed a lot these days, especially since we've been organizing. There used to be so many hardships, being a maid. Children disrespecting you, mothers disrespecting you. You were nursing the children and they were being taught the maid wasn't as good as you, and she's not your mother so you don't have to do so-and-so, and they would call you nigger. And we had to take all that stuff. That was the time, you know, blacks were humble, didn't have anything to say. Now they have more pride in themselves. They speak out for themselves.

One of the worst things was when a husband would make attempts at you if you were an attractive woman, if you looked good. Then you'd have to quit. You wouldn't stay, because you resented it. I resented it to the highest because I respected my own color. I've never been disenchanted over being black. I always thought black was beautiful. And I had the common sense to know that I couldn't question God because he made me black.

But you'd quit if that happened and you wouldn't dare to tell it, because you'd be telling a lie. And you just didn't have nobody to tell it to. Nobody would believe you. They put words in your mouth. These were some of the awfulest things that women had to go through. There's been some nasty things in domestics, back years, but thank God that progress has come in such a way that we know how to deal with it now. But it's not easy, and this is why I'm so aggravated when people start talking about maids and putting them down as little people. It makes me so angry.

The most important thing in life is finding yourself. I found myself when I first saw myself, after I was blind. I saw myself as brown, and I looked in the mirror and saw that I wasn't ugly, I wasn't made like an ape. And it's beautiful to see for the first time. But I had really learned to feel the within of others. I don't search for the outside of a person. I'm searching for the inside of people. Is there really a reality within you? If there's one in me, there's got to be one in you. So let us work to make this a reality together, instead of apart.

We bring a lot of things in, and whites have been misusing the black folk from slavery up. We were the first foundation of labor here. We were brought over here, not on our will, but somebody else's. We were made to work and slave for this country. We built this country and we are the first ones who should have a voice. The Indians were here, but they didn't work the Indians like they worked us. And we were everything. We were advisers, we were cooks, nurses, field workers, we were the maids. They got our opinions, our thoughts and we could develop anything. We didn't have to have a master's degree and we had great skill.

In 1959 I lost my sight again for two weeks, and the doctor asked me if I should happen never to see again, how would I feel? I said that I'd feel lucky. He said, "You got to be kidding." I said, "I'm not kidding." I said, "I've seen everything I think God intended for me to see." See, deep down, I was feeling really discouraged, like I didn't want to do anymore, but He was testing me. He was letting me know that if I quit He was going to take something back.

I guess I'd seen so much that I didn't want to see. Like I'd seen how the police would come around and intimidate people in the community and beat them for nothing. What can a person do if he's drunk and can't stand up? Why beat him? And I had seen this so many times. I used to be going to the store and I'd see somebody drunk and put them in a cab and send them home, because I didn't want anything to happen to them.

Then in '59, that's when Reverend King and others were . . . well, I'd seen how they were being beaten and how they were shelling them and it just got all over me. And I had heard white people that I was working for say that the Ku Klux Klan was going to get him, and how they need to get him. This one lady I was working for, I had been working there four or five years, and she was just against the demonstrations.

One day her little girl came back and told me, "Oh, Mama's glad you're not with those niggers out there demonstrating." And that just really got to me, so I quit. Before that, she seemed real nice, but it was always two-faced. It didn't bother me, I went and did my work and came on out, but I knew it was two-faced and when it really came out it hurt to see this.

So in '59 I just said, "Well, I'm through. I'll just go ahead and sit down. I just can't take it anymore." But I was going off my commitment. You know, you promise God one thing and you have to hold up to that promise. I had sense enough to realize that somebody was giving me my breath. But I was taught right from wrong, you reap what you sow. And I never wanted anybody to mistreat me and I didn't want to mistreat anybody else.

EARLY STIRRINGS OF THE CIVIL RIGHTS MOVEMENT

I had nine children altogether. I had three girls who died and that's heartbreaking. They all died right behind each other and that was a great setback to me. I drank some alcohol when I lost my oldest daughter, my first child by my second husband. I was living in at the time, as a maid, and my mother was keeping my children. My daughter died of a hardness of the liver. I think it came from when she swallowed a piece of glass. She was going on two and she was a beautiful child. She had jet black hair, a beautiful-featured face, a beautiful complexion, and . . . it just tore me to pieces. I loved her so dearly.

That was in 1947 and times were hard. You had your job but you weren't making too much. My husband was working for the express company—he's been on his job for thirty-two years

now—and he wasn't making much, but we made it. Then I lost
two more girls in childbirth. I think it came from just being
over-anxious to have children. I really wanted them, even
though first I only wanted two, I think because my mother had
two.

Well, I wasn't supposed to have these children but I had
them. I went to the hospital in '49 and stayed for a while and
took some treatments for childbearing. Then I had five children right behind each other. The oldest was born in 1950.
She's twenty-four now, and I have a girl twenty-three, a girl
twenty-two, a boy who'll be twenty and a boy who'll be nineteen. My oldest son from my first marriage is going on thirty-
six years old. So, I thank God I got all my three girls back.
That helped take my mind off it. It shook me up badly, and
not only me, the whole family. Because those were the only
grandchildren my mother had.

I almost did lose another little girl. She had intestinal diarrhea and she went down to nothing but little bones in eight
hours' time. But Grady's took her in and they found a specialist to work with her at 5:30 that morning. And then the one I
named Dorothy, she had a light heart attack at the end of seventh grade. So going through all that, I had my trials.

I kept working domestics as my kids were growing, but I
didn't sleep in until the later years when my girls were grown.
Most of the time I'd come home at about five. But I was lucky.
My husband always got off at one or two o'clock during the
daytime, and I have a wonderful husband. I was lucky to have
a husband to share the responsibility. Married couples don't
realize what sharing responsibilities really is.

When my children started school, they were never without
a parent. They'd either find him there or me. And when they
were small, days I wasn't working I'd be in school most times—
attending PTA, or checking on the children in the classroom. I
was concerned about kids dropping out of school and I was
counseling some parents. So sometimes we'd come home together, but my children would never walk into a frightened
house.

We didn't have much, because there were so many children,
but we had the best for the children. They all finished high
school and they all were A-1 students and they got certificates

for attending school regular. The girls were debutantes, they were introduced to society, and they went on to college. My oldest boy is a lieutenant in the Fire Department here in Atlanta and he was one of the first blacks to be promoted in the department. My youngest boy is already married. I think I raised them pretty well.

My mother and daddy stayed together for about twenty years, and then they separated. I think I was about twelve or thirteen then. I never wanted them to separate, and why they did, I don't know. I never did ask. But when my mother died in '65, my father came around to me and we've been the best of friends ever since. He really needed me when my brother died last year. It hurt him so bad. My brother got hit by a car and he died from a blood clot in his leg. Before he died he was in the Veterans' Hospital most of the time. In World War II he got wounded in his back and they just messed him up, digging and cutting.

I think black families are closer to each other. The tradition of love has been really flowed through the family. We were taught to love each other. We were taught to respect each other. I respect my daddy to the highest and I never would put him in a home. I want to outlive him so I can nurse him. And I think this is our responsibility to our mother and father, because they first did for us when we couldn't do for ourselves. They loved us and they gave us something that I don't think young people today want to give back. They say, "I don't have time."

And you know, in black families when a child got pregnant, we accepted it. We didn't try to have an abortion, have the child destroyed. We took the child in and did the very best we could for it. We loved that child like we loved our own. More than we did our own, because that child needed us and we knew we needed the child. We loved our children with a wholehearted love, not just a put-on love. And we loved whatever they produced. And that's why you see so many black families nursing their grandbabies. If we go to work, we want Mama to keep the child, because Mama's going to do it with love.

I really resent abortion. You're destroying the human elements of life that's trying to be created. Even when the parents say they don't want them, somebody's going to love that child. You know, the child that's born out of wedlock sometimes is the most brilliant child there is. And God never gives you anything you can't afford. You just don't want to sacrifice for it, that's the trouble.

You mean to tell me I can afford my luxury to want to receive the love from the sex that I'm having, but I don't want to receive everything that sex produces here on this earth? Because you don't have the time, you're not willing to sacrifice for it? That's stupid. I sacrificed for my children. Your mother sacrificed for you. She had to, because when you birth a baby, you go through the last area of life, and death winks at you. You have to be a strong woman to go through it.

I think day care is good. It's good for a mama to get out, but not to let the child be bound in a day care center all day. Because that child is missing the love that God has instilled within. And that child knows it and that's why he gives you hell. When he was yearning for you, you weren't there. Some people don't have patience and they want to dump an infant and that builds resentment in a child. And then the child says, "I wouldn't have a child," because he wasn't treated right in his life.

And then I feel you've got to let the child develop some on his own and you've got to help him until that child gets a sense of direction. We all have fear. I had fear that my girls might go out into the wilderness, and dear God, I want you to watch over them. Don't let them stumble and fall in the gutter.

But none of my children ever gave me much trouble and they always respected the law. I see some parents, I mean white and black, have to always go get their children out of something they've got into. I always told my children, "Now you got a brain and you better use it. You use it for you, then you can go back and help somebody. And be by yourself." I don't believe in going in droves like some teen-agers do.

I don't think any child has to run and do what every Tom, Dick or Harry has to do. Because Tom, Dick and Harry can get you in a thousand dollars' worth of trouble and they can't get you out of it. I had a tight rein on my children and I guided them like I was guided. And there was no difference between the three boys and the three girls. Everybody washed dishes, everybody made beds, washed their clothes, did the ironing. And their daddy believed like I believed. My mother had a firm hand on them too. She checked on them every single day.

Well, like I said, I was at my children's school a lot, and I happened to be there the day my daughter Dorothy had the heart seizure. I was participating in the PTA. Right that same year, she was going to graduate and go into the eighth grade. And they were moving the eighth grade out of Booker T. Washington High School. They were going to put them in the heart of downtown, at Central Junior High, which was a condemned, dilapidated school. It was a vocational training school first and they condemned it and they wouldn't let the grown adults go in the school, so I was wondering why they were going to let all the children go in there.

I had a dear friend call me one day and it seemed like her voice was way off somewhere. She sounded so pitiful and she said, "Oh, Bolden, you going to let them send our children down there to that condemned school?" And it just went all over me. And I said, "No, I'm not." Well from there I jumped up and we met with some parents of low income, and that was my first protest.

I really gave our superintendent a hard way to go. I think he was really dumbfounded to see that low-income people like us were concerned with quality education. And that was my theme. I kept him out of his office for a walk in the street to see what was happening, how many parents were out there and the type of parents they were.

He had a Mrs. Sara Mitchell on the board who was a dear friend to us. She was white and she was communicating with me. She called me one night and she said, "I want to tell you that the superintendent really admires your courage." And I said, "Tell him thank you, but I really meant what I was saying."

I organized the parents and brought the pressure down until he made a commitment. He had promised us that he was going to give us a school in Vine City out of a school bond drive that he had. We didn't get that school then because the bond issue was defeated, but he promised me the next time we got out and worked for it he was going to give us that school. And I was going to make him live up to that.

The kids still had to go downtown to that condemned building. All of them finished there. We did get the new school about six years later. It's the John F. Kennedy School, a middle school. But I don't think we would've gotten it even then if we hadn't kept on pressing. I had to go down to the Board of Education every week, because it would jump off the agenda. And once they take something off the agenda, if you don't watch them, they'll never stick it back on. I kept them kind of busy.

We had a lot of backing, a lot of people, ministers and that kind of thing, because these were low-income parents speaking about quality education. And I thought it was time that we let them know that we were searching for quality, not just to integrate. I think that's what all parents should look at—not just thinking, is my child going to integrate with someone, but is my child going to get quality education that will be beneficial to them in their future?

We're talking about not just some reading, writing and arithmetic, we're talking about how do we deal with children, with a generation that is wiser than we were, and we've got to push forward. We can't still keep at what we had ten years ago. I hate to say it but we didn't get what we needed, our children didn't get what they needed, and our grandchildren are not going to get it either until we start to think where can we open some new doors to start building a foundation. It's not just sending a child to a classroom. Clay and mortar is not education. We're going to have to let the children mix and mingle with the human elements of life.

Well, I don't know how my organizing pattern came up, or whatever you want to call it, but it was a thing that I'd been doing all the time. It just came natural to me. If anything was going on in Vine City, they just sent for me. Some people can feel your justice that you're struggling for. And I was very outspoken for the benefit of both races. Many times some of the whites had been getting a hard blow from the others and I'd stand up and tell them, "Now we just don't do those kind of things."

If you're right, you're right and if you're wrong I'm going to tell you about it and I don't bite my tongue in doing so. And I think this was the way I built myself. It was a guide from within, not something that I thought about. And I was always at the right place at the right time, when something was going on. Then people would call on me to consult with them on different things and I helped screen out the black candidates and things like this. I was doing that long before I started organizing the maids.

This story's never been told, but I worked with Julian Bond way back.* He knew me because I used to be active in SNCC (Student Non-Violent Coordinating Committee). That was the organization during the sixties that was very powerful and he was with them as a full-time job then. I was a maid then and they were asking us not to go shop in places, to boycott. So I participated and I got other people to do the same and we'd talk about it. We were still segregated then, and on the buses we'd all go to the back. Maids always had to stand up on the way home and this kind of thing.

So Julian decided he wanted to run for the House of Representatives. They reapportioned the House and created some districts for us in there and he wanted to run. So he came looking for me one Saturday afternoon. It was warm, June I think, and I met him outdoors at a church. I used to go shopping with my mother on Saturday afternoon but she waited on me this time. I called her and told her I was walking with Julian.

So I walked through the community and I told him a lot of things to do, what to expect and how to mix and mingle with people, what he should watch for to see if people were ac-

* Julian Bond, first elected at age twenty-five to the Georgia State Legislature to a new seat created by a Supreme Court decision on reapportionment in 1965. He and seven others were the first blacks to be elected to state office in fifty-eight years. Denied his seat by a vote of 184–12 in the House on the grounds of "disloyalty," due to a statement affirming his admiration for the courage of draft-card burners in light of the known penalties, and other statements opposing the Vietnam war. Reelected in two special elections in 1966, again denied his seat. In December 1966, the Supreme Court ruled that the Georgia House of Representatives had violated his constitutional rights, and he was sworn in in January 1967. Previously, studied philosophy under Martin Luther King, Jr., at Morehouse College in Atlanta; was communications director of the Student Non-Violent Coordinating Committee (SNCC) and an official until he resigned in 1966. First black nominated for the vice presidency of a major party, at the 1968 Democratic National Convention. President, Southern Poverty Law Center.

cepting what he was saying. And that was a beautiful thing. I got a kick out of that. That was his first time campaigning anywhere and he was very young. He was like a little boy at that particular time and I thought of him as my own son. And I really got sincerely with Julian. I prayed for him as I walked with him and I knew dear God was walking with us.

He got kind of upset once. He went to a Democratic meeting and they called him "boy." And he came back and he told me, "Mrs. Bolden, I feel like I'm going to drop out of this thing because they're calling me 'boy' and they're not going to ever respect me as a man." And that's the time that I told him if he dropped out I'd take me a baseball bat and beat hell out of him.

I was working myself to death and I was having a lot of trouble out of my stomach. I mean a lot of trouble, but I stood up to it and I never let anyone know it was hurting that bad. My mother was dying then and she was always telling me to go to the doctor, and I said, "No, I go to the doctor and they want to cut me. I'm going to try to bail out."

Finally, I knew Julian was going to win and he did win. But before he was seated, he came out with that statement about burning draft cards. Then they denied him of his seat and they had a big rigamarole about it and that was another big battle that I knew I had to go back through. And I told him, "If you believe in it, stick with it." He said, "Yeah, I believe in it."

I'd tell everyone, "Julian will win right on, ain't no doubt about it." And then they were trying to reelect some of the others and I'd say, "We're going to keep putting in here till we win them all. They're not going to ramrod this down our throats." There was a rally one night that I had to speak at. It was so packed with people, and Julian hadn't got there yet. But just as I was saying, "I see a man standing tall in the State of Georgia and that man is Julian Bond," he walked down that aisle. And everybody just fell out.

Not long after Julian was elected, Stokely* came out with

* Stokely Carmichael first articulated the phrase "black power" during a voting rights march in June 1966, saying it was intended as "a way to help Negroes develop racial pride and use the ballot for education and economic development." Chairman of the Student Non-Violent Coordi-

that "Black Power" statement and then, well . . . I had all these SNCC† boys to deal with. They were living across the street from me in a house Julian had over there for his head-quarters. That was in '66 when Stokely made that statement, and the street was just covered with people. The news media from everywhere was there. International press people, *The New York Times,* everybody. They had a big thing in the com-munity, all kinds of threats. Some of the community people were trying to run them out after the Black Power thing. But I couldn't turn my back on those boys.

I knew it was just a philosophy and I understood what they meant. I don't think anybody really knew what this organiza-tion meant to low-income people. Like during my demonstra-tion at the Board of Education, they weren't there at the be-ginning, but they always came in along the way. And it really made us feel very strong and protected. It was one of the strongest organizations, along with Reverend King, and it meant a great deal to see the magnificent strength of these young men. To understand a group like that you have to be

---

nating Committee until other SNCC leaders severed relations with him in August 1968, when he was prime minister of the Black Panther Party. Co-authored *Black Power: The Politics of Liberation in America* with political scientist Charles V. Hamilton. When he returned to the United States after a world tour in 1967, his passport was revoked for visiting Cuba, and the Justice Department initiated proceedings against him for advocating sedition. Went to live in Guinea, West Africa, in 1969 and broke with the Black Panthers, calling their tactics coercive and au-thoritarian. He and his wife, South African singer Miriam Makeba, were granted Ugandan citizenship in 1973. Organized the African People's Revolutionary Party in 1973 with the aim of fostering stronger ties be-tween black Americans and Africans.

† Student Non-Violent Coordinating Committee (SNCC), formed in 1960 by a group of southern black college students who staged a sit-in at a "white only" lunch counter in Greensboro, North Carolina. Within four years, penetrated most black college campuses across the nation. Held forty to fifty demonstrations a week at its height. Originally dedi-cated to nonviolent forms of confrontation. Initiated voter registration drives throughout the South. Later advocated formation of a nationwide black political party with the black panther as its symbol. Became in-creasingly militant after Stokely Carmichael became chairman in 1966. By 1969, leadership was divided and the organization disintegrated.

there working with them, observing them. This struggle really got into my blood and it hasn't gotten out as yet.

So after all that, I had to talk up the word in the community about giving them some food. And I wasn't doing too well. I was sick and all and I had my grandmother living with me then too. But we dealt with it. I was able to give them some breakfast, some of the boys, and I was able to feed them when they asked me. If they needed anything or any advice they could always come to me.

I was proud of them. They were boys that had great knowledge, great understanding of what the struggle was all about. They had more understanding than the people they were struggling for. Because sure to God, we knew some of it and some of it we didn't. I've seen a lot of people who wished they'd never started. They'd say things like, "You're going too fast, you're pushing things too far." And that really made you angry if you knew what they were really trying to do. But you couldn't express your anger, you know?

I knew what Reverend King was doing too and I thought it was one of the magnificent things. The tone of the man's voice did something to you. It electrified the inner spirit of you. It awakened the belief you had within. You had to really move. It didn't take you long to get the understanding of what he was doing if you really felt it.

Reverend King had an impact on me when I saw him in Montgomery, Alabama. I prayed hard for God to give him courage. I would see him on television and we would hear it on the news when we would be on the job. And when he had a march here, I marched. I'll never forget that day. I think it was a Sunday morning and it was cold that day. I fed my children corn flakes for breakfast and I told them to stay and don't open the door for nobody. And I went demonstrating and it really gave me great pride and dignity to do so.

We marched downtown, by the Terminal Station. Everybody marched, all the old people on my street. Wasn't nobody home but the children. And I went back home and cooked dinner, and I turned the television on and it just gave me a thrill to know that I was part of it. He's dead and gone but I still believe in him wholeheartedly.

He was a man that God gave great courage and I believe that God suffered for him too. Because God needed him to say, "You can't continue to let these people live like this." But He had to give him up. And there never will be another one of him. He was a highly Christian man. You could feel the vibrations of truth from him. God's children do have a vibration that others can feel.

And I think he helped the white as much as he helped the black. He really aroused the curiosity of whites and made them begin to think, am I doing right? It brought them a sense of understanding and it helped them to find a new belief, a belief that there must be a God. They would laugh at you when you'd say there's a God, and it really hurt. A lot of them I worked for, they'd say, "There's no such thing as a God." And all this would make you think, how do you act around these people? They don't believe in anything. And you always had to cramp it down in you.

I think Reverend King gave me the most courage that I have, because I knew what he was saying was the truth. He died a little before I began organizing the maids, but I think that all of our inspiration came from him. It's just like your courage had been dead or asleep, and this gave you something. He died for what he believed in. And the night he made his last speech, he'd been up on the mountaintop, I truly believed he had. And he said it didn't matter no more, because God had been by to tell him something. And he preached that all that week in his church.

He didn't want no big funeral. He didn't want anybody to tell how many degrees he had. It didn't matter to him about those things. "But just remember I tried to help somebody. That means more." You felt him. If you had any sense of human in you, you felt him. And it made you feel good. I always think of him and it still makes you feel good when you hear his voice now.

NATIONAL DOMESTIC WORKERS, INC.

When I came out of the Civil Rights Movement, I came out in a big force. My children can tell you, even though they were very small. But I've been my own woman all my life. I had to be, because my mama and daddy were separated and I didn't want to see my mama's head locked in her shoulders. So my little bit helped her a great deal and that made her strong.

I had thought about organizing us in 1960. We just needed more money to survive. But what got me going was when they wanted to send the children across town to an integrated school. That was in 1965 when I was demonstrating against the Board of Education. I knew that maids weren't making anything for anyone to talk about sending their children across town. We couldn't afford to pay twenty cents round-trip for the bus. And you couldn't afford to give your child forty-five cents for lunch. So why send your children out and then have to thumb a ride back and not have lunch money and a part of the time didn't have school shoes?

You're talking about poor children and you're talking about women who are the head of the household. We hadn't gotten farther than about seven dollars a day then. That wasn't any money, but it was some money to us. It was better than not making anything at all. So I was thinking about these poor women taking on more responsibility and earning so little. If you had three or four children . . . I had five in school, but I was lucky.

I just could barely afford to send mine downtown, twenty cents round-trip. And I gave mine sandwiches. They didn't get no hot lunch. I was just lucky my husband had a job, so they had fresh milk and cookies. And my mother only had one daughter, so my children were her children and she kept them supplied with goodies like apples and oranges, and cold drinks for when they'd come home from school.

She was the same way about me. And she was proud of what I was doing, so she helped me a great deal. She never turned me down on anything. If I spent my last dime doing something and I didn't have the grocery money, she said, "Come on, let's go shopping." And she would give me good advice. Before she died, we talked about the maids. And she said, "If you believe in it, go to it. I'll help you however I can." She was my sister, my mother, my dearest friend.

Also what made me strong was my husband. I had a finance supporter who took care of my children, so I didn't have to worry about where the rent money was coming from or where the food money was coming from and that's got lots to do with it. If they all needed something, I'd buy a batch of socks this payday, and underwear the next payday, and that way they all had enough until school opened up the next year. But it was geared to where Mama was helping and Daddy was doing the supporting. And this was the most important thing.

Well, when they started with this cross-town thing, I said, "Now this is wrong. Somebody needs to organize us." So I started in 1965, before my mother died, and I called several community leaders and our Civil Rights Movement leaders. I talked a long time with them, and they said they just couldn't do it. It was just too much.

Then after a while the Urban League* heard about what I was trying to do, and they called a meeting at the YMCA. We got down there and there was all types of people there, black and white. I listened to them throw things around which I knew were so far wrong. So one of the ladies said, "Stand up, Mrs. Bolden, and tell it straight to the people." So I got up and told them that they actually didn't know what they were talking about. They were giving some off-the-wall stuff. They never worked as maids, never knew how our own labor field really was. And I told them, "You don't even know the price we even want or how much money we'd start trying to get."

So then this John Stenson at the Urban League, he said, "Mrs. Bolden, why don't you go out and bring us back something you think we can deal with." So from then on, I started going around just about every night talking about the domestic. Sometimes I'd be gone till two o'clock in the morning talking with these women.

After that first meeting with the Urban League when they sent me out, we met again at the Y. Then I had to go out of town for two weeks and before I left, I wrote down, "$15 plus carfare a day." Then they started to meet, and I didn't want to

---

* National Urban League, founded in 1910, one of the most affluent and effective civil rights organizations, with ninety-five local offices around the country. With an emphasis on economic progress for blacks, it operates job training and job-development programs and works in fields of housing and education as well.

come back because I knew that if I'd been at these meetings, they were going to pick me to be the president. I thought I'd give another woman a chance to do something. I wanted to sit back and be a part of it, but I didn't want the responsibility. I knew you were going to have to give up something if you were going to be a full-time representative, and this is what we really needed.

Well, I got back and they called me and they said, "They're waiting on you this afternoon." So I said, "Well, I'll be down there later." I let them get into their meeting. They had a temporary president then, and when I walked in somebody said, "We nominate Mrs. Bolden to be our founding president." Then a lady got up and seconded the motion and I told them to take a vote on it, and they elected me that night overwhelmingly. So that put me in the driver's seat and I've been here ever since. I had to give up my job then, in the last of '68. Then the OEO (Office of Economic Opportunity) here gave me office space with a telephone and a secretary.

So we went on in '68 struggling and I set the price at fifteen dollars plus carfare and up, per day. I began passing out the leaflets every morning downtown here. Sometimes it'd be freezing out here, but I'd stay out there. Then after we set the price, you had to teach those women how to ask for it. If you were making ten dollars a day, you had to learn how to communicate with the lady and tell her about the cost of living. If she didn't want to pay it, you'd just have to find a new job that's willing to.

But I didn't want anybody to protest. We women didn't believe in it, especially in this field. Because if thirty thousand women get without a job, and that's how many maids there are in Atlanta, where else have we got to go to? So we couldn't go out demonstrating, and we weren't ramrodding anything down anybody's throat. Just if we weren't getting paid, we just walk off the job. So this is the way the fifteen dollars came around.

I had to do a lot of talking. I had to do a lot of appearing on television. But I kept the press out of this while I was organizing. See the press can be beautiful, but some things we don't need them on until you get the foundation laid. I knew they could have driven me up against the wall and just labeled me anything they wanted to label me. They could have said, "This is a radical woman here, bringing on disturbance between the employers and employees." So every time they wanted to know why they couldn't come in to our meetings, I'd say, "Well, you don't go to any garden clubs, so don't come to our club!"

The women named all of this the way they wanted it, so it's National Domestic Workers, Inc., but we're not really national. I didn't want to accept that because you get bogged down in paperwork and you never do anything concrete for the people you're developing for. You have to worry about your chapters, and then you have to worry about dues, and then they call you over here and there because they have a problem and the area's so large that it wouldn't show what I was really organizing these women for—to upgrade them. I wouldn't be here long enough to develop a new career for them. I think this was more important than me having to go across country.

I couldn't change the name after they got it, but I still go out of the city to organize. I'm willing to, when they send for me. When we were first organizing, Whitney Young* sent for me to come up to the Urban League convention in Washington and then he sent a videotape down here to have me on tape so he could carry it across to his regional offices and inspire other women to organize. Then I began to go out on speaking tours of organizing to South Carolina, Savannah, all these places.

At the beginning, I knew some harsh words were going to be said by the maids and the employers. A lot of the maids were afraid to join. They were skeptical because they knew what unions had done in the past, and at first "union" was part of the name. I don't think we realized how much "union"

* Whitney M. Young, Jr., executive director of the National Urban League from 1961 until his death in 1971. Dean of Atlanta University's School of Social Work, 1954–1961. Considered one of the most moderate black leaders. Wrote *Beyond Racism,* which espouses the creation of government-backed neighborhood economic development corporations. Called for a "Marshall Plan" for the nation's blacks to compensate for generations of economic and other forms of discrimination. Many of his specific proposals were incorporated into Lyndon Johnson's anti-poverty program in the mid-1960's.

frightens people. They think you're coming in to stampede and bargain and harass and talk about striking and this kind of thing. Some time during a maid's life, they have probably switched for a time and worked at a laundry or something, and they just didn't want to be bothered with a union. They start collecting money from you, and then "I don't want nobody communicating with my employer except me."

Then I had telephone calls coming in from employers calling me a bitch. Or they'd say, "The bitch wasn't worth that type of salary." I didn't bang the phone up and I didn't get angry. I always had kind words that would erase their little ugly words, so we would hit it off pretty good after that. I'd listen to them, and when they'd get through I'd tell them, "Now you be willing to listen to me."

It was a constant thing, all day long and half of the night. I had to stay away from home much more than I had anticipated. But it wasn't too hard for my children to adjust, because they were brought into this life that way. I remember when we first started demonstrating about civil rights. My husband would gather all the young around and they'd have the television on when I'd come in, and we'd all cuddle around it. I was usually there during the daytime. If I had to work, I'd come home at five, I'd fix dinner and he would bathe the children, and then I'd usually go to a meeting.

My husband has never been out with me any place where I went organizing. I didn't want to do anything to jeopardize him or to make him lose what he loved, and that was his job. So I used my maiden name for this. My married name is Thompson. But my being out a lot didn't bother him at all. He just wasn't that type of a person. If you had one member of a family doing something, the other one had to share in responsibility for staying with the children.

I guess the most encouraging time for me was when the women began to call for me to place them in jobs. That really got going in about '70. I give them jobs free of charge. I don't charge anybody anything, the employer or the employee. I can't, because I'm a nonprofit organization. I'd have to buy the license, then I'd have to contribute so much out of each dollar I received, and I just wouldn't want to go through that. This way I help people in the community, and we help the employers and employees by helping them find each other. And it seems we get all the advertising we need because I'm on television and radio so much, and in the papers.

It was also very encouraging when maids began to meet me on the streets and tell me, "We're so proud of you. We're so happy to have someone like you to really speak for us." I'd speak for senior citizens too. And then I started to do counseling. I was concerned about all areas of the maids' lives, not just one area. If somebody was having problems with her husband, they'd come and talk it over with me. Then some of the employers tell me some of the problems they have. So I have all types of social problems that people call on me for, and I like to be able to help people.

I have over two thousand members now. We have over thirty thousand maids in Atlanta, but I would never try to take those type of people in. We still have meetings, but I don't have them like I used to. It's dangerous now to have women out at night and they work in the daytime. But I have an executive board that meets once a month. I tell them what we're doing, how we're progressing. They want to know if we're developing things for the maids, and I let them know about the studies and proposals and things.

You have to be a developer here. You can't just elaborate on fifteen dollars a day plus carfare and up to twenty dollars, for seven years. It's a constant thing. You must know how to change it as the years pass on. The philosophy and the mold must change. You can't continue doing what you did ten years ago, or even five years ago. And I didn't organize just on money. I organized to upgrade the field, to make the field more professional.

The first program I did was for the State of Georgia in 1971. That was a homemakers' skills training program, how to train inner city housekeepers. I let Economic Opportunity of Atlanta administrate the funds for me. That's a community action program with funds from the federal government. They had the machinery already set up for the payroll checks, and I didn't want to ever have it said that I misappropriated some money. I had thirteen women working with me and that program really proved some points.

Now the Equal Opportunity is administering another grant

for a study on domestics that I completed this year. We found out how the maids felt about getting some type of training and if they would participate in the training program with the employers. See, I knew I had to go to them to ask them because they don't care what *you* want, they might not want it. You have to go to them so they could have a say in it. I got Atlanta University to put all the data and the findings together for me with a computer, and then I circulated it and I carried it to Washington.

The Women's Bureau at the Labor Department never had any statistics on black women and domestics, so I wanted my study to be A-1 plus. I don't think the Women's Bureau really knew what a domestic worker was. Then also, some years back I had created a career ladder with the Women's Bureau and I wanted to try it out here, to see if it's going to be workable. Now they have this household-technician program, but I don't agree with some of their points. Anyhow, they never really had any money from Congress to operate, and they're more concerned about the professional woman there.

Well the first thing I did when I set out to see if this career ladder was workable, I went over to observe the WIN (Work Incentive) Program. That's a welfare program. They furnish the clients and the Labor Department will furnish the program. It was supposed to be a training program but it turned into more of a testing for job applicants, teaching them how to apply for jobs. So when I saw what went on there, just a bunch of women sitting up there and you seeing what they're capable of, this is when I knew you had to do something to dress up this field, to make it more tasteable to people, to sell it.

So I had to talk about training programs, and this is what I'm still talking on now. Home management, home technician, and things like driving. I don't know how to drive, but I know you needed to drive, picking up the children and all. And so I built a new career ladder for these women. And I want to give them a beautiful pin or something to let them know they have finished the course to the best of their ability and that they are professional women.

Now I'm writing a manual for the maids. It's to give them and the employers a kind of guide for communications between them. A lot of times, people don't have understanding of this field. It has been so overlooked and overshadowed. I'm trying to give them a guide on what it's really all about, and how the relationship should be established in it—how they should work together, being two women, and that kind of thing.

I don't get any salary. The only money I get is if we have some projects going. I've been here seven years and I've been running out like this, but I always come out on top. It's just who I know and how I get around. I'm presently on the HEW Secretary's Advisory Committee on the Status of Women's Rights and Responsibilities. That was in 1972, Richardson* nominated me. But even before that, I just really got around and got to be known across the country.

I remember in 1969 when I went to the Urban League convention in Washington, and Whitney Young introduced me to Mrs. Florence Rice,† the First Lady of New York. Then Florence carried me to Mrs. Chisholm‡ and we sat down and talked to Mrs. Chisholm about introducing a minimum wage bill for domestics. Mrs. Chisholm was really the forerunner in it and I feel like she's due the credit.

There already was a minimum wage bill, but we had never been included in it. They were raising the minimum wage and

---

* Elliot T. Richardson, cabinet member of the Nixon administration: Secretary of Health, Education and Welfare (1970–1973), Secretary of Defense (January–May 1973), U.S. Attorney General (May–October 1973). After a brief stint as Ambassador to England, appointed Secretary of Commerce by Gerald Ford.

† Florence Rice, president of the Harlem Consumer Education Council, Inc., founded in 1968 to educate minority communities about their rights as consumers in areas ranging from credit to education and health. Called "the black Ralph Nader" by a New York newspaper. A former union leader, she spoke out publicly in the 1960's about widespread discrimination against blacks in the New York garment industry. Currently forming a national black consumers' organization to focus on all forms of economic discrimination.

‡ Shirley Chisholm, first black woman ever elected to Congress, from New York's 12th Congressional District—the Bedford-Stuyvesant section of Brooklyn—in 1968. Outspoken on problems related to racism, poverty and the urban crisis. A former educator and child care center director, she was elected to the New York State Assembly for two terms, starting in 1964. First woman and first black to become a presidential candidate for a major party, entering several Democratic Party primaries in 1972.

we felt we should be included. They had defeated getting us in it up to then, but she kept on struggling until she won. Mrs. Chisholm knew what the needs were. You don't have to keep pushing on her. There were maids where she lived, and she knew they weren't making a decent salary. So I didn't have to worry. She's a woman who really does her own job.

That was the time I really challenged the Urban League, at that meeting in 1969, and I believe I was the first low-income woman to challenge them. I just told them these women were not accepted in the minimum wage and that no organization had done anything for them. And they didn't have black low-income people in their affiliations across the country. I just wanted to bring the issues down front and I wanted to see the people in there. It didn't have to be me, just so they had some poor black people, especially some women.

I'm still struggling for black women. They've been the burden bearer of all segments of blacks and I think they need the opportunity to demonstrate their skills, their abilities, and their knowledge. We have some professional women that have had the opportunity to be branched out, but not that many.

In the past seven years there's been a great deal of change. These women used to be embarrassed about saying they were maids. You had to take such hardships that you didn't want nobody to know you were. Now it's different. You can't tell a maid from a secretary anymore. In the past, if a black woman was a maid you could tell by the way she dressed. Now they don't carry the shopping bags as much, they go neater, and they look more lively and intelligent. They're making between fifteen and twenty dollars, up to twenty-two dollars a day. And the heart of the Deep South like this never paid that kind of salary before.

There's so much I still want to accomplish for them. I want to leave an institution for them to be able to go through, so when they have problems or sickness, they can have someone that really can help see that things are properly taken care of. I'm expecting to leave a foundation here, an institution that will give them pride. The AFL-CIO started like this, struggling. I don't expect we'll become a union, but we'll be a strong organization, beneficial to both races. This is what I'm working for.

One of the things I want to work toward is medical coverage. They're beginning to get Social Security now, and they're more concerned about it, and this I'm very proud of. As time goes on, they will get more involved in pushing for things. We're still struggling with a lot of basic things.

The first of the week they're here looking for jobs, and then they call me about complaints they have, like "She did so-and-so, how must I deal with this?" And I'm here to give them feedback so they won't just get angry and walk out. Because sometimes minor things can be corrected if we know how to communicate with the lady.

This is the most important thing, knowing how to communicate. I don't care what type of job or what level the job is on. If we don't know how to communicate, we'll never be happy in anything we undertake to do. We should learn how to say, "I would like to have a conference with you." That's the way it should be on any job, and in family life. We even need to have conferences with our children and say, "This is to let you know how I feel." So we have to keep struggling with all this, communicating, talking to each other.

POLITICS, POVERTY, AND TOO LITTLE LOVE

I think my faith influenced me to be what I am more than anything else—what God wanted me to be. My blindness gave me my sense of direction. I'm one alone. I know that and it doesn't worry me at all if I don't agree with some of the viewpoints of people. Some people ask me, "Why don't you let somebody else come up there and learn?" I say, "I don't keep them from it. I learned mine out of the streets. God has geared me in to operate this way." I really have no other choice.

But I don't use it for no profit gain. I really resent that. If you want to get a good argument out of me, just tell me about where I can pick up some money. I'm not out here to sell my soul. I think this is what happened to Nixon, ambition to be *the* President, and nothing but *the* President. How many times did he quote that to you? He put a shadow God up there, but you don't play with God. He let him fall into a destruction of his own. He was his own downfall.

There's no man on earth that's going to get all the votes, unless you trick them into it, and that's what he did. It's like stealing. At the time, they were sending people here to try to get me in the Republican Party. I didn't want to be no Republican because I lived in the Republican days in the Depression. Hoover was the President. I'll never forget that.

For me, politics and my Christianity don't mix. I don't believe in wheeling and dealing. I go through that Georgia House of Representatives and I stand up there and look around that room. It doesn't take me any time to say, "Dear God, I never want to be in this." As I say, God has given me a foresight into things and I'm able to analyze it the minute I go in. I can feel the vibrations in there and it feels awful. I know it's not real. They are playing games with each other and it hurts. They play around with righteousness and they tramp all over justice.

Some people don't even know what justice is. It doesn't take you three hundred or four hundred years to know that we haven't done right in some categories. There's no way in the world that one race of people can control this world. None of us own anything here. We just have what we have. We came here with nothing and we're going to leave here with nothing. So why do they sit up there and say they're going to do something for people and then they don't do it? They have the power, sitting up there in that House to do it. But we don't ever have enough money to reach over to the poor. I just don't know. We've been denied of so much and received so little.

We have hunger, which we shouldn't have in this country that's so rich. They have alcohol problems. And then they fuss about the welfare. Well, the welfare system was set up at a time when nobody had any money, right after the Depression. The blacks didn't set up any system of welfare. And $109 isn't anything when you have seven children. That isn't any money. I heard a tale in the paper where welfare people can make more than working class people do. In some states maybe, but I know darn well it's not true in this state.

We got to take a look at the Poverty Program too. It didn't help only blacks, it helped whites too. And some middle class whites. They got jobs out of it and they made good money. Top money. So let's face the facts. We still have some programs going here and I have hope that the South will deal with that problem. We're going to be a showcase for others. But we've got to learn first to accept reality.

I talked about these things every time I went around to talk to the women's lib. I was very proud to see them stand up and speak up when it started. I'm glad to see any group do that when they're righteous and I know they have been denied of something. But they're not talking about the masses of people. You've got different classes of people in all phases of life and all races, and those people have to be spoken up for too.

Once I was a speaker at the Tarrytown Conference Center in New York. I think it was the National Women's Political Caucus or something like that. But it really bothered me to see that they don't include low-income women. Maybe one or two black women, but no poor women. You can't talk about women's rights until we include all women. When you deny one woman of her rights, you deny all. I'm getting tired of going to those meetings, because there's none of us participating.

They're still trying to put their amendment to the constitution, but they're not going to be able to do it until they include us. Some of these states know this, that you don't have all women up front supporting that amendment. They are talking about women's rights, but which women?

I would tell them this: "We're not on your agenda. We're not in your by-laws. We're just scrubwomen and you're not even considering motivating us." Some of them don't even want to pay us. They talk about rights, but they are violating my rights. They got to talking that they better do their own housework. I said, "Well, how are you going to do it when you don't know it? You need me just as much as I need you. So there's no use to lying and saying that we don't. We need each other."

You take a force of thirty thousand women that never asked the federal government, "What have you done for me, and I'm a working woman?" Thirty thousand domestics right here in Atlanta, and they are feeding into the economy. They're putting their little bit of money back. They are not on welfare. They are not asking for a handout. "I'm struggling and what have you done for me? What type of training have you developed for me? What have you offered me?" These are women who work every day. Working class women. They're poor but they're working class and now they're classed as a work force.

"You don't see me. You never have seen me because I'm off at seven o'clock in the morning, I'm catching a bus and I'm not off until black dark, and you're gone home and I'm probably serving you your dinner. What kind of help are you offering me?" That's the kind of thing we need to ask. We've been here since slavery, before any other class of labor. Before we had cars here or even a steel plant, we were here and we were working.

We built this country on our sweat. We wonder when they're ever going to say, "Let's grant these women some training." You've got your education, but you don't have what you need to have at home. You have to use the education you got outside of your home. I come into your home every day. And what are you offering me?

There isn't any movement ever going to be as powerful as the Civil Rights Movement. Women haven't been denied their God-given rights. I've been free to do what I want to do. It's because a woman looked up to the man. But also, civil rights had love. With the women, they're fighting over each other. The minute you go in there you can feel it. We've got to have love and they don't have it in there.

They call me and they ask me what I feel on abortion. I say, "No, I'm bitterly against it." I love an infant when he is born. If I hear him cry, it goes all over me. And I don't care if he's white or black. Whether it's that or something else, they're always squabbling with one another. And then this whole professional thing. We get too professional, always dealing with this here paper. We can't ever correct nothing when we professionalize it right here on this paper. Common sense ought to be in print too, but we don't do that.

In years to come, women may defeat themselves. So overanxious. I'm proud that women began to get up and let them know that we can shape this world into a form together, but some of them are trying to be men. If God wanted you to have everything that a man has, he would have given it to you.

A woman is a helpmaker. She's not to get up and dominate man. I can't see things like pushing a man out of a job, or say you have a man who's president of an organization and you think you should have a woman. If she is president, she's going to get the ambition the same as he gets. She could make as big a mess as he can make. And we weren't put here to take over.

I look at a man and I am his helpmaker. But I don't put him up on no pedestal either. My husband waits on me as much as I wait on him. I've been a free woman all my life. I've been making my own decisions, but I respect yours and I'll go halfway with yours. But a man is your protection. When he walks up to accept you from your mother and your father, he asks for you, doesn't he? Then he takes on the full responsibility that he's taken from Daddy. So why do you think that he's taking your rights?

When I look at the Women's Movement, there's so many little things in there I dislike. But it's not for me to tell them, it's for them to learn it. It makes sense to some extent, but they carry it a little too far sometimes. All people exaggerate sometimes. I like to see progress and I like to see a woman making a decent salary. If she's doing a man's job in an office or any other place, I feel she needs to be equally paid. Everybody ought to be equally paid on this earth for what they're sweating for. But not just to prove a point that a man is pouring cement so I want to pour cement too.

This is why men are not respecting us anymore. The womanhood has lost something. It has lost its beautiful effectiveness out of it, because women are trying to be like men. "I don't want to have babies. I don't want to have this and I don't want to do this." They have lost the effect. And womanhood is the most beautiful thing in the world.

I think the majority of men have got hang-ups about women coming in and taking over men's jobs and it builds resentment until she catches hell. She hasn't seen nothing yet. It's going to put a lot of pressure on the generation coming on now, and they're not going to be able to bear it. There's going to be a lot of backpushing from men. They aren't awake yet. They're watching it, but they haven't come to a rally yet. They can get strong, they can get tough, and they can be in control. We'll never take that power from them. And I dare not to try to struggle and fight with them about it.

A lot of people are lacking in common sense when it comes to dealing with the human elements of life. If I'd gone on to school and gotten a degree, I probably would be a different person, wrapped up in a professional life, dealing with professional people. But I still believe in that philosophy that Christ told Paul: "Talk in the language that my people can understand, not just you and I, Paul."

I know my children changed a great deal when they went to college. Maybe they do have to associate with those people on that level, from the learning level. But it takes a lot out of the gut. They didn't really change *that* much because I would continually tell them that you've got to have common sense with the book sense you have. A book was only written by a man, so you just learned what he wrote. You've got to build from your own abilities of thinking.

See, I instilled within my children that you to go school, and that's important because you're going to have to be able to deal with the other elements of life. But I don't want nobody coming back here and thinking he's better than I am. Education or money doesn't make you no better than me. I've got news for you. I've got love, and I'm a millionaire in some sense, because I'm able to do what you can't do. It doesn't take money to do some things. I've been able to prove my point because God was able to implement it through me. It may take money to rent a house, or an office, or buy clothes. But sure to God it doesn't make you any higher than the next person.

Poor people are just beginning to get into that mainstream of life. We've been denied of that so long. You had a few black people voting, a few poor whites. They were denied too, like we were, in voting rights. And nobody ever listened to them. You lived in a community you saw deteriorating, just vanishing away, and the politician came out here and he'd say all this stuff and then he's gone. We don't get nothing and nobody listens. The older generation especially feels that way, because they never were able to participate. So finally they did believe it's not going to help any whether I vote or not.

But you see, education's out here with people, seeing what each other's doing. It has to be brought out of the classroom at some point. We need a couple of hours to know how to read and write, we need some hours to know how to progress, but when are we going to ever come out to let the child find out what life really is?

We've got to do something. We're beginning to get where children are killing their parents. Parents are afraid of children now, and that's a wicked stage. Children are stealing from their parents, if they get on drugs or something. I feel sorry for parents that have this kind of pressure put on them. I don't think we're doing enough to bring the family together.

Then some kids were born with a silver spoon in their mouth just because their parents were rich and they don't have any idea what their parents sacrificed for them. I think Hank Aaron's* got a good pattern. He says, "Just because I got, don't let me give these children everything they ask for." And those are brought up like common ordinary children. And he's just a common ordinary man. I've never seen him act but like himself.

I pray to God that He will guide my children. I'm willing to sacrifice for them, but I need Him to guide them through life. You can keep on straight street or you can detour. I'd like them to walk the straight way of life. They're grown now, and they have a right to make a choice of what they want to be in life. When you get to taking care of yourself, supporting yourself, keeping your own self in shelter, I have no more jurisdiction over them. Now I can't give them anything except advice. I can't demand anything. But most of all, dear God, I want my children to respect You. Other than that, we have to wait and see how things are going to work out.

I think things are a little better for black people. We're going to keep suffering to have our justice one day, but I believe it's coming. I may not even be here, but it's going to get better. We'll never be what we used to be as a race. We can't live in this world together without recognizing one another, so things have to change.

My biggest hope is, dear God, can't we live here together as one people? You know, God teaches you how to find yourself. Once you find Him, you're going to find yourself, because He's going to help you. And you have to first learn of yourself be-

---

* Henry L. Aaron, baseball "superstar" with the Atlanta Braves; superseded Babe Ruth's lifetime record of home runs in 1974.

fore you learn of anyone else. You don't have to love that person, but you learn of that person's being, you feel him, and you respect him. We first have got to respect life, and we don't respect it now. That's where we failed. We've been disrespecting God's constitution of laws for centuries: "Thou shall love thy neighbor as you love yourself." We just can't continue to disrespect that.

A lot of people just don't know how to cope with life. And life is so beautiful, so sweet, so understandable. But we don't have time. I doubt if we'll make it to 2000. It's bad to say it, but I think we'd do good if we get to 1990. I don't know how we're going to come through all this because it's not getting better, it's getting worse. You can't trust people. Everybody's going his separate way. Don't have time, don't have time. But do you take the time out to think about your fellow man as much as we should?

● POSTSCRIPT

Dorothy Bolden's life continues at a frantic pace. She covers so much territory at such a fast clip—from her office, to community meetings, to conferences in Washington and elsewhere, and back home again—that it is no easy feat to track her down. Despite bouts of exhaustion and occasional physical problems, she maintains her pace.

National Domestic Workers, Inc., has managed to stay alive financially and continues to provide a voice for domestic workers, serving as a buffer between them and their employers and helping employers and employees to find each other. The organization is currently grappling with a rising demand from employers for the women to "live in," while most domestic workers want to be able to live with their own families. Given the current degree of job scarcity, Dorothy has been counseling women on both the benefits and the disadvantages of "working as a live-in maid."

Over the past year, National Domestic Workers, Inc., developed a counseling and placement program with a small grant from the CETA (Comprehensive Employment Training Act) program. But it has not yet been successful in obtaining a federal government grant to develop the kind of training program that Dorothy feels is so vital—one which would "really draw on these women's skills and place them in some useful jobs." Since Washington has not responded, the plan is now to approach the Atlanta city government and private foundations.

National Domestic Workers, Inc., sponsored a conference this year which had a significant outcome. (As Dorothy put it, "We've got no money so you got to put your efforts somewhere.") The conference was called around the implementation of Title 20 of the Social Security Act. This new law gives states more jurisdiction and flexibility in planning federally subsidized social service programs—particularly for families on welfare and for the aged, the blind and the disabled. It also encourages citizen participation in the planning process.

The conference was attended by women concerned with schools, housing, prisons, day care, senior citizens' programs and other community needs. They decided they needed an ongoing forum that reflected their concerns. The result was the establishment of a new organization, Common Cause for Justice for Low Income Women. The group now meets every other Saturday and has about thirty active members. In addition to domestic workers, some members are office workers, and a few are professionals.

"We're talking about what can be done to benefit *all* low-income women," Dorothy said. "We want to get women to participate in programs and to make the decisions about the programs and the things that affect their own lives. We want community involvement and we need a community base." One current issue drawing a lot of attention is the possibility of a rise in the bus fare in Atlanta—now at fifteen cents—which would create a special hardship for these women.

Dorothy continues to serve on the board of directors of the Legal Aid Society, a local radio station and community organizations in Vine City—where she sometimes carries her five-month-old (and third) grandchild to meetings. In addition, she helped establish a second new organization this year, the Black Women's Caucus.

The year also brought her another new honor. She was appointed to a three-year term on the Governor's Commission on the Status of Women. "We're just laying the foundation there," she said. "First we have to get it structured right, in cooperation with everybody. In time I'll have my chance to talk about the needs of the maids."

Betty Gagne at home in Chicago's Southwest Side.

Betty Gagne on a visit to the immunization program established by the Southwest YWCA's health committee.

Betty Gagne

IOWA'S FARMLANDS TO WASHINGTON, D.C.

I was born in Emmetsburg, Iowa, in 1923. It's a real small farming town, about three thousand or so, in northwest Iowa way up near the Minnesota border. My father's parents were landowners and he was raised on a farm there. Both my parents were born in this country of immigrant Irish parents. My mother lived in Chicago and grew up right southwest of here. Her father was a planning engineer for the Belt Line Railroad that laid the plans in the Clearing industrial district just west of here.

My father met my mother through my mother's brother. He and my father were in the Navy together. Then they went back to Iowa to live when they got married. There was a big Irish settlement there. Actually, the town was about half Scandinavian and half Irish. There were two large Catholic churches and a smattering of small Protestant congregations.

My mother had thirteen children—nine girls and four boys— and I was the second oldest. So I learned how to take care of kids at an early age, but I got out of it a lot too. My older sister was very sharp, but physically kind of slow-moving. I was the one that sneaked out the window when I was supposed to be doing things and she'd plug away! But I always maintained that I got my work done. It was just that I didn't want to stay and finish hers for her.

My father taught school for a while, but that was back in the days when I don't know how much education he really had. Maybe six weeks of normal school training or something. Then he worked for the Postal Service for forty-three years. It was a real small kind of setup. I remember him being in the finance area, selling bonds and postal savings and things. Then

· he worked the whole gamut of inside jobs—weighing parcel post, taking turns at the different windows.

Both my parents are religious. My mother has always been one to change and she's changed a lot over the years, but she still has some little stumbling blocks. Two of her grandsons were there one Friday morning and when they couldn't decide what they wanted for breakfast, she got busy reading and they ended up fixing bacon themselves. This was before we were exonerated from the Friday abstinence, and that really upset her. I mean she just beat her breast over that.

The Irish and the Scandinavians in our town mixed well, except when it was time to go to church. Aside from that, there were never any real strong lines drawn. We really had a hard time, though, with one of my brothers when we were growing up because he just thought anybody that wasn't Catholic was no good. We didn't like that. My parents, above all, didn't like it and they always tried to impress this on us. In fact, everybody that was any kind of minority in the town was their friend. I can remember when we were kids they sent home a family history sheet at the beginning of the school year. Every time they asked us what nationality we were, my mother was insulted and she would say, "Write 'American.'"

I think St. Patrick's Day was the greatest thing that happened all year in our town. Everybody celebrated, Irish or not. They just joined in. It was always a school holiday and a lot of businesses were closed. It seems to me it was kind of carnival time and it went on and on all day. They had kind of Irish talent shows, as I remember. In the evening there would be a dance, and the kids would just be dying to sneak in.

One of the nicest things about growing up there was you knew everyone and you knew what niche they fit into. My parents knew everyone, and I mean really knew them. It was almost like a family relationship, the concern that people showed for each other. You might see that in the city sometimes, like on a certain block in a neighborhood, but you don't see it in the same degree.

During the years when we were growing up, people just didn't get around. My dad had some first cousins that lived out in a farming area near our town, but we didn't have a car for a good many years. Even public transportation was practically nil then. We'd have an occasional visit from Grandpa or Grandma when they'd ride up in a panel truck with the mailman. Most of my aunts and uncles were farmers and they would occasionally come and spend a Sunday with their families, but it was like seventy-five or eighty miles. And that was a long way in some of those little cars.

As we grew up, people became a little more mobile and I think the kids in our part of the country probably were driving cars at a much earlier age than they were, say, in the city. We had kind of an advantage that way. The kids from the farm always had cars and we went to dances and ball games and the like. So after we got older, we had a lot of opportunities to get back and forth, simply because the geographic layout of the community was such that people had to have their own transportation.

When I was growing up I could probably see a lot that I thought my parents could have done differently, but basically I admired them and I enjoyed them. I remember that in spite of the fact that my mother had a large family to take care of, she did find time for other things. And I really reveled in that.

She belonged to one group called the Fortnightly Club—"the girls"! They did things like read books and review them and discuss current topics. And I think through the Fortnightly Club she probably got enlisted in the kinds of things we do through church groups. I remember going on the first Mothers March for Polio that Roosevelt sponsored and that sort of thing.

My mother was a Republican until Roosevelt came along and she turned Democrat. Then after him I think she went back to the Republican Party. This was a terribly interesting aspect of our lives because our mother was working for the Republican Party much of the time and my dad was a dyed-in-the-wool Democrat. They were very individual and, still, there was such unity there that it was admirable.

My mother was a very strong person. I never thought of her as that until I got to know her when I was an adult. In fact, I think that was part of my really getting to know my father, too, when I came to realize how tender he really was and how he tried to hide it. He was the disciplinarian, you know, but then he was always very affectionate. He'd read the paper with two babies in his lap. Somebody had to take care of the discipline and it just wasn't Mother's suit at all.

I remember when the Depression came. We didn't have penny candy like all the other kids had, and I think it was a kind of a discipline with my parents. Everybody was poorer than we were then. We felt like the richest kids in town, and still I know we didn't flaunt it. We just had such a sense of well-being and I think it was probably because our parents gave us a good understanding of the difficulties that other people were encountering and just made us feel very secure at that time.

Money was always a problem though. I think my mother worried herself sick most of her life. We always had plenty of food, and it was never a problem in the sense that we were ever looking for help. But it was always a serious consideration. We saved and we managed to get around it in other ways, like clothing. We wore a lot of second-hand clothing. I think most kids did in those times, more than they do anymore.

My dad had an acreage on the edge of town, a plot of land where he had a barn and he had some registered cows that he had invested in. He and a farmer friend who had a bull used to breed them and we were real interested in this. My dad would hire a truck to take the cows out to the farm at the right time.

Then, of course, we always had milk and we always made our own butter. And there were a lot of responsibilities, especially for the boys, that they wouldn't have in a city home. When we were kids, it was the boys who cleaned the barn and they fed the cows and milked them and that kind of thing. The girls had their household chores and we didn't envy the boys their work at all.

One thing that always stands out in my memory from childhood is one time when my mother was home in bed with the seventh of us. She gave birth to a number of the children at home, with the help of practical nurses, they called them, but they were nothing but midwives, really. I think it was a matter of her being there to manage the household.

Anyhow, I was down the street at a neighbor's and I stepped out on their back porch and saw the roof of our house on fire. And it was a big house, two stories with an attic. I saw those flames whipping away at the roof of the house and that was really traumatic. I don't even remember how I got home. I don't know whether I passed out or whether I just drew a blank. But we all suffered, I'm sure, some little scars from that. I remember going to sleep at night and smelling the charred wood for a while after that.

Our school was really archaic. It was run by the Sisters of Charity, BVM. We had fun, but they were strict, terribly strict as a matter of fact. But we were awfully close to some of the nuns because we lived right across from the school grounds. It was a big block of property with the school, the church, the rectory, the convent. They had a football field and tennis courts too. The nuns used to visit my mother a lot so I really didn't grow up with any terrible fear of them. I think probably in those days I got along with them on their own grounds, and then later on I learned that they were human beings. As kids you just have a notion about them, like they weren't real, you know?

All thirteen of us went to that school. Of course, then it wasn't the hassle that it is now. I remember at one point—I was working at the time—my parents lost the home we were living in and they moved into the other parish. Since that parish didn't have their own high school, they paid something like five dollars a year for the kids in our family to go to the Catholic high school back in the other parish. That was the extent of the cost, except that we did actively get out and work in fund raisers to help pay for our school. But there was no per capita tax hanging over our head the way there is now. It costs us $250 for our two little girls in grammar school. And last year our Tom finished at St. Lawrence High School and his tuition was $530. It didn't even cost that much for our parents to send their kids to college.

There was a great interest in college there. A lot of people would be surprised to realize how many farm boys went to the State Agricultural School in Iowa in order to be good farm managers. But it didn't necessarily follow that they all went back to the soil. Some of our farm boys went on to other things. There were and there are a lot of well-educated people in the community.

I think people who could afford to, people who could see their way to it at all, sent their kids to college. And I don't think there was a great difference made between whether they were girls or boys. There was a smattering of girls who stayed on in town, but there was nothing much really for them to do at that time, except be waitresses and dime store clerks, grocery clerks. On the whole, I think they came from some of the poorer families.

My dad had wanted me to go to college. Oh, he just pushed so hard for it. My older sister had already gone into nursing and I was the second. But I finished high school before I was eighteen and I immediately got a job in a lawyer's office. It happened to be open to me and I wanted a job. I liked it but it was only for a few months. I was replacing a woman who left to have a baby, so when she came back I was going to be without a job. But then the lawyer was on the board of directors at the bank and he got me a job there. So I was very fortunate in that respect. I really never went around begging for a job.

I didn't like that job at the bank, though. It was posting and teller work and secretarial work, just everything, and I found it very wearing. I stayed there for about two years and I guess by then my dad had given up on me going to college, but he didn't want me to stay in a small town. His idea was that there just weren't the kind of opportunities there that he would like to see us have. And my mother worked just as hard as he did at encouraging us to move out.

Aside from myself and one sister, all the kids had some kind of further training after high school. And we all did leave, though some of them went back for a time. One of my sisters worked for the county there after college. Then one sister married a young lawyer from near our home town, just by coincidence, and another married a lawyer from Des Moines, where they eventually settled.

I remember my father asking me one time if it ever bothered me that I hadn't had any college work, and I said, "No." He said, "You know all your brothers and sisters have"—all the ones who were old enough at that time. So he asked me was I sure about that, and I said, "Well, they're my brothers and sisters, and we've always communicated well, and I never saw any real difference in that way."

My oldest brother, Jack, was the one that my dad really had a hard time getting rid of. He went into the service and came back and went to a junior college and worked in a meat market. He never did get a degree, but he ended up working as a sales manager for the Armour Packing Company and then for a meat company back in Iowa. My brother Bill is in the home offices of Mutual of Omaha. He's worked for them all through college, but he's very disillusioned with big business. I wouldn't be surprised any day to hear that he had bought a small farm out in Colorado or somewhere and taken his family out there. My brother Rog is a doctor, a urologist out in Rapid City, South Dakota. And my youngest brother is working for his doctorate and does counseling at the University of Nebraska. Four of my sisters are nurses.

Anyhow, I was working in the bank and my father wasn't satisfied with that. Part of his assignment with the Post Office was that he was an examiner for the Civil Service Commission for a few towns in the area. He finally convinced me to take the exam and he got one of the other fellows to examine me, but I didn't fare too well. I was extremely nervous. But he still wanted me to get out. He'd always say, "There are so many attractive jobs available."

So I went to the FBI in Des Moines and applied and told them I wanted to go to Denver. The first thing I knew I was in Washington, D.C., classifying fingerprints. I was about twenty then, and that was a terrible, boring job. And there was virtually no advancement. So later, through people I had gotten to know, I got a job with the War Labor Board in the personnel department, and that was much more satisfying to me.

I'd gather information for personnel journals—backgrounds on people, what their advancement had been within the Civil Service structure. That was my first job there. Then I went on to a job supervising and editing all their field journals, the ones put out by people who worked in the regional offices all over the country. I had done some writing for a regional newspaper in Iowa during high school, but that was just a penny ante thing. I enjoyed it and I always liked to see my stuff in print. I think that was most of the gratification connected with it. That's what my dad wanted me to do. He thought I really wanted to get into writing. But I don't think I ever wanted to very badly.

CHICAGO'S SOUTHWEST SIDE—
BEFORE AND AFTER THE CIVIL RIGHTS MARCHES

I met my husband just a few weeks after I was in Washington. He was stationed there in the Navy and he was going out with a friend of mine. We were married about a year later. I was in Washington two years altogether, and I worked right up until we left. Bernard was going overseas and I was pregnant, and I didn't want to be there alone when the baby came, so I went and stayed with his parents in Philadelphia for about a year until he was discharged. The baby was a few months old before he saw her.

When Bernard came back, he finished up school in Philadelphia. He's an embalmer and you have to have about a year of technical training after two years of college. Then we went up to Maine to live. He had family in Maine and his parents had never really put down roots in Philly. They were there supposedly only temporarily and they always said they'd go back to Maine. Both of his folks are French-Canadian and they had always been with family until they went to Philadelphia. They never really felt at home there.

We were only in Maine for about a year and then Bernard was called back in the service during the Korean war. Since he was in the embalming field and had background in biology, he was put in the hospital corps and he was in a reserve unit that was the first one to be called back after it was discharged. When he was called, I was in Iowa visiting with my folks and we had two children then. So he came out to Iowa and got me and we went back to Maine. We were still living in an apartment but we had bought a piece of property and we were planning to build. But then we decided to sell it because we didn't know whether we'd ever really put down roots there or not.

So I stayed in Maine and sold the property and shipped our belongings out to Iowa and I got a little apartment there until he got out of the service. Then he came out here and got work and we lived in Gary, Indiana, for a while and then we bought this house here in Chicago. That's getting rid of a lot of years in a hurry, but that's how it happened! Seven kids, and it'll be thirty years we're married next month.

Bernard works for a funeral home that's about five minutes away from here. It's walking distance so he comes home to lunch, except when he's working five to midnight, of course, like now. That's kind of a regular thing if you work for a big outfit in this business. They're a very busy firm. There are three regular embalmers, and they have to always have one on duty. I think he got interested in this field as a kid through an old bachelor that was in that business in his neighborhood in Philadelphia. Bernard liked him and he used to hang around his place a lot.

I can't imagine myself having stayed on working the way I did for very long. Having a family was what I really wanted to do. I have one sister who was married ten years before she had her first child, and I think it was extremely difficult for her. She did personnel work and she was very interested in her work, but I always felt terribly sorry for her. Emotionally she wasn't as well adjusted as any of us during those years, and I figure it was because she didn't have a family.

Since we've been married, I guess we've always been involved in the community in some way. When we came to Gary my husband was a scout leader so I inquired about the women's groups but . . . well, I wasn't much with the women's groups. I've never liked church women's groups either. The sunshine letters, that's my favorite. I heard it called that one time and I think that epitomizes it. You know, where they send letters or cards to people in the hospital, and they tell how many sunshine letters they wrote.

But after we moved to Chicago we did get into a couples group with the church that was part of the Christian Family Movement. It was really an action group. It was small and very interesting because of the people who were involved. It was a kind of a leadership-formation type thing. On the inside, we organized some things to do with our own liturgy. And on the outside we did things like a study on racism in the neighborhood.

The Christian Family Movement was a federated organization. We did things like we had interparish meetings with a group from a black parish just east of us. We had a lot of exchange that way. The actions we took were nothing earth-shaking, you know. We didn't go out thinking we were going to solve any of the major social problems. They were more or less helpful and enriching for ourselves and kind of moved us along in the direction things were going at that time in this community. It was really just a little bit ahead of the things that we were approaching.

At that time they were kicking around open housing in the state legislature and a lot of people were afraid. We had a fairly young priest that we became very close to and I remember his telling us that people in this neighborhood shouldn't be worried. They should go out and work for open housing. People just figured that their neighborhood was going to be taken over if there was open housing, but he said, "No, no. The blacks aren't going to stop here. If the right is established for them to move where they want, they're going to move all over the place and the class that belongs in this neighborhood will be here." I thought he was terribly right myself, but there weren't very many other people who did.

He also talked about a neighborhood organization, and it was many of the people who were involved in the CFM at that time who were instrumental in getting the first organizations in the community here, like the Council of Lawn Neighbors, a very local group. The CLN became part of the Southwest Community Congress, a kind of umbrella group. The whole group has been active and they've taken a role in many other movements that were important. Over the years I've been on committees for both, although I don't claim to be part of the group that spearheaded it all.

Well as I said, the CFM helped prepare us a little for the changes, but what happened here during the Martin Luther King march was horrible. I was ashamed and I was scared. The inhuman way that people behaved was unbelievable. And then of course, it was right here in our back yard. It was all described as Cicero and Gage Park, but they were marching right down here on Sixty-third Street and in the park, Marquette Park.

We couldn't allow our kids to go out and some of the kids in the neighborhood were saying terrible things and there were people who were panicking and telling stories that weren't true, you know, like "They're right here on our doorstep, they're ready to turn our corner," and this kind of thing. We had to try to fight the psychological aspects of it and at the same time be very careful for our own security and the security of the kids. And it was really hard to tell our kids why they shouldn't be down there and at the same time keep them from realizing how upsetting it was to us. I'm sure there were people they knew that were down there, throwing rocks and things. We didn't know who they were, but there had to be some they knew. It was just a terribly difficult time.

I remember I got on the phone and called this one black woman I knew and found out her husband was in the march and I tried to kind of explain to her some of the reactions. See, I was sympathetic, to an extent, with some of the people who were so frightened that they would go out and do those things. People who had lived here all their lives and put everything they owned or earned into their homes. It was understandable that they were a little insecure. But at the same time I didn't feel it warranted that kind of action, you know? They just felt that an army was marching in and taking over the neighborhood, that was all. They wouldn't accept the fact that it was a demonstration in the true sense of the word. It was a war to them and they had to defend themselves.

Well, I think there were probably repercussions of that march for three or four weeks. Then, in addition to that, we had the added enhancement of having the American Nazi Party demonstrating and taking over the parks, attempting to get permits to have meetings in the parks and using the marches as leverage because *they* were allowed. And of course, they were doing nothing but rabble-rousing and attracting a bunch of young people that really didn't understand.

The awful thing about it was, there were elements in the neighborhood who were supporting it. They had an office not far from here and they're still going now. The thing that was really upsetting to me was that the people who followed them from the neighborhood seemed to be mainly people from Europe who had had hard times, and they seemed to think somehow that this group was going to be their salvation. They really seemed to admire this white Nazi party that was forming. It was really sad when you talked to them.

Apparently the anti-Communism was what caught them, that was one of their big things. But isn't that always the top rung? The people didn't seem to see anything else. But then they were fighting the blacks and the Jews too. I know this one woman who kept going on and on about it. I think she thought my boys were a bunch of renegades because they weren't over there throwing rocks. It was really rough around this neighborhood for a while.

I remember when Marty, who's twenty-one now, was over at St. Rita in his freshman year and this priest who's now in the City Council was teaching there then. He's the one who advocated drawing a line down the middle of Ashland Avenue at one point—white on one side and black on the other. Marty was just starting high school and he came home one day so upset and said to me, "Why do people hate each other?" And he just sat down and started to cry. Apparently this priest's views had gotten so much play in the newspapers that the black kids had started to come over to the bus stop right in front of school and hassle the white boys there. There were things like that going on all the time.

After the marches, a lot of people threatened to leave, but then things kind of settled down very gradually. There are still no black families right here, except one that's lived in an alley house for I guess a generation. But generally I think that the people in this immediate area are much less frightened about it all. I don't know what to attribute it to, but I know it's got to be a fact.

I used to have a neighbor across the street who was in a wheelchair with arthritis for quite a number of years. She's been dead now for several years, but I was talking to her one evening and she said, "I was sitting here on the porch and one of the neighbors came along and said, 'Helen, we've got blacks moving in over in the next block.'" And Helen said, "I just couldn't believe it." And I looked at her and said, "Why?" So she said, "Because a couple of years ago they would have come and told me that there was a race riot on the next block, before anybody would tell me that somebody had moved in over there."

And of course, it was one of those things where people jumped the gun. They had black movers over there. What happened was, the woman who had bought the house had moved from a neighborhood that had gone entirely black, and she had rented a truck and some black neighbors of hers moved her things for her. So there was no black family involved at all. But still, that was the first impression and before they killed them they went around and talked about it.

I think the changes that have taken place here are changes that people didn't really expect. There are Arabs and Mexican families moving in, and all they had ever thought about was keeping the blacks out. Some people who live a few blocks from here had a white family living next door to them for years that were nothing but trouble and dirt and what have you, and all of a sudden they sold to a Mexican family. We've known these people for years and I just couldn't see them tolerating a thing like that. But they stood still and watched to see what was happening. Well, the house was completely done over, a good deal of money put into it and they're just so pleased about it all.

This community has always been really mixed. Lithuanian, Polish, Irish, oh everything. And I remember this one priest we used to have would say to us, "Have you forgotten the days when Marshall Field's would advertise, 'No Irish Need Apply'?" That was very real to him, because he was raised in the city here and that was what it was like when he was young. It's amazing how things have changed in that respect.

We had a lady come out to the Southwest YWCA last week, a wealthy white woman, to talk with us about fund raising. And she told us right out that because we were described as white ethnic, she said, "My kind of people wouldn't touch you," you know. She was very, very honest with us. What she meant was, we're the sinners, we're the racists. And that stamp is on all of us now.

I don't know how convincing I am at telling people that I'm not a racist. I really don't, because I'm not sure that my experience speaks too well. I just haven't had enough of it. I think that's the inadequacy I feel. But with some of the other people here, I don't really think it's that they have an axe to grind with the blacks. I think it's that they've had difficult times themselves financially and that they felt threatened by some of the things that have happened in this neighborhood. We all did. That was the only time, during those marches, that I ever felt insecure in the neighborhood.

It's about a fifteen-minute walk to where I work now, and as close to me as that I hear people saying things some days that I'm glad I don't have to listen to all the time. Comments about movements, you know, the line shifting, that kind of thing. Maybe they're right on the edge or in an area that has begun to change. It's been described to me as a cancerous movement and I think that describes it very well. It seems that it's done in one-mile areas, more or less, from east to west. Like right near us, the eastern edge is becoming all black and the western edge of the area is mixed. Then, when that mile becomes all black, it jumps across the main artery and it starts to become spotted on the eastern edge of the next one-mile area.

It doesn't worry me a lot, but it's true that the value of real estate has declined terribly. We're having our problems right here because insurance companies and savings and loans and all these people kind of look on us as suspect. I think they've begun redlining here. I know a fellow that works with my husband just sold his home. I think he got $27,000 for it and it was a really nice home. I guess blockbusting is a lot of it too.

Catholic Charities has started organizing people on the parish level now, along the same lines as some of the things that the Southwest Community Congress was trying to do. The Catholic Charities thing is known as the Federation, and they're doing what they call greenlining—trying to pressure the local banks and savings and loans to reinvest the people's money in their neighborhoods, threatening to take their money out and put it elsewhere if they don't. It's really a tactic for getting them to stop redlining.

I think what worries people most around here now is the economy. There are an awful lot of people who are in real bad trouble already, particularly in the building trades. The lack of work has been really noticeable this summer, during their peak season. But even people who are working and families where there are two people working are having difficulties.

I sense it in groups when you hear them talking about . . . well, not just meat and potatoes, because those things we're all sensitive to. I think everybody just hates having to pay too much for groceries and I don't care what their income is. But I see it like in our health committee at the Y. People need to be reimbursed for things like local telephone calls, so they must be really feeling the pinch.

You look up and down the street here, and there are police-men, city workers, factory workers. There's a really strong con-centration of city workers in this area. I guess a lot of the people make somewhere between $14,000 and $17,000 a year. And I'd say that the majority of wives on the block work too, although it's probably a small majority.

I see in organizations where I'm active that there's a large majority of women who work. I don't know why that is. It seems that the people who are home would be the ones that would be carrying the organizations. I remember the last year before I went to work it was so hard to get volunteer help for anything, and I used to say, "Gee, everybody's working." I had the notion that people felt that the ones who were working had a good excuse to do nothing else. And I found out that they really did have a good excuse! But it seems like it's often the ones who work that are also the most involved in other things.

BACK TO WORK, SEVEN CHILDREN
AND TWENTY-EIGHT YEARS LATER

Bernard is a real putterer. He's great with machines and gadgets. He fixes all kinds of things. And if he walks through the basement and there's a load of clothes to be dried, he does it. Or he'll pick up in the kitchen and start the dishwasher. He takes a lot of initiative around the house. I don't ever have to ask him to do anything, really.

If I'm working during the day, he'll take the kids out for a hamburger sometimes, just for a treat. Our kids boycotted Mc-Donald's during the last election, because they made that big contribution to Nixon. And it was funny, because they used to be slaves to McDonald's. But you know how it is. You always eat crow.

Bernard just does things like that. My boys are real good too. But I think my big problem as far as that's concerned is that my husband will do what needs to be done and the kids very often don't get their feet wet. Maybe just by the fact that they have the example of cooperation, that'll go a long way.

Our oldest child, Pat, is going to be twenty-nine and she has three children. She lives in an integrated area in the city, a beautiful area not far from the suburbs. She's a registered nurse and she has worked, on and off. She worked in a hospital at one time, she's worked in drug rehabilitation programs out in one of the suburbs, and she talks now about maybe going into the school system.

It's interesting about our kids and drugs. Marty, the third oldest, at one time had a little brush with a group when drugs were really big here in the neighborhood. Pat was working actively to help people who were having that kind of problems, and Mike worked with a group on the North Side as a volunteer. Marty has never been associated directly with any drug program, but I think he's probably done as much good as any of them. He'd just talk and talk and talk with some of his friends.

The second oldest is Mike. He's the joy of my life, but he wants somebody to fight with him all the time. I never argue with him, I just listen to him a lot, and he always keeps looking at me to see if he can read my reactions because I always just say, "Uh huh." He doesn't get the kind of rise out of me he expects sometimes. I guess I think some of his philosophy is kind of tongue in cheek and some of it'll change.

For a long time, Mike was really too serious about school and about work. He was never without a job from the time he was a sophomore in high school. Then he was in accounting in college, and I think he could have made a better selection of the kind of work to get into. He's very artistic and very creative, and accounting is pretty much of an exact science for a guy like him. But I feel that one of these days he'll decide where he's going. He has lots on the ball and he was a really good student. He dropped out with one semester left before he had his degree, so I guess maybe he's proving a point.

I always told him if he was going to be a carpenter to be a good one. The funny thing is, that's what he wants to do now. He's been redoing an apartment now and he's just so involved in it. He put skylights and this rough paneling in the bedrooms so that it looks like a treehouse. He's always talked about doing things like that. He had a little tiny bedroom upstairs here and he used to tell me about these effects he wanted to get.

Marty is twenty-one and he's a pastry chef. He started cooking before he was out of high school at greasy spoons and the like in the neighborhood. He was a hotheaded little kid and he always told us that when he was eighteen he'd split. So when he was eighteen, we celebrated his birthday and we kind of laughed about it, but the next week he went and moved out.

Then he was cooking in a place up north, but he had terribly little respect for the job he had at that time. He was there for three or four months and he called me one day and he was crying. Oh, we used to worry so much about him because he was so young. I'd ask Mike to go look him up, even though he was living with some other kids. I just felt like he was a little boy and I felt as if the ones that need you most are the ones that are slowest to admit it, you know?

Well, then he went to work at the Bakery for a year. It's a gourmet restaurant, one of the few in Chicago. Then he began to specialize in pastry and he went to the Drake Hotel, and now he's at a men's club downtown. He's been there for about a year and a half now, but he always makes me feel as if tomorrow is the day he quits. He says things to me like, "You know, I'm sick and tired of being a productive human being."

I think Marty finds a real outlet in pastry because, again, it's very creative. He made his sister Pam's wedding cake and it was really something, the way he went about that. For two weeks he worked at marzipan roses. He must have made four or five dozen of them and then he made lovebirds and the whole thing. It was beautiful. Our kids just have the attitude that anything we can do for ourselves is better than anything we have to have done.

Pam is twenty and she got married this June. Her husband is a community organizer on the North Side. When she was in high school, she began working in a day care center with retarded children. She did a lot of decorating and cartooning kinds of things with the kids and realized that they responded well to color and design and that sort of thing. Then she got to the point where she didn't know whether she wanted some education courses with the idea of working with retarded youngsters, or whether she wanted to go into cartooning. But she may be doing something ten years from now that is terribly new and different.

Now she's working at Kroch's and Brentano's in their party goods section. She sets up the department and she's gotten a couple of awards for doing windows and that kind of thing.

Our kids really are creative. Maybe it's because they've been encouraged to try things. I think too many kids are stifled in efforts like that.

Tom is number five. You wouldn't believe Tom. He was eighteen in May. He's working in a factory on the four-to-midnight shift now. He wants to go to the Goodman Theatre School. One stumbling block is that they're not allowed to work and go to school at the same time and it's quite expensive.

Every year they do one major theater production at the high school he went to. In his sophomore year he was in *Jesus Christ Superstar*. Last year they did *Fiddler on the Roof*, and this year they did *Enter Laughing*. It's a comedy and he played the lead and everybody was telling us how funny he was and what a kick they got out of it. My reaction to it and my husband's too was, "That's our Tom." He was just up there on stage, that was the only difference.

Well then, Therese is going to be thirteen and Mary is nine, and that's all seven. They're both in parochial school now. Mary is really something. For Pam's wedding, it was funny. Everybody was saying, "What's Mary going to wear?" So I said, "Well, I haven't been able to pin her down on that yet." And she looks for Pam's approval for everything she does, so Pam said to her, "You know, Mare, you're not going to be able to wear jeans to the wedding." Then Mary wanted to be part of the wedding party and I said to one of my friends, "Just watch, we'll have the first nine-year-old female ringbearer that anybody ever saw." And that's what we ended up with.

There were a number of hitches with things all the way through the wedding. It had rained all week so the yard was soggy. The flowers didn't arrive on time. Then the musicians didn't arrive on time, so they were forty-five minutes late getting started. One of my cousins told Mary he'd give her two bucks if she'd go down to the microphone and announce that the ceremony would proceed when the musicians arrived. So she went halfway down the aisle, then she turned around and looked at us and shouted something. My cousin just pointed and Mary went all the way down to the microphone and made the announcement. What a kid.

You know, for some reason or another, people have made remarks to me at various times about how our family is so beautifully spaced. And I know that they're insinuating that it was unnaturally so, but it wasn't. I didn't believe in birth control for myself. I don't condemn other people for using it, but it's just a matter of my own personal feelings.

I think my kids feel pretty much the same way I do. They are all anti-abortion, very much so. But as far as birth control is concerned, I don't think it would bother any of them. As a matter of fact, I know my Pat used the pill. She was advised to, because of medical problems. But then on the other hand, two or three years ago she told me, "You know Mom, I never want to get pregnant again, but if I should, I'll take my lumps." You know, abortion would never occur to her.

Even though I don't have any real problem with birth control, I'm really for freedom. I don't feel as if any group of people or any individual should be singled out and told, "Well, look, you have enough kids." And frankly I'm a little afraid of this because I think little by little people's rights—especially poor people—can be taken away from them. In fact they are being taken away from them with some of these sterilization programs and other things going on. Maybe those things happen to open our eyes and make us see that maybe we shouldn't let down in those areas at all.

But I can't really see abortion for any reason whatsoever. We had a group come to the board at the Y not too long ago about sponsoring a pregnancy-testing program and, despite how I feel personally, I went there with the idea in mind that we can't just fight this thing on that level, you know. We have to give it a hearing and see what things are favorable or not so favorable.

Well, it was very unprofessional. I had no idea of the makeup of the group until I went there. What really shocked me was there were two girls who were under eighteen, then there was one who was probably twenty, and then there was a young married woman with a child. The thing that occurred to me was that the three younger ones must have felt like they were doing some kind of a big adult thing, claiming this kind of freedom for themselves. I thought it was pretty sad to think they felt themselves capable of rendering that type of service.

We have some very young people on our board. Out of twelve board members, we have about four girls who are college students, on the lower end of the college level. So we have a really wide age mixture and varied opinions on things and I went in there thinking this is the time I might really have to fight. But when I got there, they had been questioning them for some time and I was amazed at the fact that the younger people were really very negative about it. I sat there and listened and I realized that a lot of people were thinking the same thing I was. They were asking for information and records that the group couldn't produce.

They touted the fact that they had a working alliance with a local mental health center and so forth, so I said to them, "If my twelve-year-old daughter were to come to you and you tested her and found that she in fact was pregnant and she hit the panic button, what would you do?" And you know they looked at me as if, well, what do you think we'd do? Then one of them said, "Somebody always has a car." Like that was going to save my twelve-year-old. They didn't give any indication of what they would do with her, except that somebody always has a car.

The board voted something like ten to two against the sponsoring and I was really proud of that group that night. More than half the board is Catholic, but the national board of the Y is pro-abortion. So as I said, I wasn't too sure when I went in. But I think that sort of makes obvious the kind of thinking that's going on among some groups of young people these days.

I think if one of my own kids got pregnant it wouldn't be terribly important what I felt, if I could see that they had thought it out seriously. I do think that there are alternatives. The old-fashioned way is make them get married, and I don't believe in that. If she decided she wanted to give up the baby, I think I'd have to help her through that. On the other hand, I don't think you can take a mother's baby away from her unless there is an awfully good reason to think that she has no right to it. All ways, it's difficult.

In some ways, I think my daughters' lives will be different from mine. I see them, for instance, continuing their education after marriage, which I didn't do. There was a time when I no longer had to be at home taking care of little ones anymore and I thought seriously about it, but then I thought maybe there were more important things for me to do, especially in the community. But I see taking courses and going on with their education as a healthy thing. I think it's good for the marriage and I think it's good for the community and anybody else that's lucky enough to get a corner on it.

In this day and age I don't feel that people are necessarily mature at twenty-five years old. I don't see any of my kids as being through exploring life or exploring their own talents. And I've never really pushed them. Maybe some of them would have gained some—quote—honors if I had pushed them a little harder, but I don't know that it would be worth it. I just don't put too much stock in that sort of thing.

I'd just like to see them be productive and be happy with what they're doing. I'd like to see all of them have good marriages. And I'd like to see them be able to make themselves felt a little bit in anything for the betterment of people. I would enjoy something like that, and I've had little smidgeons of that sort of thing right along through them.

It's funny, but I got so busy in the community before I went to work that my husband was saying things like, "She's on the go so much, I told her that she'd better go to work so I know where to find her." I used to spend two days a week at school, our parish elementary school, St. Nick's, where I'm on the board too. And then the Y, and I was getting real busy with the health committee there, and just generally I was involved in so many things.

There were two programs at school I was involved in. One was the religious ed program for kids that are on released time from the public school. They'd come to our school and I taught the basics of their religion. For about five years I did that one day a week. And then we had a learning center which was kind of a new concept in primary education. We had audiovisual equipment and we worked with individual kids in math and reading. Then they started having the aides go into the classroom and work with a small group of children. I went into math on the sixth grade level and I just loved it.

I think it was like going back to work with me now. I enjoy it because I know I don't have to do it, you know? I can really relax and get the most out of it for myself, and I suppose by the same token I'm putting something better into it. But when I decided to go to work, I had to give up helping out at school and that really wrenched me. The rewards of working with kids are just the greatest thing in the world. There are six-foot-tall boys now who call me by name that I wouldn't know from Adam, and it just makes you feel so good all over.

Actually, I applied for the job as a lark. I was out of the job market for twenty-eight years. Then a couple of gals who worked in my program at school were working at Talman, the savings and loan, and they said, "Why don't you apply? They're always hiring." And so I did. And I filed the lousiest application you've ever seen in your life. It asked for previous work experience over the past twenty years and I wrote "none." And it asked, "Who do you know here?" and I named two people and I'm sure I knew fifty.

Well, a year later we got home from our vacation and there was a note over the phone to call a Mrs. Wright at Talman. So I called her and she said she'd like to interview me. She mentioned files and I thought, Oh no. I went there thinking that I wasn't going to like the job but that at least maybe an interview would be more favorable than the application was. Actually it wasn't filing. It was research and I really enjoyed it.

I think I had come to realize that basically this was something I'd be trying for myself. Whether or not I'd like it was another question, but I'd always been involved in doing things for other people. So when I was offered the opportunity, I thought it might be a good idea. I started to work about a year ago, and generally I work four days a week, nine to four.

First I was on a temporary project and then they put me into an area where we interview new accounts. You counsel people as to how to set up their accounts and the kind of certificates to get into, depending on their circumstances, and I just love it. When I'm sent down to the reserve room, where I work out of, all the girls talk about is recipes and new clothes and it drives me out of my mind.

My boss is the reserve boss and the girls in that room all have some training in a number of areas in the association, so they can be sent to fill in when they're needed. And then there are job orders that are sent down there to be done. When I go back upstairs I don't care how hard I work. Four periods a year I'm liable to work twelve hours, two days a week, but I love it. At dividend time, everybody has to take some extra load. I wouldn't say I'm not exhausted and wish I didn't have to go back in the morning, but I enjoy the work. And it's the kind of place where if you make a typographical error or some other mistake, well, that's what happens after ten hours. People are so understanding. And you find out so much about people.

Some of those women downstairs really have problems. They relate very well to one another and some of them are the ones I enjoy being with most, but then there's a group, you know, that just doesn't think about a lot of things. I've never liked gossip and I always tried hard to get along with people, and there are girls there who just find it extremely difficult to work for certain people. As I see it, it's our job to be adaptable to different situations there.

There's this one girl who has two young teen-agers. She's a beautiful girl and she has a lot of capability as far as the work goes, and I'm sure that she must get on beautifully with the customers. And still I have never sat down to lunch with her but what she was complaining about one boss or another and saying, "If I didn't have to be here I wouldn't." And I feel sorry for people like that.

Then you'd hear her being paged for outside calls two or three times a day. Well my Mary called me at work one day and said, "I don't want to go to dancing." I was sitting at my desk upstairs interviewing and I said, "Well I'm sorry, honey, I thought you were old enough to make that decision for yourself, and when you've made it, either go to dancing or put your shoes away and forget it." And I hung up.

That night I came home and everything was sweet as could be. So after a while I said, "Mary, what did you do about dancing?" And she said, "Well, I didn't go because I really had a headache and I'm awful sorry I called you and cried over the phone because you were working," and all this stuff. Well, I don't know how people can take it when they have to put up with that at work. I'd be torn to shreds. And then to have to say, "I *have* to be there," too, it's really sad.

You know in June, after Pam's wedding, it was really a letdown for a while. I had made my own dress and little Mary's and the bride's dress, and I had all the sewing done before I took my week off to get ready for the wedding, and it was just nothing but excitement and parties and everything.

Well, the Monday after, I went back to work and they stuck

me in the insurance department, bringing policies up to date, throwing out old ones, and transferring information and filing. Oh, I was just miserable. And there is this real great gal that was hired when I was and she's Jewish, and if I have a meeting of minds with anyone there, it's with Lena. She's different from the other people there. She thinks about other things than what's at work and what's at home.

So Lena was stuck down there with me and we were crying on each other's shoulders and the second day we were going home I said, "Lena, if I had been a very impulsive person I would have quit last night." And she said, "But you're not and you're still there and you'll be back on Thursday." And I said, "Yeah, I'll be back Thursday, but boy I'm feeling for the tones that we're going to be needed upstairs."

I said, "I just ache and I sit there and I've gone through fifteen letters of the alphabet and all of a sudden I think, what have I been doing for the last hour and a half? My mind is miles away from the place." I said, "I can't stand it." So she said, "Well, it's not just the work, you know that, don't you?" And I said, "Yeah, Lena, I know its psychological and I'm trying to wind down and it's a little bit of loneliness and it's this and it's that," but I said, "It's still a lousy job and if they expected me to do this all the time I wouldn't be here." But by the end of the week we were ordered out of there, so it wasn't really all that bad.

But my attitude is always, I'm not here because I have to be here, but because I enjoy being here. The pay is terribly little, although there are girls making a living at it, so I shouldn't say you can't. We got a raise recently and it's a little over three dollars an hour now. But it's been really great for me. It's not in any sense a means toward an end or a permanent situation. In fact, I just might see some change I'd like to make or something else I'd like to do.

I think there probably still are a lot of women who are stuck with the old stereotype that you work, and you go home, and you keep house all by yourself, whether there's a husband in the house or not. It seems like there are an awful lot of women who are just knocking themselves out trying to do both. But of course that's going to be a long time coming because men have been relegated to that lazy role for so long!

But I do think some things have changed for women, particularly probably in employment—in the business world—and I suppose it has to start there. I wouldn't say they've changed a great deal, but you can see indications of it and I think we're going to see a lot more change. Some of the banks and some of the other institutions have already been affected by it. There's been a lot of publicity and the like, and I think others are bound to start rethinking some of their policies.

Undoubtedly the Women's Movement is responsible for that, but I don't see any personal advantage in it for me at this point in time. Employment just isn't that important to me, but I do realize it is to a lot of other people. I guess I'm more concerned with things like health and education, which are also problems that all women share. But I don't see that the movement has ever influenced me in any way. I don't know, maybe I was too well started in the direction I was taking on my own.

I think in a lot of ways the movement has missed the boat. One thing is some of the people who are representing it just aren't acceptable to a lot of other women. I think first of all that the person who is conveying the idea has to be attractive to you as a woman. And I don't think there's any getting away from it, a lot of them haven't been. I think they've been just too coarse and, well . . . unladylike! I know that's not a good term anymore.

But I just think that if they're fighting for women, in order to get support from women, they have to be like women. I was just turned off by the way they presented things. And of course a lot of the ideas they expressed were contrary to my way of thinking, too, just a real departure from my feelings about myself and about other women. I think this is why from middle age on up they've found it hard to penetrate groups.

WOMEN'S HEALTH
IN A WORKING CLASS NEIGHBORHOOD

Before I got involved with the health committee at the Southwest Y, I really didn't know much about what was going on there. One of my friends called me one day and she said, "We're having a program-planning meeting and I'd like you to go." And I said, "Phyllis, I'm not even a member," and I had all these excuses, because I was really busy. So she said, "Is there anything that you'd like to see done in the neighborhood that isn't being done?" And I said, "Sure, you know that." So she said, "Well, why don't you come for what it's worth."

So I went over there and there was a crowd of about twenty women sitting around in a circle in this small room. They started at the door and asked everybody what they would like to see done by the Y and it ran the gamut from a softball team to reducing classes to crochet lessons. When they got to me I said I had a feeling that women in our community weren't too well covered healthwise, and that if there were any others that had the same feeling, I'd like to have an opportunity to talk to them.

Well, no nibbles. Except there were some other girls that called the Y and said they'd like to talk about women's health, but really they were interested in Lamaze, the natural child-birth method, and the La Leche League, that supportive group of nursing mothers. It's an international thing and Grace Kelly has been in Chicago for their conventions. Anyhow, they were highly organized and I figured people who belonged to a group like that are pretty well founded as far as their own health is concerned.

See, I had always felt that a lot of women in this area were terribly unaware of what went on with their bodies. They worry a lot about it and they talk a lot about it and they don't do much about it. You hear so many women talk about irregularities and how they hemorrhaged, you know. You hear this kind of stuff being talked about on street corners. Sometimes I wonder if they know what the word means and they really have a serious problem and they're not doing anything about it or what.

Then at the same time, I've had problems myself. I had surgery, and I finally had to have a hysterectomy, and I always had a very good sense of well-being because I had a lot of faith in the people who took care of me. But then I had a cancer scare. Mary is nine now and it was right after she was born. I went back to the doctor for a regular examination and I had a Pap smear and I called to get the report on it, just routinely you know, thinking that if he had anything to tell me he would have called me. So he said that there were some suspicious cells, he called them, and that he'd like to talk to me. I really hit the panic button and I just felt, well, why in the world didn't he call me?

So I did go in immediately to see him and I'm lying on the table and he examined me again and he's talking to me with his back turned to me. So I said, "Where do we go from here?" I had all kinds of questions and I worried about it a couple of nights when I could have been sleeping. So he said, "Well, it's really nothing to get excited about. I'd say that in a couple of months you should come in and we'll do another Pap smear." Here I was with a new baby, carrying suspicious cells around.

So I talked to my sister, who's an RN, and she said, "How do you feel about what he told you?" And I said, "I feel like if I wait until January I'll be in the boobyhatch." I said, "I want to go to another doctor and find out what goes on here." See this man is an OB man and I really had great faith in him, but he was afraid . . . he couldn't talk to me about it. And I thought, here's where I have no more use for you! I just couldn't afford to be sentimental about it at that point.

So my sister made an appointment for me, and my daughter Pat was in nurse's training at the time, so Pat said, "The three of us will go." So we went down and I told Dr. Towne the story and she said, "Till January, huh? And you're supposed to take care of seven kids and a husband, cook three meals a day, with this on your mind? Uh uh." She said, "We'll take a smear and we'll give it special handling and in the meantime I'll set up a surgery date for you."

So, this was action and I came home happy. But boy, those days went by slowly. I kept thinking, well, should I leave them with new carpeting at least? Oh, weird thoughts come to your head. You can't imagine. The day that I was to call the doctor, a friend of mine came over to be with me. I called and she said, "Congratulations!" She told me it was perfectly clear, but she wanted to do more smears every couple of months, set up a whole kind of schedule, and I sailed through that. So like I say, I have always had access to sound medical advice and with this Y thing, I just felt here might be an opportunity to either make women more aware of their needs or to give them services which would help alleviate their worries.

Well, after that first meeting, I think that was in '71, nothing happened for about a year. Then there was a St. Patrick's Day party at our church and Phyllis and Judy Jager, who's on the staff at the Y, were both there. So Judy says to me, "I've got a job for you." And I said, "Another job I don't need." Then Phyllis said, "I think Betty is one of my more liberal friends." She said, "I really think she thinks pretty much the same way I do and I think she'd make a good replacement for me on the health committee." And Judy says, "Oh fine, we're glad to have you." Well, I was really resisting it like all get out because I didn't have the time, but at the same time I didn't even know they'd started a health committee.

So I went to the first meeting and then it just all evolved. First the immunization program that we set up through the Board of Health, and then comprehensive medical exams for school kids, and then from the very beginning we gave out information on health services in the area. When I started they had been in existence a very short time really, so we took about six months establishing priorities while we were working on the immunization center, which was a lot of politicking with the city.

And then we started organizing toward getting low-cost health care for women—particularly pelvic exams and Pap smears. We sponsored a program with our local hospital to have low-cost pelvic exams and it was really amazing. Hundreds of women responded. We had advertised in the local papers and church and PTA bulletins and things of that sort.

We had 240 women examined the first time and then we were left with a waiting list of about 600. And there were a lot of angry responses when people found out that the hospital didn't want to repeat it. So now we've been busing people out of the neighborhood to another private hospital that was willing to do the testing and they're doing breast examinations too. We're going to send the third busload soon. We got a great deal of publicity on the busing, which may or may not have been helpful.

Our long-range objective is to have that kind of a program here in the community permanently. As a matter of fact, I objected to them sending people to the other hospital for that reason, because it is outside of what we feel is our community here. I felt that, although it might be frustrating and take us longer to do it, maybe we should work on putting pressure on our local hospital to serve their own community. But the waiting list has been hanging there for almost a year and a half now and we're hoping to get to all the women on it.

We're trying to reopen negotiations with the community hospital now and we have the backing of women's groups, PTA's, church groups, about fifteen different groups in all. We're not asking the hospital necessarily to donate their facilities, but it seems to me the least they could do would be to help us in long-range planning for some kind of program. And at this point, they're still denying that the reason women don't get these examinations is because they can't afford it.

The hospital is saying that all they got was their own patients, their own doctors' patients, and they're saying that the women went just because it was cheap and all we did was take the private fees away from their doctors. So we refuted all this by doing some surveys that were really painstaking. There's just a big void with many of the women when it comes to medical care. We've got all these survey sheets and so that's something we're quite sure of.

It may be slow with the institutions but we're keeping at it. As we plod along, little things happen. Like we got a note from one woman who said that she wasn't able to get in for the first testing, but she did go on her own and she was writing us from St. Luke's where she was in for cancer surgery. So at least we're able to publicize some of the things we're doing and we're developing some degree of awareness in some women who haven't really had good care.

These are not welfare people, they're working people. Some of them may be in a class where they figure if it's going to cost them twenty dollars for an examination, well, maybe the kids need shoes worse. Or maybe there's a party coming up that they know their husband would like to go to and, if he doesn't say anything, they'd rather buy a dress with that money. It's like, "There are a lot of things that come before medical care for myself this week," you know?

That's why they talk on the street corners as they do. They're looking for support. They're looking for somebody to say, "It's nothing. Everybody has it." That kind of thing. And one of their greatest securities, when they get to be in their forties, is

"Well, I guess I'm going through the change, and you can expect anything in the change."

Well, the doctor I went to said, "Don't ever let anybody tell you you can expect anything in the change. Menopause is the cessation of the menses and it doesn't mean you're going to start to hemorrhage or have a period every two weeks or any of this other foolishness, and if there is extracurricular bleeding it should be examined." She's a real preacher. All the time you're in her office she's telling you all this stuff, and I know she's exposed to the same thing we are out here in the community, through her practice.

I think all of this is tied in with the feeling that our women in our community have about going to the doctor at all, really getting to the bottom of the thing that's bothering them. When they do go I don't think they're terribly fussy about who they go to. And I think a lot of women in general aren't. They figure if they just go to *a* doctor and get *an* opinion that's all that's necessary. But if they still have the same ache or the same bleeding, what good does it do?

I guess what it really amounts to is that people are satisfied with too little for themselves. And if you're satisfied with just any doctor you run into, you should be satisfied with just any treatment you get. A lot of women aren't getting good medical care, but I don't know why they don't move on, what it is that inhibits them from feeling, "Well, I can leave this man. Maybe I owe him my friendship, but not my life!" But people are that way. I've had people tell me, "He's been our family doctor, my mother's family doctor and my grandmother's," and so on. But what they've said about him . . . well, if they said the same things about mine, I wouldn't like it one bit.

I really think there are a lot of good doctors around and women should make it their business to find them. It's true that good medical care is too expensive, but it seems that you pay just as much for poor care. One of the things that I really objected to in the book *Our Bodies, Ourselves** was the putdown of the medical profession. I just can't believe that they're all

* *Our Bodies, Ourselves: A Book by and for Women,* a thorough exploration of issues related to health, reproduction and sexuality from a feminist perspective; written by the Boston Women's Health Book Collective in 1971 (New York: Simon and Schuster, rev. ed. 1976).

that bad. Also, I suppose I think it's just too radical, too, just so divorced from the way I look at things.

I think in a way I feel more personally involved in the health committee than in any of my other community involvements. I guess it's because I feel so close to the situations. And then we're kind of socially oriented in our family and I think that health . . . well, it's so important. I have four sisters who are nurses and a brother who's a doctor. I never wanted any part of it myself professionally, but you see it kind of follows.

Also, I think being involved in this made me really see how people accept being short-changed. I can see it more and more clearly and in recent years it just really bugs me to hear people say, "Well, that's the way it is," you know. I just feel like that isn't the way it has to be, or that at least you should be restless about effecting some change, if that's the way it is.

I guess I have changed a little in the way I do things since I got involved in the health committee, too. I remember we were in existence probably a year when Goldie Lansky came as a staff person. She was a work-study person and I think she had a lot to do with stimulating people in the committee. She was such a driving force.

She came in here one day when we were decorating the house, and I was up to my elbows in paint. I told her the office had called and this man from the local hospital has been trying to get hold of her. So she called and found out that he had brought himself over and plopped himself down and was waiting for her to come. So Goldie had Judy Jager paged at the Y's headquarters downtown and Judy said, "Don't go alone. Take Betty with you 'cause she's community."

Well, I'm not the type that likes to fight. I always try to barter with people rather than come right out and say how I feel about what they're doing. But he started lashing out at Goldie and I loved Goldie, and I didn't want to see anybody getting rough with her. So I knew it was time I step in.

He was public relations at the hospital and he had told us he was in trouble with the administration because we had called a press conference about the testing program. He felt that if anything like this was to be done, that they should do it. The hospital was very perturbed. They wanted all the credit. And he was telling us it might cost him his job and all this.

He knew better, you know, but he just sat there anguishing and wiping his face and carrying on about how he was supposed to be out on the golf course. And I really got annoyed that day and I talked kind of nasty to him. I said, "Oh gee, if I had some salve I'd soothe your wounds for you," and I was harassing him all the way out the door.

I was really surprised at myself afterward. But we had been dealing with this man all along and we knew his game. His personality had come to irritate us and we'd been trying to hold the line. At this point it was just a few days before the program was to be carried out, and it was an exciting experience for us. So when he pulled that, it was too much.

We kind of got bad press in *The Southwest Herald,* the local paper here, that may hurt us when we try to reopen negotiations with the hospital this fall. It was the sort of thing where they used a headline that didn't state really what was in the article at all. It was just kind of a summary of a survey on the testing program that we sent out as a news release, but they treated it as if we were opening fire on the hospital. They do very well at copying our articles because they're too lazy to rewrite them, but the captions they put on them are terrible.

We got the same thing on the abortion issue. That was really bad. We had discussed the board's thinking on it and we had decided that we just can't turn people loose if they say they want an abortion, without giving them some kind of counseling. You don't know what people are going to do or where they're going to go, and you feel responsible. So we decided to come up with a reputable listing of people that they can go to.

Anyhow, I opened up the paper one day and saw this headline and I thought, boy, oh boy, are we in trouble. It said, "Southwest YWCA Takes Anti-Abortion Stand." And we never did. We still haven't taken a stand on the issue because we'd be losing an opportunity to do a lot of community work if we did. We seem to have as many people on either side of the issue, so the only thing we can do is not touch it. And it's been brought up again and again.

Anyhow, I feel the health care problem probably will be a long hard fight. But I think the fight is challenging and interesting and I really do have hope that changes can be effected. In retrospect you can always see little things that we might

have done differently or places where we might have saved energy, but let's face it, there aren't many people doing things
like this so we had no pattern. It was all kind of a trial and
error thing. We had nobody's experience to use as guidelines,
and in a sense I think we've accomplished a great deal for what
we've had to work with.

At the same time, I don't feel any large measure of success
in this yet. There are little things that happen all the time that
we kind of gloat over, but what I'd really like to see is some
kind of a clinic set up where women could go and have comprehensive physical examinations, not just pelvic and breast
exams. Sometimes I think about the fact that there are other
forms of cancer that are getting to people and here we are
still chewing on our little bone.

But it's what we started with and what we've been fighting
for, and I feel as if it's one hurdle that we have to cross. Really,
though, the long-range battle is to make people realize that
the women in a community such as ours just can't—because
we're told to do it—we just can't always find it possible to go
for a checkup once a year. Even though people might understand it's a good thing to do, they just don't always get it done.

I think in general the plight of the working class community
is virtually unexplored. I know it is, just from my contacts
with people from outside this community in trying to get things
done. There's very little understanding of what goes on with
the people here and what their needs are. And their needs just
seem insurmountable sometimes. We badly need organization
in a community like this. And first of all we need funding, in
order to have organization.

Probably the first priority of the people themselves would be
things like education, and then of course health—mild hang up!
But health keeps coming back to me. Oh, there's just a whole
bag of problems, so the solution to even a few of them could
add an awful lot to the quality of life of the people. They are
hard-working people and taxpayers and so forth and all down
the line, and it always seems that they have too much to get
help from the government and yet they have too little for a lot
of the better things. So it's a constant struggle.

I think a major stumbling block in the way of organization
is the fact that these people are so hard-working that they're

easily discouraged, and they're prone to come home and sit down and put their feet up at night. So they have difficulty being heard. Maybe it's that they've never come to appreciate their worth, as far as getting things done for themselves that they can't accomplish through their livelihood.

And then probably the fact that there were racial problems in this area has turned off some of the people who might have given us an ear earlier. Like I mentioned before about us being labeled white ethnics, the bad guys. I think they blame the people for their insecurities. They don't understand their insecurities and so they blame them for the things that have gone on.

Then another problem is that you just never get people organized in a community like this to the point where they can make somebody stay until they'll really listen or sympathize. I don't mean you never can, but it's been tried. Maybe it'll work out in the future, but there've been some real good tries that haven't worked out.

I think there's a nucleus of people who will be organized and who will try to do things. But I think for the most part they're a little different in some ways from the majority of people. Maybe what we're trying to accomplish through the Y, or through the health committee particularly, is to do things for people—or to help them to do things for themselves is more accurate—hopefully showing them how they can do it and showing them things that they really are entitled to. Maybe with a few successes, people would feel that it was worthwhile to be organized. I think you have to have a success in order to convince people that they can have some power. And I think that's so terribly important in a working class community.

One of the things we're really lacking in is leadership. You know there've been times when I was so disgusted with local politics that I maybe said that if they couldn't do better than that, I'd run myself. And I caught a couple of people taking me seriously and I realized I wasn't ready for that!

I don't really think of myself as a leader. I mean, I know that there are people who value my opinion of things and I know there are people I can influence fairly readily. But I don't think I have any large following! You know, I don't think of myself as the kind of person who could say, "Hey, this needs to be done," and get forty people marching with me. I may be able to motivate a few people, but I find it difficult to just plow in with something new and sell it. I'm not that kind of person.

I don't know what it is really, but sometimes people say things to me like, "Gee, I really admire you for what you've done," or something. Maybe I'm gifted with an interest in people that everybody doesn't have. Maybe that's the whole essence of it. Because it has never made a whole lot of difference to me what need it was that people were talking about. If there was one, I've been interested. So maybe it's that.

But as a matter of fact, I've been trying to sort of phase out of things for some time now. At the health committee meetings, I've been talking about expansion and nobody catches on to what I'm talking about! But the group does well on its own and now that we have a staff member that's assigned to the committee I think we may have more of an opportunity to expand. I would like to take a less active role.

When I got back from our vacation, I got a message that one of my brothers is dying of cancer and the doctors had told him he had two months to live. And my mother has had cancer for years and is just barely hanging on. And then I have a sister in Oak Park who has multiple sclerosis and she's taken to walking with a cane. And I just feel the pressures of wanting to do more for my own family. Of course I think there's always room for something outside, but I really want to make myself more available to them.

So I declined my seat on the board of the Y this year, and I also backed out of my assignment at school. I want to remain active, you know, but last spring I know I postponed going to see my mother in Omaha because of some of these outside activities and I got to the point where I was beating myself about it. So I decided it was time to just kind of cut loose from some of these things. Believe me, I hope that the opportunity will present itself for me to get involved again, but there are just too many personal things pressing right now.

Also, these responsibilities can be very confining as far as my own personal life is concerned. I called my pastor one week last spring and I said, "I'm going to miss my first school board meeting." And he said, "Oh, I'm sorry, are you ill?" And I said, "No, but my husband is home this evening and I'm going to spend it with him!" And I think he was shocked.

I really look forward to seeing Bernard be able to get into an easier job one of these years—to kind of get ready for retirement. He's worked awfully hard and I'd like to see him find something that would be less taxing. I'd like to see him work maybe eight hours a day, five days a week like a lot of people do. Now he works forty-eight hours, six days a week.

Anyhow, I've always enjoyed the things that I do and I just can't stand the thought of not being involved in some few things. I've never done anything for any period of time that I didn't enjoy doing, and I guess I've been lucky that my judgment has been pretty good before I went into any of these things. I just really was never unhappy at any of them for any long period of time. But over the years I remember people saying to me so often, "How can you do all that?" And I felt like saying, "How can you not?"

● POSTSCRIPT

Despite her expressed desire to free herself from community commitments, Betty Gagne's nature evidently prevents her from doing so. The untimely death last year of one of her brothers caused her to further reevaluate her involvements. She decided to try to confine her activities largely to her family and to "her first love," the health committee. However, rather than becoming less active, she accepted the post of chairwoman of the committee, with the hope of being relieved of that responsibility in the near future.

Betty is both exuberant about the health committee's successes over the past year and concerned about how much more needs to be done. The committee was able to persuade the Chicago Board of Health to initiate a program offering Pap smears and pelvic exams in the community—once a week and by appointment. But they are not satisfied with the scope of the program and continue to work toward the goal of establishing a comprehensive health program for women.

The health committee also spearheaded a successful drive—involving PTA health committees and community organizations over a large area of the Southwest Side—to petition the Board of Health to expand its School Physical Exam Program.

The board extended the program from two months to three during the summer. But the health committee's goal is to have the program operate at least one day a month during the rest of the year, to provide physicals for school athletes, kids in scouting programs and parochial school students, whose physical exams are required in the spring.

The neighborhood immunization program initiated by the health committee celebrated its third birthday last fall. Betty wrote, "Things are going better than ever there. We could almost forget we ever had anything to do with it, except that occasionally we go in where a snag develops and help out until things are running smoothly again."

While her term on the school board expired last spring, Betty still feels the need to be closely involved in the school's affairs, especially since it has been facing a growing number of problems. "I am sure I will still be vocal enough," she wrote, "but the commitment is a little different."

While still at the same job at the bank, Betty has increased her work hours over the past year and is gaining broad experience in different facets of the operation. But she remains on a part-time basis, "because I enjoy knowing that I can take time off if I feel the necessity." She and Bernard have been giving a great deal of thought to retirement lately and are hoping to ease into it gradually within the next few years. They plan to remain in their neighborhood, "because it seems so convenient for our family to come here in crowds."

A recent headline in a Chicago paper reading "Two Experts Claim the Baby Boom Is On" caught Betty's eye and is now posted on her refrigerator door. She has a new grandson, whom she sees several times a week and enjoys enormously, and two more grandchildren are on the way.

Betty's son Marty was married last year. Therese, her second youngest child, entered high school this year. "She gets super-involved and is really an interesting person to watch." Mary, the youngest, was looking forward to finally being the oldest in the Gagne family at her elementary school. "I could kill her at times," Betty wrote, "but she is such an independent and capable young lady that I have no sentiments about seeing my baby grow up. She's already a liberated woman and a very sensitive human being at the same time."

Joining the Ranks:
Unionism and Feminism

Cathy Tuley

Bonnie Halascsak

Cathy Tuley at work in her former office in Highland General Hospital's billing office.

Left to right: Tom, Nicole, Cathy and Becky Tuley at home in Castro Valley, California.

Cathy Tuley

MISSOURI TO MARRIED LIFE IN CALIFORNIA

I was born on August 28, 1950, in Kansas City. I was the
oldest child and I have a sister who's a year younger than I
am. My mother was a war bride, you might say. She was born
in Birmingham, England, and moved to North Wales when she
was pretty young, and my father met her over there during
the war. He's a native Missourian, but his grandparents were
British, and I think his parents were born there.

Before I went to school I was more into the British tradition.
I think you're affected by the kids around you a lot. But when
I was real small, I had a British accent. And just the way my
mother raised us was British. It's hard to describe exactly but
she still carries on a lot of the traditions, which I like. Christmastime we have a lot of the type of food that they eat there—
trifles, plum pudding, Yorkshire pudding, things like that, and
Christmas caroling. She really kept that going.

It was hard for my mother when she first came here. It was
so different for her. My father was raised in a very, very small
town in Missouri, and when she came here people didn't
understand her. They didn't know she was speaking English!
She really had a heavy accent. Some people still think she
does, even though she's been here for almost thirty years.

There's quite a few other English women who were in a
similar situation of being war brides and they formed a club.
She's still friends with a lot of them and they meet regularly,
so it's not like she's cut ties off completely. There are about
twenty or thirty who belong to the club in Kansas City and
we got to know them. We traveled back there with the whole
club one time. We got to go there twice and I met my mother's
mother, and she came here once, so I knew her a little.

People always think British people are reserved, and maybe my mother fits into that one characteristic. A lot of times I felt that maybe people misinterpreted her, because she was a little more private than some of the other women she was friends with. She wasn't as close as some of the other neighbors were to each other. It's the way she still is. I guess she likes it like that. In that way I feel like my sister and I are much different.

My mother still hasn't become an American citizen and she never will. I don't really know why. She's gotten so involved in community things, yet for some reason she doesn't want to completely become a citizen. I don't know if that's her way of saying she's British, or what. It's kind of strange, after being here more than half her life.

She's a saleswoman now, and that's really the only training she's ever had. Sometimes she feels like she's a little inferior, because in England, when she grew up, they quit school at around fourteen unless you were very wealthy and were able to go on to college. There were five kids in her family and my mother missed out. She started working very young as a sales-girl, and then she came over here and did the same kind of work.

When we were pretty young my parents had kind of a hard time financially. My mother wasn't working, so my father was supporting us. I guess she felt that she should be at home with us or something. Then she started working and kind of sup-plemented things. But they weren't that hard up, really.

My father works for the water department in Kansas City. He checks up on pollution controls and things like that. It's a city job. But that's something he's done for only the past ten years. Before that, he was a metal spinner for about twenty years. They made nose cones for missiles, space equipment. Then it seems like the industry kind of went out of business, and it moved, too, so he was out of work. He had a choice of going to Florida or staying in Kansas City, and well . . . he listened to us and he stayed. So he had to start all over again when he was pretty old, in his late forties, and that wasn't easy for him.

I never thought I was like my mother, really, until now. I don't know if that's part of growing up or what. You say you don't want to be like your parents at all sometimes, but at times now I feel that I am, even though I don't necessarily mean to be. I like being like her in the way that she's very energetic and she's always been active. She never just stayed at home. For the ten years she didn't work while we were young, she was always involved in things.

She was very active in Girl Scouts. She was a leader and on a council, so we were Girl Scouts too and we went to summer camp, which I really enjoyed. She helped out at all kinds of school functions—carnivals, PTA, this type of stuff. Then she taught church school at the Presbyterian church we went to. Sometimes I felt like she was pushing us too much, but I was pretty active in the church till I was about fourteen or fifteen, and I think it's because she started us when we were two or three.

The other side of being like my mother is I feel that maybe I'm too overprotective of my daughter, like she was with us. I thought she was a little too strict, and in areas like sex and dating it kind of hampered me, I think. She wanted me to date, but under her own conditions, like being in at very early hours, which to me . . . Well, I just didn't even want to go, I'd be so embarrassed. I'd just as soon forget it.

I had trouble talking with boys, expressing myself, in high school. I don't know why, I just felt that they were so different. I don't know if it had anything to do with her, but I just felt like I couldn't communicate with them very well. It took me a long time.

Also my mother's got these old ideas about marriage and what a woman's role should be, and she's not going to change. She just really believes that you should listen to your husband all the time. She's tolerated a lot—too much, I think. So she thinks I'm strange because I won't tolerate that much. And if she knew how many meetings I went to . . . I don't tell her about all of that!

We lived in a suburb with tract homes, all pretty much the same. Lots of kids. All white. The only ethnic group in Kansas City that stood out were the Italians. They were more or less the most wealthy people. They had some of the most fabulous houses that there were. Otherwise, where I lived the people seemed like they were all the same, all grouped together, with similar houses. And it still looks like that. But it was a lot noisier when I was there. Now when I go back it's so quiet I just can't believe it. The kids have all left. It's the type of neighborhood where I guess the parents just stay on.

A lot of my friends' parents were very prejudiced where I grew up and my parents weren't. I don't know why they were different, but they were. They taught us to be a little more tolerant of other people and not to judge them based on the way they looked. I didn't realize it when we were growing up, but it really has affected my sister and me.

I think I'm much more able to accept people than some people I know that have grown up with this kind of conditioning, where you're not supposed to associate with blacks or people of different backgrounds than yours. Even though I never really got to associate with them till I moved out here. The situation was that there just weren't any there.

There were about 2,500 kids in my school and I felt that that was too many. It kind of split between the kids that were the athletes and in the cliques and all that stuff, and the ones that were the rabble-rousers. And I was kind of in-between— never in one or the other. I had friends and we did have our own group, but for some reason we wanted to belong to one or the other of these two groups and we just weren't the type.

The rabble-rousers were the troublemakers. They'd set fire in the cafeteria, skip school a lot. They had hot rods and all that stuff. They dressed differently than the others, too. There was a definite difference in what you wore if you were in this one group than if you were in the other. They wore the tight jeans and the T-shirts and the pointed shoes. You know, slick, greasy hair. The others wore the penny loafers and the madras shirts and their hair was a short Princeton, I think they called it. And they wore their lettermen jackets, too! Now that I look back on it, I guess that in the group that were the athletes and the stars, their parents were the prominent people in the community. The others' weren't.

I was active in quite a bit—the pep club, the girls' athletic club, the drama club, language club and things like that. I always participated, but I always had these expectations of myself that I shouldn't have had, I guess. Like being a cheerleader was something I always thought was neat. But I never could have been a cheerleader. You were voted in on a popularity basis so I don't think I would have stood a chance. It really didn't matter how good you were, because the pep club just voted you in.

There was one good friend I had that I think kind of helped me to be more confident of myself. For a while I really wanted to write poetry and she was the only person I'd show it to, because she wrote, too. I guess she just made me feel that I was more capable of doing something, you know? I don't know why I was so shy, but it really hampered me from expressing myself. I had a hard time vocally. I was more able to do it on paper.

When I was in high school, it was the thing to do to be engaged and married practically on your graduation day. Some kind of pushed it aside and went on to college, but a lot of them got engaged and went to college like with the guy, together, not setting out on their own. Some of my friends went for a short period and then they'd drop out, mostly because of marriage. There were a lot of early marriages in my high school, too. Forced, you know, pregnancies and that type of thing.

My parents really pushed me to go to college, and it started from when I was very young. I think they were disappointed, very disappointed, when I quit. I went to Central Missouri State College. It was only about an hour from my house, in a very, very small town called Warrensburg. The classes there were kind of on a junior college level and I felt like I wasn't really getting anything out of it. And I was in a hurry, too. Too much of a hurry to decide what I wanted to do. I just really didn't know what I wanted. I think that was fifty percent of it.

I quit because I was tired of being broke, too. I had worked my way, in my brief time that I was there. In high school, I worked in a library, and a 7-11 Store during summers so I could save up. And it was really hard to find jobs, so I did baby-sitting and stuff like that. Then once I was at school, I just wasn't able to get a job at all.

Now I'm taking night courses and for the first time I'm enjoying it. I took a humanities course and a chemistry course and a course about retarded children. I'm just going now for stuff that I want. I don't really care about credits and things.

I don't have that on my mind anymore and I think I felt a little bit too pressured about that before. Someday I might decide that I want to continue and go after some particular thing.

After I quit, I came back home and lived with my parents. That's something I didn't really want to do but I was trying to save some money to get out. I wanted to get an apartment and take LVN—licensed vocational nurse—training. But at the same time, I really wanted to have a car. So I went and bought a car, which was dumb.

I worked as a clerk then for the federal government. First I was at the Social Security Payment Center in Kansas City for about six months, and then I transferred to the Air Force. I'd been getting out a lot at night, going out with my friends. So even though I was living at home, I was paying room and board and I had my own car, and for some reason that made me feel more independent.

At Social Security they told me that if I'd have stayed a few more months, I could've gotten a raise and a promotion, but it was so boring that I just didn't think that getting a raise would really do that much for me. I was at the point where I just could not stand coming in there and doing the work, it was so tedious. I was in a typing pool, typing up form letters on a production basis. It was really awful.

Then when I worked at the Air Force as a clerk, the problem was I didn't have enough to do. I was the only clerk in the office and there was a lot of times when it was very slow, and I just had to sit there. And that's as bad as having too much to do, you know? I would try to find my own ways of improving things, but I wouldn't tell others about it. I'd just do my own thing.

During all that, I kept hoping that I could save enough money to go to school, but it seemed like such an impossible thing to save enough so that I could live for a couple of years the way I wanted to and not have to scrounge around the way I did when I went to school. It seemed like such a far-off thing, but it was something I kept thinking about a lot, and it kind of helped me through sometimes.

Those kinds of jobs are really deadening. I found that there were very few women that would just stay in them, like this typing pool, even though they weren't organizing to form a union or anything. Most of them wanted to get ahead. They wanted to get their promotions and get out of that office and go on to something else in another area. But there were a few that just stayed and stayed. I think they were the type that were just afraid, you know, to do much.

I met Tom about six months after I quit college, when I was twenty. I met him on a blind date through a friend of mine who went with a guy in the Air Force. They were stationed together. We didn't like each other at all the first time. Then we just accidentally met again about a month or two later. We didn't know each other very long. We just got married after a few months.

Three months later we transferred out to California. Tom got out of the Air Force early and he went to school for a short time when we moved out here. That's the reason they let him out early. He went to junior college and we knew he wasn't going to be able to support us, but he wanted out of the service really bad. We came out here because this is where he's from. His family is still in San Leandro.

Tom got a job but I was pregnant so I couldn't work. He worked in a can factory for about seven months in Hayward. It was a seasonal job and he was just lucky to get it, but all of a sudden they laid him off. That's when our financial problems started and I had to find a job real fast. My baby was three months old when I started working.

I worked at a private hospital in Oakland for a month and a half. Then I got laid off. It was very small, and I was the last hired and first to go. It was two weeks before Christmas. That was one of the most depressing things that's ever happened to me. I think they had eleven patients in the hospital at the time and they just weren't making any money. It was a really small hospital, only thirty or forty beds.

Then Tom got a job as a truck driver for a gardening place. It was really crummy. They paid something like two dollars an hour. A few months later, he got a job at International Harvester, which is where he still is. So it wasn't really that long that we had financial problems, but it sure seemed like it at the time.

Then I went to another private hospital. A month later, I

just happened to get that. I was a medical records clerk. But then fifteen people were laid off six weeks later, and I was one of them. I also had a clash with my supervisor and I think that had something to do with it. She was a tyrant! A real tyrant. She used to go through the wastebaskets and stuff like that, looking for mistakes. She really expected a lot out of me, I thought, and I told her that. I was really just trying to voice my opinion on my workload, not in a hostile fashion at all, but she thought I was mouthing off. The next day I was gone!

I'd taken the civil service test and I'd been turning down certifications. That's when they reach your score on the test, they send out notices from different job sites throughout the county saying that they'd like to interview you. So I turned down quite a few of those because I thought, well, I've got this job, maybe I can stick it out for six months and then I'll go see about the county, because the pay is a lot better than anything private. So I just told them I wanted my name put back on the active list, and a week later I got the job that I have now at Highland General. That was about two and a half years ago.

I've always been really interested in medical settings. For a while I thought I wanted to be a nurse or a social worker, that type of thing. I still wonder about it sometimes, you know, especially when we get so bogged down in paperwork. Probably the same thing happens to them, too, but it just interests me. It's a lot more interesting than the kind of jobs I used to have.

I don't have any direct contact with patients, but I do see a lot of them and we're right close to the mental health ward. And in the union work that I do, I come in contact with other clerks that work in different areas so I find out about their patients and their problems and stuff. I really would like a job with patient contact. Hopefully, that's something I'll get one day. I could have had it if I'd stayed on, but I'm going to be quitting for at least a year when I have my second baby, about two months from now.

Right now I feel very isolated. All I have in front of me is a piece of paper. It's like assembly work, is what it is. I worked in a factory once for about three months, and I just couldn't do it. This was in Kansas City, and I did piecework at Western

Electric. I was doing diodes, plating. They have to be put in an oven and then they have to be plated. I was boxed-in in this little area with these special gloves for using tweezers.

Well, they expected you to put out a production report and they expected your rates to be very high, and I felt like I wasn't progressing as fast as I should. Three months really wasn't that long. I probably should have given myself more time. But it was a night job, too, the 10:30 to 7 A.M. shift. I used to sit there and go to sleep behind the machine!

Well, on this job we process bills. There's about eight of us in outpatient and three or four in inpatient billing, and there's two county hospitals in this area that we do the billing for. We have to know all the Medi-Cal requirements and all the rules, and we're expected to do so many a day and put out so much money. So we have to total up and make out production reports daily, and in the last six months they've been putting a lot more pressure on us. They say we're responsible for keeping the hospital open and all that stuff.

Sometimes I feel like my work is just so many little details. I really resent some of the problems that take up a lot of your thinking, that shouldn't have to. Like really dumb computer problems and ways that you have to compensate for errors. It's just endless, the amount of ways we're expected to compensate for things going wrong.

And sometimes I really have trouble disciplining myself to do all the little things I'm supposed to be doing at my desk. All the rules, like "Before you do this, you have to do that." And when I ask questions like, "Why do I have to do this?" nobody seems to know the answer. "You just have to." And I say well, "I don't want to," and they accuse me of corrupting other people when I try to find easier ways to do things. Like why should you have to dig through a box to find out the times that a person had their lab tests? I just make them up!

There's a lot of rules that we have to follow that I think are ridiculous. So there's that, and also getting there on time and taking my break on time and just being rigid. I have trouble with that, and with putting out the exact same amount of work each day. My production report goes up and down. It depends on how I feel. Some people are more capable of adjusting to it I guess. But they must think I'm worth something, because I'm still there! It's getting to the point, though, where I think they hate to have me ask questions.

The best thing about my job is that we're all close together—the insurance billers, the Medi-Cal billers, patient billers, and then the people that deal with the public, and they really do allow you to move around a lot. I've been in about three different types of billing areas, so I've gotten to know quite a few people that way.

ORGANIZING CLERKS IN ALAMEDA COUNTY

I met Kay Eisenhower* the first day on my job. We were in the same section. She came about a month before I did, and she was kind of like the lead clerk. We have a pretty high turnover! So we just started having lunch together and talking, and she was interested in organizing a union.

I don't know if she has her master's or what in political science, but she was really active in student movements and in and out of the women's liberation movement, that type of thing. I think she thought that, rather than teach, which is what she would have been doing, she wanted to meet people and work with them and get to know their politics.

Kay was probably the biggest influence on me. She had been involved in politics for a long time, and at the same time she always worked almost alongside me, in the same area and everything. I don't think I would have become as openly involved in organizing if I didn't have somebody there to push me. I might have, but I think it would've taken a lot longer and I might have been more afraid. I just wasn't the type to start doing it on my own, and she made me feel I could contribute something. Before that, I never really felt I could.

* Kay Eisenhower, civil rights activist in the South in the mid-1960's; active in Berkeley (California) community politics and the Peace and Freedom Party. Involvement in Oakland Women's Liberation and women's health issues led to an interest in organizing hospital workers, with the realization that "the only way any real changes were going to be made was through the activities of working people." Became a member of the Executive Board of Local 616, Alameda County Employees (of SEIU); is an active member of the Coalition of Labor Union Women and Union WAGE.

We started off talking about problems in the immediate workplace. Our supervisor let us organize the work pretty much the way we wanted to. Kay is very good at that, and I was interested in it, too. So we talked about trying to get things running smoothly, problems with various other workers, supervisors, that type of thing. We really just spent a lot of time sitting around analyzing things.

Then we just felt that we could do more if we were all in one organization—things like getting a contract and having shop stewards, that we never had before. In general, just getting better working conditions. The employees' association they had at Highland then was not representing the right people. It was really representing management more and it was more like a social group than a union. They had picnics and this type of thing. And when a clerk would call in to the association for help, they would notify her supervisor that she was calling and she would get jumped on for calling in without going through the channels.

Well, then SEIU—the Service Employees International Union—was organizing hospital workers in the area—maintenance people, LVN's, social workers. Kay knew quite a few other clerks, and SEIU started having organizing dinners, trying to get us to join and help organize the clerks. So Kay invited me and we started going to these dinners and talking about our problems at work, and I started finding out more about unions.

I'd never been a union member before and I felt I had a lot to learn. This was my first association with it all. Before, the word "union" always made me think about blue-collar workers and men. My father was in one. He never talked about it that much. I guess he didn't participate much. But his being a man and a blue-collar worker, I guess that's why I made that association.

In my previous experiences being a clerk, I was never aware of things. I just went and did my job and went home. All of a sudden I was aware of problems between supervisors and workers and the kind of power games people play. In fact, that was the kind of thing that really started us organizing.

We had a supervisor who was an older woman, in her later fifties or early sixties. She wasn't that organized herself, but she was the one who let us do our work the way we wanted to. She never hung over our shoulders or anything. Then a younger woman came in, younger than all of us, and she kind of took over as our lead clerk. Her husband was a supervisor in the same hospital in another department, so she always went to him with her problems, instead of this woman who was her immediate supervisor.

Well, things got very tense in our unit because of her. I think she was envious of some of us. She knew that we had better ideas about doing things than she did, and she resented it. Anyway, our supervisor started being harassed and she really felt like her job was being threatened. She ended up dying very suddenly one day in the office, and just a couple of days before, she had told Kay how she felt.

There was a lot of feeling that she was pushed to her death by this man and this woman. He's my supervisor now and I just can't help but think of this sometimes, especially when he sits there and does his crossword puzzle all day. And I mean, being objective, this woman wasn't the best supervisor I've had. But they purposely tried to get rid of her and it was very evident. That was one thing that really stuck in our minds.

So SEIU was trying to get us to join, and this employees' association was trying to get us to join them, too. For a while we kind of worked on our own. We called ourselves Clerks' County—a name we made up for the clerks in Alameda County—and we put out a newspaper that was our original organizing tool, saying why we were thinking about either joining SEIU or starting our own clerical union. We didn't want to join this association.

We started that in about June of '72, and then one day in Feburary of '73, the association joined with SEIU very secretively. Suddenly, after all this time of us telling people not to join the association it all becomes one union and we were right in the middle of the whole thing. We had to completely reverse what we'd been saying.

I think what happened was the association was in the red. They were going downhill financially, but they had quite a few members. And this was a chance for SEIU to get a lot of people all at one time, without too much effort. So there was something in it for both of them. But we really felt taken. We had been working toward having an open election that was supposed to be held a month after the time that they made this secret affiliation.

So we were all thrown together and now we are in a union with professionals, semi-management-type people. But we have a separate clerical unit where we're able to do things ourselves we couldn't do before, like bargaining. There's about five or six of us who were in it from the original organizing point, and we've added people to our caucus as we went along.

We still have our Clerks' County newspaper that the SEIU organizers helped us start. They had a woman who showed us how to do layout, and we used different locals' mimeograph machines. Then those of us who had never written would team up with someone who had written for some other newspaper or something, and then we just all took turns. We're all responsible for distribution. We set up our own distribution centers throughout the whole county. Most of our caucus members are in the major worksites where most clerks are—the hospitals, welfare centers, libraries.

In our shop Kay and I have gotten almost everybody to join the union. There's about 2,500 clerks in the county and about 40 percent are members of the union now. But in terms of negotiations, that's not enough if you want to show your power. And that's what management relates to, your power. I have people telling me, "Look, I'll join if you get this and that at negotiations. I'm behind you all the way." But I say, "It doesn't help to be behind me, you have to join the union and participate."

It's hard for people to realize that management relates to us in terms of numbers, and they keep very close track of how many members we have. Also, I would just like more people to join so that they can know their rights. And I think the union is the best way to learn them.

I think maybe it's harder to organize clerks than some other kinds of workers, because sometimes they feel that they're halfway into professionalism, like maybe they have one foot in the door. The way it works within the county, you can get a promotion and all of a sudden be management if you know the right people, and that type of thing.

Also, maybe because they're women, they're not as aggressive. They have been taking things the way they are for so long without saying anything, whereas the men . . . Well, like if Tom blew his stack and cussed somebody out at work I think they would accept it more. Sometimes I'd really like to say exactly what I feel when something happens, but I have to kind of control myself more. I feel that if I said what came to my mind, it would probably go on my record. It's more structured, the things that you're allowed to do as a clerk, the things you're allowed to wear. There's the public out there, you know, and all this junk.

I've been a shop steward for a year and a half now. We were the first class, several of our Clerks' County caucus. We all took it together. It wasn't really much training, just four sessions. But we learned union language, and we talked about how to process grievances, becoming familiar with the contract, things like that.

A lot of people come with questions about sick leaves, maternity leave, things which we try to have them look for in the contract themselves. Then there are workload problems and personality clashes between people and their supervisors. I've had quite a few of those. We try to do things informally and not file formal grievances, because this means you have to go through each supervisor, each step.

A lot of times I ask around where vacancies are in other departments, and then I'll ask the clerk, "How do you feel about going to this person above your supervisor and we can talk about another job? Maybe you don't like your job." They frown upon personality clashes as a means of transferring. So the approach of "My job isn't that satisfactory, I'd like to be doing something else" seems to work better. Also, management doesn't want to bring these things out in the open. If you do, they want all kinds of evidence and facts to back it up and a lot of times, people aren't willing to go into that.

The shop stewards have four hours a week to handle grievances. People just drop by, but sometimes that's a problem because there are some very anti-union supervisors in our office that clock us in and out and get real sticky. In the contract it says you can handle grievances four hours, but it doesn't say you can pass out literature or do leafleting. So we try to do that on our breaks and lunch, which means a lot of times we don't get lunch or breaks, because we've been reported.

I guess being a shop steward has helped me have more self-respect, just being able to help people. But it's really hard sometimes to be objective about problems and not help people just because they want the help. You have to be able to see what's really going on. And then when I don't like somebody I have a really hard time talking to them.

We're having a big problem now with clerical job reclassifications in the county. The Civil Service Commission called in the State Personnel Board and they created the whole thing themselves. Then they consulted each department head after they had already written up the job descriptions and they asked the department heads to recommend what each clerk should fit into. There was no input from clerks on the job descriptions, but also the department heads did not consult the clerks about how they were going to fit them into it until several months later.

All the clerks, 2,500 are involved in this, but not all were really affected by it. Most people just had title changes, that's all. No wage increases, and they made it harder to transfer and advance in some areas. But many of them were reclassified at a lower level and a lot of people have been hurt by it. Especially ward clerks, who have some of the hardest jobs, and most unit clerks in the welfare system. We feel the county's just doing it to save money. They would claim that's not true, but we did a study on it and the last reclassification was seventeen years ago. So all these people, the ones that were demoted, had been working out of classification all this time, for seventeen years. It's very strange.

Also, throughout the county they use intermittents, people that are hired temporarily. They're paid on an hourly basis, while we're on a monthly basis, and in many areas they do exactly the same work that we're doing. They hire them for two to three months at a time, and this is a very cheap way of getting people that have no rights. They have no bargaining power, no sick leave, they don't get paid for holidays. They get no benefits unless they were hired before July of last year, but then it's only after a certain length of time that they're entitled to benefits and they lay them off right before that time. So we're trying to fight for them, too.

A lot of people are very unhappy about all this and the union is the only place to turn right now. Chances are, if you go to management on your own, you're going to get shot down. If you go through the union, you have a much better chance of working it out with more support behind you. Because of this we have a lot of new members.

They elected me chairperson of the reclass committee. It was an honor, but I didn't realize what I was getting into. It's a lot bigger thing than I first realized. I've really tried to put a lot of time into it and study all the classifications and the changes that were proposed by management and get around to all these different worksites. It's hard, but I've developed a lot of contacts all over the county through it that'll help in the future, I think.

I think all of this has really helped me to develop myself, my personality. I've become a lot more vocal and aggressive, too, and I'm not as gullible as I used to be. Now, you can tell me something, and I want it proven to me. Sometimes it's kind of rough when you do that to your husband! "Give me the facts," you know. "Prove what you just said."

The first time I had to speak in front of a group I was really shaky and nervous. Maybe glad that I did it, but wondering how I sounded to other people, still worrying about that. That takes a long time, to forget about what they think, you know. It's easier for me now, but I've always had trouble getting up in front of people. I still really get shook. It's better if I do it spontaneously and not have to think about it for a long time. That just makes it even worse.

When I first started going to the organizing meetings, I felt for the first time that maybe I could really do something to change things somehow. Before, I never even thought about trying to. So it was a big change in my whole attitude. Also, I think being recognized as a valuable worker helps, too. I was able to do more than my share of work and do it accurately, and I think they kind of recognized me for that and started listening to my ideas about changing things.

Also, being a shop steward, it helps to be able to keep up

your end of it, or else they won't listen to you at all. Some of the supervisors really expect a lot of you. They'll do things like use our ideas, saying that they're their own, and then if we come in late or something, they'll say, "What kind of example is this that you're setting for everybody else?" That happens to me because I'm always late!

I've always wanted to work with people in some way that I could help them. And I think this organizing has kind of given me the attitude that you just can't give up, even more so, and that things don't happen overnight. For me, that's been the hardest thing to learn. I can see people becoming more aware of themselves and their rights. These changes are happening. But sometimes you're just so involved that you don't see how much. And you just cannot change a whole structure of a union overnight, which is what we're trying to do!

TOM TULEY ON HIS WIFE'S CHANGING ROLE

I was born in Oakland and grew up in San Leandro and always lived in this area. My mother is full-blooded Portuguese. She was born in Massachusetts, but her parents came from the Azores. My father came from Oklahoma. He's part French, part Irish, and half Indian on his mother's side. Him and a friend of his decided they were going to come out here when he was about seventeen. So they took off one day in a junky old truck that broke down in Arizona or somewhere and they hitchhiked the rest of the way. He went to high school up here for one year and my mom and him got married.

They've been separated since I was about fourteen but they just finally got a divorce. My mom worked until I was about five. Then my dad made her quit work. She started again when I was about sixteen. She worked for the federal government when I was a baby. A runner, I believe is what she called it. Then later she worked in factories—for Brothers Cookies and then for a glass company.

I worked in a can company after school, but I went to college too, for a while. My dad wanted me to go because he said he never had a chance to. My mother really never said much about it. I tried. I was working graveyard at Continental Can in San Leandro and going to junior college out here during the day. It used to be a real drag.

I'd just go home, eat breakfast, shower and go to school until about 1:30. Then I'd come home, sleep all afternoon until about eight o'clock, get up and study for an hour or two, go out for a while, see if the world was still here or not, and then I shot off to work again. Did that for almost a year.

I saved quite a bit of money, but it was still rough. One nice thing about out here is the county pays for everything except books. No tuition, nothing else. You just jump right in and hope you make it. I studied commercial art. At one time I wanted to get into that, but right now the field is real tight.

I left school because I was going to be drafted in the Army and I had a choice of that or going in the Air Force. So I went into the Air Force with my uncle's help. He had been in for over twenty years. I spent three and a half years in the service. Then I went to school for a while afterward until finances became difficult, and then I started working very hard and diligently!

I've been thinking about going to school off and on for quite a while now, but I can't get myself to go for some reason. I have friends at work that want me to go with them, nights. I'd probably take up art, drafting, and I'd probably take up a little bit of ecology and things like that. Learn something about where I live.

Right now I'm what you call an assembler. I help build the trucks at International Harvester. The parts come in, you put them together, put them on the truck, and then hope to have a complete check at the end. It's like you have three parts to put on and that's what you put on, those three parts. I have what's called the motor mounts. That's what holds the engine in the frame, keeps it from falling out.

It's a production line, and before this work slowdown we're having now, we had thirty trucks a day. If you get thirty trucks done by two o'clock, you shut the line down and everybody just goes and does what they want to do. It's not a hard place, like Ford or Chevrolet. It's a fairly easy, even pace and it's constant, which is nice.

I wouldn't say I like it, but I do it because the pay is good. I make $5.58½ an hour right now. Plus I have most of my dental and all my medical paid for, for the family, too. The benefits aren't that bad for a married man. That's why it's kind of hard to give it up sometimes, even if it is a very tedious and boring job.

I've been there two years and eight months now, but I've had several different jobs, so it really hasn't been too bad for me yet. There are jobs in the plant that are really nice to have, but it's rough to get them. You have to be there ten, fifteen years, or you have to know somebody. Like the electrical shops—wiring, troubleshooting for the plant. And then there's the maintenance guys who fix hoists, fix the line, the air guns. Jobs like this are nice because you can set your own pace and you're always working on something different.

In my opinion, our union isn't good for much. For the UAW, I think it's one of the worst locals they've got. I just pay my dues and read the literature they pass out and that's about as far as I get carried away with unions. I just can't find interest in getting into it, like shop stewards, like my wife. You get into being a social worker. That's more or less what you are in the plant. And if a guy is goofing off and you know it but you have to help him, I can't see it. I don't believe in this. So I just voice my opinion when it comes time to vote.

But it seems like the candidates are normally the same people. For the first two years I was there, I never saw any of the officers change. Finally, in the last election, they got ousted. But I haven't seen anything drastically change yet. Maybe in the next year or so, as these new people get into what they're doing, it may change. But I don't know. Have to wait.

In the meantime we pay $11.57 a month in dues. I believe it's two hours plus a dollar, is what it amounts to. It's a lot, especially when they take it out in one big paycheck. It cuts you down. You know the time it's going to come, and most guys will try and work a few hours overtime to make up for the difference.

I was in the service when I met Cathy. We were all pretty hard partyers then. She either had to be a hard partyer like the rest of us or fall out, so she kept up with us. Us drunks, like we were. She was pretty noisy sometimes, very outspoken like she is still. Maybe she was shy when she was a child, but not when I knew her. She didn't let people try to cut her down or anything, and that was good.

She's changed a lot since she's been working at Highland. She met a lot of kinds of people she never had much contact with until she came out here. People back there were pretty . . . modest, I guess you'd call it. They have their simple ways. But out here, the way we are, we just voice our opinion and do whatever we want to do.

Since being at Highland, she's really gotten interested in a lot of off-the-wall stuff. Like the union. She's really gotten into that union. And the newspaper. She's helped build it up with several of her friends. And she's gotten into black and white relations, which I know she didn't have much to do with when she was back east. Now she's always watching how I talk and stuff. And her personality has changed as far as a lot of things. She'll speak right up now, where she may have held back earlier in our marriage.

With the union and all that, she's usually gone two nights a week. So it's not too bad. Becky and I, we do see her. Some nights she'll leave at 5:30 and be home about 8:30. The next time she'll have a late meeting, so she'll come home and have dinner with us first. So Becky does get to see her without going to bed and wondering where's my mother and stuff like that, like a lot of kids do, growing up and not seeing their parents.

I don't mind helping around the house. Cooking, I've always liked to cook. When I was younger, I always got up and made my own breakfast. Always had my own hot plate when I was in the service, when I didn't want to eat the garbage. So I've always been into that. It's all right. I like it. It's fun.

To me, what Cathy does is like social work. But like I said, I think it's good for her because I think it's helped her personality. And it doesn't bother me when she's away so much, if she doesn't get carried away. Like three or four nights and then an emergency meeting, which happens occasionally. When that happens, it kind of starts bothering Becky and she irritates me, and I have to get on Cathy. So it's like a circle.

Otherwise, it's usually not too bad. It doesn't irritate me very much. But when she starts bringing her problems home, that's when I'll probably make a real cease to it, if she ever does. It's fine if she takes care of her union business during union time, but don't start bringing it home and laying it on me or my daughter. Like I say, I'm not into social work.

I know it doesn't sound like it but I love people. People are fantastic. Just as long as I don't have to carry their woes along with my own. And this is more or less what a union person does, as far as I'm concerned. I like just to have friends, and get to know people and talk and have a good time. But my problems are my problems. I shouldn't be burdening you with them. You know, "This guy's picking on me or that guy's picking on me." Well, pick on him back. That's my philosophy. There's always a way you can get back at somebody, with or without a union. At least where I work.

After working all day in that plant, it gets to be nerve-racking. So I like to kick back on the week nights. Evenings when Cathy's at a meeting I'll usually take Becky to my mom's, or go visit my old friends I still have from high school. I like to sit around, diddle with my camera. I just like to loaf, relax. Weekends we usually go shopping, try to find stuff for the house, go to dinner, things like this. I'm not a guy that likes to make things in the garage, or that stuff. My dad was that way, but I never got into it.

Camping, I like that. If they had warm season all year round I'd probably go at least once or twice a month if I could. That's about the only thing I really like, and maybe fish once in a while. When I go camping, I just like to walk around and enjoy what I see. We go to different areas. At this one place there's just a large stream up there and it's eight thousand feet, so you're pretty much up there where the air is rare. It's pretty hard to breathe the first couple of days. I usually take a fishing pole and trout fish, walk around, fall in the water, things like that!

I still enjoy art. I doodle sometimes. It just depends on how I feel. I like to go to art shows, look at art, things that people make. That's what really interests me. People that have the gumption to sit down and make something. I think, wow, that's pretty neat. I might do that someday. That's what I keep telling myself. One time I was into making rings, then I got tired of that. Then I made little posters, got tired of that.

I just become bored very easily for some reason. I have another brother that's into art too, and he has the same problem. He'll be going great guns and all of a sudden, yuk. He throws everything away and he'll start something new. My dad is the only one in the family that ever started something and kept with it. I'm an Aquarian, but I'm right on the cusp, and I have a problem with the Pisces in me. I have a lot of problems with that Pisces part . . .

CATHY: STRUGGLING FOR EQUALITY

I really didn't know what to expect of marriage, I guess. I had to compromise on ideas and ways that I wanted to do things, but I think that's part of marriage, anyway. I don't think that you can be aware of all the responsibilities you have until it actually happens. When that first hits you, it's kind of hard sometimes. There really is a lot more—like budgeting and planning things that you don't have to do a lot of times when you're single. And it was hard getting used to having somebody around all the time, since we hadn't lived together or anything before.

I feel that Tom doesn't like me doing what I'm doing now, going to meetings and things like that. I don't know if it's that he objects to those kinds of activities or if he just wants me to stay at home. I think he doesn't exactly realize sometimes how he's reacting to these things. It's hard. I feel I'm straight with him about things and sometimes it's harder for him to be more open. I think it's basically because of the way he was brought up. His parents were not that open about their feelings toward each other and maybe he can't help but be the same way sometimes.

I've tried to explain to him that he's going to have to accept me the way I am, you know, and I try not to interfere with his life, but I feel that he doesn't seem to want to do that much for himself, outside of work. We just seem to have a lot of different ideas on what we like to do, you know? Just going to work and coming home is not enough, for myself. That's why I've taken classes and gotten involved in union activities and stuff. And I wish that he felt the same way.

I guess I was different when we first got married four years ago. I mean he knew that I probably would be taking night classes and stuff, but we never realized that I'd be getting into union activities the way I am now. And it seems like it does get more and more, in terms of time.

Sometimes I think Tom really objects to how much time I'm away and I think at times it kind of slowed me down. And sometimes he uses the thing about I'm not spending enough time with Becky and I think he might use it more when we have two children. That's what I'm really worried about. But talking to the friends I have in our Clerks' County caucus who have similar problems has helped me a lot, because I felt like I wasn't the only one facing that problem.

I've tried to have open discussions with Tom about it, saying, "You know, this is the way I am. I will try to limit my meetings to maybe three nights at the most and if you feel I'm doing too much I'd appreciate it if you'd tell me every once in a while, or if you feel I'm not spending enough time with Becky." Because I do feel he has the right to tell me that. So I think we kind of got it out there in the open a little bit, but every once in a while I feel that he kind of is holding me back.

I think I feel much closer to women in general now, because I find that the men I know aren't able to express themselves in the same way. They're not as vocal. I don't feel that that's their fault, but maybe that's the way they were brought up, unfortunately. I feel that Tom, well . . . hopefully he could change in that way.

Another thing is thinking he's not as good as other people and worrying about what other people are thinking of him. I think maybe that's a lot of the problem that men have. The ones I know, they really are aware of how other people think of something. Like maybe what I'm doing. Somebody might say, "Wow, look what she's doing. How come you're letting her do that?" That type of thing. And it would be a reflection on him. I think he gets a lot of feedback from his friends on that, even though he doesn't tell me all the time.

I feel that people don't know enough about marriage before they get into it. I wish there was some way that you could tell people, "Don't get married!" Sometimes I wish I hadn't gotten married. I feel maybe I could have maintained more independence if I hadn't. But then having to end it with a divorce is really traumatic, I think. I used to think that being separated, halfway between being divorced and married, was like you really weren't standing on your own two feet saying, "Look, I want this or forget it." Or, "If we can't agree on this, we're going to just end it all." But now I can see where some people just separate because it's just not that final.

There's something about changing your name too that really . . . like it changes your identity. Maybe it shouldn't, but somehow it does. My name was Cathy Boone, and I still don't feel like I am really a Cathy Tuley! How can you all of a sudden change your name and just fit right in, you know?

I don't know if I would be as strong as some people have been that go ahead and say, "The hell with everything. I'm going to make up my own name, I'm going to have as many kids as I want, and I'm not going to get married." I really admire them. I know it would be much rougher on kids and it will be a long time before that changes I think. But some places you can do it easier than others. Like out here I think you could do it. I know a lot of people that lived together that got married when they had kids because they didn't want their children to be harassed or anything like that. And that's too bad, that they are.

I don't see that people are getting married that young anymore. I don't think that's so much the problem. I think it's just the fact of expecting changes from the other person, drastic changes in their personality, and it's just too much to take. Especially like when you're supposed to clean house, do this, do that, go to work, watch the kids and all the rest.

To me, being a mother is kind of an unsure role. A lot of times I don't know if what I'm doing is right, or what type of effect it will have maybe ten years from now, you know? I'm kind of afraid of molding Becky in some wrong way that might drastically affect her. Even at three, she asks a lot of questions. I mean she wants to know why people have different color skin and that kind of thing. She's very observant, like most kids are. I just don't want her to pick up the wrong things, and it's really hard to do.

I hope as she gets older I'll be more open to her ideas than my parents were toward mine. I mean, if she wants to do the kind of thing that I'm doing, that's fine, or whatever she wants to do. But when she's a teen-ager or so, I want to treat her a little bit more like an equal than I was treated. I felt like they always thought I was a kid all the time. They still do!

If my next baby is a boy, I'd try to bring him up the same as Becky, but it might be harder, because my husband and I would be pulling him in different directions. Tom really would like to have a son, but in his family they have much different roles for men and I think it really is hard for him to break away from that. I know he tries, but at the same time he kind of falls back into it every once in a while—wanting to be waited on, something like that, his ideas of what women should do.

I really like to be busy, to keep my mind busy. When I don't have anything to do, I find myself just really being bored, kind of wandering around, not knowing what to do with myself! I just think the busier you keep yourself, the more you'll enjoy life. And I like to experience different things. I think for most women it's probably good to at least participate in something, the community, whatever. I don't think it's such a good thing to spend all day, every day, just staying home with children.

There's a lot of day care centers in this area, so it's really no problem. Some are government and some private, but the government ones are pretty restrictive. I tried to get my daughter into one, and I made too much money. Would you believe it? I guess I'm lower middle income or whatever, and I feel they don't have enough for what I am. It's more for people that are poor or single parents. I make about $670 a month, with our last raise. It's not enough, but actually I think it's pretty good.

When I quit work to have this baby, I'll probably stay off for about a year. And I'm kind of wondering what's going to happen, you know? Whether or not I'll go back to what I was doing before or what. It's all kind of in the future, so I don't know exactly what I'm going to be doing or if Tom will be stopping me in any way.

He doesn't really try to stop me, he just won't show any interest and sometimes that's almost just as bad. I don't think he realizes a lot of what I'm doing. Sometimes I try to include him in things. Like when I'm writing articles and stuff, sometimes I'll ask his opinion on them and then he shows interest. But unless I approach him, he won't ask me any questions or anything. But he won't ever say that he won't baby-sit or anything like that. And I think actually, just being around some of my friends, he has changed a little bit, whether he realizes it or not!

I'm really going to miss all of my union activities. That's why I keep thinking about going back to work early. It's just so much of my life now that when I quit, even though I know I won't have that much free time with the new baby and everything, I keep thinking I will and that I'll be bored. I'd like to take a few classes. I've kind of thought about the idea of going to school full time for a while, studying nursing, but I haven't really decided on that yet.

I think in general I feel more comfortable out here. Sometimes I really would like to go back to Kansas City, though. I get that feeling especially when things get so hectic and I feel like I'm getting crowded. But whenever I think of going back, it's only in terms of a few years and always thinking of coming back here. Here there's more activity and I find that most people, at least the people I associate with, are very friendly and not as conservative.

A lot of towns around here are pretty conservative, though. When I first came out here I lived in San Leandro, which is very conservative. There's about one percent blacks. Then we moved to Hayward, where there's a lot of Chicanos and some blacks, so it's different. We lived in a Chicano neighborhood about two blocks away from the can company where a lot of people worked.

Then we moved to Castro Valley and here I see two types of people. There are upper class white professionals, and kind of lower type white workers. There are some really nice expensive homes here. It's kind of a nice suburb area, but then there are some really crummy apartments. I used to live in one of those, where a lot of people are on welfare, until we moved a couple of weeks ago. It's still mostly white here, but there are a few blacks and other minorities.

The way things are now, every once in a while I really feel resentful that I have to work and Tom has to work in order for us to keep going. I just wish sometimes we could stop for a year and maybe travel or something like that. I'd like to see a lot of places in this country, just kind of camp all the way across the country, that type of thing. But the way things are, that would be almost impossible to do. There's always having to do this and having to do that, having to pay these bills—water bills, gas bills. Why do you have to pay for stuff like that, you know what I mean?

The way the economic situation is now, it really worries me a lot. The finances—how to stretch the money and all that. Sometimes I feel maybe we can go over our budget and do with less. But we were talking about it last night, about how we like to do things—go out to eat, go to good movies, take trips sometimes. All of that takes money, but then you have a lot of good times to look back on. So it doesn't really bother me that much that we're not saving like to buy a home. I'm not really that interested in that.

Sometimes things just seem so unfair in this country. Like food prices are so high and wages are so low, and yet some people are really making money and others have to live under very bad conditions their whole lives. I think I'm fortunate in some ways. I'm not really rich or anything, but I guess I'm enough in the middle that I can change things. Some people are so poor they're just unable to get out of it. That's what I find really depressing, because after a while I guess they give up hope, and that I think is bad.

But I think that the people in the lower income classes will be making themselves heard more in the future. Different minority groups have chosen different ways to express themselves—some violent, some nonviolent. But they are beginning to come through and I think that they will have more of a voice in the way things are going—as far as prices and wages, and maybe kind of breaking down some of the barriers between the classes that we have now.

I think one problem with the Women's Movement is that some groups of women do have definite advantages, because of their positions and education and bringing up. I think that might always be the way it is, that some people will have an easier way to go. I think it'd be nice to see women accepted as equals, regardless of what type of training they've had and all that. But I think it would be difficult for that to happen, the way things are structured.

I think in many cases a man might go by a woman's achievements in different areas, say like writing a book. They might say, "Wow, she really did a great job and I admire this woman." But at the same time, they might have their wives at home and they wouldn't say, "Wow, I really appreciate what you're doing for me," or "Gee, I'd like to help you sometime. I'd like to help you fix dinner, or vacuum the house or something."

Recognizing women for different things kind of separates them I think. But then the same woman who might get recognition because of some achievement might not be recognized for a lot of other things. She might just be known for only one thing, and she might not be recognized as a wife or a mother or things like that, in an equal sense.

I guess I've been pretty much influenced by the Women's Movement because of the people I work with—the clerks in our caucus and in the union. A lot of them were in that movement, so I've become more aware of it that way. I've just become much more aware of being a woman and the rights a woman should have. And also, some of the things that single women have to go through. A lot of my friends are single or divorced and they really have a rough time, especially when they have kids and their ex-husbands won't support them.

Before, what I knew about the movement was really limited to just what I saw—people in demonstrations and the type of women who were professionals and their side of things. That's what I think was published more than anything else, so that's all I really picked up on. Also, they seemed to go in for legislative actions, that type of thing, which I didn't relate to. So it didn't mean that much, because of the type of people that were being publicized. Like the woman that started that magazine, Gloria Steinem?*

I think the way she looks is hard to relate to. And also, I think her education put a barrier between her and people like myself. I don't know, maybe she had to go through what we've had to go through, but it just doesn't sound like it from the

* Gloria Steinem, co-founder and editor of *Ms.* magazine; president of the corporation. Leading advocate of the feminist movement; founder and board member of the major national feminist organizations. Formerly a journalist, magazine editor and civil rights activist.

way she talks. I feel like maybe we've had to deal with life more realistically, having problems presented to us that maybe were never presented to her. And I think the type of men that we meet and deal with would be different from the type of men that she would. Somehow I cannot picture her going out with an auto worker, or someone like that.

Maybe I have my own stereotype of her, but I think maybe she looks above us. I feel she's fighting for women like herself, professional women, and that she's not thinking of women in the whole sense, just part of them. So I don't consider myself part of her movement. I think, the way that it's been presented in the past few years, that there are probably two movements going on. And getting them together is hard.

Groups like WAGE—Union Women's Alliance to Gain Equality*—I think have made a move toward that. The first meeting I went to there was the first time I ever saw such a mixture of working women. There was a woman lawyer who gave a presentation, then there were some women from an auto strike, but they were all working together. And that really struck me as kind of unusual.

There were older women, younger women, professionals, clerks, and here they were, all working in the same organization, which I thought was really good. People were willing to let each person talk, and they would not be criticized because of where they were coming from. The reactions were based on what they were saying, not because this one was a professional and that one was a clerk.

I haven't been in WAGE that long, but after just a little I've noticed that they have people working on both ends

---

* Union WAGE (Union Women's Alliance to Gain Equality), founded in 1971 at a NOW conference in California by fifteen women who protested the lack of representation of working women on the program. First group to demonstrate for extending protective labor laws to men, calling for "men's rights," in order to protect benefits for women (which were eventually lost). Works to raise the minimum wage and improve working conditions for all women workers. Publishes a monthly newsletter, now circulated throughout the U.S. and to twenty-three foreign countries, as well as a series of pamphlets, including *Organize: A Working Women's Handbook* and *Labor Heroines.* Now has three chapters and two in formation, all in California.

of problems. Like a lawyer might work on the court end of a law for farm workers, supporting it in her way. At the same time, the other women might be passing out leaflets or going to rallies or benefits for farm workers, so they really do work together. It can be done, if you can think of it as a whole in whatever project you want to do instead of separating it.

At first, you know, you tend to get involved in your own little group. But then I think you have to get out and see what other women are doing, so you don't isolate yourselves. If you do just work within your own group and don't see what others are doing too, chances are you might not last long. So I feel like that's helped me. And it's nice to know you can help somebody just by being able to tell about your own experiences with something they've never done before and want to learn how to do. Also it's nice to know there's someplace you can go if you need support and help for what you're doing.

Sometimes some of the women make you feel uncomfortable, but not often. It depends on how they speak. Using vocabularies that people would never understand, or the armchair type views of things, you know. Just constantly using their background, maybe, to make you feel inferior. Like you're not equal to them because you're not like them. Some people might do that on purpose, some people might do it unconsciously.

Within our Clerks' County caucus we have people that have extensive educations and also people that don't. When we print something, we look at it together, and after working with this group for so long I feel I can say, "I don't understand this. You're using terms that I don't understand, so if I don't, I know somebody else won't. So I feel you've got to go at it this way." I mean, I'm willing to learn, you know. I think the best way you can learn is by experience, really, anyway.

I haven't run into too many people who try to put other people down because of their education. But I feel like you should be able to communicate with all people, not just people who have the same background as yours. Because I would say the vast majority of people in this country don't have an understanding of a lot of words, like a huge vocabulary. And maybe it's not their fault.

CLUW—the Coalition of Labor Union Women*—has been hard to get started out here because the people that are in charge of it are creating special rules of membership. Like you have to have a union card to get in. At the last WAGE meeting I went to, a woman told how many women were organized within this country, and the percentage was tiny. So what good is it to have a group like CLUW that are just union members? Why can't they include people that want to be union members too? At the first conference out here, a lot of people, like clerks, were criticizing the leadership about the way things were going, and it didn't seem to solve much.

No resolutions were allowed because we hadn't formed our chapters. Well, the only way you can form your chapters is to have a certain amount of members, and you have to have a certain amount of members from so many different internationals, and then you have to apply for a charter, and some people have tried to do that, and they've been waiting for months and months. Chapter meetings have been going on, but they haven't been officially named as a chapter.

I feel that eventually CLUW will get on the right track and include women that need help and get strike support and things like that going for women as a whole. It's just that to have to start off like that is kind of bad. The good thing about WAGE is that it doesn't restrict you. It doesn't have all these different rules about who can participate. But WAGE is a Bay Area thing. It tries to do things at the state legislature and it's good to have it. But CLUW could become a national thing that could really put pressure on the federal government.

Maybe I'm optimistic, but I think things are changing right now for women and it's going to get better. They're allowed to go into different fields now that were mostly dominated by men before, like carpentry, engineering, auto factories, that

* Coalition of Labor Union Women, founded in March 1974 at a Chicago convention attended by 3,200 union women, representing fifty-two international unions. Goal is to establish an interunion framework to deal with the special concerns of women as workers and union members. Major purposes are: organizing the unorganized (less than 12 percent of female workers are union members); affirmative action in the workplace; increasing participation and leadership roles of women in unions; and political action and legislation. By December 1975, there were over forty chapters across the country.

type of thing. And they have more of a sense of themselves and because of that, they're letting themselves be known in different kinds of groups. They're speaking out in different ways.

I think when Becky grows up she probably won't have as many barriers and the kind of breaking-out-of-the-shell type thing that I've gone through. Maybe she won't have to go through that and she'll have less guilt feelings. Hopefully she won't be as restricted when she's older so that she can do what she wants more freely without always having to think, "Is this the right thing? Am I hurting somebody by what I'm doing?" That kind of thing. But there's still a lot of catching up to do for women to be on equal terms.

I guess I've always tended to side with people that are being taken advantage of, but since I've gotten involved in organizing I feel like I have to contest things people say sometimes about minority groups. Now I do much more defending. I don't like to hear people say things that they can't back up and that's where I run into trouble sometimes, clashing with people.

I mean people can have their own ideas, but I don't think you can find out what the truth is or really change your opinions unless you work alongside people. I have a lot of close friends now that are black and Filipino, in the union and also at the job site. And sometimes with certain nationalities or groups it takes longer to get close to them, but I don't think you can make a big thing about how different they are if you want to be close to them. There are definite obvious differences between groups, but I don't think I'd want to see everybody the same anyway. As long as they're able to accept my ideas, I'm able to accept their ideas and I think that's really great.

I would really like to see people accepting each other more instead of separating themselves by their backgrounds, their cultures and stuff like that. It just seems like such a waste of time and really petty. We're wasting so much energy, with so many people doing this constantly, cutting themselves off from other people. I'd really like to see people talking to each other more, getting to know each other and their problems, working together.

If I do come back to work, I think it's possible that I might even get more involved in union things. But I don't think I'd ever want to be a full-time organizer for a union. I think that we can get more done the way we're going right now. And that's kind of an isolated job, the way I see it, in relation to people I've met that are organizers. You can become part of an organizing caucus to some extent, but you're never completely part of it. And I don't think you're ever completely trusted either, no matter how hard you try.

Also, it seems like union organizers don't follow through with the whole thing. At a certain point, they disengage themselves from some of the movement. So they start it, then leave, go on to something else, and never become fully part of it. And I don't know if I could do that. The way I feel, to just pick up and leave like that, you have to be thinking a little bit more of yourself or of the union itself, than the people you're organizing.

I feel a lot better about my job than I used to. I used to really hate it because it was so boring. Now I have these other activities that kind of take up some of my work time! I mean, I get a lot of phone calls and visitors and things like that, so that helps. And I'm also doing a much more interesting job than I was when I first started. Now I do Denta-Cal and Medi-Cal billing, and insurance billing, which involves quite a bit of math. It's kind of like accounting.

This is the longest I've ever worked at one place—two and a half years. If it wasn't for the union, I think I'd be jumping around from job to job the way I used to. You know, working, getting bored, looking for something else and moving on. I think I'd probably still be doing that, not really committing myself.

Before, I used to be kind of afraid to commit myself to anything. That might have been part of my problem, not wanting to see things through. Also, I guess I'm not as romantic as I used to be, thinking oh, things are going to be better this time, you know? Thinking like, well, someday I won't be doing this. Someday I'll be doing something that I really like. And maybe things are going to just change by themselves . . .

Now I really see things differently. And I see so many people criticizing the way things are, yet not trying to do anything about it. I feel you're just wasting your life when you do that.

People can do things that will help change conditions, if they want to.

It's really hard for me to say exactly how I might have helped change things, you know, to describe them one by one, but I feel that maybe I've helped a little bit. Especially with organizing our new local. And I feel it's a good thing because I'm helping people to express themselves and to say what they think, and basically to help themselves. So I believe in what I'm doing and I guess that help. me to be optimistic.

● POSTSCRIPT

The spell of boredom that Cathy Tuley anticipated during her planned maternity leave never materialized. Her second daughter was born in October of 1974. "I enjoyed staying at home," she wrote, "not having to live by a regular schedule, and not having to deal with the everyday hassles of a job you don't like." But in February of 1975, Tom's plant closed and the company relocated in Indiana. Although unemployment compensation and sub-pay benefits were due for a year, Cathy felt she should return to work because, "I don't like not knowing for sure if a paycheck is coming and Tom was thinking about going to school."

Cathy "reinstated" with the county but didn't want to go back to her former job. Instead she took a job as an account clerk at the Welfare Department. Two months later she took a promotional test and landed a job as a medical clerk at the county hospital she had worked at previously. She's now working as a ward clerk, a job she finds quite satisfying except for those days of extreme pressure.

As she describes it, "The phone rings constantly so I have to remember who's on hold on three lines (I usually forget who's who), I copy doctors' orders on the nurses' cardex, make out medical cards, handle admissions and discharges, and try to keep the station running smoothly by notifying nurses, doctors, patients and admitting of what's happening. I'm learning very quickly that this job requires flexibility and aggressiveness too."

While on maternity leave, Cathy continued to attend conferences and Clerks' County meetings. When she returned to work, she again became quite active in Clerks' County, whose recent newsletters have focused on "the relationship of federal spending policies to our jobs, and also on how we should support other unions on strike."

She also became a union shop steward again and now belongs to the Labor Relations Council. The council brings together representatives of different job categories in the union for monthly meetings to discuss current issues throughout the county and keeps people at all the worksites informed, especially during negotiations. Currently the council is organizing actions against a countywide job freeze which management has linked to the union's recent wage increases.

Cathy expressed great enthusiasm over her recent election as a member-at-large on the Executive Board of Union WAGE. There are now four WAGE chapters in Northern California and the organization is becoming recognized outside the Bay Area. During the past year, it sponsored two conferences for clerical workers. Cathy also serves on WAGE's publicity committee and is now helping to plan a speakers' training course. The goal of the course is to enable more of the membership to respond to the many invitations that WAGE receives for speaking engagements.

Before returning to work, Cathy took a women's literature course at a local junior college and read a series of autobiographies. "It's a good way to educate yourself on women of different backgrounds," she wrote, "and to value and appreciate where these women are coming from. And it's good that they're speaking out because they represent large groups who most people haven't really understood or related to. Maya Angelou's books have been my favorite."

Tom is having a difficult time adjusting to being unemployed, although he's taken on much of the responsibility for raising Nicole, their baby. Cathy has been attempting to convince him that she would prefer his going to school or training for a job, rather than taking a job he knows he will be dissatisfied with. Although Tom did attend college recently for a while, he finds it difficult to seriously consider alternatives to full-time employment.

Cathy continues to wrestle with the problem of limiting the number of meetings she attends and balancing outside commitments with her responsibilities at home. "But I think I'm doing fairly well," she wrote, "on deciding which meetings are priorities and then skipping others and not feeling bad about it. Sometimes I absolutely burn myself out and then I'm no good to anyone."

Bonnie Halascsak outside the guard shanty at her former gate at U.S. Steel's plant in Gary, Indiana.

Left to right: Bonnie, Cathy, Leonard, Julie and Lenny Halascsak on their front porch in Hobart, Indiana.

Bonnie Halascsak

NEVER AT HOME IN SMALL TOWN INDIANA

I was born in Gary in 1943. My dad was born in East Chicago, but he had moved there to find work in the steel mills. We rented a home there for many years. The people in the area were all pretty much in the same class. A lot of them worked in the mills. Then when I was a freshman in high school, my parents built a new home in Hobart, so we moved, but I didn't feel as comfortable there. It was a newer area, very few people around.

My father's a mixture of Scotch, Irish and a little hillbilly. My mother's German, but she was born here, too. On both sides, we had lots of aunts and uncles and grandparents around. I always felt very comfortable with my father's mother and I still do. She's a doll. She's more easygoing, like my dad, and I could talk to her about anything. My brother was the same way. Whenever he needed someone to talk to, Grandma was always there.

I was raised Missouri Synod Lutheran and sent to parochial school from kindergarten through the eighth grade. The atmosphere was extremely strict. It was really a parochial school, right to the letter, and they can have much too much of an influence on your life. Then, of course, certain kids were the best in the class and others were constantly put down. I always felt put down by those teachers.

It was really traumatic when I moved from that small school, where I had gone to class with the same twenty children and had the same three teachers for eight years of school, and moved into a high school where there were hundreds. Four hundred in my own class and a different teacher every fifty minutes. I was absolutely thrown. It was a tremendous adjustment for me and something I'd never do to my own kids.

I was very much a tomboy when I was very young. I loved sports and there were mostly boys in the neighborhood. There was only one other girl, one year younger than I was and we were both tomboys. We'd play dolls and stuff occasionally, but we wanted to play football and high jump with the boys. I did join a 4-H Club one time and I really enjoyed that.

I remember my brother was in Little League and he had music lessons and things like that, and my parents were involved in a lot of his activities. It seems like I didn't do much, really. I really wanted to play the piano very badly, but by the time I was old enough to get into music lessons, my brother decided he didn't want them anymore. So they felt it was a waste of money for him, and I wasn't allowed to have lessons because they thought I wouldn't follow through either. That upset me very much.

I guess my mother is what you would call a typical housewife. She cleans and shops. She's a hard worker as far as anything around the house goes—washing walls and windows, working out in the yard, anything along that line. But she's not involved in any activities. She belongs to no organizations or anything. She stays home. She's bored, I think. Very bored. She's never been out in the world, so her own world is very narrow.

Maybe because I was raised with that, I guess I'm a little bit the opposite. I never considered myself rebellious, but I never agreed with everything I was told, either. I think I was always questioning. If somebody told me, "This is the way it's going to be," I wanted to know why. I just was always that way and I still am. When I was younger, whatever my mother said had to go. I had to listen to her, but I resented it all my life. And I guess I was independent in character enough to always know what I wanted to do, even though I couldn't do it until I became of age.

My father is more like me. He's strong and independent. He and I are still real close. He needs somebody to talk to once in a while, and I guess I'm the only one he has. My dad's really pretty open-minded. He backs what I've been doing to a certain extent. Sometimes he thinks I carry it a little too far, but he works out in the mills also, so he knows the situation, the way women are discriminated against. My mother, having

never worked and never been out of the house, can't understand. She thinks that all women are supposed to do is stay
home and take care of their families and clean.

When I was growing up, all that mattered was the cleanliness of the house. You know, shoes off at the door. I could
never do that to my kids. It's their home and I let them live in
it. Like on Sunday mornings they'll come in if we're sleeping
late, and Lenny, the oldest, will ask if they can make a fort out
of the couch or something. So the cushions are off the couches,
blankets all over. We never could have done that in my mother's house. Everything was just perfect. But I can't live like
that.

Hobart's a very conservative town. It's strictly a white area,
like a suburb of Gary, and it's mostly Protestant. There is a
Catholic church in town and it's quite large now, but it wasn't
at one time. Most of the men here are steelworkers, but some
of Hobart is rural so there are some farmers too.

In my own family, my husband and I both work at U.S.
Steel, my husband's father retired from there, and my father
works there. This is the steel area. That's the only place you
can make money. My father is in production planning. He
takes orders from the sales offices and does scheduling for
the mill.

A lot of the men . . . a lot of your white males here are
really supremacists. And they're not in favor of integration,
either. They work with black people, but if one moved next
door, this town would panic. It's a shame, you know. I live here
and I don't feel that way at all. But how do you move from a
section like this and move into an area where the crime rate is
high? I'm afraid to make the reverse move because of my children's safety, so I live in a community that tolerates discrimination. It's kind of ironic.

At one time, they were talking about cleaning up Lake
George. We have a beautiful lake in Hobart, which is very
polluted. You can't swim in it or anything, and there was a
large fund-raising drive to clean it up. But many people felt
this would bring blacks into Hobart, to the beaches, so they
dropped it.

My husband and I went to a sorority social the other day, a
fish fry. Several of the men are realtors and they were talking

about this, the blacks moving into their area. One of my sorority sisters said, "I'd sell. I'd sell and leave in a minute." And my husband said, "It wouldn't upset me at all if a black family moved in right next door."

I knew he thought that, but he's rather quiet and reserved, and it surprised me that he would pop up and say something that controversial in this area. If you see a black person in Hobart, you know he doesn't belong here. It's been this way since I was growing up and it hasn't changed a bit. I know the first ones that move in of course are going to have a fight and I feel sorry for the ones in that situation.

When I was in school, my grades were good enough that I did take the college prep course. I didn't know what I was going to do, but I thought maybe I'd go into nurses' training or something like that. I think most parents wanted their sons to go to college at that time, but to send their daughters was unimportant. I remember I was called in by the guidance counselor and told that I was very mechanical, very high in math, and some other things. But then they told me these were not women's fields, you know? Typical prejudices. I can still remember that.

I finally did go to college, just part time for a couple of years, but my parents didn't want me to go at all. I don't even have a year all together, but when I was going, they wouldn't help me out at all. I lived at home and paid them room and board. I did everything on my own, really. My mother thought I should get married, have kids and stay home. She was upset when I went back to work after having my kids, and she was very upset when I took this job. It's not a woman's job! But she doesn't think women should work, period.

I guess I was always independent. I think I wanted to get out and be with people at the time. And the jobs I had after high school bored me. I worked for about two years before I began at Indiana University, at the extension over here. I worked as a bookkeeper in a bank, but I don't like sitting behind a desk, so that just wasn't my thing. Then I began working at the hospital in Gary and I loved that, but it doesn't pay and it just wasn't enough of a challenge for me. I was a ward secretary, working right on the floor, handling medicines and things, clerical work again.

So I started college and it was pretty rough for a while. I went four nights a week and worked full-time. Got up at five o'clock in the morning, went to work, went straight to classes till ten o'clock at night. Then I went home, went to bed and got up and did it all over again. I spent weekends studying.

College really brought a new awareness to my life. We'd get into some really good discussions—into the why's of things, not just "this is the way it is." And I enjoyed the challenge of that. Also it brought me into contact with more people and I think I needed that, living in Hobart. I needed to get out and see what the rest of the world was about. Even when I was younger, I felt too confined here.

I guess I was beginning to broaden my own world when I was working at the hospital, and college definitely helped. A very good friend of my husband's and mine was Mexican, one of my best girlfriends was from New York. There were people from all over. I was only going part time and I knew it would take quite a while before it would help me to get a better job. The main thing I wanted was to meet people and learn about the world.

Then I met my husband. He was a student at I.U., and he belonged to a group of friends I belonged to there, and we ended up getting married. I was twenty-one. Before that, when I was dating, my home life in the last few years there was pretty bad. As I look back now, I know I wouldn't have stayed. But at the time, nice girls just didn't leave home and get apartments. There was a lot of friction, but I stayed. I was afraid to move out on my own.

When I met Leonard, well . . . he wasn't even allowed in the house. He was Catholic for one thing. So there was a lot of friction about that. If the phone rang, my mother wouldn't even answer it if she thought it was Leonard calling. He'd tell me what time he'd be by to pick me up and I'd go out. Everybody said, "You shouldn't do that," but my mother wouldn't let him in the house. What was I going to do?

My father would sympathize. He understood how I felt and he would talk to me when we were alone, but at home it was the same thing. So we pretty much avoided talking. It was that simple. Live there and if you had to say something to somebody you would, but for two years it was a bad scene.

Then I converted to Catholicism. Another rebellion on my part, I suppose. When I started going with my husband and several of my friends were Catholic, I ended up seeing other sides. I was open-minded enough to look into other religions, where my mother can only see the one. So this of course caused quite a bit of trouble between us.

We're not very religious anymore. When I converted to Catholicism I think I really needed that, the structure. But I've kind of branched out a bit now. I mean, I don't disbelieve in God or anything like that. I'm not an atheist, but I don't really believe in structured religion as much anymore. I don't think you really need that. I think it's the type of life you live that's important and that's what I'm teaching my kids. Leonard feels the same way. So we don't go to church anymore.

I disagree quite often with the Church's teachings, too. Like I was never against birth control. That was one aspect I never could believe. But I don't have to worry about that anymore. Ever since Julie, my third child was born, I've had trouble and the gynecologist finally insisted that I have a hysterectomy, so I did.

When it comes to abortion, I don't think I could do it. But I don't think I have the right to sit in judgment of anyone who chooses to. If they feel that's the best solution, then that's the way they should handle it. Some people are not ready to be parents and they're not capable. I think the trend nowadays is to have the children and put them in foster homes until later. And I think I would prefer to see that. It might be more emotionally satisfying for many people who I don't think could cope with abortion. There needs to be more counseling.

I'm really not a joiner, but about five years ago, just about the time I was going back to work, I joined a national sorority. It has local chapters and it's philanthropic. You raise money for charities like Tradewinds, which is a handicapped children's school in the area, the cerebral palsy center here in the area, the National Kidney Foundation, cystic fibrosis, American Indian education, out in Arizona.

When I joined, I felt I needed to get out and do something. And I thought it was going to be more of an individual type of basis, where you can help people. But it didn't turn out that way. It turns out that you have two big fund-raising projects a

year and donate the money. You really don't have the contact
with the people you're helping, and that's more or less what
I wanted to do.

I was very active for a while. I hated all the bickering but I
believed in getting in there and doing things, you know, to
help change things. I was treasurer for a while, chairman of
many committees, a model for the style show, did a lot of
handicrafts to sell at bazaars and things like that. But I quit, I
went inactive, because I just don't have time for it anymore.
And the pettiness of it, I couldn't take that. Going to meetings,
sitting down and discussing really unimportant things.

The women around here don't feel the same way I do about
things. Like the neighbors around here, I'm the only one that
works, except for one older woman who's a realtor. The rest
are like my sorority sisters. I was the only one that worked
there, too. They have their own little worlds. Most of their
husbands are college educated and maybe a little well off. This
is a football area—a lot of scholarships. But I don't think they're
so inclined anyhow. Most of them are very passive and not
very free-thinking.

Most of my close friends from high school are gone. One's in
Florida, one's in Angola, Indiana. There's one here still in town,
but I hardly ever see her. We have nothing in common anymore. I think everybody goes their own way after high school.
But it was ironic when we went to the class reunion. I found
that the same people were still in their little cliques. I guess
they still need that security.

U.S. STEEL'S FIRST WOMAN SECURITY GUARD

Five years ago, I was very reserved, very quiet. The most
important thing in my life was home and the kids. I hadn't
really looked beyond what I was going to do when the kids
got older. My life was just built around this. I was stuck out
in the country with two kids in diapers and no driver's license.

I had worked at U.S. Steel for the head of the employment
office when I was first married, and the day I got my driver's
license, I brought a neighbor out to the mill and tried to get
her a job. That was in 1969 and I had been home for about a

year and a half after my second child, Kathy. The head of the
fire station had asked the employment office to find a woman
clerk for them, and they talked me into taking that job!

I was the first woman ever put on in the fire station. The men
never stayed long; they'd move out into the mill in higher paying jobs. That's why they decided to try a woman. It was a
union job, too, Local 3061, so I was the only woman in our
local, and they weren't too happy about that at the time either.

They're all men in the local, and their jobs involve protecting the steel mill—plant security officers, fire equipment inspectors, firetruck drivers. I worked there for three and a half
years and I really liked my job. I worked hard to organize it.
They never had anyone in there who really knew what they
were doing before.

I had figured approximately three hundred pages of tabu-
lated typing, listing extinguishers, automatic systems, and had
gotten the job just about organized to where it was quite easy,
so that I didn't have to retype everything. It was just a matter
of filling in the dates. And I assumed a lot of the boss's duties
because, while I was there, one of the bosses was out sick for
a long time and then he died.

Well, then the head fire equipment inspector was promoted
up to assistant fire chief, so instead of three of us being in the
office, there were just two. I took over a lot of his work—a lot
of the safety contacts, the scheduling and the overtime, and
all the reports that he had done before. So I was actually doing practically two jobs.

I really liked my job though and I was very happy there.
Eventually you learn to win the men over. At first they were
against having a woman there, but after a while we were all
real happy. Then the merger happened. That was in 1970. U.S.
Steel made the two separate plants into one big plant. Gary
Sheet and Tin is where I am and the other side is the Gary
Works. One is a finishing mill and the other makes steel. I'm on
the finishing end. The steel comes over to us and we put out
the finished product. Now it's all called Gary Works.

At one point there was a line right down the middle, and
there are various union locals on one side and different locals
on the other. So when they merged the two sides, of course
this merged many departments. They merged plant security

and there is still friction about this because there are non-union guards on the other side and union guards on our side. This happened in the fire station also. There was a union clerk on one side, which was my job, and no clerk on the other side.

I'm sure what they originally intended to do was to transfer my job from this side to the other side. But they didn't want it to be a union job because they're not unionized over there. So it was a process of elimination. They moved the records and everything to the other side, and my job was eliminated.

When they moved the job, I was told at one o'clock one day that I was eliminated at four. That's how much notice they gave me. They told me that they were going to call me in for an interview, and when I asked for the right of union representation I was told I wouldn't need it. They said there was nothing important going to be discussed. But I don't trust them that far, so I took my union president with me.

So we had the fire chief, the superintendent and the assistant superintendent from one side, and the union representative and myself on the other side. With the union rep there, they didn't make the salary offer I'm sure they had intended to make, because that's blockbusting. See, they cannot offer a union worker a job with salary. It's called breaking the union. In fact, the fire chief had mentioned how he needed a clerk, but he knew he couldn't hire a union clerk. If I had been willing to go without union representation, I could have transferred, I'm sure, as a salaried worker to the other side. But I didn't want to lose my union rights.

They had told me ahead of time that they would list job alternatives for me, but with the union rep sitting right there beside me, they couldn't offer me the salary job. So they gave me only one choice. They said, "Of course you have the right to promote to plant guard," which is the next step up on the promotion chart. Technically, I suppose, I could have done this three and a half years before, but I was happy where I was. So I said, "Is that it?" He didn't answer. So I said, "If that's the way you want it, and I don't think you really do because you don't have any women guards, but if that's my only choice, I'll take it."

Well, they made a big joke of it, and I really think they were surprised when I said I'd take it. But the only other choice was to file a grievance and hopefully get my job back, which is the route we chose to go. The union had said it could possibly take a year, but we were definitely going to get that job back. We were quite sure and I still am sure that they couldn't legally do what they had done. But they did it.

Anyhow, since I decided to file a grievance, I had to stay within the union. Within the local, in fact. I couldn't transfer anywhere else in the mill. I couldn't take a salaried job or another clerical union job somewhere else in the mill. But I wanted that job back badly, originally. It was really important to me. They took it away from me with ten years' experience at the mill as a secretary in many departments and with a beautiful work record, and they gave it to a guy who had never worked a clerical job before. Didn't know the first thing about records, didn't even know how to type, in fact.

I had to stay within the local, and these were all traditionally men's jobs. So they put me out on the guard force. It was a challenge, but at the same time I was really afraid of crashing that barrier. Probably no one likes to be the first one. At least I didn't. I knew I was really going to be in for it. I knew it was going to be a long fight. That was in June of '72.

They put me in a three-week training program that they have, and the training officer took me to Chicago for uniforms. They had no uniforms for women, so they got me policewomen's uniforms. He got me skirts, he said, "because you won't be working out with the fellows. We'll put you at a desk somewhere."

It turns out I didn't want to work the desk somewhere. I happened to like it out working on the truck gate and everywhere else, walking patrol, driving car patrol. They couldn't discriminate, so it ended up they had to get me slacks too and put me outside. I'm sure they regretted it after they made the move because it really blossomed into something they didn't expect.

Also, they put me in the truck gate which is called "discouragement gate," for over a year. It's the hardest job in the department. You take the bills and weigh the trucks, every steel truck that goes out, anywhere from five hundred to seven hundred a day. It's not a physically hard job, except that you're on your feet, you're out in the hot sun or the cold, with the wind from the lake. And you supposedly get a lot of abuse from truck drivers. I never had that problem with them. I got along better with the truck drivers than I do with management.

They put you on this gate where they can watch you closer, because there's the head guard and several management people down at that gate. They made it quite difficult. I was watched constantly. I knew I had to go by the letter. Maybe the fellows could be nice and smile and let somebody go past them without showing a badge, or let something out in the car that they shouldn't. I just couldn't afford to take those chances because I knew I was being watched.

One night at a dance I ran into an investigator and his wife. I didn't know he was married to her at the time, but I knew her. Her daughter and I went to school together. So we were talking with some people and one fellow asked if I remembered him, the night he asked if I would let them out early. So the investigator popped up and said, "No, not her. She wouldn't let you out early." So I said, "You'd know, wouldn't you?" He said, "Yeah, we've been watching." So he actually made the admission. This is the way our department operates.

So I was kept for over a year at this one gate. I was supposed to get discouraged and quit. I'm quite certain this is what they had in mind. In terms of salary, it wasn't really a promotion. I made a dollar a day more, but before that I was working straight days. As a guard, I had to work shiftwork. I got a shift differential, just what the fellows got. They didn't discriminate in pay. At the time, though, I didn't think it was that much of a step up for me. But now I wouldn't go back. I ended up loving it.

The company really dragged out the case before it got to arbitration. There was a purpose in their dragging it out too, because you could not file a charge with the EEOC—Equal Employment Opportunity Commission—until you had gone through all other possible channels. It took over a year to get our arbitration decision.

Our local was strictly behind me. They helped me an awful lot. Some of it was that I had a good relationship with them, but mostly they didn't want to lose the job. There's still a lot of animosity between our side of the plant and the other side, and they didn't want them to take one job. They were afraid if they got one, they'd try to take more. It was really a test case since the merger, and I kind of got lost in the shuffle.

When you actually get to arbitration, the international handles those cases, not the local. So the local president went with me, but he and the international staff rep that went do not particularly see eye to eye. The international guy would not put our local union president on the stand, so I pleaded my own case. All the international staff man said was, "Now, you know you people from the company violated the contract. It says here you shouldn't do this." That's all he said!

He really didn't fight that case like he should have. He didn't do any cross-examination, and one man made a couple of statements that were false and he wouldn't even challenge him. He stated the job at the fire station was created for me, when in fact there were five male clerks before me. And the international knew that. But this particular staff man, I think he was bought off. The arbitrator listened, but he really only heard one side. Inadequate representation is what it really boiled down to. So we lost it.

Well, I was the only woman guard for a year and a half, but since I had gotten on, two women from the mill actually went as far as the Department of Defense to challenge U.S. Steel because they would not put any more women on. After they hired me, they hired several men guards, but no more women. I think they really thought they could discourage me and they'd get rid of the one woman they had, and it was all going to blow over. They certainly didn't intend to hire any more women.

The two who filed charges are a mother and a daughter. One was a truck driver and one worked out in finishing, and they wanted to be guards. They had jobs where they were out physically working in the mill, they were both dirty jobs, and I think this looked a little more glamorous to them. It's a lot cleaner. So they fought it and it took a year and a half, but they got on and they've been on six months now.

They went to the Department of Defense and they contended that U.S. Steel was not complying with the law and so they shouldn't get any government contracts. And the Department of Defense agreed that they were discriminating. So the company was of course then forced to hire more. They put on four women at the same time—one more on our side and three on the other side. So two are in our local and the three on the other side aren't in any union.

Since then, there have been a lot of changes in the department. Before, they were really giving me a hard time. They told me they'd never put me alone. See, many of the gates were set up where the guard would leave the gate after shift change and check the men's washroom and the wash houses in the area, to keep people from sleeping in there, or to check for break-ins in the lockers. They had no trouble in the women's, but the guard always checked the men's.

So I couldn't work on any of those gates. I couldn't work car patrol because I wasn't qualified to be an ambulance attendant, which I had been. The company had trained me at one time, but your card elapses after three years, so I had to demand to be retrained. Then I demanded to drive car patrol, demanded fire training. I demanded to walk foot patrol. Now I'm going to be starting Emergency Medical Technician School, to be a paramedic, for when we man the ambulances. The captain I worked for helped me out a lot.

There are two management people in charge of each shift, a lieutenant and a captain. My captain felt that any job any of the men can do, I can do also. So they gave me the opportunity to show that I could. At first, when I was stuck out on that one gate, I didn't get the opportunity. Not until this fellow moved me out to a different gate, put me on foot patrol, had me in a car. I've been on ambulance calls, fire calls, and I love it. So I guess in my case, it was just a matter of being backed into a corner and either standing up and fighting or sitting down and crying. And I wasn't about to sit down and cry about losing that job, even though I'd really liked it. I guess I turned out to be a fighter, even though I sure didn't start out that way.

My husband has really been behind me in all this, even though we didn't actually know what the job entailed. I had never paid that much attention to what the guards did, either. But shiftwork was going to be difficult for me, with three children. And we were in the process of building a house. It was unpainted and we had just moved in. So we knew it was going to be difficult, but he left it up to me whether I wanted to quit right there.

I was really very angry about what had happened, and I had a breakdown a couple of years before. So he didn't know how this was going to affect me personally, whether it was going to be the right thing for me or if it was going to upset me. I used to be very much in a shell. Do you believe that? I was very bashful, very quiet, and if somebody had so much as said something to me that I would take as derogatory, I'd have probably cried. No way I would stand up and fight.

I think the breakdown was really a combination of many things. I had always been out in a public relations type of job, in the employment office and in industrial relations, and I really liked dealing with the public. Then suddenly, two children in two years. The first two are twelve months and three weeks apart. We lived out in the country at the time and I didn't even drive. My husband was going to school four nights a week and working full-time. And I was just climbing the walls.

So they suggested I go back to work. My doctor thought that would help, and so I did. But I really think that it was just too much pressure and it finally got to me. I felt the discrimination all the way along. For the first year I was at the fire station I was constantly proving myself to the men, proving that I could do the job. I guess I was back at work for about a year and a half, and then I was hospitalized for thirty days.

I was extremely nervous and I kept everything inside. I hadn't learned to speak out, to say what I really felt. But eventually I learned and evidently I was a little bit successful! One thing I can remember very clearly was one day when I was in the hospital and I was having migraine headaches at the time. The doctor would come in the morning and then they'd have these group sessions. So I asked him before the session this one morning if I could have something for a headache. He said, "Bring it up in the group."

Well, I never talked in the group. I just sat and listened. I just couldn't bring myself to say anything in front of all those people, you know? So after the group session was over, I went up to him and asked him again for something for my headache. He just said, "I told you to bring it up in the group session." Well, I was reduced to tears. I just fell apart. So he said, "Well that's exactly what we're going to work on."

At that time, they had a chairman of the group that had to kind of lead the discussion and everything, and he was going home in the next couple of days. So the doctor said, "I'm going to appoint you chairman." So I said, "No, I just can't do that." I couldn't even bring myself to talk, much less to speak for others and try to lead the discussion and the activities that they planned.

It was a private hospital and they have a very good program there. I think everybody, even people who aren't depressed, should go through it. They would come out much more understanding individuals. They force you to learn an awful lot about yourself and how you really feel about life and everything else too. It's a beautiful experience, it really is.

So he appointed me chairman of the group and I was scared. Oh, was I scared. But I learned to speak up. He said, "I think that's what you need." He said I had the potential and I wasn't using it. I wasn't even sure I had the potential! But I learned to try.

Well, I was out for probably another month, and then I went back to work. My boss at the fire station was great. They're friends of ours, he and his wife. He was very understanding and helped me a lot. I was still under the psychiatrist's care for about a year, just learning to speak out. He kept telling me over and over, "Say what you think." And I had to learn to, as difficult as it was for me.

After I went back to work, I got pretty involved in union activities, which I hadn't done before. At that time I was the only woman in the union and I was self-conscious and I felt, well, the guys don't want me there. I didn't feel I belonged down there and I thought the fellows might resent it. And I really never had anything that important to say at the time anyhow. Now I don't care if they want me there or not! I'm going to be there.

I'm on civil rights now for our local. I went to a women's rights seminar in Gary dealing with discrimination and this man from management got me so angry I cussed him out afterward. He stood up and said, "We had some women who filed a charge with the Department of Defense stating that we discriminated." He said, "We were so anxious to settle this that we hired not one, but we hired five women into plant security."

He said, "We've had no incidents yet, so we don't know how they will react when they run into a troublesome situation. They've never handled a drunk or worked alone or anything like that."

Well, I was sitting in the audience and I was really upset. Here I'd worked a one-man gate and I walk patrol and I've been subjected to everything the fellows have for two years. I've had a dope addict, I've had drunks at three or four o'clock in the morning when I'm there alone, and it really upset me to sit and listen to this man stand up there and tell the heads of corporations that they don't know if women can handle the job.

I couldn't get the floor then. They only had about three questions and answers and then they adjourned. And I'm sure they did it on purpose because they knew we were there, the Steelworkers NOW. We got no chance at all to challenge him on any of his statements. But afterward, I went up to him and I just really told him off. I just couldn't let that go, when I've done my job and everything the fellows have done. And, in fact, I think women can handle some problems a lot better than men.

A woman's best weapon is her mouth. Usually I've found you can talk your way out of things. Once I had a guy who was high on dope and he'd been in the mill for five hours, and he wasn't scheduled to work. He was leaving, and the canteen had been broken into while he was in there, so he was a suspect and he had to account for his whereabouts. He wasn't going to at first, but he ended up doing it!

When I worked the truck gate, you get a lot of drivers who've been in the mill anywhere from four to eight hours trying to load one load of steel, and they're a little uptight when they come out. Some of them are hiked up on uppers, because they're driving long hauls, maybe for twelve or twenty-four hours straight. So they come to the gate after getting the runaround all over the mill, and if they don't have the right paperwork when they get to the gate, they're not too happy.

But ninety-nine percent of the time I have no trouble with them. With the fellows, it seems like they'll clash with another man, where usually I can talk them around it, talk nice to them. You have to have a little bit of personality, or try, any-how. A person who's ready to fight right away is in trouble on that job.

I had one truck driver tell me one time he was going to wipe up the scales with me. He was very upset and it was ten o'clock at night and I was the only one out there. He's going to wipe up the scales with me! And he was a big guy, and what was I going to do? I don't want to pull a gun on somebody unless I'm going to use it and I didn't have Mace at the time, so I just looked at him and said, "Just go ahead. It's been that kind of day anyhow."

Well, he looked at me like, "You dumb broad." But then he started to laugh about it. I said, "Now, come on, you. Let's talk it over." So you can pretty much talk your way out of a situation. He would have busted any one of the guys right in the mouth. Really. But usually you can bring them around to your way of thinking.

I had almost no training. Very little. They gave me a gun. I wear a thirty-eight and we have target practice, so I can shoot. But when I first asked for Mace, I was told it was too dangerous. I was sitting there wearing my thirty-eight and they told me that Mace was too dangerous. So I said, "Do you think this isn't?" They just laughed, but they weren't going to do anything.

Then I asked for training to protect myself, some sort of physical training like karate or anything. They said, "No, that's your own responsibility." And Mace is too dangerous. So I pretty much just took it on my own then and I got myself some Mace. Evidently, they just weren't going to give me whatever it was I wanted when I first went in.

Well, after they put the five women on the department, they came around and gave us all a can of Mace. So I said, "I guess it's not dangerous anymore!" I thought it was rather ironic that once they had five, they finally had to accept us, I guess. When they just had one, I don't think they would have cared too much if something had happened.

I still get a few jeers, but very few. I've been on two years now and the others have been on six months, so they're pretty much used to seeing women. Every once in a while, if I work a different assignment or on overtime or fill in for somebody, they'll do a double take because they're not used to me. And of course you get a lot of comments, you know, like, "The guards are getting better looking" and that type of thing. But that helps break the ice between the two of you.

As I said, my husband has really been understanding. But the way we look at it, I need to work. I can't afford to quit. So if I'm going to work, he has a job, I have a job, and we both have the one at home. He can iron and wash clothes and everything else, so he helps. He's not exactly fond of it, but it has to be done! He didn't always. After my breakdown he started. I think he realized then that it was too much for me.

I think I had resented it for a long time, you know. I had two jobs and he had one. But I had never said anything. I didn't let it show, what was bothering me. So we had to learn to hash it out between ourselves and finally he began to understand how I felt and I understood more how he felt.

If I didn't work, we couldn't afford this house and the taxes on it. We couldn't afford to eat out occasionally. A lot of things. The last two years we took vacations and we never did before that. This year we splurged. We really went all out and went all the way down to Florida, camping. We wouldn't be able to do that if I wasn't working.

But also I need a sitter from Tuesday to Friday every week. On midnights or day shift, either way, she comes in at 7:30 and leaves whenever I get up or get home, which is usually around three in the afternoon. On three to elevens, I only need her from one to five, but I pay her the same—eleven dollars a day. And during the school year she only has the baby. It's a lot of money, but I don't think I'm really ready to put Julie into a nursery school. She's three, but I'd just as soon wait at least another year and I think I can afford that until she gets into school.

We just transferred to salary. With the last contract, we're salaried union instead of wage, and now we make $395 every two weeks. And we're paid for being off sick. That's just about the only benefit we got in the new contract besides the raise that all steelworkers got. Being wage, you don't get paid when you're off sick. You have to be off seven days and then upon doctor's certification they have to start paying you from the seventh day on for six months. Now, when you're off sick, you get paid, period. Up to six months. All salaried workers have this. But as the fellows start abusing it, I'm sure we'll need a doctor's slip every time we're off!

Leonard started working as a standard checker while he was going to school. It was shiftwork, an industrial engineering job. He dealt with bonuses, figuring incentive rates. You observe how they're working out in the field and you either cut their bonus or add to it, based on productivity and how hard they're working. It's a salaried non-union job. They couldn't have a union person doing that job.

About three years ago he got his degree in industrial engineering, going to night school. Now he's in costs for new construction and things like that—setting standards for larger projects. He's kind of concerned with the whole department of production, whether they're making money or losing money and cutting costs. That's salaried non-union too, so he doesn't have the union protection we have. It's one step under management.

I guess we both work pretty hard. Other than his job and finishing our house, he also does some small contracting for other people. He enjoys doing anything with his hands. I think he'd make a better construction worker than an industrial engineer. He's more that type of person. He really built this house from scratch, starting with digging the foundation. I was the mortar mixer when he needed the blocks!

There are times when my husband and I have talked about whether I would want to quit working, and I really don't. He once told me I was a better wife when I'm working. I said, "Does that mean I'm a bad wife when I stay home?" He said no, that he just feels I need to be out with people. He understands that my own type of personality is I don't like being cooped up in a house. I'm not the typical housewife that likes coffee klatches and lounging around.

And when the challenge came, Leonard stood up to it just as much as I did. He's just very broad-minded and he's against any kind of discrimination. I couldn't do what I'm doing with the Steelworkers NOW and all that if he wasn't behind me. It takes a lot of time on both of our parts. When I go to meetings and make trips to Chicago and get myself all involved in things, he's baby-sitting. So I just couldn't do it if he didn't help.

I really didn't expect to get as much support and encouragement from him as I did, because it does take a lot of time away from him and the children, and I'm sure at times he resents that. But he doesn't say too much, just things like, "Don't get yourself over-involved." I think he's afraid more for my own sake that I'll overdo it and get too worked up. He knows that I take things very seriously. When I get into something, I really get into it. So he doesn't want me to become over-committed and then get frustrated if we don't accomplish what we want.

STEELWORKERS NOW

The story I first heard about the women at U.S. Steel getting together with NOW—the National Organization for Women—was that Mary Jean Collins-Robson, who's the president of Chicago NOW, said some men had called her. One was a big official of what we call our large local, 1066, the wage workers. My local is small. We only have sixty-five members and now two of us are women. See, in our contract, the guards have to be separate from the workers they're guarding, so 1066 is where most of the workers are.

I know most of the people in 1066 and some of them had been talking to me down at the gate. They asked if I was interested in going to this NOW and I said I certainly was. And I got another girl, Marie Scott, who's a friend of mine from out in the mill. She's a member of 1066 but she wasn't active in union activities. So just a few of us kind of got together and went up there for our little meeting.

We went because we wanted to stop some of the discriminatory practices against women, period. Not only ourselves. By that time, what they had done to me was pretty much over and done with, and Scottie never had any problems. But we knew the problems existed and somebody needed to do something about it.

I missed the first big meeting. That was right before Christmas in '73 and I was in the hospital having surgery. But I've been to every one since. And there've been a lot of women there that were loud and clear that there is discrimination in the mills. Each meeting we get more and more women there and lately we've had several from other plants who read about us in the paper and heard about the consent decree.*

Some are from Bethlehem Steel, some from Inland, some from Youngstown. They want to know what they can do and they're hoping that what we've called our Steelworkers NOW— a chapter we're trying to organize—can help them if they want to join. There are lots of things wrong in their plants too.

When we started, we tried in our own plant to get coopera- tion from the unions. We wanted mailing lists of all women employees so we could contact them, but we've been unable to get that. At one time they told us that they didn't have it broken down by sex, it was strictly initials. Then right after they told us that, they sent out a booklet about the new con- tract and it had individual first names on it. So it was just their way of putting us off and not giving us what we want.

The unions just don't seem to want to push this too much! And then there are very few women in the mill who are union to begin with. Most women that were hired since the war are hired for clerical jobs and a lot of them are content there. They're hired mostly into accounting, and this is the type of job they want. So they're not too concerned with the women out in the mill who are fighting and having some problems.

At first when we started to organize, the men thought it was funny. But I think they're beginning to see that we mean busi- ness. I can mainly talk about our department and our local,

---

* Consent decree, signed in May 1974 by the United Steel Workers of America, nine major steel companies, and the U.S. Departments of Jus- tice and Labor and the Equal Employment Opportunity Commission, to bring employment practices in the steel industry into compliance with Title VII of the Civil Rights Act. It established new rules for job trans- fers, training and promotions aimed at opening up seniority channels to black, Spanish-surnamed and female employees. Under the decree, $30.9 million in back pay was awarded by the companies and the union to members of those three groups who were victims of past discrimination. It also established numerical goals and timetables for their advancement into the higher paying trade and craft jobs and apprenticeships, formerly dominated by white males.

but the majority of men in the mill are white and they're not too behind us. Some are, but most see women as a threat to their job out there in the mill. They're very upset about this new consent decree that we have. But I think for the most part the black males have really helped us. Maybe they can understand the oppression more and feel this need to demand your own rights.

Since that initial contact with the Chicago NOW, we haven't gotten much union cooperation. It turns out that this was purely a political move within 1066. They had a lot of women that were really pushed around a lot before the assorting department was eliminated. Quite a few are older women and a lot of them experienced an awful lot of discrimination through the years. And a lot of them stood up and fought.

At one time, the assorting room was where they used to check the tin sheets. They called them tin flippers. During the war, they hired over three hundred women there because they couldn't get men. Afterward, they kept all the women in this one area and they really didn't hire women into labor jobs, period. There were very few women anyplace else in the mill. A few janitors, but that's about it.

Well, when the assorting room went down, they retired a lot of women. Tried to get rid of them. Some they gave clerical tests to, to see if they were smart enough to take a clerical job. You know, this was the attitude. I was in the employment office at the time so I know a little about this. But many they just transferred temporarily out into labor jobs in a department. And for the longest time, unless these women went on their own and got a permanent transfer, they didn't even belong to the department they were working in.

We have women who had been out in various departments working labor jobs for five, ten years, but they were supposedly still working for the assorting room. This was before it was permanently closed down. That was management's way of keeping them from promoting. They'd stay on the lowest classed job. So the company could hire someone off the street, put him on a labor job and he could promote all the way up to stocker or crane man. She had to stay on labor because she was subject to recall.

Well, we finally stopped that. This is one of the things that the NOW has done since we've put some pressure on the union. One of the local agreements in this last contract was that if you work in a department for a year, you become a regular in that department, a permanent employee, unless you don't want to be. This means you can go on to a seniority unit and promote.

I don't think 1066 intended for the NOW group to blossom as large as it did. I kind of got that impression at the last meeting. NOW wants to expand to the mills around here that are interested and any other unions that feel they have problems that we could help them with. But this one official who has a lot of power in 1066 wants to keep this strictly within the locals on our side of the plant.

True, he wanted the women in our locals here to stand up and fight some. But he never intended for us to go into the EEOC and file a class action suit, which we did. Or for us to start holding these big meetings and getting people outside the mills involved and getting the publicity that we got. And I'm sure he's getting the company officials breathing down his back to stop it.

Before NOW, I had intended to go by myself to the EEOC at one point and my union president, Leonard Tomajewski, was strictly behind me. But if I had filed charges myself with the EEOC, it wouldn't have been nearly as effective. There's supposedly a four- to five-year backlog of cases to begin with, so it wouldn't have come up for years.

But also, NOW was instrumental in getting us in the consent decree. They were not considering women at all at first. It was only black and Spanish-surnamed Americans. Baloney on women. But we made a little bit of noise and the NOW went to bat for us, putting some pressure on some people. I'm sure this is the only reason why we were included. I couldn't have done that alone, by the way. I'll take on a lot, but I won't take on the whole government!

What we did was, about twenty or twenty-five of us filed a class action suit with the EEOC. Then we went down to Birmingham, to the federal court there, to challenge the consent decree. It seems we may get back pay under this decree, which the NOW told us we're entitled to because they have to pay for past discrimination. But at this point, we aren't sure of the status of our charges. It seems like they keep changing their mind about how they're going to implement it.

It's all very confusing. The way they told me, it covers only people hired before January 1, 1968. But the way I read it, it says that blacks and Spanish-surnamed Americans hired before that date and women hired as of the date of the signing of the decree—in May of this year—are covered. I was hired, rehired actually, in March of '68, so if they interpret it one way I'm not covered, nor are any other women who have been discriminated against for the past five years, which is what they contend—that they didn't discriminate before five years ago!

At first, when the NOW told me I was involved in Birmingham, I wasn't upset about it at all. I figured all of us were in it together. I had thought Judy Lonnquist, NOW's lawyer, would take the whole group, you know? But at the last meeting here, I found out that was not the case. She chose three individuals to represent us and I was one. So I'm sure I'm tops on U.S. Steel's list again!

One is a woman down in Birmingham who was terminated because she was married shortly after the war. U.S. Steel didn't hire married women. During the war they took anyone, but afterward they fired them. They gave the jobs back to the men who were coming back from the war. This woman still had her termination slip and several other things, so she represented all past employees who were discriminated against.

Judy chose me to represent all present employees who are not covered by the decree, the way she interprets it, because I don't have the five years' seniority that would entitle me to back pay, since I had left for a while when I had my first two kids. So this was a way of pointing out how the decree is inadequate. And then evidently there's another woman who represents future employees.

When the decree was finally signed, it named both the steel companies and the union, the international. It says that the nine major steel companies and the international will have to pay $30.9 million in back wages. It sounds like a lot, but it's really nothing for those companies. And from what I've heard, the union's payment will come out of what's supposed to be our strike fund, so it won't hurt them either.

The company has really been stalling about implementing

the decree. And none of the people on the committee to implement it are the people who are directly concerned. Two of the fellows are white and one is black, but he's a very staunch union man, more than he's a black, I think. And then there's the government man. So there's no woman and nobody out front representing minorities. I think the international set it up that way.

It's unfortunate, but I think most of your women in the mill are afraid to really push. They're afraid of harassment. They can make it really difficult on anyone if they want to, you know, and women have had it difficult enough. When they get into a department and everything gets calmed down, they pretty much want it to stay that way. I think we have up to seventy-five women maybe who have attended one or more of our Steelworkers NOW meetings. As far as regulars, maybe fifteen that we could really count on. It isn't nearly enough, but they're hearing about us now and we're growing.

Many of your women out in the mill are your older women, and then they did hire quite a few black women three or four years ago. I think a lot of these women are afraid that this is a radical group, even though we aren't, you know. Also, most women feel they have their union to go to, even though their unions haven't done much for them. They don't know what outside sources they have and they're not that trustful of organizations they would consider more radical.

From my point of view, many of the girls that have helped us, I don't think are radical enough. They're concerned about their own problems in the mill, but that's it. They're not concerned about the whole scope of women's problems, which is why we've run into the problem with the union that we have.

At one of the meetings they proposed a bill of rights—some of the things we're fighting for—that the NOW and the women steelworkers got together on. Well at first they didn't include anything about pregnancy leaves and I thought they should. The mill treats a maternity leave separately; they don't class it as a disability. So you get six weeks' pay, but they force you to take a leave.

I was working all three times when I was pregnant. With the first two, I was forced to quit at four months. So I was out

five months before and two months after, and for seven months
I got a total of six weeks' pay. The third time I was allowed to
work seven months. But when you go on a maternity leave,
your insurance ends the last day of the last month that you
work. When you go on any other type of disability, your insurance is carried for six months. Now this is discrimination!

So I brought this up under the bill of rights, that this is
something we needed to work on changing. Hmmmm. Well
most of them were past childbearing age to begin with, so they
weren't too concerned about it. But surprisingly enough, there
were two that were very vocal against it. You know, "Anybody
that's foolish enough to get pregnant doesn't deserve to get
paid," and everything else.

But we ended up getting a majority and it passed. I had
learned in sorority, and I found it in every other organization,
the guy that gets his pitch in first usually gets the victory. Nine
times out of ten, if you can get your argument in first, you've
got the battle three-quarters won. I think the majority is a
silent majority, kind of wishy-washy, and they don't know
which way to go, so you can often swing them to your side.

I'm sure that most of those women there felt, you know, we
don't need to bother with this. We've got other problems. But
I had my plan pretty well thought out to begin with. Actually,
we ended up with a modified plan. I said I wasn't asking for
full pay for maternity leave, even though I personally think it
should be that way. But I don't feel that U.S. Steel is ready for
this. That will be our next step. Sometimes you have to take
things a little bit at a time. So what I said was that at least the
insurance should be paid for the full time you're off. They
finally went along with that much of it, so it's a start.

What we've gotten so far through the NOW has really
helped us. The local issue regarding the transfers into the departments and becoming permanent employees. That won
quite a few women over. They saw we actually accomplished
something. Then of course the fact that we intervened to get
women included in the consent decree and some of them are
going to get some money out of it, hopefully. And they realize that if the NOW had not gotten on this they would not
have been included. But how involved they're willing to get,

I honestly don't know. I don't really think we have too many feminists in the mills. If we do, I don't know where they are. But there must be some somewhere!

There are three of us that are pretty much leading the Steelworkers NOW group. But we're having a real organizational problem. The other two who are in 1066 have not experienced the type of situations that I have, and I don't think they're ready to stand up and fight as much. They don't want to make waves. I want to get a real chapter started with women in other mills and even community-wide, but the other two aren't really that interested. They want to keep it strictly within their local and I'm sure they're getting some pressure from their union officials to keep it small.

What I'd really like is to have an organization like they have in Chicago, the NOW there. That's an organization I could join. I can see where they go with a group to talk to their congressman and they stand behind what they believe in, rally behind it. Like they demonstrated against an employment agency that was discriminating. I think that's great when they get out and do that. But so far, what can I do as an individual? You can just take so much of the pressures alone, you know? It gets to where it feels like you're fighting just everyone and you get very tired of that after a while. We have to get an organization going here first.

The NOW women in Chicago were trying to help us get set up as a functioning organization right away. But the other two women claim it's too much work if we get larger and they don't have the time to devote to it. So they asked me if I would handle it, the Chicago women did. It does involve a lot of work. And it's going to be doing a lot of bucking. Some people aren't going to like it.

My own situation is a little precarious to begin with. A lot of the women in the mill don't trust me because of my job. A lot of people just mistrust any type of authority. You know, anyone who carries a gun is a policeman. So a lot of people kind of steer away. I don't have any trouble with the men in the mill, but I guess a lot of the women resent having to show a badge.

I'm stricter with the women than the men guards are. Most of the guys are more lenient. It's, "How're ya doin', cutie!" and on in they go. So they resent having to dig for that badge for me. But I can't afford to do different. If I were doing favors for the women employees, right away I'd be suspected.

The ones who get to know me as a person, at meetings or something, don't sense this. But the ones who only see me on the job, it's two completely different personalities. My job doesn't really fit my personality too much. You have to have that authority and you have to be a little strict and you might step on somebody's toes occasionally. Hopefully, most people can see beyond that, but some can't.

I've learned to not take it personally though. A few years ago, I couldn't have done it. I would have been crushed if someone said something. But you learn to realize that they're not talking to you as a person, they're talking to you as a guard. You have to learn to completely separate those two identities. It took a while! It's going on two years now, but with experience you learn to disassociate yourself from that guard there that's giving them a hard time.

I think competition between women is another factor here, in our NOW group, and I didn't want to see it. I was hoping that this organization wouldn't be that way. I don't know why I expected it to be any different, but there is a lot of pettiness. I think if there are differences, you should be able to take care of them in private, rather than getting in front of the group and saying something sarcastic or derogatory, you know? Have a time when you get together and settle it before the meeting. But I think, on the whole, women don't do that. The Chicago NOW does and I was encouraged to see that.

I think there's a little animosity there. I honestly think sometimes that they resent my job. It's a public showmanship type of job, which a lot of women find extremely glamorous. It has a lot of disadvantages, but it's a good job for a woman. To have a thousand men go through the gate and everybody call her by name and say something nice, a lot of women look at this and they're jealous of it.

But I think our main problem is that our aims are completely different to begin with. They just want a little union subcommittee and I want a whole organization. One of the leaders from 1066 is a very dynamic person, very good at getting up in front of a group and carrying on about something.

But she's not a feminist. Definitely not. All she wants is equal rights for women on the job, and that's the scope of the way she wants the organization to go. But on-the-job problems are handled mainly through the union. We can only do so much in that area at this point.

A COMMITMENT TO CHANGE

If our NOW group did become a community effort, we could get into things like day care. That's a definite drawback in this area. There's nothing, and baby-sitting is very expensive. See, in an area like Hobart, it's a small percentage of women who work, so they don't push for these things. Now I'd say your black women in Gary itself, they're really pushing for this. This would be a good place to start.

I brought up day care at the last meeting we had. We were talking about U.S. Steel sponsoring a day care center like some companies do, where you can bring your kids who aren't in school yet and you can see them at noon. But there was a total lack of support for that, through U.S. Steel. And I don't think our unions would ever get into that. We are such a minority within our locals that they're not that willing to go all out for women's rights. It's just not a politically advantageous move for them.

Well, where we go from here, I don't know. I've pretty much left it to the Chicago NOW to discuss, because they know the friction we're having here. And they want it to expand and they know I feel the way they do. But a few weeks ago I met two girls out here at the county fair and now I think maybe we have a chance. Before that, I was a little afraid you know, because I had no one else to help me. But these two girls were very enthusiastic and said they knew a lot of others they could contact and we could get a group going in Highland, the Gary area. So maybe the light has been lit for us. Then we could have women from the other steel plants and from the retail outlets like Sears, and from all over.

If we do get going I'd like to be able to work with young girls and their problems. Just from my own experiences, I know at that time I needed someone to talk to. And I think young girls today, the situation in the world is such that they need even more emotional guidance at times. Things like what they want to do with their lives. If their mothers are browbeating them into the old mold, and if they don't feel they can fit into that old mold, maybe they need some encouragement to be their own type of person.

And counseling, too, for girls in school. Just like what happened to me. They told me I should be a mechanic, but . . . ! Or let's say if a girl is pregnant and needs counseling on whether to have an abortion or have the baby or what. This is the kind of thing I'd choose to do if we ever can get to that point.

I guess I was always interested in the Women's Movement. There's a show on Sunday mornings, *Feminine Forum* I believe it's called. In fact, some of the NOW girls have been on there. There are always the few radicals, you know, but on the whole I always felt I could associate with them.

I listen to debates occasionally and panel discussions on television, and it interested me from the very beginning. I kind of followed it in the papers too. I think I just happen to believe in human rights, not just women's rights. I just believe that all people should be treated equally and everybody should have the right to decide what they want to do.

After that first NOW meeting up there in Chicago, I came back and told my husband that they were the most down-to-earth people and that we shared so many of the same ideas, that I really felt very comfortable with them. I think as long as I had been going to sorority, I didn't feel any of them were really my friends. They're social friends and that, but if I needed someone to talk to, there wouldn't be a one I'd really feel comfortable with. They're too disapproving of too many of the things I believe in.

The NOW women are just nice people. I didn't find any of this high-handedness at all in any of them. In fact several people that have this attitude about them, well I wish they could meet some of the girls, because until I met them that's kind of what I expected too, I guess. I've only had about one semester of college, which is nothing, you know. But I've been out in the world a lot. So you kind of combine the two, and you get your hands on everything you can and start reading. You try to become informed, even though you haven't had the education maybe that some of these others had.

I mean, I didn't know anything, really. I was going in completely unaware of what could be done—the proper agencies, the proper channels, what actually your rights were. All I knew was basically just what I had read in the papers. But then the NOW put me in charge of complaints for our steelworkers' group, so I had to know what our rights were. I had to do a lot of research, and they gave me a lot of literature, and that helped me. It encouraged me a lot.

I probably have changed a lot. I'm not sure if it's a result of all this or as a result of my job. Probably a combination of the two. I'm sure I'm much more composed, for one thing. I couldn't ever get up in front of a group and speak before, or do anything of this sort, and the job I have now is more or less a show job. I'm in front of people all the time. And I've learned to adapt to that, where before I would have been very self-conscious and very uptight about the whole situation.

I don't do much speaking in front of groups, but when we've had our meetings and I've had something to say, I don't hesitate at all. If I had to make a speech or something, maybe I'd be a little bit nervous. But, like when we were proposing the bill of rights, I had come up with three or four amendments or changes and no one else had any. It seemed like I was pretty much leading the discussion. I just kept jumping in there and I was kind of surprised at myself afterward!

I think maybe I have more of an awareness of some things than some other women, possibly because it's been forced on me. Maybe I've been through a little bit more than some, and it's just the experience, the fact that having been through it I can see it all a little more clearly. In this general area, I think women are pretty content as they are. But when you get out of Hobart itself, there is quite an awareness that hasn't hit here yet. Hopefully it will.

I think there's been a lot of changes in the past few years. If nothing else, women are more aware of their rights. There's been a lot of publicity, and a few people working very hard to make women more aware of what their rights are. And I think some women are becoming more restless, less satisfied with their own lives and looking further, searching out something that's been missing.

I hope my daughters' lives will be more like my life the way it is now. I think they're both very sensitive. My son is also the same way. And I don't think they have these stereotyped ideas about people. They seem to just like people in general. We've tried to explain to our son that women are the same as men, can do the same things. Already he hears other children downgrading women. He's only eight and it happens already. Kathy, who's seven, has been encouraged to do anything she wants to, even if it's something boys do supposedly, you know. I tell her there's nothing she can't do if she wants to and I think she's responded to that real well.

I really do believe that when you're more of an individual, more of a person, it can only help a marriage. It sure has helped mine. I think that unless a man is threatened by it, and then he has problems, it can't do anything but help. And if it can help marriages, it can help the whole country, the whole society.

I guess I'm always trying to change things in some way, to some extent. But you take a corporation the size of U.S. Steel, I've learned you just really can't buck them. It's a lot of work. It's a real concentrated effort. And it's the same thing with the government. It takes a lot of public pressure to get anything changed. And it takes an organization, not an individual.

But I do have more hope now. I've seen that there are others concerned and I think this is the problem of the silent majority today. They feel they're alone. And yet when we get together, we can do a lot. I used to feel I couldn't do anything because I was just one person, but the more I began talking with people, I found out that there was a real need out there and that if you get to the right people you can accomplish a lot. So it gave me a lot of faith.

But I don't push how I feel about many things. Oh, once in a while I'll throw in something in a conversation, but I don't try and push what I believe in. Everyone has the right to their own ideas. So maybe I don't make a good leader, you know? I don't think it does any good to try and cram anything down anyone's throat. If anything, I think it gets their back up.

I think the only way you can really prove things is to do your own little part as an individual. Like when I first took this job, I had to prove to them that women could handle it. Before this, I had been brought up to think women were inferior and I believed it. It wasn't actually until I started doing what they considered a man's job and found out that I could do it just as well that I actually began to believe this. And I found men to be no different. They're just as petty as they say women are!

I know I'd never make a very good politician. I'm too blunt. I'm not afraid to speak out and say what I think, and a lot of people resent that. In a leader they want you to be kind of wishy-washy and I'm not that way. You have to learn to go all the way around things without ever saying head on what you really believe, to please both sides. I know I'd have a difficult time doing that.

It's interesting, but evidently this big official in 1066 feels that I have some support, because a while ago he came to me at the gate. He comes and sits down in the guard shanty and wants to talk to me. Then he started on about how he wants my support for Sam Evett in this coming international election. I don't know if you heard, but there was vote fraud in the last election for the district director of the Steelworkers. So they went to the Department of Labor and they're having a new election.

Now 1066 admitted vote fraud for Evett and this guy was going to clean it up and everything. Well, he comes back and he wants my support for Evett after all this, because he says that Abel* and the rest of the international in Pittsburgh will not give us anything if we go for Sadlowski,† Evett's opponent. So it's strictly a matter in the union of "don't make waves."

* I. W. Abel, president, United Steelworkers of America, since 1965. Moved up through union hierarchy. Helped organize the first Congress of Industrial Organizations (CIO) local in Canton, Ohio, in 1936. Elected a vice president and executive council member of the AFL–CIO in 1965; chosen president of its industrial union department in 1968.

† Edward Sadlowski, at age thirty-five won control of District 31, the largest local of the United Steelworkers in America, by a two-to-one margin over Samuel C. Evett (backed by I. W. Abel) in November 1974. The U.S. Labor Department closely monitored the election, due to widespread voting fraud in an earlier contest between the two, the results of

So when this guy came to me I said to him, "Evett did nothing for me when I needed help." You know, when my grievance was taking place. "Well, I'll tell you," he says, "he hasn't
done anything for women's rights, but he's going to." I said,
"Oh, really. I can't vote on promises." But this guy honestly
felt I should vote for Sam Evett because he wanted me to and
it would be politically advantageous to us.

So I told him, "You show me what he will do and then let
me talk to Sadlowski, and you let me decide who's going to do
what." Because Sadlowski had been much stronger about wom-
en's rights from what I'd heard and what I'd seen. So I said,
"I want to do some research on it." People don't look into candidates. Local 1066 says, "Vote for Evett," so everybody follows.

So many times, people just sit back and let things happen.
They don't want to get involved. A lot of times they're not well
enough informed and they hear so many conflicting things that
they don't want to have to make up their mind. There's the
newspaper, the television reports and everything else and I
think sometimes they get confused and they'd rather not think
about it.

I hope Watergate will change all this a little. I think the
politicians are going to be watching each other very closely.
Especially if the Democrats get in, the Republicans are going
to try to do the same thing to them. So maybe they're going to
keep each other in line a little bit more. And I think the people
are going to keep them in line. I don't think the people are going to put up with this again.

You know what I'd really like to do? I'd like to be a police-
woman. I really would. But there are none in Hobart, and I'm
not too anxious to be the first one and go through all that hassle again. Also, my husband is not too fond of the idea. He

---

which were voided. Due to his repeated criticisms of I. W. Abel, his
election was seen as a sharp rebuff to the union's international leadership,
and tensions persist. A third-generation steelworker in District 31, he
makes frequent visits to workers in the plants, in the belief that the dues
payers—the rank-and-file members—should be giving advice to union
leaders, instead of the other way around. He attempted to hire additional
staff representatives, including a woman for the first time, but his request
was refused by USWA leadership.

thinks it's dangerous. I suppose it would be more dangerous than a guard's job.

Otherwise, I think I'd do it. I feel I need a commitment to the community in some way, and I'd like to work with youngsters. I think they're the ones that need help today. I'm quite concerned about the dope problem and even the drinking problem. And the lack of guidance that I think a lot of them have in the homes. Gary is a big drug area and, because we live so close by, I think the drugs are readily available. In Gary they have some programs for kids, but around here they pretend it doesn't exist. The children know it does, the high school kids, and they know who the pushers are, but of course they tend to stand up for each other.

The parents seem to resent it if a teacher comes and says, "We think your child is on drugs." They refuse to believe it and they take it personally, that they have done something wrong. It seems like the parents are not as concerned about the welfare of the child as they are about their own image. They get angry at the school board. There was a case recently where parents were going to sue the school board for saying that they thought that this child was on drugs. I would thank them if they told me about a child of mine and I didn't know it.

The only thing I know of outside of Gary is a phone rap line, Contact Cares, where youngsters can phone in their problems and discuss drugs or abortion or anything they want to. And this interests me a lot. I wish I had some time to devote to it. Maybe I should make time. In a couple of years, the kids will be a little older and I hope I'll be able to do that. I'm happy with the freedom I have now and I love my job, but it would be nice to have a little more time to pursue some of the things I'd like to do.

I do hope that things will be a lot better for the next generation. I think they might, because the young people today are more aware. They're striving harder and they won't put up with a lot of the shimsham business that's been going on. I have great faith in the young people of today. Hopefully they'll correct some of the mess we've gotten ourselves into.

• POSTSCRIPT

Bonnie Halascsak wrote recently, "My life has changed so drastically since our interview that the first draft of the transcript hardly sounds like me. In the end, I just got fed up with the rat race. I've had a long hard fight and I'm tired."

In the middle of 1975, Bonnie left U.S. Steel, at least for the time being. She didn't want to have to endure the "hassles" she had on her last job. Continued problems related to sex discrimination on the job coupled with internal political struggles left her exhausted, depressed and in poor health. She may eventually decide to work part time at a different type of job, since Bonnie doubts that she can ever stop working completely. She is now looking forward to the opportunity of staying home for a while and taking some college courses, but she may have to postpone this "temporary retirement" due to the mills' economic problems, which reduced her husband's work week to four days.

In addition to on-the-job problems, Bonnie felt disappointed by the Chicago chapter of NOW, which had originally organized Steelworkers NOW. While she and some other women at U.S. Steel were trying to organize their own chapter, they ran into conflict with an existing—though inactive—chapter in the area, which claimed that the steelworkers' group could not organize a chapter within industry.

The Chicago chapter of NOW had understood that the local chapter in question was nonexistent. A great deal of confusion and an angry exchange of words followed. Bonnie described the experience as not being "particularly sisterly." Then, for a reason not fully understood, the Chicago chapter "dropped us like a hot potato." The upshot was that she and the others abandoned their efforts to form their own chapter. As Bonnie put it, "End of Steelworkers NOW and my attempt at being an organized feminist."

Reflecting on the more positive aspects of her experience, Bonnie feels that she accomplished her major objective: to prove that a woman can handle a so-called man's job. U.S. Steel Gary Works now has seven women in plant security and she believes that through the efforts of both Chicago NOW and Steelworkers NOW, the job situation has been improved for many women.

"I don't feel that my quitting is the end, but rather a beginning for me," Bonnie wrote. "I'm ready to move forward and that means continuing my education first. It's time for me now to decide what type of career I really want, and the job I had isn't it. There are many things I'd like to do with my life but first I need to regroup. I want to spend more time with my family, before the kids are grown and gone, and less time under pressures and schedules. Len and I decided we were just too busy to live life the way it should be done. Anyway, my doctor has slowed me down from a run to a walk and for once I feel at peace with the world. I see many things I don't like about the world we live in, but I no longer feel it's my duty to change those things alone.

"While I'm no longer organizing a community NOW chapter, I'm probably just as much a feminist as ever. I will certainly find time now to devote to our cause, although I don't know exactly what course I'll follow. In essence, I'm freeing myself to do what I want to do without the confines and limitations of a demanding job. I'm much happier, but wouldn't have missed the experience for anything. I've gained an awareness of the hardships women face in today's job market, but also I've gained a confidence in knowing that we can and will succeed in overcoming the many obstacles placed in our way. Whether we band together in a group or go it alone, we each have something to contribute."

Practical Politics

Rosalinda Rodriguez

Anita Cupps

In the Cotulla courthouse, Rosalinda Rodriguez and a legal assistant prepare for the challenge to her election as City Councilwoman.

Rosalinda and Roy Rodriguez at their home in Cotulla, Texas.

Rosalinda Rodriguez

A FAMILY OF MIGRANT WORKERS

I was born in Ohio on February 17, 1948. I think my father had a migrant job, but I don't really remember. I was too little and I haven't really asked. I was one of five in the family, four girls and one boy. I was next to the smallest. And we had one dog. I guess I've always liked dogs and cats. And flowers. I like to think I have a green thumb and can make things grow. You could say I like nature. I like to go out and walk and see all the different things.

My mother was from Artesia, Texas, about fifteen miles south of Cotulla. And my father was from Laredo. They were both born in the States. I guess my father was in the service and that's where he met my mother. Since my mother was divorced from him a long time ago, I don't really know that much. We lived in Laredo for some time and then we came to Cotulla. I was in third grade at that time.

My mother and father had already separated and my mother came here looking for work. She was a waitress and she was offered a position here in Cotulla. In fact, I think she won some little medal for being the best waitress in Laredo. She's liked that job a long time. She got married again when I was in the third grade.

Now that I'm married my father visits me sometimes. But then, when they first separated, I couldn't even remember his face, his features. When all of us were growing up, my mother had to be both parents to us until she met my stepfather. And then we had a lot of problems with my stepfather. He was the type where, instead of him disciplining us himself, he would go to my mother and get her to do it. Then he liked to drink a lot and he would push our mother around a lot. We would see that when we were little, and so that even pushed us further away from him.

When my stepfather came into the picture, I always thought they favored my older sister, the one just older than me. She's very different from us in color of skin. When we were younger, we always used to say that she was the milkman's daughter because she was so white compared to us. She's all freckled and really looks different from us, even though she talks just like us. Well, I felt they used to favor her. They'd go off with her and leave us home to clean house and all that.

When we came over to Cotulla, I must have been nine or ten. I remember I was very, very shy. I was retained a second year in the third grade because I was so shy. I knew the answers, but I just wouldn't talk, so they held me back. I'm not sure what made me that way, except maybe that I never had a close relationship with my mother. And then with what had already been happening at our house, I guess I didn't think I could trust anybody.

Then we had to migrate and that held us back too. We would go to Wisconsin and Illinois. We migrated usually in March, and school didn't finish until the last few days of May, so we would usually lose about three months. I guess that's why I graduated high school when I was already twenty. When I came back from up north, they usually put me in a slow group, so that really hindered my education. I went all through school with these different problems.

I must have been eleven or twelve when we started migrating. I remember I was real small because I couldn't even work. I guess my mother just couldn't make enough being a waitress to support us all, so we had to migrate too. We met somebody from Cotulla over in Kenosha, Wisconsin, who knew this nurseryman. So my mother and my stepfather and my brother, who was very young, too, and my older sister before me, they would all work in the nursery. They would transplant little seedlings into boxes and baskets and different things. And my stepfather would drive the truck all over to deliver Easter lilies and other kinds of flowers.

The oldest daughter of the family stayed back in Cotulla. She was seventeen and she was going to graduate that year and, by then, my mother and her were having family problems. I guess my sister wouldn't accept my new stepfather. She was closer to my father. So there was a real split there. Then she graduated and got married that year and migrated up north with her husband.

I remember we did the nursery and at one time we did some field work too—potatoes and tomatoes. Then I think it was in July that we'd go up to the northern part of Wisconsin, around Green Bay, and do the cherries. All the kids could pick cherries. But I know from March to June up where we were they wouldn't allow us to work because of the law. We had to be fifteen or sixteen. But since we were working in the nursery most of the time, there wasn't a very good chance of the law seeing us, so we could work some. Then when I was thirteen I couldn't work at all because I was sick. I got rheumatic fever. They treated me like I was real fragile because it affected my heart, even when I felt fine.

Except for missing school and friends, migrating up north was really fine for me. We would go in a car or in a truck and you got to see different things from one state to another, between Texas and Wisconsin, and that's what I liked most. But then my stepfather was so strict that, when we came to Wisconsin, all we did was work. Other friends who migrated would say it was like a vacation for them. They would work and then they'd go out to the dances and visit different places and they didn't really feel away from home because it was like a home over there. But we would work and then we lived around the television because there was no other activity.

We lived in one house that was so small it's hard to believe. There was one long room like a trailer house that we considered our living room. We had a sofa bed and some of us slept in there. Then we had another room where two double beds just fit with about two inches between them and some of us slept in there. We lived there from March until July every year. By then we knew this farmer, and we were guaranteed work there every year so there was no problem.

Since I couldn't go out to work, I was left at home to clean house. Sometimes I'd do the wash, sometimes I'd do the meals. That's mostly what I did from when I was thirteen till the last year we migrated, when I was about eighteen. But also I'd work in the nursery a lot because you don't do any real physical work there. You just stand there and transplant. We didn't have much field work where you'd have to carry heavy loads. We were migrants, but not in the sense you usually think of the migrant workers who go out in the fields all the time.

As far as the cold, we didn't feel it that much because we were inside the greenhouses a lot and they always had it warm in there. But in our house it was never warm enough. We had one of those gas heaters with the big pipe, but our employer used to pack straw in our houses to keep them warm. It was poor housing for where we lived, because we weren't like out on a ranch. We lived in the town. One of the main streets went right in front of our house. But I guess it wasn't really that bad compared to stories I used to hear from other migrants who came to the nursery. Some of them lived in really terrible conditions.

Then when I was about eighteen, in 1966 or 1967, we stayed home. My mother bought a restaurant and we got set up in business. She managed it and I helped her. To start off, me and my younger sister were the waitressses and she was the cook and we kind of managed that way. Then the following year my younger sister got married and all the others were married already, so that left only me. I still did the waitress bit and my mother was still the cook, because in Cotulla it's hard to find cooks unless you really pay them well. And along with paying them well, you have to go along with the air conditioning in the kitchen and good working conditions that are expensive.

The restaurant wasn't fancy, but it was big. It had a lot of Mexican food, and steaks and beer and different things, and it had a lot of business. The Anglos could come there and relax, and it was like a party house for them. There were three or four other restaurants in Cotulla, but I think they had a little more liberty there. My mother didn't set down any laws like they have now. Then you could come in any way you were dressed, even without shoes, and you didn't have a limit on how many beers you were served. The Anglos more or less ran it the way they wanted to and I guess they were a little spoiled.

My mother finally sold the restaurant. She was having trouble like with the waitresses, especially after I got married.

She was doing most of the work herself and it was ruining her health and there were lots of little disappointments. So she sold it and they moved to a small town outside San Antonio where she could get a good job and she wasn't under that much pressure.

My mother is Catholic and my stepfather is a Jehovah's Witness. But neither one was really that religious so there was nobody to tell us we had to go to church or to teach us the different customs. I remember one time when I was eleven or twelve we went to the sisters' house for Bible school during the summer here. What I remember now is that we had fun and I think that's the only reason we went. It was like a party, but besides that they taught you the Bible.

At that age I really didn't learn much. I would have liked to have gone on and that's what I'm trying to do now. I've started reading the Bible. I've got the Catholic one and the Baptist one for young adults and I'm comparing the chapters— the different wordings and the different ways of presenting things. I like to learn about the laws and the different things that happened then.

Even though I'm Catholic, I've considered other religions like Baptist or Methodist. In our church, the priest goes through the same thing every Sunday, every mass, and there's not much from the Bible. I noticed when we were invited to the Baptist church here that mostly everything is from the Bible. And I'm just realizing now that what happens in the Bible repeats itself and how you can read it to understand some of what's happening today.

I think I'm searching for something that I haven't found yet. I guess I was turned off by the Church so I hadn't been going and I had been getting to watch the evangelists every Sunday on television. There's this one that comes on and seems to preach the Bible pretty well. I know I get real emotional when I listen to him and some of the others. Something moves inside me when I hear them. But I haven't found that in the Catholic church.

I think being involved in the church is a way to bring people together more. I missed that when I was young and I still miss it. Before we got this last preacher at our church there were two who were very involved in the community and wanted to help the poor people. But the last one was from Spain and he started getting involved in politics, going over to the Anglo side. Religion and politics should never mix but he mixed them and he was even turning the young people away. Whenever Chicano families that were in need went for help, he could never help them. The Catholic church is one of the richest churches in the world but the Church in Cotulla has never helped any of the people that I know of.

Like I said, I was real shy in school, real quiet, just kind of embarrassed to talk. When people asked me something usually I would just answer "yes" or "no," so I didn't have that many friends. My sisters were a lot more popular than I was. One of the only teachers I ever liked was the teacher we had in the fourth grade. She was really good with the different crafts and she used to encourage me to draw a lot. I haven't drawn in a long time, but I really like to draw. I'd like to learn to be a cartoonist, but I don't think I'll ever get that good.

I had three classes of homemaking different years at school. Every year they'd get new stoves and the only time they ever used them was when they had a bake sale or a school carnival and they baked cookies or something. We never learned anything. But when I went up north to Wisconsin to the school there, that was a real homemaking class. They really let you cook. There were four in a group and we cooked and set the table and washed dishes like a little family.

In the Chicano family we're real informal at the table. We don't have a place setting for everybody. We hardly really use the fork and the spoon. Usually we use the tortilla. And we just use the cup, we don't use saucers. But like when you go out to a restaurant and you have all that silverware . . . well, if you're not taught it at school, where are you going to learn?

The teacher here in Cotulla used to spend most of her time telling us how she grew up and how her husband used to help her with the dishes. Then we had a homemaking cottage with the living room and the kitchen and a washer and dryer, but they were never really used. Some of us were used to sofas and things like that. But there were some kids who had never seen a washing machine or a dryer and didn't know how they worked, and we never really learned.

I guess school was something I had to do until I was sixteen, and by then I was already in high school so I thought I might as well finish it. We had already gotten so anglicized, it was like we were brainwashed into thinking we could really make it if we finished school. I always used to look down on somebody who would drop out of school. Also, I didn't see any other alternatives. My mother had her business then, and if I was at home I'd probably have to be helping her out. And they were so strict at home that school was a different kind of freedom. It was somewhere to go. We didn't get to go to dances, but once in a while we could go to a party or something. So school was like an adventure, I guess.

I think I would learn much more if I went to school right now than when I did go. We were young and it was mostly play. I know I barely got through some of my classes. I just didn't like school, period, and I didn't think I'd learned enough to make it through college, so I never thought much about going. I didn't see how college was going to help me at all.

Our school counselor was an Anglo and she was only interested in pushing the Anglo students ahead. Most of them went to college and that was mainly what she was there for—to look into colleges and help them get jobs or grants or something. You couldn't go to her with a problem and have her work it out. I didn't have that kind of confidence in her. She wasn't for us. In fact, I think she was a little against us.

I guess I'd like to be growing up now. There are so many different kinds of freedom. I remember when we were in school, we had to wear our dresses down to our knees. And there would be special meetings in the auditorium if the principal told the counselor he thought the girls were wearing too much makeup. And here she was, she'd sit with her legs wide open and she'd wear all the makeup she could get on her face.

But now, the girls go to school with shorts or with pants. And then we couldn't talk Spanish at all. Now they're much more at ease about that. But there weren't even any Chicano teachers then. I couldn't tell you if they have any better teachers now. I thought we had about the worst you could get, like the typing teacher who was an alcoholic and would drink right in front of us. They probably aren't much better now. But I think that I would learn more now.

MARRIAGE AND CHICANO POLITICS

When I was real young we spoke only English in my home. It wasn't like we were Mexican at all. Even the holidays. The only one we really celebrated was Christmas. The only celebration I remember in the town is the Sixteenth of September, when Mexico won its independence from Spain. It's like the Fourth of July. They usually celebrated three nights.

In August they'd choose three or four girls and then they had like a popularity contest for beauty queen. But usually you didn't win by popularity so much as by how much money you could raise more than the next girls. The girls had little cans with their pictures and names on them saying they were running for Sixteenth of September Queen, and they would leave them in the different stores and you'd put in a nickel or a dime or whatever you had. Then they'd work real hard to get their family to donate money.

The one who came out with the biggest amount was queen. One of my sisters won one year. Being crowned queen was a big deal. On the Sixteenth they had the crown and gown and the girls who came in second and third were like the princesses. They made this big court and they set the queen up on a throne in the plaza. There was lots of dancing all three nights and they had food stands and the cakewalk and bingos and all.

We still celebrate the Sixteenth now but we leave out the queen bit. We have a little fiesta out here in the plaza and the dances and the different stands and games. And the Raza Unida Party is trying to have the state make it an official holiday, or at least the city. We want to have school out on that day like Columbus Day. So far they won't do it, but we're going to keep on trying.

When I grew up I had already forgotten my Spanish but, when my mother remarried, my stepfather didn't speak English and he'd say, "If you want anything you're going to have to tell me in Spanish." So we learned to speak Spanish again. But even to this day, when my older sister tries to talk it she has an accent like you would and her words are kind of choppy. Her kids are growing up just with English too, so there's a real division there. She understands what we're trying to do with our movement, but she doesn't see it from where she lives right now. She lives up in Illinois and there's Anglos all around her. They accept you a little more there.

When I was in high school here in Cotulla, you weren't allowed to talk Spanish. If you talked it in class they'd punish you. I remember one time we had an exchange student from Mexico. We were seniors and she'd already finished school in Mexico, so she came over here to learn some English. We were in a history class and one day she wanted to explain a chapter or something but she didn't know English well enough so she started to say it in Spanish. Our teacher then was also our principal and he cut her right down and said, "I don't want to listen to any Spanish in this school."

At that time I felt very proud of myself because I knew English and I think I kind of looked down on her because she didn't. You know, this is the way we were brought up. Now I wish I had learned Spanish well when I was little. I can't even write it and there's still a lot of words that I don't know. We spend a lot of time now talking with the older people who speak it correctly.

In Cotulla, it's more like a slang. We're talking what they call a Tex-Mex Spanish. If you talk the correct language here a lot of the people won't understand what you're saying. But when we campaign, the speeches are mostly in Spanish. Most people understand you, but also what we're fighting is the gringos.* If you talk in English, you're going back to their language.

My mother used to say that I was always quiet and I'd listen, but when I was ready to say something I'd say what I'd be feeling. And I'd say the truth about everything that was going on. Well, now when I think back about some of the things that happened when I was younger, that kind of keep pushing me on in my political involvement, I always remember this one time in my mother's restaurant.

One night there was this real rich rancher in there who liked

*"Gringo" literally means "white foreigner" in Spanish. It is used pejoratively by Chicanos to refer to white Americans who are either bigoted or unfriendly to their cause. "Anglo" is the positive counterpart.

to drink a lot and he was kind of rowdy. We had one section in there where you came in and you could drink and get hamburgers, and another one which was more like a dining room where the families would go. I was the waitress then and we had a cook for when my mother was off in the afternoon. She would cook all morning and then she would come in late at night and play waitress while I would go out and rest.

Well, this one family came in and sat down and were real quiet. The man was a border patrol and he was in uniform. I knew from other times that my mother said to kind of keep the noise down for the families, so that was what I tried to do. The rancher had been drinking already for a while so I asked him to keep his voice down because there was a family in the dining room. So they quieted down for a while, but in a little while they were up again real loud and I asked them to keep it down. I was the only person there and I didn't know what else to do, so I thought I might as well leave it at that.

Well, I guess the border patrol heard me ask them to keep it down, so he came over to their table and he said, "This young lady has asked you to be quiet, so why don't you try to be quiet?" The rancher mumbled something, but it was right there in front of all his friends and I think he was embarrassed. That all happened just before my mother was scheduled to come back.

When she got back, the family had already left and the rancher was still drinking. So I told her what had gone on, and I guess he thought it was up to him to tell her too. He was a regular customer and when he came he brought friends and they ate steaks and spent a lot of money. So he must have threatened to not come back when he told my mother and also my stepfather, who had come in too.

My stepfather is very anglicized. His family had always worked for the ranchers and been under the Anglo influence and they still had the idea that you had to be very courteous to the Anglo, especially since this guy was a rich rancher. So when they heard the story they came over to me and they said, "You go tell the man that you're really sorry about what happened and that the border patrol came over himself, you didn't go tell him to."

So I went and did this for them. I don't know why I did, I

just went and did it. But when I came back, the rancher was still mumbling and grumbling. I guess he wanted to put me in the bad position and, since I had to wait on both of them at the same time, he probably thought that I had asked the border patrol for help. So he kept on mumbling and my step-father said, "Well, go tell him again." And I said, "I already did." And he said, "Tell him again because he's a good customer here." They kept pressuring me and pressuring me, and I think that's what pushes me on in what I've been doing.

I never went back to tell him again. I'd already gone once and he had been told more than once to keep his voice down. And I didn't think he was any better than me or the family. He didn't have the right to just refuse what I had told him. And I always go back to that incident now and think about it. It was like a lot of things we did when we were young, that I really didn't notice till I got involved in things politically. Now I want to change all that.

Before I married Roy, I wasn't really politically aware at all. My mother could vote, but I never knew of a time when she went out and voted. I knew by hearsay that so-and-so had won an election, but the Mexicans I knew made no effort to go and use their vote. That was when you had to go out and buy your poll tax.

I met Roy sort of by accident, before school started one year. We had just come back from up north and my mother was setting up housekeeping. She'd bought this big TV antenna and we lived in one of those old houses built up on cement block. There were posts, like stilts, about a foot or two off the ground so we needed help with the antenna. My mother knew a friend of Roy's and she called him up to come over and Roy happened to be along in the group.

So they came over and Roy was clowning the whole time. I guess he was trying to win me over. We started talking and we both talked English, so I guess we kind of got along. Then I was so shy and he was real outspoken and he had been to places that I'd never been to. He had migrated over there, too, but his mother allowed him to go out all over. He was just more aware of things, more sophisticated, and I was a quiet, hicky girl! Well, we started to go together that year, when he was a senior and I was a sophomore.

Then for some reason I was in the pep squad at school. We did all the different yells and all to encourage the teams. That was the only way the Chicano kids could get out to see the different games free, because the school took the pep squad, so all of us joined. Roy always seemed to be at all the football games and at halftime, the pep squad was given a break to go down and drink a soda and rest for a while and that was when I usually saw him. One time during the halftime I wanted to speak to him, but he was like me. He felt so insecure that he always wanted to stick with his friends. So he didn't want to speak to me that day and the next day I told him that I didn't want to go steady with him.

See with the Chicanos, when a girl starts going with a guy, right away you go steady. When you go out with the same boy more than one time, either you're fooling around or you're going steady. The Anglos had much more freedom. The boy asked the girl out and he'd come to the house and you go out. With the Chicanos, you're not able to go out with a boy unless you've got this understanding that eventually you're going to get married. If you didn't, you always had to meet your boyfriend on the secret. Either you say you're going out to the store and you stay out there for fifteen minutes, or you go out there five minutes and you're back home.

Well, in that way I was going steady with Roy and I told him then that I didn't want to anymore, but we would still see each other off and on. Then I left in March, when it was time to migrate to Wisconsin, and we started corresponding. I guess I had been influenced by him because I never went out with anybody else. I could never see myself with another guy who was trying to make time with me. I would always compare him with Roy, and I couldn't see it. And I didn't like to fool around like some of my girlfriends did.

At the end of my junior year, Roy came back from up north and he asked my mother's permission to come and take me out—to date and all that, like the Anglos. It was strange because my sisters always had to meet their boyfriends on the secret, like I said. They were never allowed to come to the house just to visit. But my parents liked Roy and this is kind of funny to me now. Before I got married, they were always in disagreement with my brother-in-laws and they favored Roy.

Now it's the opposite, because they're opposed to what Roy is doing politically.

In 1968, at the end of my senior year, we were married. That was the year he went up to Chicago for the Alinsky training program* where he met all the different people. He came back with long hair and he didn't wear shoes sometimes and he was considered a hippie. In Cotulla, they've still got the ranchers' attitude, with the crewcuts, you know, the chopped-off hair. They don't like anybody with long hair and they consider them radicals. They say, "These young, long-haired, inexperienced punks."

Roy's personality, compared to mine, was always very different. I couldn't really understand why we were attracted to each other. But when he came back from Chicago he was even more different. He had already started being aware of what had been going on—things he hadn't really noticed when he was in school. Actually, there were always things we both noticed, but we had been brought up to respect the Anglo.

All the teachers and principals in school were always Anglo, so if we were punished for something and we told our parents, they'd say, "You probably needed it." They always thought the Anglo was right. We didn't have the parent involvement that we're starting to have now. So we could see things, but we knew we couldn't get any help from the parents. I just kind of accepted it that way, since I was always so quiet.

---

* Saul D. Alinsky, trained as a sociologist, concerned early on with social pathology, the poverty cycle and need for reform. In 1938, formed the Back of the Yards Council, a citizens' group in a poor area near the Chicago stockyards, to pressure for social reform. Using peaceful direct-action tactics, it succeeded in improving the neighborhood and establishing the concept of using political and economic power to achieve legitimate ends. In 1940 he established the Industrial Areas Foundation as a reservoir of funds and expertise for community organizing, which he directed until his death in 1972. He undertook community organizing efforts in poor and powerless neighborhoods across the country, always at the invitation of local groups and with the intent of developing local leadership and instilling the notion of self-help. Worked with Mexican-Americans in California, as well as with blacks in urban ghettos—notably Chicago and Rochester, New York—and later in low-income white areas. His *Rules for Radicals: A Pragmatic Primer for Realistic Radicals* had a profound impact on the field of community organizing.

Anyway, before Roy went to Chicago he was working in the State Highway Department. When he went away, they found out that he was going to organizing school, and there was a lot of talk about him—he was going to be an agitator, he was going to come back and disrupt the community. I really don't even think I knew what it meant then. I wasn't that aware of what he was doing. The community was always the same to me. Nothing had ever changed. And I didn't know what was going to change later.

When Roy came back he got more and more involved. Then in 1970, our candidate from the Raza Unida Party won the election for mayor and Roy won as a write-in candidate for county commissioner.* That was when I started to be more involved and go to some meetings. I thought it was my job to ask questions, because I didn't want to be always in the dark.

But even when I was a senior, I had already started to see what they were doing in the schools—like we couldn't use our own language and the way they taught us about Pancho Villa, that he was a criminal and a rapist and he went around burning everything. I kind of thought that Pancho Villa was to the Mexican family like this legend about Robin Hood. He robbed from the rich to give to the poor, too. But we only learned the bad side of men like Pancho Villa. I went along with it, because that's what I read in the book. Now I say, "Never believe what you read."

Then Roy began to tell me about the true story of Mexico. He loves history and he knows a lot about it. And he pointed out what they did to the Mexican heroes and how they idolize George Washington, the father of our country and all this. Well, now I hear there are books out about men like Jefferson and the slave women, and it isn't at all like they have them in our textbooks. Washington might have been like another Nixon, for all we know, but they make him out to be godlike, like a saint, while they attack all of the Mexicans in history.

Well, I was twenty when I got married, and Roy was twenty-two. Sometimes I think I should have waited, but

---

* Roy (Roel) Rodriguez, elected county commissioner at age twenty-four, was the youngest elected official in the history of the State of Texas.

probably I wouldn't have been as happy as I am now. I think I would have gone in a different direction. By that time I had already gotten into believing anything my parents said, and they're against what Roy has done politically.

Marriage for me was like an escape from something. I felt about Roy that this is somebody who really cares. My mother probably wasn't so happy about it because she was pressed for workers then. But Roy's politics didn't upset her that much yet. He was already involved, but not publicly in the community where it would affect me or her.

About one year after we were married, my mother actually told me, "It's affecting my business." That was when Roy joined MAYO—the Mexican-American Youth Organization—and they were starting to do things in the community. Then a couple of years after that, in 1970 when he ran for county commissioner the first time, she said to me one time that some man had walked up to her in the restaurant and told her he learned from hearsay that somebody wanted to kill her.

She kind of made me think they said that to scare Roy or me to where we would kind of back off. I kept asking her who it was but she wouldn't say. We compared notes with the waitress who had been working that night and we called the FBI and asked them if they'd check on it, but we never found out how true that was. I'm still not sure—maybe she told me that just to scare us off.

I don't know how she feels now. I do know that when I ran for City Council this year, she came to Cotulla to vote for me. After all, I am her daughter. But as far as what we're doing, I'm sure she's still very much against it because of her job right now and also, like I said, my stepfather was very anglicized and he's influenced her a lot. Otherwise, maybe she would be glad.

A lot of the older people are really glad about what we're doing. They're using us and using their vote to get back at the Anglos for the way they were treated when they were young. They could never speak against them for fear that something would happen to them or their families. So now they're glad that somebody's speaking out. Even though they didn't do it when they were young, they can help us now and we can help them.

ROY RODRIGUEZ TALKS ABOUT
THE RAZA UNIDA PARTY

Growing up in Cotulla, the Chicanos were always the majority, but we didn't realize that. We weren't politically oriented. We had always been told to act very gentlemanly or womanly in front of the Anglos and never to talk back at them. And we got to be ashamed of our own parents.

It's the whole educational system that makes you feel inferior, starting in the first and second grade with the readers they have. We would have Puff and Tim and you know, wow! They were our heroes! And then the pictures of the fathers with a briefcase all dressed up in suits, petting the dog and kissing the wife, patting the heads of their kids. Our parents weren't like that, you see? So we started to feel inferior and we wouldn't tell our parents about PTA meetings because we were ashamed to have them go to class and meet the teachers. I didn't realize what was going on until my junior or senior year in high school.

We went to what they called the zero or the preprimer when we were six years old, so we didn't get to the first grade until we were seven. But before the first grade they used to give us a literacy test—and this was in an all-Chicano neighborhood, at a Chicano school. In fact we called it the LBJ school because Lyndon Johnson had taught there. The gringos thought he was too Mexicanized because he used to live in a Mexican part of town, but the Chicanos loved the guy. It's like JFK, you know?

Well, anyway, I knew a lot of English because we used to migrate up north and we used to hang around with a lot of kids in the Midwest when we went to pick the crops. So by the time I was about five or six, I could survive in English. Well, they gave us this literacy test where they'd show you an elephant and you're supposed to say it in English. Now I know what *elefante* is, but why would I know it in English?

Then they'd give you things like washing machines. I'd never seen a washing machine in my life. We saw our mothers washing clothes in a tub with a scrub board. They take you one by one to a room and they give you all these little cards and if you don't know words like that, they classify you as a slow learner or mentally incapacitated. They stopped doing that, but they still do other similar kinds of things.

I never ate in a lunchroom at school, except maybe on Thanksgiving for turkey dinner or Christmas, when our mothers could afford the twenty-five or thirty cents. We used to take our lunches and we were . . . I guess you could call it ashamed to be seen. The white kids would bring in their lunches in big bags, sandwiches and potato chips and all, and we had our tortillas. We'd fold them in our pocket and they flatten out, you know? Then we hid way in the back of the industrial arts class and that's where we'd eat.

Then about my sophomore year we started realizing there was a profitable deal with tortillas because the white kids liked them. You could go to a white kid and say, "Hey man, I'll give you two for your whole lunch." We had kids coming up to us before lunch period and saying, "Hey man, I got some ham or roast beef." And we were very arbitrary. We would say, "But if you don't have this or that . . . " And they'd say, "But this guy has that. We can trade." Before you know it we had a whole concession going and we were trading tortillas.

I was never home as a kid. I was raised all around the neighborhood. My mother was a housemaid and she used to work all the time, and my sister used to stay with a neighbor, so I was always roaming around. I was born out of wedlock so I was raised by my grandfather, who was very hard with me at times. But he was a strong influence because he was very politically oriented in his own oppressed way.

My grandfather was a crew leader. Cotulla's a very agricultural area—onions, carrots, potatoes and tomatoes, stuff like that. He used to have two trucks that he used to take people to work in the fields in. He was like a boss, so he knew a lot of the gringos. He might not have been very educated, but he had the common sense and experience enough to know how to act with them. He knew them well, and at the same time he hated them.

Before he got real sick, he used to tell me that whenever he died, he wanted to have the Mexican flag draped around his coffin. He didn't want no relationship with the system. They didn't say all the rhetoric that we say now and maybe they didn't put all the things together like we do, but it still came out. Why does he want the Mexican flag? Because of the system and his feelings against it. Even if he was one of the supposedly "good" Mexicans, as they saw him. They respected him in a lot of ways because he wasn't scared of them.

It's hard to explain, but the older people have a more militant reaction toward the gringo than we do. I mean we can live around them, but the older people can't stand them, because of the Texas rancher attitude. Like maybe you were walking or standing in the downtown area and all of a sudden here comes a rancher who needs three hands. He just picks up his gun and says, "You're coming with me." The people had no choice. Sometimes they didn't even know where they were. Then they'd be paid a dollar or a dollar fifty a day.

I guess you might say that we're in that era where people are more aware of the social movement, but we don't get publicity about a lot of things that are happening around here. What's going on in south Texas needs a lot of publicity. That's what the gringos don't want because they're scared they'll be discovered. That's why they react against us the way they do.

Well, the educational system in Cotulla only divided the Chicanos more. Especially the dropout situation. Maybe one out of ten of us Chicanos graduated high school and we really felt superior to the ones that dropped out. Those guys were working in the fields and here we are, still going to school and supposedly going to do something with our lives.

Then it hits you, man. Graduation day and then boom! Next day out of school and that's it. Nothing. That's when everything started coming to me more. It was a very heavy scene for me. Like God, you want to hit a wall or something. You start to evaluate yourself, and you start learning that you're nowhere. You wake up and say, "Well, what do I want to do now? Buy a truck? Go in the Army?" You start thinking about algebra, geometry, biology and it just doesn't relate. Now you start to sympathize with the kids that dropped out of school and why they did. Then I realized that I was the one that was being used because I was more or less going to be an example for the white saying, "Look, he made it."

Finally I got a job at the State Highway Department as an engineering technician, they called it. They had high hopes for me. Two or three more years and I'd be going to Texas A and M probably—technical school to get an engineering degree. But I wasn't interested. I just wanted to stay here in Cotulla because I had met a bunch of guys and they had an organization called the Mexican-American Youth Organization—MAYO. We were a whole bunch of young kids just out of high school. Our mind wasn't set on what we were going to do, but finally I had something that I was really interested in: politics. Something that my grandfather had been doing for twenty or thirty years, but differently, not openly.

Starting to organize in Cotulla was really something. I remember I had the sticker "Don't Buy Grapes." I put it on the bumper of my car, and I put the car in the parking lot of the State Department. It didn't take more than two or three hours, and I was already on the blacklist of subversives. And we hadn't even started organizing yet.

We started with a guy who was a VISTA worker here in Cotulla. Since then, by the way, the county commissioners voted that VISTA's are no longer allowed here. We started trying to organize the high school kids and we didn't do that much, but the establishment saw that we were trying to do something. Then they started putting pressure on the State Department to fire me, because I was getting too involved. Eventually I quit, but not before I antagonized them.

That was in '67 or '68 and they were really paranoid. First of all, they heard about Chavez.* Then they heard about a guy

---

* César E. Chavez, California farm workers'—largely Mexican-Americans —leader, who since 1965 has won widespread national support for strike and boycott actions against table-grape growers. A migrant farm worker himself until the age of twenty-five, he joined a grass roots political movement—the Community Service Organization—formed by Saul Alinsky in the area of Delano, California, where he worked in voter registration and rose to position of general director in 1958. Resigned in 1962 to devote full time to organizing a union for field workers, generally exploited by both labor contractors and seasonal employers in the areas of wages, housing, working conditions and education. Became executive director of the United Farm Workers Organizing Committee, AFL–CIO, which he was instrumental in forming, in 1966. Employed civil rights and dramatic tactics, like long fasting periods, to bring grape growers to the bargaining table. Wine-grape growers finally agreed to sign a contract in 1967, but it took an amazingly successful nationwide boycott of California grapes and four years before the table-grape growers agreed

saying, "Kill the gringos." They didn't know that we had a definition of a gringo and an Anglo, which is two different things. But there were all those news media things and they started connecting everything. Then MAYO started coming out and we marched and helped with the school boycott in Crystal City. And your picture eventually comes out in the paper somewhere.

Before I quit, I had vacation time and I had a good friend in Austin at OEO Regional who had this connection with a guy at the Industrial Areas Foundation in Chicago. They had a new program there. They called it community development or something. Anyway, they were going to send OEO-type guys that work in community centers to train with Alinsky. It was really weird because I didn't fit in with them. They were going to go back and work in a little office and organize. My train of thought wasn't the same as theirs.

The first time I went up there was about a year after high school. It was during those radical years, the war and stuff. There were a lot of white radicals, some Berkeley types, some blacks from the South. Before that, I never had that much contact with people with diversified ideas and things. Where I come from, we never considered talking across the table with a white guy. I guess I finally realized there were some white people that I could relate to. And blacks too. It's always been known that blacks and Chicanos don't like each other. Like in Chicago, most of the gang wars are between Puerto Ricans or Mexicans and blacks like the Blackstone Rangers or the Disciples. I guess two oppressed people take it out on each other instead of the system that's screwing us both.

But it was really something. I'd been around white people all over in the South and the Midwest or wherever I was working, but not in that environment, that friendly feeling. Like having drinks together and once this professor guy from the University of Chicago invited us to eat at his place. I had a very negative attitude toward going. We never go to a gringo's house in Cotulla. The attitude was that all whites are the same.

---

to sign a contract. The momentum generated by "La Causa's" successful strikes led the UFWOC to organize workers in the truck-vegetable areas of California, and then other states, where it has engaged in territorial disputes with the Teamsters.

We never thought we had people that could relate to some of the problems, that could help you.

When I came back to Cotulla I was helping organize MAYO, and then I started working with Nueva Vida, which started right after OEO started. This priest of ours helped the community organize into a development corporation to bring in some monies, not in a political way. First it was mostly older women and men with no youth influence at all, and the median age in Cotulla is twenty-five. The youth were really dormant then. But then Nueva Vida started to bring in VISTA's, and that's when it really got going. They were Anglo kids, and they were going into communities, forming co-ops and things like that.

Then I saw the chance to work with the VISTA's and really begin to organize to get political control of the City Council and the county. I learned that over 75 percent of the people make it in America. I thought wow! Where have we been? Things are happening all around us, but we're not benefiting. Then we got different people together and we formed Barrios Unidos—like a barrios betterment association. That was political, but before the Raza Unida Party.

Nineteen-seventy was the first time we tested our political strength, but we weren't very serious about winning the election. We were just going to give them a scare. We only started organizing about four weeks before the election, and we never had any real political training—registration drives, block work, that kind of thing. Also we didn't think we could win because the majority of the people just weren't politically inclined yet. But groups like MAYO were very instrumental. I guess MAYO was the first militant Chicano group in the State of Texas. Raza Unida grew out of that.

I remember a meeting in Crystal City one night when we were planning strategy for the school boycott and then we started talking about a Chicano political party. We talked about some names, like the Chicano Democratic Party, but that didn't sound too hot. Then José Angel Gutiérrez, the leader of the group there, had a piece of paper with a Mexican eagle on it and somebody wrote La Raza Unida under it. Then some guy said, "That sounds too militant. The people are not going to swallow it." José Angel said, "Well, they can get used to it," and that's how the Raza Unida Party really started. They had it in California already, but we weren't affiliated with it.

Well, the name stuck, even though we couldn't get it on the ballot that year. We had our people running with no political party. I ran as a write-in candidate to finish out someone's term for county commissioner. After just four weeks of campaigning we won the mayor, two councilmen and two school board members and I won too. The reaction of the people was just incredible, after forty years of having nothing.

It was eight o'clock at night when Samora won the mayor, and the whole town exploded. They were dancing on top of pool tables in the cantinas, which were bursting with people. Everybody was singing in the streets, dancing, honking. We invited everybody that went by to a party or gave them a beer. It lasted for about three days and it scared the gringos so bad they organized. Up to 1968, the total vote cast in the city was under a hundred. In 1970, it was close to twelve hundred and it's going up.

The ranchers are really scared. They saw what happened in Crystal City where the Chicanos took over the power, and they're afraid the same will happen in Cotulla. They've been fighting us so hard in the city that, before they knew it, we were right behind them in the county. See they're so used to being able to buy enough votes. Like with my grandfather, they'd buy the poll tax. Now they buy them license plates for their cars or give them money. If you're really poor, that can decide how you're going to vote. And the ranchers are rich. They control the economy.

It's really funny, them complaining about us being on welfare. Cotulla's one of the three poorest counties in the nation and about the poorest in Texas, not counting the valley. We get about $555,000 in AFDC (aid to families with dependent children) monies and aid to the old and stuff like that, and the government subsidizes the ranchers over $4.2 million. And that's so the agribusiness won't grow things, so the land sits fallow and there are no jobs. It's incredible. They say, "Oh, those Chicanos, they don't want to work." Bullshit! They're the ones on welfare.

Everything is political in Cotulla and the gringos control everything, even who gets the few jobs there are. So if they can't get you politically, they'll get you financially. The financial pressures are tremendous. I depend on Rosa a lot. If it wasn't for her, I just wouldn't be able to hack it.

Our son, who's five, is very politically oriented already. He understands what Raza Unida means, and when Rosa was running for City Council, he'd walk up to people and say, "Did you vote for my mother already?" When we won, the outburst of emotion was incredible and he understood it. Then, when we started having City Council meetings, he couldn't understand why the gringos were against us. We never taught him to hate, but he saw it himself and now he understands there's two different types of white people—the gringos and Anglos. All the young kids seem to be oriented to this already, I guess because of the influence of the people they've been around.

Ever since I met Rosa, we were always on the same line of thought. But I told her what I wanted to do and asked her was she going to be able to cope with it. And then her family had a very negative attitude toward my involvement in politics. But I kept telling her, even after we got married, that she could check out anytime she wanted to if she felt it was that bad.

I was never really surprised that Rosa got so involved and decided to run for the City Council. She was. I always pushed her to do things because I knew she could but she never did believe me. She always felt inferior. You know, it's mostly the woman attitude. I always saw things different. I was raised by my mother and she was very strong, and my *madrina** too, so maybe that's why I think this way. But the kind of pressures you get in a political fight are really bad—especially being a woman in a racist town.

But Rosa's political awareness was really of her own doing. She started looking at all the injustices and she saw that we were being screwed. And she saw my attitude and my reactions when I came home, and then she started going to meetings with me, and then this campaign started and she was stronger than I was at the time. It got so strong that when she said her second speech, some of the Chicana women cried. They were wanting for so long to hear something like that.

We had a rally in the plaza. I remember I was running a

* *Madrina,* Spanish for godmother.

stand or a bingo or something, and they called her up to the platform. This was a few days before the election. She didn't have a planned speech but she started talking and saying things like: "It's about time that the women come out of their kitchens and the men get out of their cantinas and start talking about politics with each other in the streets, because that's where it's really valid." She said, "We have to be more aware and get more involved and we're not doing it for ourselves, but for our kids." And that's what really got them.

She started saying that men should have more respect for the things that women did and that they should work together all the time, because that's the only way we were going to get things changed. And we were doing it for our children, and our parents, and our grandparents. It just all came out of Rosa, and tears started coming down the women's faces, because here was a woman speaking out for them for the first time.

The men were surprised, and it really hit them emotionally because it was true. Finally, somebody came out in the open and said, "Look, we've been apart for so long in our thinking and in our lives." Chicano men have always kept women where they want them to be. They get married and have kids, but the women aren't considered equal when it comes to making decisions together, unless it's a crisis. Then the men need the women because they're a lot stronger in coping with a lot of problems. Men are very naive when it comes to giving a position of respect to women or giving them a role. They fear that if they let the woman do what she wants, she's going to leave. Then they threaten them—they're going to send them back to Mexico with their parents or take their kids away. Always keep them worried or insecure about something.

That's why the men around here respect Rosa. She doesn't stand for that. She's very frank when it comes to saying her mind. And women here . . . well, they're not supposed to argue with a guy or tell him what she thinks he should do or criticize him. At the beginning, even our politics in the party was like that. They wanted only men involved. Me and another guy thought we should have some women candidates, but most of them didn't want any. Even though if you called a meeting of Nueva Vida or Barrios Unidos and a hundred people went, seventy-five or eighty of them would be women.

But Rosa's speech really hit them hard. Especially the reaction of the people—the honking of the horns, the women with tears in their eyes. The men realized how important it was. And the women . . . well, finally there was somebody saying what they've been thinking and what they've always wanted to say for a long, long time. When she was speaking it really got to me. An emotional feeling just came over me. And I thought, if I'm feeling this way, I can imagine how other people in this town must be feeling too. But I still think Rosa doesn't really realize how much impact it had. She's very down to earth and she's not about to talk about it that way. Well, I guess maybe that's Rosa for you.

FRUSTRATIONS AND CHALLENGES OF A CITY COUNCILWOMAN

I really can hardly believe where I am now. I guess it started with going to meetings with Roy and campaigning with him. The people knew me a little because of that, and then they needed a new president of Nueva Vida. The president was a man who was ill and wanted to resign. Also, he was against the Raza Unida, and the president should at least be impartial. Nueva Vida is a poor people's organization for community development, and it's registered with the state as a nonprofit agency, so we can't be involved in politics at the meetings. That's the only way we can get any projects or funds from the federal government.

What happened was, the woman who was president before that man was very involved with the party, so she didn't want to be president again. She wanted to stay in the background and influence people politically, so she asked me to run. She told me she'd do all the talking and all the work if I'd just be president, and she's a real talker. She talked circles around me and made it sound like a bed of roses and pushed me into a position where I couldn't say no. So the night the man resigned, my name was raised as a candidate and they elected me president. That was in October of 1972.

All of a sudden I was forced out front where I didn't want to be. If I had known what it would be like I would have been scared, but I went into it blind. I was so shy and afraid to go out in a crowd and talk. And then all the people came to me for help. Like the old people, who needed medicines they couldn't get in Cotulla, and the people on food stamps. And then we were right in the middle of a boycott of the stores in Cotulla because of the high prices of groceries and everything.

The boycott was more like a political attack. The store owners almost never had sales and they could keep the prices high because the people had no choice where to shop. So we would have bingos and other little fund raisings to pay for a bus to take the people out of town to shop about twice a month. It cost us about a thousand dollars a month, but that was the only way we were going to put pressure on the local merchants.

Well, it was my responsibility to see that the bus was gassed up and didn't need any repairs. Then they usually loaded from my house, so often I had to go and pick up the people who didn't have a way to get to my house. Usually we made sure to take the people who were on food stamps and welfare, and there was a bunch of women I'd always contact the first of the month to let them know when we were scheduling the bus.

After a few months we were making such an effect on the stores that someone began rotating the dates when the people were supposed to receive their food stamps to kind of hold us back. They weren't coming on time anymore. The boy that interviewed people for stamps is the son of the Anglo mayor we have now. Also, the local merchants threatened to get the highway patrol to stop the bus. Finally we had to give up the bus, because we couldn't raise enough money to keep it going.

But we're still continuing the boycott. The people who can are still going to stores outside of Cotulla to buy their groceries. We have a Nueva Vida membership card, which is like an identification, and in some stores the people can get a little cheaper prices. I think the Cotulla stores felt the pressure but they haven't really lowered their prices. One store which has the lowest prices of all has had some pretty big sales, but still not like the sales in San Antonio. What we're working on now is to bring a large supermarket chain here and we've collected signatures from hundreds of families saying they would buy there. We found a site, and the Texas Migrant Council might help with the financing. See, our thinking is, why help these local merchants by giving them our money when they're using it to fight us?

We had between two hundred and three hundred members in Nueva Vida and I guess the people knew I really wanted to help them. I would accept everybody for the bus project as long as they paid the membership dues, which was three dollars for lifetime. And I didn't pressure them to pay right away, because a lot of the people have four or five little kids and they're poor and, since it was a lifetime membership, they should have a lifetime to pay.

So, because of Nueva Vida I was forced to be out there in front. Then our chairman of Raza Unida in Cotulla came out with a speech that we should have more women in politics and by then, some of the guys in the party knew me. Like Roy said, I'm frank about what I say when we're talking politics and, at the meetings we have, I'm about the only girl who comments and I go against some of the things they say. When there's a conflict, they'll tell me, "Well, it's the Women's Movement!"

I'm with the Women's Movement when it has to do with the community. I like to have an opinion and be able to disagree without having somebody looking down their nose at me, even if they do it in a joking way. One day we went to visit a friend of Roy's and there was something about the Women's Movement on TV. And he says, "You know, women are pampered." So I argued with him about how much work we really do at home, and I guess he didn't expect it. I guess I'm about the only woman who does it, and I show them about as much respect as they show me as a woman.

Well Barrios Unidos, which is like Raza Unida's local branch, was screening candidates for City Council and the chairman had made that speech about women. They had about three or four names and I think deep down they were kind of like daring me to put myself in the position of a candidate. They had asked me the year before to run but I didn't want to. I guess I didn't think I was capable, so I had refused. I was nervous and scared and I didn't think I could go out and make speeches in front of large groups of people.

This last time I didn't really think I could do it either, but I didn't feel I was in a position to turn them down again. They had asked for more women's involvement and, also, the way I understood it, indirectly they were daring me on to accept the nomination. The time before, in 1972, they put up my name along with a young girl who was involved in the community, so they thought she'd be recognized. This time they went through and screened about twenty or thirty names of people who were the most involved. Some of those had been candidates before and lost. Well, they pulled out my name on a secret ballot along with five other names, all men.

I told them again I thought I couldn't do it. I knew it would have to be a man running against me, and I didn't think I could handle a man attacking me, even in words. Usually when it nears election time, I've noticed that the speeches get kind of dirty, kind of personal. I didn't think I had any skeletons in the closet, but still they could bring up something irrelevant to the campaign and I didn't think I could take that. So I told them I'd think about it, but that must have given them the impression I was going to run. After that, there was no way of saying, "I thought about it and I won't do it." So I could only say that I'd try.

I really never expected to win. My opponent was the strongest candidate of the opposition. As it turned out, he didn't make any personal attacks. And the only platform he had was how much he had done for the community. But really, he was already a councilman, and there was no evidence that he did anything. It was all just words. He was in charge of the fire department, for all that means. And then he was involved in having the airport repaved.

The airport is for the ranchers, like when deer country opens and they come in in their helicopters. Or like when Lyndon Johnson visited Cotulla, a helicopter brought him. That was the first time we even found out we had an airport! And I used that in one of my speeches, that my opponent was involved in using all this city money for an airport, when we don't even have any transportation and our streets aren't even paved. I said, "There's never any value placed on our community, where we live and what we need."

Johnson came here I guess for a political thing. He said he had been in Cotulla when he was young, when he taught school here, and he hadn't been here for about thirty years, and it's still the same. I think he had sent some money to the school district. They never made any repairs until they heard he was going to come. Then they had the whole school painted and fixed up.

This is the school where all the Chicano kids used to go from grades one to six, all the kids they thought were slow and retarded. Then you were transferred over to the Anglo school. It wasn't until 1970 that they made it integrated and the Anglo parents got all upset because they didn't want their kids mixing with the Chicano kids. They felt too good for us. But we didn't mind. We were used to that already, and being blamed for anything that happened at school, like a fire or something.

It seems like nobody from the outside really believes what happens here in Cotulla. We've had people from Washington come and research us—the social problems and housing and health care. Barrios Unidos had written a proposal to get a clinic to help the poor people, because you can't get any help now in the one hospital here unless you pay in advance, and the people can't afford the services. There is a lot of sickness around here, but now a lot of people are going back to using herbs, because they can't afford medical care and the hospital won't give us credit anymore. So the people from Washington come with big talk and they seem shocked and they say, "We want to help you." And then they go away and we never hear from them again.

During the campaign I talked about a lot of things and I think we had the first speech on the radio, and then our opponents began to use all the same points that we were making. I talked about how bad our schools are and how the kids don't have buses and the roads are a wreck. And when it rains, they have to walk through floods to get to school. And the mothers have to worry about all this and then paying the bills.

Most of the kids leave during the summer to do migrant work, but there's nothing to do for the kids who are here. And I talked about the need for jobs, especially on this side of the tracks. We need industry here so people won't have to keep migrating. And we have no sewers, so when it floods the people have to bail out their houses with buckets. But the worst thing is there's no progress in Cotulla. The Anglo kids go to college and then find jobs in other towns. Even the teaching jobs are so low-paid that people will work somewhere else if they can. We keep encouraging our kids to go to college but also to remember the poor people, to come back and help the community. But then there are no jobs, so it's a vicious cycle.

Like I've said, everything here is political. I have this friend who kept encouraging me to run, but about a year before the election, her family was still a little neutral about the party. Now their son is running on the Raza Unida ticket for county treasurer. But his father is an independent deliverer of bread, so his politics affects how much bread he sells. They're probably happy for their son, but still they were holding back because of the business. It isn't doing that well and now he's being pressured like us.

And the pressure is not only here in Cotulla. The Anglos know the business people in the other towns and they can influence them. Like they might say, "Are you going to let Raza Unida sell in your store?" I guess they're really afraid of losing power. Or maybe it's so they won't lose face with their own kind. Anyway, these friends of mine had to look out for that too.

But now, they surprise me when I go over there. This boy's aunt is always encouraging me and telling me that I can get to the people's heart. She kind of pushes me ahead all the time. Maybe they got a little more encouragement because of what Roy and the party have done and they're not as afraid as they were before. I would always go to them and say, "What will I say in my speeches?" And they would give me ideas, and they helped me figure out how to start off when I had to tape that speech for the radio, to get the people's attention and all. And then they'd help me write it in Spanish, since I can't write Spanish, and they'd go over it with me.

It was like an ad on the radio that they'd run every so often. First I would state my name and that I was a candidate running for the City Council. Then, as a mother, I felt I was sensitive to the needs of the children and the women in the community, and I thought I could be a good spokesman for the women who had never had the chance to speak out against the city and all the problems we have. Then I brought out the different points that the party was trying to make, but from the point of view of the woman. And at the end I would mention the other Raza Unida candidates for City Council, give their names and positions, and that was about it.

I still can't believe that I really won. Every time I had to get up there and say anything, I felt so nervous about it I couldn't remember anything I said. People told me afterward. I'm still real bashful, I guess. At that rally Roy told you about, I think I was the last one they called up to speak, after the mayor and the other candidates. And mostly they had already said what I thought should be said. I kept asking myself, "What am I going to say?" even while I was walking up there. I guess I just talked, without realizing what I was saying. It was so awful talking to a crowd, especially on a microphone where you hear your own voice reflecting back. Before that time I used to serve food at political rallies and hope that I'd be passed over.

Well, evidently the people liked what I said. Don't ask me what it was. I just opened my mouth and talked. But I still prefer to listen instead of talking, and to be in the background. During the campaign I kept thinking, what am I doing out here? But here I am, a Chicana, the first woman elected in Cotulla, and so young, and we didn't think I'd win because I had such a strong opponent. It was a big boost for the women. They were carrying me on their shoulders. I guess I give them encouragement. I'm still surprised. And I'm happy because Roy believes in me, and that I can do it, even though I'm not sure myself.

Now I guess I'm really in the spotlight because of winning the City Council, but I would rather be in the background so that more women would become involved. If I'm always taking the stronger positions, I'm going to be handicapping the other women who should be coming up and speaking out. And one of the reasons I got involved was to help women have a voice. I think the woman feels that the husband isn't supporting her in what she believes. Like Roy had to encourage me a lot, because I wouldn't have done it myself. When the husbands don't support the wives, it's because of the machismo.

Chicano family life is centered around the woman. A father and the kids isn't considered a complete family. But I guess we're still a little backward. No matter how modern the Anglo woman and the Anglo family are going to get, we're still going to respect the man as the head of the family. I don't know how modern Roy and I seem to you, but still I'm going to let his decision overrule mine if we can't agree. But the machismo is still a problem for Chicano families. If you tell a man to help you with the dishes, well . . . that's the woman's role and they feel the machismo is falling down. And they think if they don't show that machismo, then they're letting the women wear the pants in the family. But with some of our friends, in the more modern and the younger families, the husbands do help with the housework.

I'm for the Women's Movement as far as the family goes. I think the woman should be recognized in making decisions, like where they're going to live, and financial things, like about going out to borrow money. The way I grew up, even though there were discussions at times, it's always been the man who decided. And I think it's about time the woman and the man share the decisions. So I think women should have a little more freedom of speech in the home.

But as far as what we saw on TV when the Women's Movement first came out, well some of it was ridiculous. The burning of the bras and everything, to be equal to men. With jobs, if you can do it, okay. We're equal as human beings and I agree that we should be getting the same money if we're doing the same job. But I don't see myself going out and being a miner or a lumberjack. I don't think I'd want to. If I'm educated to become an airline pilot, well okay, if I can do the work. It's fine if they have the brains and education to do certain things. But then I heard about this one woman somewhere who was in the fire department, and she was married, and she thought she had the right to sleep in the same room with the men. Well, I don't see it that way, maybe because I'm married.

From what I've seen, the Women's Movement hasn't really changed anything here. It's not helping the Chicano family, but it's not hurting us either. I don't think it helped me win at all. What helped was the fact that I'm involved in so many organizations in the community. It's the party that has opened the minds of the people, and the political involvement of the different families. I think that's the main thing that's changing people.

The hardest thing about being a candidate and then winning is when it comes to helping the people. As soon as I won the election, one woman called me up and she said, "Where's your office?" And I said, "I don't have an office." The City Council only meets once a month and there's no salary or anything. But the people were already coming to ask for help even though there's no way I could give them help. They need help moneywise, you know, and I have to explain that I have no control over the monies. Like Roy is constantly being called for financial help, but the Commissioners' Court has to approve what they spend. It's the same with the City Council. There's no emergency fund or anything. So there's no way we can help them, even though the monies are supposed to be used for the community, and that's so hard to explain.

And now I don't even know how long I'll be on the City Council. When I won my seat last April, the Raza Unida candidate for mayor and another councilman won with me. And there was another Chicano too. Altogether there's five councilmen and the mayor. So we had a good chance of changing things in Cotulla. But then the Anglos decided to contest our elections. They're saying that some of the Chicanos who voted for us were aliens, that they never got their citizenship papers in order. These are the same Anglos who used to go out and pay the poll tax for the poor people years ago when they only needed less than a hundred votes to win. Now I guess they're scared. They're beginning to see that the Chicanos can use their power.

Roy says the contest might take a year or two like it did in Crystal City, the same kind of thing. The Anglos' lawyers got a list of all the voters and then they asked some local people who were the people born in Mexico that didn't have their proper papers. Then they sent a list of people they thought were aliens to our lawyer, who's a Legal Aid lawyer in Crystal City. He has to prove the residency of these people and then what we're probably going to do is challenge the Anglos' residency, all those ranchers who don't really live here.

Anyway, the law says that at the first City Council meeting after the election, any new members are supposed to be sworn in. Well, before the swearing in, they were discussing at the meeting that the old City Council had the right to say whether or not the mayor could be mayor, because of the vote challenge. They wanted an Anglo to be mayor pro tem for the meantime, even though our mayor had been in office for two years already and it wasn't until his reelection with us that they challenged him. After being mayor for two years, now they're saying he wasn't eligible!

Well, there was a big argument then and the City Council walked out. And it was really packed. All the women were there, friends of mine who had given me the encouragement to run and were glad for me being the first woman to win. They were all there to see us sworn in. But it was packed with Anglos too, and as the City Council walked out, all the Anglos walked out too. Then I guess in an effort to heckle them, the women started to clap.

Then there was an incident that gave us the impression that they had planned the whole thing. As they were coming out, one of the border patrol hit a bystander in the stomach. They expected this man to react, to hit back, but he just didn't do anything, and I guess that angered them even more. They had made Roy a city marshal, so he happened to be right there when it happened. And he said to the justice of the peace, "Did you see what just happened?" The justice of the peace is a Chicano who's anglicized and the sheriff is an Anglo, and they all said, "We didn't see anything." And they all took off.

I guess that was all planned, because by the time I got there before they walked out—I was about two minutes late—there were peace officers all over the place. I was so surprised to see so many of them, I thought maybe something had already happened. Well the justice of the peace didn't want to be involved. He had already gotten into the position where he had to do the Anglos favors to stay ahead, so he just denied he saw anything. Then the man who was punched in the stomach filed a complaint at the county courthouse, and at first the justice of the peace there accepted it. Then, about a day later, he said he couldn't accept it. Obviously, he was being pressured and that was right before the primaries. He was running against an Anglo and we got the idea that he felt he was going to lose out. So there really is no justice for us here, and there never has been.

The election we just had was really no help to us, because still we can't do anything in the City Council. They have the majority. They made sure they would, even though they did it illegally. What happened was, there were two Anglos on the council and there was going to be three Chicanos. The third Chicano didn't run with Raza Unida. He was already being anglicized. Ruiz is a businessman, like most of the council members, and he was being pressured from both sides.

His vote was the deciding one, and we tried to talk to him so he would help us to bring in new projects to benefit the people. If he voted with the Anglos, that would be three to two and they'd kill our projects. Still, we were a little optimistic about how he would react inside the council, where he would have to be facing the Anglos. But he said, "I probably won't vote with you or against you. Probably I won't go to the meetings at all." He didn't want to be the deciding vote. But he said he wouldn't resign either.

But by then we had already gotten into the issue of the court deciding on the mayor. Our mayor, who had won by election of the people, wouldn't be there to help us, to be the deciding vote. If Ruiz resigned, it would be us two, and the two Anglos, and the mayor pro tem from the old City Council, who's an Anglo. So he promised us he wouldn't resign until we had settled the position of the mayor in court. But at this last meeting we had, by the time I got there he had already resigned. I guess he couldn't take the pressures from both sides.

Ruiz was worried about his restaurant business, and also he delivers beer. That's why we're having this big beer boycott now. We're trying to get everybody not to buy his beer. Because by resigning, he hurt the poor people. He broke his promise to us and then the mayor pro tem had the opportunity to appoint someone else. Naturally, he appointed another anglicized Chicano, somebody they knew was going to vote in their favor. So that left us out again. We really want the boycott to work and hurt Ruiz's business badly to discourage the same kind of thing from happening in the future. Some people think he got paid off by the Anglos. Well, we want them to know we mean business now.

It's so frustrating. The people want to know why the man they elected mayor isn't mayor, and it's so hard to explain. It's so complicated and a lot of them are illiterate. A lot of the older people were scared to vote the Raza Unida ticket to start with. Now they're questioning whether it's worth it to vote after all. Their mayor isn't there, and now some of them are afraid of being called to court, the ones who might have to prove their citizenship.

The Anglos got what they were pushing for this time. It doesn't really matter whether me and the other Chicano go to City Council meetings or not now. The vote will always be three against our two. They passed a motion that the old City Council's mayor pro tem will be the acting mayor until there are new elections in 1975.

That's why it's so important for the Raza Unida to organize. For this November too, for the county elections. Roy is in the same situation there, with the ranchers in the majority. There are about eight or nine posts up that are all held by Anglos. They've been in them so long they could probably get pensions—county judge, county clerk, the commissioners, justice of the peace. Roy's the only Chicano now, but the party is putting up candidates for all the offices. We really have to organize so we can help the poor people.

There are so many pressures because of being involved in politics. The worst is the financial part. Our whole income is Roy's salary for being a county commissioner, which is five thousand dollars, and neither of us can get other jobs, because of Raza Unida. That's just coffee money for the ranchers who are most of the commissioners, but that's all we have to live on. As I told you, they control everything, and when you go to apply for a job, they screen you politically to see which side you're on. And they censor what you teach, too.

Once I was being interviewed for a job as a school aide and they asked me who my husband was. Then they said, "Don't call us, we'll call you." It happens to all our friends too. The Anglos use the school and all the other jobs for their politics. Even the first mayor we had who ran on the Raza Unida ticket, he was forced out by financial pressures. He was a teacher with a master's degree and he couldn't get a teaching job in Cotulla. He had to travel forty miles each way to the job he got. And there's no salary for the mayor either, so after one term he just didn't run again.

Right now we're in debt and I know that we're not going to

get out of it very easily and the pressures are coming from all sides. I'd like to have three kids, but I'm not even sure we can afford a second one now. Then also, that was the reason I was a little reluctant about running, but I guess I couldn't find the words to tell the guys who were pushing me to run. It was hard to explain that it's different for a woman, especially a young woman. Here I am on the City Council and if I get pregnant, well . . . you get really big and uncomfortable and here are all these men watching you and I think I'd be embarrassed going to meetings.

Then it's hard to find a baby-sitter here. We lived with my mother-in-law to start off and she helped raise my little boy before she started working regular as a cook. And now she still takes care of him when I can't take him along for some reason, but I make an effort to take him along most of the time. Now that little Roy's going to be in school, I'm relieved because I'll be able to do different things. If I have a baby, that's going to hold me back.

A day care center would be a help here, but as far as sending my own kids, I think I'd prefer to take care of them myself. I guess because of the way I grew up. I was alone most of the time, and I didn't feel my mother was really that involved with us. I know I felt that I was her kid and she had a responsibility to me, but I didn't feel that love. My sisters and I are trying to be less strict with our kids, and a little more concerned about them.

Now that little Roy is starting school, I'm going to get real involved in it because so many things need to be changed and so that he'll know that we're there and we love him and he can come to us with problems. If I had another baby now, I guess I could leave it with some friends, but I don't think they could take care of it as good as I would.

We have a Planned Parenthood here in Cotulla. It's mostly for the poor people on welfare and I have to pay, but I think it's a real good idea. Not only the birth control for the young girls and the married women, but it also takes in the Pap smears for cancer. I noticed that no young girls like in junior high school go. If I had a daughter, I would want her to go and I'd go with her. They show the different organs of a woman's body and all about natural childbirth, and I'd like her to see all that. I never really understood the facts of life, you could say, until I got married. It was very different than what I expected.

If I had a daughter, I'd raise her with an open mind to different things. And I'd want her to be sensitive to the different people, like the rich and the poor people who are needy. I wouldn't want her to be a snob, even if she had all the advantages that other kids didn't. I'd probably want her to have the best clothes and the best everything if we could afford it, but I wouldn't want her to look down on other kids that didn't have that. I didn't have that, so if she looked down on those kids, then she'd be looking down on me.

Roy never got to go to college, except for San Antonio Commercial College for a year or so. It's like a trade school. Now he can't go because of the money. Every year he says, "I'm going to go to night school," and I think he'd like to be a lawyer, but he never makes it. Even though I didn't have the money, I never really wanted to go. But Roy is already pushing little Roy to be a doctor. And I always say, "Well, let him be what he wants to be. Why a doctor?" Maybe he won't want to go to college.

If I had a daughter, I would want the same thing for her as I want for my son. I think most of all in life, I would like to die of old age and to see all my children grown. To see them in college or some kind of profession, and to see that they're settled and in some way working for the people. And as I said, not to be snobbish or selfish or stingy. They're probably never going to be millionaires, but they should be able to give.

I guess I agree with the Planned Parenthood people that a child should really be wanted. And there's no reason why children should be brought into the world to suffer if the parents can't financially take care of them. But I still can't see abortion. I just don't think I could do it, unless maybe for medical reasons. With all this birth control going around, people shouldn't have that problem. But if a woman is poor and she's pregnant, I don't see any reason why she can't go ahead and have the baby and give it up. There's a lot of people who would like to have a baby and can't.

Customs have changed and I guess women have more advantages these days, though you don't see much change in Cotulla. But men have more advantages too. I read in the newspaper where in some state there's a new law that men no longer have to pay alimony and it's up to the women to go out and work and support the kids also. And I think that's fair. I know there's some women who get divorced or separated and the men are left to pay all the expenses. Sometimes the women are off fooling around and they leave the kids alone or with a neighbor, so the father is playing the parent role but the mother isn't doing her part. Then often there's the opposite too, where the father just neglects the kids.

I really haven't stopped to think what the major differences are for women. I think going away to college kind of opens up people's eyes to a lot of things. But here in Cotulla, most of the people haven't been to college and they haven't been outside the community. They haven't even been to other towns where they could have the opportunity to see different things. Most of the kids have never been out, unless it's like a special field day to the zoo or something. So we're not that aware of things like you would be.

When I go to some of the conferences with Roy, or like when we had the VISTA's here, most of them had gone to college and seemed more aware of things. I felt like I really hadn't learned anything. I think when you go to college it makes you realize that you haven't learned anything in high school. But then I've met a lot of people who've gone to college and I've heard them talking with Roy and they'll come out with: they know so-and-so—some real well-known person—or they're a member of such-and-such. And I don't know if they're really telling you the truth or they're trying to impress you. I really can't distinguish it. It doesn't really impress me, but then sometimes I feel what I say doesn't interest them, because they know so much more and have been so many more places.

Sometimes we think about leaving here, mostly because financially we can't make it on the salary Roy gets as a commissioner. I don't know if there's anyone else as strong as Roy in the precinct, who could withstand the constant pressure, but if he quit, we were thinking of moving to Austin. He could get a job there and there's probably a little more opportunity for me too. I'd like to work with kids, probably as an aide or something. I did volunteer work when my son was in Head Start and I enjoyed that.

In Austin, the people are a little more liberal than right here in south Texas. They're not backward like here. I've gone there so many times already and I love it there. But if Roy and I left Cotulla, I don't know if it would be good for the people. It would be like we were giving up. If Roy was the only one, that would be one thing. But now there's two of us in the family who have run under Raza Unida and, if we moved away, I think it would kind of set the people back a little.

I try to analyze myself once in a while and I think that all along, from the time I was a young kid, I've been the type that when I start something I want to finish it and do it correctly. And I think a lot of people right now are depending on me, even though I may not feel secure and I may not think that I can do it. It's a pressure, and I'm a little queasy about it, but still I think probably if I really set my mind to it, I can do it.

I think I'm still shy, but not as shy as I used to be. If I'm asked to speak, I think I'll be a little more intelligent about what I say. And I think the people know that I say what I really feel instead of a speech like the President makes. He has the writers with the different points of view who write the speech and then he just reads it in front of the people. It's not really himself talking, what he feels. I think the people know that when I speak of the different things I would do it's because of what I feel, or what I think is right or wrong.

From now on, until the third party is strong, we're going to have to be organizing. That's why I don't see how we can leave. We've come this far and it was hard for the people, especially the older people who couldn't read and didn't have as much education as our generation. They were always Democrats, so the third party was very different for them. We had to have a big education campaign and teach them how to find the names on the ballot. Usually it's Republican, Democrat and then the Raza Unida, so we teach them to vote straight ticket. Since Raza Unida started, we've never had a candidate for President, so we've never voted for President. And as far as that goes, whether you like him or you dislike him it doesn't seem to make much difference. The only thing that concerns me right now is the community, anyhow.

I never had the slightest idea that I was going to run for an office. I never would have believed it. But I had to be involved, since I was Roy's wife, and then, well . . . I was just there. I had to be at the different meetings with him and I had to show some kind of encouragement for the people, especially when we were only starting and we didn't have that many people who were willing to go out and talk to the people. Roy did most of the talking, but then people come and ask you things and you have to know the answers. A lot of the women would stop me in the street. They weren't very politically aware either, and you have to explain to them. I guess in some way I was really campaigning for Roy.

But then something changed in me and I started to remember different things, like that experience with the rancher and a lot of other things that happened to me when I was growing up. I knew I couldn't correct them because they had already happened. But I think I was trying to prevent other things like that from happening to Chicano people in the future, especially to young kids growing up now.

I don't know if things are really changing for the better. I would like to hope that instead of going to the moon and spending so much money on things related to wars that there could be some way to find cures for all the diseases that are killing so many of the people. Especially for cancer and TB and all these heart diseases. I guess because I've got a heart disease. I'm not at the point where I'm going to die any minute, but most of the deaths I've known about have something to do with the heart.

Even before I started reading the Bible, I more or less concluded in my mind that we're going to have a double amount of all those evil things that supposedly came out of Pandora's Box. Like the drinking and the drugs, and I think we're going to have a bigger war than all the ones we've seen up to now. I may sound like I'm pushing religion, but I think now's the time for a lot of us to get involved with the greater being, you know, upstairs. Once before, you know, the entire world was covered with water and it ended in the flood. Well I have this belief, and so do a lot of others, that the world is going to end in fire this time.

But I guess things are changing for the better here. The people are becoming more aware and demonstrating their anger. The young people are getting really involved in the party, especially since the eighteen-year-old vote. Now they sit down with the elders and ask questions, and find out how the political system works. Some even skip school on election day to get out the vote, which isn't really too good since the teachers give them a zero for the day.

Even the old people are changing now. At first they were horrified by what we were saying about the Anglos. They had grown up with the system of oppression and they accepted it. And they were really afraid of what we were trying to do. But now they sit and talk to us, and some of them have even better—or maybe I should say even worse—stories than the ones I've been telling you.

● POSTSCRIPT

Several months after an historic election—as both the youngest person and the first woman elected to the City Council in Cotulla—Rosa Rodriguez lost her seat. The opposition challenged the citizenship and residency credentials of some of the people who voted for her, contesting her right to hold the position. After a bitter contest, the votes were recounted and Rosa lost to her opponent by five votes.

Members of the Raza Unida Party and lawyers friendly to their cause anticipated that the judge in the case would not be fair. According to Rosa, he was blatantly partial to her challengers. A few of the people who voted for Rosa did live outside the Cotulla city limits; others had not become naturalized citizens, even though they had lived in Cotulla most of their lives. But there were many "illegal" voters on the other side as well, including ranchers who lived outside the city limits or had official residences in other states. The date the judge set

for the hearings did not allow time for Rosa's defense to sub-
poena testimony from the ranchers and others who were "out
of town."

As a result, after what seemed like a major victory for the
Raza Unida Party—one that would give them a fighting chance
to bring about change—the City Council in Cotulla remains in
the hands of the old power structure. There is now only one
councilman who is identified with the party and he can accomplish virtually nothing against an opposition of four.

Party activity diminished markedly in the past year. Many
activists have moved to other places in search of educational
and job opportunities. As Rosa put it, "We tried for the past
six or seven years to change things in Cotulla, but they've
been breaking our heads and ruining financial opportunities
for us too." What particularly angered her was that the "anglicized Chicanos," who were benefiting the most from the
party's efforts, continued to oppose them.

Rosa feels that what happened to her discouraged a lot of
people. They frequently ask her, "Why should we even vote
if they won't give us a chance to win?" And the few party activists who are left in Cotulla are beginning to think the same
way: "We have to get out and make a living and forget about
politics and the people for a while." The financial bind many
found themselves in became untenable.

Rosa and Roy moved to Austin late last summer. Before they
left Cotulla, Rosa worked for a short time as a clerk in a new
county-sponsored program—the Women, Infants and Children
Program—that provided monthly milk supplements for needy
mothers, pregnant women and children under four. She also
started to organize women in the Raza Unida Party to raise
funds for the next city and county elections. By the time she
left, they had raised close to two thousand dollars.

The Rodriguezes moved to Austin primarily because Rosa
was pregnant and Roy had to find a job. Due to her heart
trouble, Rosa needs regular checkups and the kind of medical
care that is unavailable to Cotulla's lower income families. Because she was pregnant, she was refused a job at the Austin
telephone company, where she had hoped to work for a while.
Roy found work at a construction company and plans to enroll
in the University of Texas.

They return to Cotulla fairly often to visit relatives, and Roy continues to attend the monthly meetings of the County Commission (his term does not expire until next year). But both are staying away from politics, at least for the time being. "Sometimes I go to Cotulla and I don't want to come back to Austin," Rosa said. "But I'm glad not to be in politics anymore. I'm glad to get away from the hectic pace and all the pressures. Still, I feel bad about letting everybody down."

Anita Cupps in the office of the Selma Project, which served as headquarters for Alabama Women for Human Rights, in Birmingham.

Left to right: Johnny, Jenny, Anita and Sherry Cupps at a mine site where Johnny formerly worked.

Anita Cupps

RURAL ALABAMAN ROOTS

I was born on July 28, 1948, in Warrior, Alabama. That's in the northern end of Jefferson County, about eighteen miles out of Birmingham. We lived there for several years but then we moved quite a bit and I attended four or five different schools before I was ten or twelve.

A lot of times things were hard, but we always had a good time and Mother and Daddy always made sure we ate. It might be biscuits and gravy, you know, but we ate. Often you could tell they were worried and didn't know where the next rent payment would come from or something, but I can't remember a time without feeling the love they had for us.

We went through some hard times when Daddy was opening up Rickwood and he didn't have another job. Rickwood was a hole in the ground, is what it was. It was a cave that Daddy found on one of his outings when he was a Boy Scout leader. He got this dream—I guess you'd call it a pipeline dream—of opening it up and turning it into a tourist attraction and that's what he did. It was called Rickwood Caverns. It still is, but the state has bought it now and turned it into a state recreation area.

We spent from about 1954 to 1966 there. There were these caverns, like a big cave. Daddy built us a home there and then he built a concession stand and we had a park for the kids and a swimming pool and a camping ground and the rest. We just built it up to a family attraction. He started it in 1954 and we opened it, I believe, in '56. I was there till I married in '66.

I have a sister, Sharon, that's eighteen months younger than I am and my brother, Butch, that's thirteen months younger than Sharon and we all had jobs to do. We drew a payday! I was chief cook and bottlewasher in the restaurant, and I lifeguarded, and we took tours through the cave and took up tickets and cleaned up the parks, picked up papers and washed the tables off. You name it, we did it. We had other hired help and we did just what they did. There was no difference. We got paid the same, too, and that was a good way to earn your money for your school clothes and things like that.

When we first moved to Rickwood, we all five of us worked. Up to then, we had always had someone to come in and help mother with the housework, while she worked in the caverns and all. But then I got to where I really had a lot to do in school and I told them I'd just stay home and do the house and all. So I did that and I got paid just like Butch and Sharon did, and then I worked on Sunday just like the rest of them. There was no big deal about it, though. You did what you wanted to do. If you'd rather stay home, Daddy'd let you stay home. That was just no money in your pocket.

In the winter, you didn't have much business except maybe on the weekends. But summer was really an everyday affair. You met a lot of new people, you made a lot of new friends and you got to meet the public. It brings you out of a lot of shyness and after a while you get to learn to meet new people. It was an experience I won't ever regret.

We had people from all fifty states and from countries all around the world. A lot of them spoke foreign languages and it was just really an experience. We made a lot of dear friends like that, that would come to camp every year. They became like part of the family. We had campgrounds all over and we had enough room for several hundred campers a night.

Then we lost it. Daddy turned it into a corporation to get the necessary funds to enlarge it, so we could build the swimming pools and the restaurant and all that. But the corporation lost a lot of money and went out of business. They ended up by selling it for taxes on the place and just recently the state bought it. Daddy put so many years of his life into it and then he lost it. But I think he's finally reconciled now to what happened.

After Rickwood, Mother and Daddy moved back to Warrior. Rickwood is not but about five or eight miles from Warrior, so we've always been around this area. Daddy was raised there and his father is still living there. Mother was born and raised in a little town called Kimberly that joins Warrior's city limits. I don't know where they all came from originally, like way back. They've all been right here so long, and that's all I've ever heard.

Butch has a tire store in Warrior. He sells tires and has a service station, does grease jobs and mechanic work and things like that. He was doing real good working as a diesel mechanic for a trucking company in Birmingham. Then he got an opportunity to go into business with my uncle, so they bought them the tire store and Butch runs it. He does real well and he likes to be on his own. And people like him. He's a good kid. Sharon lives in a little town right on the outskirts of Warrior. She's a dental hygienist and she has two little boys, five and three. Her husband's the assistant director at a city park.

A lot of families here tend to live right in the same general vicinity, not very far apart from each other. Usually in a small town like that if you find a big family they're all pretty close-knit. It's good in a way, but sometimes it creates problems. It's nice in that you have a lot more things to do, a lot more fun, like the family get-togethers and all. Also you know everybody, and you know who married who and how the family's doing and all. It's really like your next door neighbors are part of the family too.

Right before we moved where we're living now, my husband, Johnny, and I, one of his sisters, two brothers and their families, and his mother and daddy lived together in this one little area, with a big fence around all the houses. We spent five years down there and it was an experience! The kids all played together, and everybody more or less just stayed at home and minded their own business. But when one has problems, you all naturally feel it if you're living that close. And when it comes to making decisions, you don't really want to go against the grain, so it can get difficult trying to get everybody to agree.

We left there because we didn't have any land. We have a few head of cattle and two horses and, the way it was, our cattle had to be kept off at someone else's place. Our little girl really loves them and we wanted them close to her and so we found us a place with a pasture and we decided to move and have all of our family together, cows and horses and all!

Daddy's working for an insurance company now in Birmingham. It does him good to get out more. He was a Methodist minister for several years and he had several different churches while we were coming up. I was eight or nine when he started pastoring church and even while he had Rickwood, he had his churches. But he has to kind of go easy on his religion now. It gets on his mind and worries him a good bit.

Mother works with Butch now at the tire store. She's worked all her life and she'd rather be out working and meeting the public than staying home. Daddy has odd hours as an insurance agent and he's not there a lot and Mother gets bored at home. So she works and she gets to see old friends. They've made a lot of them in the time that they've both been working. And since there's not much for her to do at home now, it gives her a way to pass the time.

Our family's always been real close all of our lives, but I guess Daddy had the stronger influence on me. I was the oldest and I always liked to do things that he likes to do, like playing ball and swimming. He likes to get out and go hiking and scouting and I always went with him and always just had a good time with him. Mother was always there for us, you know, but I was strong-willed and Daddy could do more with me than Mother could!

I really enjoyed school. We graduated from Corner High School, which is right out from Warrior. I think there were eighty that graduated from our senior class, so they were kind of small but they were good schools. We had a good time. I was a cheerleader for three years and editor of the yearbook. And I was in the Future Teachers of America—we were just general teacher aides you might say. Just a lot of different things.

I never did take a subject that I didn't like. Science courses I guess would be my favorite. But I love reading and working math problems. I just liked going to school. It really was an experience that I looked forward to every day. I never did get bored or tired of it. I had applied for a nursing school in Birmingham and then, well, Johnny and I just decided we'd go ahead and get married. We both started Corner together in the ninth grade and we started going out and we got married the summer after we graduated. Then we both went to work and I never did go back to school. I think I would've enjoyed nursing. But right then you couldn't tell an eighteen-year-old a whole lot, so we just went ahead and got married.

I got a job as a service representative for the Bell Telephone Company in Birmingham. I'd talk to the customers who called in to have their telephone connected or order something, or if they had a problem about their bill. It was a demanding job. You have a supervisor there and then you have observers that are listening to you while you're talking to the customers, and you get sort of graded, according to how you talk and what you say. You're constantly under observation, but I was really lucky because I had a lot of good supervisors. I really loved them and I hated to leave because of that reason.

I was there for two years. I quit when I was about five months pregnant with Sherry. I had been sick a good bit and that job plays on your nerves a lot. You're under a lot of tension, so I thought maybe if I'd quit work I'd get to feeling better. After the baby was born they called and wanted me to come back, but I had gotten used to being at home and I didn't want to leave my baby to be raised by anybody else, so I just told them no.

A lot of the girls I worked with that stayed have gone on to supervisor positions, so chances are I would have too. But I don't think I would've wanted that. You're under a lot of tension from the higher-ups. You catch it from them if your service is not up to what it's supposed to be. And then a lot of times the supervisor doesn't have a good relationship with their girls, you know, and I wouldn't have liked that. I don't like being put in the position of telling the girl what she has to do. She ought to have the initiative to do it on her own.

When I went to the phone company in '66, the first black rep trained right after I did, in our division at central headquarters. We were all wondering how it was going to work out, but it worked out real well. At first there was a little anticipation on both sides, black and white. But she did real well and then other blacks started transferring from other departments, bidding on service rep jobs and coming into commercial. If I had stayed, I might have bid out of commercial. I would've liked to work in the plant, be a dispatcher or something like that. I don't like management. I'd rather work with people than work above them.

ANITA AND JOHNNY CUPPS
ON COAL MINING POLITICS

JOHNNY: My whole family is coal mine. My father's retired now, but he worked thirty-five years underground. I got eight brothers and three sisters, and all my brothers but one are in the coal industry. They're bosses, miners, strip-miners, operators, some kind of deal. But I didn't start out in the mines.

After high school Anita and I got married on August 12, 1966, and then the tenth of October I had to go off to the Army Reserves and I stayed gone six months. Then I went back to work at Genuine Parts Company where I worked before I went off. That's an automotive parts company and I stayed there five years. I went from the warehouse to a truck driver and from there to a counter salesman and then to a store manager. Then I went to a junior college, night school, and I wound up working there as a salesman the last six months.

I wanted to be a health, physical education and recreation major so I could be a high school coach. And I was doing real good. I was going to Jefferson State, this little junior college that was on the 3.0 system, and I had a 2.81 average. But then when I took that job selling with that company, they sent me to Chicago for two weeks to go to school. So I dropped out of college that spring and never went back. I just lacked a few hours to finish the second year.

I told Anita the other day, I don't think I'll stay in the coal mine forever. I've always wanted to go into law. I hate a smart aleck lawyer, only I really admire them. Some of the politicians here in this county especially are just jackleg, smartass lawyers. We got to get rid of them sometime, and one of these days I'm going to go back to school.

When I came home from Chicago, I worked with this company for about six more months and then I went to the coal mine. I just wasn't cut out for sales. Too much pressure. And then the driving back and forth about forty miles each way and the driving on the selling route. So I got a job with U.S. Pipe and Foundry and I've been there four years, first day of this month.

Now I'm just underground labor, they call it. Anything that

has to be done. First two and a half years I worked underground, I was a roof bolter. You got a machine and you drill holes in the top, just like a ceiling. Then you got these pins that are anywhere from three to five to seven foot long, depending on how good the top is, and you put them in there and tighten them up and that holds the roof up.

I'd been working in this little mine that we nicknamed "mini-mine." We just opened it up and it's maybe 300 feet deep at the most. But the big mine, now I went back to the big mine just this morning and I guess I'll be there for a while, and it's 532 feet straight down. Have to ride an elevator down. It's easy work though. There's nothing to it. It's all mechanical.

On July the twelfth of 1973, I went to work for the international mine workers' union as an organizer. I worked July, August and September in Jackson County, about 134 miles from here. There's a big strip mine up there I was trying to organize and we stayed there about three months. We didn't get them. It was either us or the company, and the workers chose the company.

The day before the election, the company put out some of the best smut material you've ever seen. It's a division of Peabody Coal and they're plenty smart. I bet they spent ten thousand dollars to have newspapers printed up. They had Tony Boyle's* picture, you know, and everything the union ever did rotten.

Most of the union's hospitals and clinics are located in Birmingham or Jasper, centralized in the coal area. It's a hundred

---

* William Anthony Boyle, elected president of the United Mine Workers of America in 1963, after a career as a miner and local union official in Montana. Opposed for the presidency in 1969 by Joseph A. Yablonski, who represented Miners for Democracy, a rank-and-file insurgent group. Shortly after Boyle's reelection in a bitter contest, Yablonski, his wife and daughter were found murdered in their Clarksville, Pennsylvania, home. The U.S. Department of Labor obtained a court order invalidating the 1969 election, shortly before Boyle was defeated in his 1972 reelection bid by Arnold Miller. Attempted suicide in September 1973. In December, indicted and convicted of using union funds for illegal political contributions, he began serving a three-year sentence in federal prison. In April 1974, found guilty of three charges of first degree murder in "ordering the assassination" of Joseph Yablonski, his wife and daughter, for which he also had diverted union funds to pay three hired gunmen and two intermediaries.

and some miles up to Jackson County where a lot of the mines are. And also at that time, the welfare fund in Washington had been on strike. So they had a picture of one of the clinics somewhere that was closed with a big picket sign on it, and it said in their paper, "After you drive 105 miles to take your child to a doctor in Birmingham, this is what you'll find. Is this what you want for your family?"

Anyway, this company got it better than any union dared to be. They pay all their hospitalization, all their medication, and they give them a few thousand dollars a year into a trust fund as a retirement fund. And the miners there were getting about a quarter better than union scale. So it was tough trying to organize there. We got beat seventy-five to thirty-six. So I went back to the mines that December. I'd planned on staying with the union as long as I could. It just so happened that . . .

ANITA: Tell it like it is.

JOHNNY: Well, when I left the mines I didn't have any intention of going back. I'll tell you just like it is. See, we was in the miners' campaign down here in District 20, which covers all of Alabama. Miller* won against Boyle in '72 and this was the following year. So it was the Miller faction against the Boyle faction and we was Miller folks. Not so much in being Miller people, but wanting change in the thing. So we were fighting the Boyle bunch and they're a bunch of dirty rotten bastards that ever lived. They're strong-arm people and if they couldn't beat you they'd try to whip you. Or kill you.

The whole time I was in Jackson County working for the union, the campaign was going on. I'd come home three and four nights a week, sometimes every night, and get Frank Clements† to get out and campaign. At first we thought Frank was a good guy, and we thought he had a good chance of win-

* Arnold R. Miller, succeeded Tony Boyle as president of the United Mine Workers of America in 1972. Ran as a reformer; was a co-organizer of Miners for Democracy with Joseph Yablonski in 1969. A coal miner for most of his life. From 1970 to 1972, president of the Black Lung Association and member of the Board of Directors of the Appalachian Research and Defense Fund.

† Frank Clements, executive board member of the United Mine Workers of America from District 20. In the 1973 district election in Alabama, his was one of three positions on the pro-Miller slate; the other two were president and secretary-treasurer of the local.

ning for executive board. Really we didn't know, but we spent a lot of money to get him elected. He's a Miller man, one hundred percent. He's a yes man's what he is, and I don't care if you put that on the front of your book.

First, let me tell you how Frank first got his job. See when Miller ran against Boyle in '72 he got only 23 percent of the vote here. There was very few people in this district that supported him.

ANITA: Or in the whole Mine Workers. We had family conflict about him for how long? How many months?

JOHNNY: Oh, maybe a month or two. See Miller promised all what he was going to do, you know. "I'm going to give you five to six hundred dollars a month pension, I'm going to give all the disabled miners' and their widows' hospital cards back," and it was all just a dream, you know. But a lot of people swallowed it. Anita swallowed it.

ANITA: No, I just wanted Tony Boyle out of office. Our union was going to pot, here and everywhere else. When he was president, there were things like his daughter was attorney for the Mine Workers in Montana and she used to draw a big salary. His brother was president of the district out in Montana and he drew a big salary too. Then everybody in Washington had those limousines. That kind of thing was going on all over.

So we were getting reports about how the union was going broke and how the hospital cards were going to go. And you could see it. What mainly was my concern was our youngest little girl, Jenny. She had just been born and she's got several serious problems and we knew that we were going to have to have the hospital card to make ends meet and to get her the help she needed. That was my biggest concern, and that Boyle was going to rob the union blind and we wouldn't have anything to rely on.

We still had our hospital card at that time, but we were really afraid that the fund was going to dry up. And we realized that we had to rely on the union to save our little girl's life. That's where I decided I didn't want any part of Tony Boyle. So Miller, he seemed at the time like he had a good platform and at least he would make an honest effort to clean it up. So at first, I was for Miller and Johnny was for Boyle.

JOHNNY: No, here's what it was. See there's a hell of a lot of young miners here and all over the country, been there one or two years, and most of them hadn't been around a union, didn't know what was going on. And the old fogies, the old illiterates around the mine—and that's what they are—they were Boyle people. You know, the sun rises and sets on Tony Boyle's butt and all this kind of stuff. The young ones didn't know and hell, they just . . . well, that's the way I was, too. I didn't know any better.

It's the old ones that had the influence and they could tell them it's raining out there right now, Tony Boyle could, and hell they'd put their raincoats on. What people don't realize is the mentality of coal miners. I don't know how it is in other parts of the country, but I'm sure it's about the same as it is here. The educational level of a coal miner in this district is something like the fourth grade. I've got people that work at my mines that make $250 a week and can't read. Hell, some of them can't even sign their check.

The biggest reason they liked old Tony Boyle was that he got them a good contract last time and they make good money. But what they don't realize is inflation ate it up faster than we got it. We're not any better off now than we was three years ago. Maybe a little further back. Except the hospital card. There wasn't any changes there, but it covers everything. Little Jenny has to have medication every day and that's covered too. Well, I just didn't know any better, so I would've voted for Boyle.

ANITA: A lot of these coal miners, they're not interested in who runs their union. They've never made good money like they do now and they're satisfied to go and put their forty hours in, get their paycheck and go home and figure out how much they're going to spend on groceries this week. They don't care about the things that go on around them. They like their paychecks and that's it. They don't want to get involved.

After those murders, the Yablonski murders, before anybody was arrested or anything, I figured Boyle had to be the man behind it. And I really think Johnny thought so, too. But it wasn't until he got involved with this friend of his that . . . Well, go on, tell it.

JOHNNY: Well this friend that works at the mines, he's forty. He's a Miller man, or at least he was. Dick started out to be Mil-

ler's man down here during the '72 election. He's got guts, ain't
no joke about that. They went to a union meeting one Sunday
when I was still going to vote for old Boyle. I didn't say nothing
to him about the way he believed because it's a free country and
you can believe the way you want. So he went down to this little
wide spot in the road about thirty miles from here and they had
a big union meeting. Old Frank Clements and a couple of others
went too.

It was a pro-Boyle meeting and Dick got up and he wanted
to speak for Miller, try to get him a few votes. And hell, they
wouldn't have no part of it. They cussed him and called him
a fool and all. And one of the union officials here in this district, he just kicked Dick's butt, right there in front of about
250 people. He took a running leap from the back of the room
and just run up and kicked him.

Then they stuck knives and guns up to their throats and
they were fixing to kill them right there. They wouldn't let
them out of the place. It was bad. Finally they changed their
mind and decided they'd get in a big mess of trouble and they
just let them go. But they cut the tires up on their cars and all.
Oh, it was hot.

Well, Dick and them hit the papers with it and they even
telegramed J. Edgar Hoover, Nixon and Lord knows who all
else, asking for protection. I didn't really believe Dick and the
story they was telling, but it just so happens that my brother's
wife's brother was at the meeting and he said it happened just
like that. And I've known him all my life and I know he
wouldn't tell me a lie.

So that's when I got involved. I said, well hell, if the sons of
a bitch'll go that far, they'll do me the same way one day. So
I decided I'll just do what I can to help, and we've been in it
ever since. The Miller election was almost over then, but I
done what I could, campaigning, going to rallies and stuff
with Dick.

ANITA: I didn't really do a whole lot in the Miller elections
either. What we mostly got involved in was the District 20
elections. That picked up early in '73, right after the Miller
election. They were trying to get Miller's people in office
where he could have someone he could depend on and work
with from the different states. So we decided we'd work with

Miller's people here and we worked from that January till the first of October '73. A lot of states had their elections that same year and Miller lost a lot. I don't think he's got control of the executive board even now.

JOHNNY: Let's back up for a minute to show you how Boyle had the thing messed up. District 20, which is Alabama, was supposed to have an executive board member from Alabama. And you know who it was? Albert Pass* from Middleburg, Kentucky. He's the one convicted of the Yablonski murders. Boyle just appointed him. Executive board member wasn't elected then. So he just said, "You go down there Albert and keep them straight." That was one of the reforms Miller campaigned for, free elections, and the '73 election was the first one like it ever here.

Well Arnold took over in December of '72 and they had Pass in jail then, so District 20 didn't have an executive board member. So Arnold decides, well, I've got a lot of pro-Boyle people on this board, I need to get some people that'll be on my side. So we was at work one night in the coal mines and he called the motor pit and he asked for Dick. So Arnold said to Dick, "I got this job and I want you to come here and take it." And Dick got mad and he said, "I didn't get in your campaign for no goddamned job." He said, "I don't want it." That's just the type of person he is. He doesn't want anything for working for what he believes in.

So Arnold said, "I've got to have somebody, Dick." This was to fill the seat until the election the next year. He said, "If you can't get anybody to come, you be here." So Dick said, "I'll be there if nobody else will." Then Dick called up someone whose judgment he respected and told him the situation and the guy said, "Yeah, I know a man. He's a black man." And Dick said, "Well, call him and tell him we'll meet him at the union hall in the morning."

The guy's name was Sylvester Marable. He was a miner and a Boyle man, but he was supposed to be a good man with honest judgment. So they talked Marable into taking the job.

* Albert Pass, convicted of first degree murder in the Yablonski slayings in June 1973. Former assistant to Tony Boyle, international executive board member of the United Mine Workers of America, and secretary-treasurer of District 19 (Kentucky).

But evidently word got back and the Boyle folks put the thumb on him. Probably threatened to kill him. Nobody knows, but the next morning, less than twelve hours after he said he'd take the job, his wife answered when Dick called and said he wasn't going to take it. Here's what the Boyle folks were probably shooting at. Thirty-four percent of the miners in this district are black. Marable's a black leader, so if he had taken that job, he would've had a lot of influence. So they scared him out of it real quick.

So then we finally get to Frank Clements. He was working where I work and he was going to a little trade school out here on his G.I. Bill. He was a good friend of Dick's too, so Dick called him out at the school and asked him, "Frank, do you want that job?" And Frank said, "Yeah, I'll take it." So that's how Frank Clements got the job. He was third choice.

So now, coming on up to the District 20 election in '73. Bill Shamblin—he's an organizer or like a campaign coordinator— he showed up in January. That's when we began to lay the groundwork for the election. We talked about how much money you'd have to have to run a campaign and we wanted to publish us a newspaper and all that kind of stuff. We started writing letters to the editors of the *Birmingham News* and the *Post Herald* and the *Daily Mountain Eagle* in Jasper, just ripping these district officials up, the Boyle folks. So it just rocked along like that.

Here's what the slate was. Dick was going to run for president. He didn't want anybody to give him anything, he wanted to run for it. So Frank was going to run for executive board member, to keep that. And we figured that if we got a black man that was a leader to run for secretary-treasurer we could pick up some black votes. So we went out to Harold Underwood's house one night and we talked to him. He said he'd think on it and he stayed up all night drinking coffee and talking with his wife, Frankie, and the next day he said he'd run. Harold was the first black candidate in a miners' election in Alabama. So that's what our slate was. From then on, it was just go and push and work and cuss and be cussed.

ANITA: And campaign night and day. But see, the Alabama miner don't believe women ought to be heard or seen.

JOHNNY: That's the Boyle people now.

ANITA: Well, Frank felt that way too. That it's best to do all the work behind the scenes and, you know, not be seen. Me and Frankie, Harold's wife, and Frank's wife, Dorothy, we did some work. But it was kind of limited as to what we could do. We got making phone calls and writing letters and organizing rallies and picketing and setting up meetings. Then we were always running back and forth delivering things to newspapers, calling editors and things like that.

The men's attitude got kind of aggravating because you worked your head off. We got up, what time, at six o'clock in the mornings? And a lot of times at one and two o'clock the next morning we'd still be up discussing campaign issues and what we needed to do and what the men needed to do. Then, you know, when Frank or somebody'd say, "You can't do that because a miner don't want to see a woman out campaigning," or something, it got real aggravating at that point.

But I enjoyed it. We had a good time. It was a lot of hard work and some of it was . . . well, it wasn't really dangerous, but a lot of situations you didn't know how you should go about getting into. We kind of had to be careful. They sliced tires here and there and a couple of them had knives put on them. It was a hot situation all during the campaign. And we had a campaign trailer that was our headquarters and it had been gone through a time or two. And most times, it was just us three women there.

We had some people from Tuscaloosa help us some. There was a Mrs. Marchant, a strong union lady, and some others who worked that end of the state. And then we'd get some miners' wives to do things here. Like when Miller came and we had a rally, we had miners' wives and hospital employees that helped fix refreshments. Then we got the bands and made posters and things like that. And then we went to the clinics and handed out literature, at the union clinics where the miners can go for medical care.

We'd have meetings to discuss what all we needed to do, usually just the women. Chris* would come down for some of them. Then we had some kids that were out working and we

---

* Chris Hintz, organizer of Alabama Women for Human Rights, on the staff of the Selma Project. Formerly a community organizer in the Boston area for the Cambridge Ministry in Higher Education.

supervised them. We just did more or less what had to be done. Not ever being in politics before, I guess I went back to what I learned at Rickwood. We did advertising and all there. So I had a little experience in that, how to get the people's attention and what appeals to them.

Then Johnny and them would give us some ideas if we were running short. But he was out in Scottsboro organizing for the union all week, except during the summer when he'd come home every night to take Frank to the mines to campaign face to face with the miners. Frank, he was in Birmingham and Washington most of the time. Harold worked until the last six weeks, and then he was out every day doing things. The candidate for president, Fuller, he was in Scottsboro with Johnny most of the time.

JOHNNY: I forgot to tell you that we picked up Charles Fuller when Dick backed out. Dick got mad. See, we knew it was going to cost us a lot of money to run a campaign. So along about the time that we picked up Harold to run with us, that's when Andy and Chris from the Selma Project* came into the picture. Andy said to us, "Well I know some liberal-minded people that we can get some money from." They were some of the same ones that gave Miller money for his campaign.

So we're just common people. We haven't got the kind of money it takes to run a campaign, so everybody says, "Well, okay. Go ahead and see what you can do." So Andy wrote to this woman in New York who's a rich Democrat and she sent us a three thousand dollar check just that quick. And everybody was just thrilled to death when Andy showed us the check, except Dick. He said, "Goddamned New York money. I don't want none of it." He said, "I'll just quit." That's the way he operates. He never heard of this woman before.

So we picked up Fuller. Spent as much money on him as we did for Frank or Harold. We gave him the same amount of

---

* Andy Himes, married to Chris Hintz and director of the Selma Project, a nonprofit service agency devoted to the struggles of poor and working class people that grew out of the Civil Rights Movement. It was begun in response to a landmark voting rights drive led by Martin Luther King, Jr., in early 1965, where more than 3,000 were arrested, along with King. It moved to Tuscaloosa, then to Birmingham, and in 1975 ran out of funds.

publicity in the papers, handed out his literature with the others and printed his bumper stickers. Each one of them had two thousand bumper stickers printed. Fuller'd give all his away and then he'd get mad and say he didn't get as many. Hell, it didn't cost him a nickel to run his campaign.

We spent $13,000 on the whole campaign, for all three of them. In a roundabout way we got help from Miller. They helped us get $4,500 from the Auto Workers. Then we got another $800 from the woman in New York and $800 from the Episcopal Church in Atlanta. But we never did raise enough. The campaign still owes about $4,000 that'll probably never be paid.

ANITA: Anyway, Fuller wanted votes off both sides, Miller and Boyle. He didn't seem to want to take a firm stand on any issue. And his wife wasn't able to do anything, or she wouldn't. So it was more or less the three of us up here, and then Mrs. Marchant and another miner, Jerry Hubbard's wife, Linda, in Tuscaloosa, that did all the work.

Every day we were at it. Mostly in July, August and September. I'd usually take my kids with me. My little niece came down and stayed with them some. We kept on working out what we'd do, and then we'd tell the men, because they weren't here most of the time. See, mostly what they did, they went to the mine sites and talked to the miners, which they didn't want us to do. They thought that was not a woman's place to come and talk at and that the miners would resent that.

I don't know if they were afraid the miners'd think that women were helping run their campaign or what it was. Frank thinks that miners resent women doing anything like that. But what he didn't realize is that a lot of the miners confer with their wives on how to vote. And we've had a lot of them tell us when we were out campaigning that they really appreciated the wives taking an interest. See, it was as much to the wives' concern as it was really of the coal miners. The wives are the ones that manage the paycheck usually.

There's a lot of old-fashioned ideas that they think the coal miners have, but really, they don't object to a lot of things. See, Frank is under the impression that women's job is to stay home, have their children, go buy groceries and have his meals on the table. He thinks women ought not to interfere in what men are doing. He really doesn't want women around him. But even though he didn't want Dorothy out there, she did some work. She probably felt like . . . Well, see, I didn't have a husband that was running for office. Johnny was just working his head off for Frank. So I felt like if he was going to work like that, that's the least I could do because I also wanted the union to do better than what it had been doing. So Dorothy felt like, since I was doing it, she should be too.

Well, after all this, the results were we won the executive board, but the president and the secretary-treasurer got beat. Frank was the only candidate who's won and then he's turned his back on us. But a majority of the miners didn't even care enough to vote, it seems like. The voting was at the bath houses where they bathe when they come up from the mines, so they couldn't have missed it. They'd have to walk right by it.

JOHNNY: The first day of October '73 we counted the votes. I was on a five-man committee set up to help the Labor Department count the votes and I held my breath all day, it was that close. Frank won by a narrow margin. It was about 2,100 to 1,900. There was a third guy who had about 800 votes. I believe there was 4,800 votes cast out of nearly 10,000 miners. Harold got beat by 600 and Fuller got beat by 200.

So that was the first of October and on the tenth of October we lost the election in Jackson County at the big strip mine. So we left there, then I went to Tuscaloosa for two weeks, doing a survey on other mines down there we were going to try to organize. Then we left there and I took Nita and the girls, and Frank took Dorothy and two of their little boys, and we went to Black Lake, Michigan, for a week. It was at the Auto Workers' Family Center. And it was beautiful. We went to school during the day to learn how to set up an international convention, but it was a vacation for us all.

While we were there, I got a telegram to go out to Wyoming. So as soon as we got back home, I left again for two weeks in Wyoming. Then I came home and went to Fort Payne, Alabama, for two weeks. And then the international convention started. All the elected delegates from every local union in the country come together to rewrite the constitution.

It's every four years. It was in Pittsburgh and I was supposed to go, but I didn't get to go because everybody else was gone from the district office here in Birmingham.

So the District 20 delegates was there, a bunch of pro-Boyle people and several Miller people. They had a meeting with Arnold Miller one night. Frank was in there, but it turns out Frank's got a lot of backbone, just like a jellyfish. And see, one of our union officials here, he hates me because I put hell on him during the campaign. He was pro-Boyle. I gave him more static during the campaign than anybody. I was a spur in his side, simply because I know what he is and I don't like him.

Well, anyway, the delegates had this meeting with Arnold. And Arnold—well, I think our three-year-old Jenny's got more backbone than him too. So this official just got up and he told Arnold, "I want Johnny Cupps off the international's payroll." So Arnold just said, "Okay." Arnold would've had to stand up to him and I guess he thinks this guy has a big following. And Frank said nothing.

ANITA: You know, everybody that worked for Miller and for Frank in this last election has said they'll never work for them again. Miller's the nicest fellow you'll ever talk to just to talk to him, but he just doesn't seem that strong. And Frank, we can't keep Frank in Alabama long enough to talk to him about what the problems are here in District 20.

JOHNNY: So I went back to the coal mine. But Arnold had told me in the summer of '73 that the international was going to form this coal miners' political action committee, COMPAC, which they did. And he told me, "I want you to be the COMPAC member from District 20." See, I'd met him when we took a busload of miners to meet with him in Washington after he was elected. Most of the people here didn't know him from Adam. So we just decided that since we couldn't get him down here, we'd just go and see him. That was a wild trip.

So then we had a big rally here on the twenty-eighth of July in '73 that actually started our campaign last summer, and we had Arnold down. What was really going on was a black lung rally. The federal government had approved a bill that there'd be three new pulmonary function clinics here in Alabama. So we was being political and we wanted people to see our candidates with Miller, you know?

Arnold remembered me from putting pressure on him up there in Washington. I guess he figured, well, there's that old rednecked hillbilly again! He came into Birmingham on Friday evening and I guess we had a hundred miners out there to meet him. Held a press conference at the airport and got him on TV. Got him a key to the city and all this kind of rot.

The high school over here holds about four thousand people and we had it full. We had people lined up around the walls. Had people outside who couldn't get in. And it was 115 degrees if it was one degree. We had one of our U.S. senators down here who's always been anti-labor. Had the vice president of the Auto Workers here, Levi Daniel. We had a tremendous meeting and that was the biggest crowd that Miller has ever spoken to, right here. Me, Nita and Bill Shamblin put it on together. That was about it, just the three of us. That's when he promised me the COMPAC job.

ANITA: We did all that organizing mainly for our local candidates. We thought we'd have around two thousand people attend. That's what we were planning on really. I was amazed that so many came. But we had done a lot of publicity and a lot of calling. So a lot of people knew about it and were interested and we were really pleased with the turnout we had.

They kept Miller up till three o'clock Friday night with our candidates, and talking to local officials. Then they went to visit the shift change at a bath house that night, one of the largest mines in the state with over a thousand men. The next morning he went to a union meeting and then that evening we had the rally and that night we had a reception in town. And Sunday he went to Jackson County where Johnny was working and talked to the men up there in the strip mines.

JOHNNY: We kept him busy, that's for damn sure. And he promised this job. But when this local union official put a little heat on him, hell, he forgot all about it. I don't forget things either. Their day's coming.

ANITA: And so Johnny went back to the coal mines. Frank has not called us, and every time we try to call him he's out of the office or he's in Washington or Hawaii or somewhere else. You know, Johnny had tried to call Frank while Frank was at the convention in Pittsburgh, to let him come up and tell Miller his side of the story. Frank kept telling Johnny that he would talk to Miller himself but the way we heard it, he never did. He just tried to put Johnny off so he wouldn't come talk for himself. Now he won't have any contact with us. I guess Frank doesn't want to create any opposition, so he just follows what the others say.

We've learned a lot from this last campaign. We've learned to not take people at their face value. We did Frank, and we thought Frank was a good person. And he was, as far as I know, when we started working for him. But when he got in office, I don't know if he thought he got there by himself, or if he just didn't care who helped him get there. But he doesn't have anything to do with us now.

And you know, since Miller and them took over, there doesn't seem to be any difference in anything. I think there's still just three doctors at the clinic in Jasper. And within a fifteen-mile radius of it you've got at least three thousand miners and their dependents, don't we, Johnny? In the last ten years there's been about forty doctors who've gone through this one clinic, so there's bound to be something wrong with the administration. They spent about a half a million dollars remodeling it last year and they've still got three doctors in it.

We're really lucky with Jenny because with her problem we don't take her to a UMW doctor. We take her to a specialist and the union pays him. We have an endocrine specialist that got her when she was three days old and he's taken care of her ever since. And we just couldn't find anybody better. She was born with a genital defect and then there were problems with her blood and well . . . They didn't expect her to live. But Dr. Cunningham's worked with her ever since and he really has performed miracles with her.

If it hadn't been for the union, we would've been in bankruptcy I imagine, don't you, Johnny? They've never questioned anything that we've sent them. They've always paid it. So we're really lucky that way. She's had several operations and they call in the best there is to operate. We just couldn't receive any better care than what we've got for her. See, we knew after she was born that we'd have to have the union's backing to get her through.

But actually, the politics of it was first, because we were already into that even before Jenny was born. After that, it made it even more a personal fight. But we were already into the politics. She was born in November of '71 and they were on strike then, about the union contract. The miners struck all over the country and they'll do it again this November, when the contract's up.

JOHNNY: We always go on strike. The company just drags their feet on negotiating the contract. Most of the time the plants and the people have got a supply of coal in front of them for a month or so, and hell, they don't give a damn. But when the coal pile goes to getting low, well, then they'll talk seriously. Right now what we make isn't all that good. I get $236 a week. The hourly wage is around $5.90, but other crafts and labor unions here make anywhere from $7 to $10 an hour. So we're one of the lowest on the totem pole.

ANITA: And the others have a lot more benefits, like retirement and other things, than the mine workers do. The only thing the mine workers really got going for them is their hospital card. You can't improve on that. But there's no workmen's compensation, no dental care, nothing like that. Dental care used to be included with the medical a while back, but not since we've had it. Supposedly it was abused, so they took it out. But with Jenny and all, I guess Johnny'll be staying with the UMW.

JOHNNY: Unless I become a $200,000 a year attorney, see, and then I could afford to pay the medical bills myself.

ANITA AND CHRIS HINTZ ON ALABAMA WOMEN FOR HUMAN RIGHTS

ANITA: Chris and I met on the twenty-eighth of July last summer. I remember because it was my birthday and the day of the rally for Miller. Setting up that rally was really our first major thing. We had already decided on some of the things that needed to be done, but we hadn't gone about really planning them carefully yet. And that's when we met Chris and her husband, Andy.

CHRIS: That was just a couple of weeks after I moved down here from Boston and Anita really had a lot to do with my organizing the conference that turned into Alabama Women for

Human Rights. Some of the other miners' wives, too, were upset about things like Frank Clements saying he didn't want women out campaigning for him because it would ruin his image. We had a lot of conversations about that. Then at the same time, the Gulfcoast Pulpwood Association was on strike and an injunction was brought against them that they couldn't picket. So a lot of their wives had gotten together and they wanted to go out on the picket line for them and the men wouldn't let them. It wasn't their place, you know . . .

A lot of that kind of thing was happening all over and that's kind of how the idea came about for the conference. It started mainly around labor struggles and then moved into other things, like day care. There were lots of things beginning to happen all over the state, so the idea was to have a meeting where women from around the state could come together and talk about what they were all doing. It was in January this year and about a hundred women came. We had no plan for an organization at first.

ANITA: The idea was trying to learn from each other's experiences—what kinds of problems we all had and how to overcome them. There were women there from all different kinds of groups and interests. Prison reforms, health and education, day care, labor.

We had a workshop on labor where I was a discussion leader and the women told the problems that they had faced and wanted to know if we'd had any similar and what we had done about them. I talked about our campaign some and we gave some advice from that, and everybody contributed as to what they could do to solve their problems. Mostly it was a group from Mobile that were on strike against the Del Champs Supermarket and they weren't really getting any support.

CHRIS: The women again had really been the backbone of the strike. The Teamsters had crossed their picket line and all kinds of nasty things were happening. And the Del Champs people own half of Mobile—the politicians and newspapers and everything. So the workers and the women weren't able to get their story out and nobody else had heard of them until they came to the conference.

ANITA: I think the conference was a real success in more ways than one. I really enjoyed it, because you met women from every field that I had been accustomed to seeing men in. And they all have similar kinds of problems, you know? When you compare with other women, things that they went through and things that they had done, you realize you're not fighting a losing battle by yourself. You start feeling it can be won. It gives you a lot of hope.

At the conference we also set up different regional groups and we've organized one in Birmingham. It was a real success in that way, too. We're trying to stay in touch with the state-wide things, so we can go to each other for advice or help when we need it. Chris puts out a statewide newsletter now and we're trying to contribute regionally. We're working on setting up our own little projects too.

Frankie Underwood and them in Jasper are doing some work with sex education in the schools, and I think that really needs to be done in our schools here. Then in Birmingham they're working on health and welfare programs—food stamps and things like that—that we should do here too. In the rural areas there's so many things that the people don't know and that they should be informed of. They'd be so much better off, the ones who need help in areas like this.

And I'm interested in prison reforms. We don't have any-body in our regional that's really working on that, but I'd really like to do something along that line. I guess my interest started with the Jefferson County jail system. I know how bad ours is and I can just imagine what they're like on a statewide level. My father's had a nervous breakdown a few times and the only way we can get him help is, he usually has to go through the county jail system first. Mental health care in Ala-bama is really so unbelievably poor. There's so many road-blocks you meet trying to get someone some help. I hate the thought of sending a mentally ill person to the jail before you can get him some mental help. There's just so much need for prison reforms.

CHRIS: There's a new group that just started that has a chapter in Birmingham called Families for Action, and an-other group called something like the Prisoners Survival Com-mittee, started by a black man who'd been in jail for thirteen years and just got out last year. Hopefully some of those peo-ple will become part of the core group of AWHR in Birmingham, just to let people know what's happening and what kinds of things they can do.

Families for Action has really done some good organizing all around the state. Prisoners' families have really gotten into it in the past couple of years and I think the reason is that there's just been so many killings of prisoners. The wardens and the guards beat them up or shoot them. So now the parents are scared that their kids are going to get killed. It's different from them just being locked up in there.

ANITA: It seems it probably happened all along, but an organization hasn't come along until now. Now they're bringing it before the public. The average person is beginning to know more about it. Instead of just pushing it under a rock, we're getting information about it.

That's what was so good about the conference we had. We learned so much about what was happening in these different areas. And they're a real nice bunch of ladies. They've all had problems that relate to one another directly or indirectly, and every one of them wants you to know that they'll help you in any way they can, doing work with you or sharing past experiences. They're all trying to work for a better Alabama or a better chance for women.

I believe if we called on some of them for our next elections in District 20, they'd come through. I have no doubt. Because they know what we've got to go through yet. It's a fight in Alabama to start something when you don't have a lot of support. Especially in the rural areas like we live in.

We're just laying the groundwork for AWHR here in the Birmingham area now. This will just be our third steering committee meeting in August. I'm on the steering committee along with Frankie. We take turns going from Walker County. We're going to be looking to get other women involved, but really it's hard to explain to somebody unless they're working for a cause or they need help. Women are not going to get involved unless they have a reason to be in it.

CHRIS: AWHR is really completely different than other women's organizations. It's not a feminist organization in any way, like the Alabama Women's Political Caucus or NOW, which are made up of middle and upper middle class ladies, university-type people. They're both very small in this state.

AWHR is not dealing just with women's issues, and particularly not just with women getting better paying jobs, because their husbands don't even have well-paying jobs. We're really talking about class issues more than women's issues. Sure, you'd like to be able to make more money if you work, but you want your husband to be able to make more too. And most of all, you want your kids to be able to lead decent lives when they get older. You're concerned with making the whole community better, rather than just some individuals making it big.

I don't really think the Women's Movement had any direct effect on the women in AWHR or the fact that we organized it. Except the literature that's been written is real helpful, like the book *Our Bodies, Ourselves* that we handed out at the conference, women's labor stories and a lot of informational things about what's happening in different places that it's nice to know. I think it's a real boost in some ways, but I think that women have been active for a real long time and the kinds of problems that they have now are not that much different from ten years ago, during the Civil Rights Movement. Probably more women here were actively involved in things then than they are now. Black women, anyway, and some white women who were involved in the movement.

ANITA: I was still in school during those days, and in a rural area we didn't really get that much of it. We've always lived out in the country and we never really had many blacks in our area. But I never did believe in segregation. I've really enjoyed working with Frankie and Harold and getting to know some more black ladies through AWHR and other things. Frankie is a terrific person and Harold is the same and we became close personal friends during the campaign and still are. What hurt them really hurt us.

When we were coming up, mother worked a lot so we had to have people come in and help. And we had this one black lady that we loved with all of our soul. When we would see her coming, we'd run to meet Dessie and she would bring us all three in the house and there was no feeling that she's black and I'm white. And Dessie'd fix our dinner and Mother might come in and Dessie'd say, "I'll eat out front," and Mother would say, "No, you're not, Dessie, you eat with us." So I never felt like that.

As far as the Women's Movement, to me, well . . . Daddy always told me that I could do anything that I wanted to do, and I just always took it for granted that I could. He never did make a lot of difference between me and my brother when we were coming up. Then I married right as I left home, and Johnny never has treated me like he was anything better than I was, or like he was going to be the master and I was his slave. So I've always been more or less independent and I never have experienced that sort of thing.

I've always done what I wanted to, how I wanted to do it, and when I wanted to do it. Of course I considered my family and my husband, and Mother and Daddy, but I never did get any conflict or kickback from it, like a lot of other women might have had. Even with AWHR, Johnny thought it was a good thing, too. He likes Chris and knows what kind of work she does, and he saw the possibilities in it.

One thing I really do like is working with women. With the campaign, when we started organizing, I think that was the first time that a group of women worked together on something like that. I had worked with mixed groups before, but it's not the same. We'd have our meetings while the men would be in the other room drinking beer or something, and I really enjoyed it.

When you work with women, I feel like I can express my opinions and they'll be more accepted. Men don't give you a whole lot of chance to say what you think. They kind of talk you down. But with women, you don't have any fear of them saying, "No, we're not going to do that because I got a better idea and my idea is going to go." With us, we more or less compared ideas and then we worked out a plan that we thought was best for everybody concerned.

It was the same feeling at the AWHR conference. You knew that the women there had probably experienced some of the same things that you had, and they were willing to listen. A lot of men aren't willing to listen to what you have to say. They think it's unimportant. We met several like that, didn't we Chris! But we just overlooked them and did what we thought had to be done anyhow.

We really learned a lot from that. Besides campaigning for what we thought was right, we learned a lot about people, the public. We'll be better prepared next time because we'll know how to avoid the mistakes we made this time. We learned first that you can't take people at their word in a campaign. You have to take what they say and then throw it over your shoulder. Then you learn where your support lies, what campaign issues work best in what area. A lot of people don't relate to certain things in different areas. And with a black candidate, we learned a lot about the black vote. A lot of black folks wouldn't even go to the polls. I guess it's fear and also the feeling that it doesn't really matter anyway, that they can't win anyway, you know?

CHRIS: Also this is old Boyle country. I mean it's rough. There are threats on people's lives all the time. Somebody's wife got run off the road and they'd tried to kill her. You know, nasty little things like that.

ANITA: We got some phone calls, but not really threats. They would just tell us that we were on the wrong side and to switch sides and quit campaigning and things like that. I'd just hang up. They'd never give an identity with it. Just a lot of people that were too chicken to tell you that to your face, so it didn't scare me. I didn't take it seriously at all.

CHRIS: The black vote was a real important aspect of the campaign, which I don't think we've really figured out yet. In the beginning, we just took it for granted that Harold would get the black vote and we wouldn't have to worry about it. But then near the end, Frankie started coming back with stories about how even some of their friends weren't going to vote for him. Part of it was jealousy. They had just bought this beautiful new house and Frankie said some of them just didn't think he should get elected to this thing too. We still don't really understand, but we laid some groundwork and we learned a lot.

ANITA: I think Harold learned more than any of us. Some really sad lessons. He put a lot of money, time and effort into the campaign, more so than either of the other two. If the blacks had just gone out and voted, oh, it would've been a runaway.

The campaign was a lot of hard work. There were very few rewards to me personally. I had a lot of hard feelings after it was over, but you have to overlook those. I guess you're going to find those in any campaign you go through. I don't really know, this was our first. But the bad feelings are mixed with the good ones. You make a lot of new friends and then you find out a lot of things about your old friends that you didn't know, so it kind of evens itself out.

I don't think it really changed me much. I don't think I've ever run away from anything. I've always stuck to what I thought was really right. But being in that campaign did make me want to get more involved. Since I got out of school, I hadn't been involved in a lot of things. That's why when Chris decided to have this conference for Alabama women, I thought it was a real good thing. It would give you something to work at. You sort of lose your perspective on things, just staying at home all the time, raising the kids and washing and ironing. It gives your life a little bit of purpose.

Usually, in this area, if you're not working, you stay at home and take care of your family and you don't have a lot of time. But I have an unusual husband and he likes me to be involved in these sort of things. So his encouragement helps. But anyway, I couldn't . . . or I don't stay at home all the time and just do my everyday chores. It gets old. Still, I'm really just an ordinary housewife.

CHRIS: I think that nobody in AWHR really sees themselves as special or unusual. But I think the fact that people get involved in things makes them special. That kind of puts you up on another level, it broadens you. You've done some things and you've gotten more self-confidence and you have experiences to tell people about. Getting involved takes exposure to certain kinds of things, and being in the right place at the right time, and also being personally affected by something.

We've had a lot of discussions about this and nobody seems to see themselves as being exceptional in the sense that they're smarter or that they know more. The only people who see themselves like that are the university-educated women. But to try to get at the things in a person's life that make a difference, well, husbands are certainly one of them. If your husband makes you stay home all the time, that's pretty hard to overcome.

ANITA: I think things are beginning to change a little about women getting more involved in things. Your average coal miner's a younger man now. More and more younger men are going into the mines, and maybe their mothers worked or they're married to a working woman. So they kind of accept it more than the older miner did, whose wife just stayed home and took care of the house and the babies.

Today in Alabama, a lot of women have to work. If you want a few extra things, more than what a miner's salary can make, a woman has to go to work. So I think the younger men accept this more. And working in the community is kind of the next step. There's a lot of things in every community that need to be done, not just ours. And the men don't have the time or won't take the time and effort to do it. So that's left up to the women.

Most husbands of the women I know here, they like to fish and hunt and things like this, and any time they have off, they're going to do this. That leaves us by ourselves in this community a good bit, you know, while the husbands are off deer hunting or playing baseball. I'd just rather be off doing something than sitting at home. And I guess it's probably true, the men don't care as much.

NEW PERSPECTIVES

I guess what I most enjoy in my life is my children. I enjoy being with them, doing things with them, and I like being at home. And I like my church work, community work, things like that. There's nothing about my life I really don't like. I mean you get discouraged and downhearted, but everybody has those periods. As a whole, I enjoy my life.

I think child-care centers are great, but I guess I'm too protective of my children to leave them with anybody else. I mean, I could if I had to, but I'd rather not. I guess I've been around mine too long and never left them. But child care has been terrific for Alabama. It's put a lot of mothers to work that needed to go to work but didn't have anybody to keep their kids.

As I told you, I was raised up in a family where my mother worked. And I believe it does the mother a lot of good sometimes to get away from the family and to hold an outside job. It releases a lot of pressure and tensions, and I don't see where that would harm a family in any way if there was really a lot of love in the family. But I couldn't leave mine unless I had to, to have the income.

If I had to go to work to support them, I could, but I'd rather not till they get up in school. They've asked me at the hospital where Jenny goes if I could do some volunteer work with other kids there and so I guess I'll do that when Jen starts to school. But I don't know, I enjoy staying at home and having free time to get involved in other activities and all. So unless it becomes a financial necessity, I don't guess I'd hold a full-time job. If I did, I guess it would be something dealing with the public.

I've gotten real involved in church work recently. What happened was, my brother-in-law had started going to the Empire Baptist Church, and we weren't going to church anywhere at the time. He had been taking Sherry, our older daughter, with him for about a year to church and Sunday school, and I started feeling guilty staying home. If she's going to get any religious upbringing, it ought to be up to me and her daddy. So I just thought it was time that I ought to assume that responsibility and start going, so I did.

We have a good preacher. He's young, he's twenty-four, but he's got a lot of energy and he's really done a lot for our community. He's been there two years now and we're in the process of building us a new church. Since he's come, he's built it up so that we've outgrown our old church. Brother Brown and his wife Sandra, they've got two small children, and you know, it involves you when you see other people with small children. I just felt like I ought to be . . . I felt like the Lord was calling me to the church and so I joined the church and was saved.

I just believe that the Lord washed my sins away, you know, on the day that I told Him that I was a sinner and I wanted Him to come into my life. And I believe that He just made me a new person. Being brought up in churches and all, here I had quit going. And I had an ugly mouth. I cursed a lot and said a lot of things in front of my children that I wouldn't say again and that I was ashamed of. I guess I believed that I had become bad enough where I needed something else and the Lord was what I was looking for. So since the day He washed away my sins, from that day on I had a new life that I had to account for with Him.

Johnny'll go on special occasions, like Bible school gradua-
tions or Christmas plays or Easter programs, or he'll visit every
now and then on a Sunday. But he's not ready, I don't think,
for the church. He says he's not, anyway. But it's a personal
thing between him and his conscience and the Lord, and that's
something he'll have to work out himself.

I have a terrific Sunday school teacher and we have a real
good turnout of parents in Sunday school. Every week we have
a lesson that deals with different passages of the Bible. They
write lessons on them and then we discuss them and our
teacher puts her thoughts to them. We just have a good time.
It's a lot of Bible education and I need that right now, being a
new Christian in the church.

After I joined I got real involved. We didn't have a lot of
people that wanted to or had the time to work with kids then.
Being at home, I have a good bit of time. I have a group now
called the G.A.'s—Girls in Action. They're nine, ten and eleven
years old and we meet once a week on Wednesday nights.
While our church has the regular prayer meeting, we take the
kids and go downstairs. Mostly what G.A.'s is concerned
with is teaching about missions—what our missionaries deal
with, and doing mission action projects, doing things to help
out in the community.

We support our missions overseas and our home missions
too, through giving and praying. Like on Christmas, we have
the Lottie Moon Offering, which is to help our missionaries in
foreign lands. The girls save what nickels and dimes they have
and we send it to the Lottie Moon Fund. Then at Easter we
have the Annie Armstrong Offering, and that's to help our
home missions all over the United States. We have language
missions like in Spanish-speaking areas and other places where
people speak a foreign language. We have missionaries that go
to teach the love of Christ and talk with them in the language
they speak and teach them English too.

The G.A.'s are a part of the Women's Missionary Union program in the church, and that's how we support our missions.
The Baptist Young Women is part of that too and we meet
once a month. Every member of the Baptist Young Women
subscribes to the magazine *Contempo*. It has a lot of good

written material and we usually read from it at our meetings and then discuss the different things that our missionaries are doing. But mostly what we subscribe for is it has a prayer calendar. Every day, there's a list of missionaries, what they do and where they're serving, and they ask that you pray for them every night. They believe that through prayer God will answer their needs. I fall down on that a good bit, but I'm trying to do better.

Three weeks ago our whole Baptist Young Women from all over the state went to Chocco Springs in Talladega for a weekend. We talked to some missionaries that had actually been in the foreign mission field and the home mission field. You see that their love for the people in these places and their love for God is entwined, and it warms your heart. It breaks your heart really to realize the needs that they have. And you know, you try to do a lot better when you get home from places like that. It was just an exciting adventure and I wouldn't take anything for it.

Johnny's real good about me going to things like that. I haven't been away a whole lot, and if I do, I usually take the kids. He goes with me sometimes too. But he thought that that weekend would do me a lot of good and it did. You know, when we first got married, that was eight years ago, I was working and he was working. Now eight years ago, men were a lot different in Alabama than they are now. They didn't believe in helping women with anything and, if you worked, you did your job and then you'd come home and do your housework. But Johnny was always good to pitch in and help. He's always been like that and I don't think I could ask for a better daddy for either one of my girls. A lot of times we have conflicts and his ideas don't agree with mine, but either we work them out or he does what he thinks is right and I do what I think's right.

I don't remember needing the Women's Movement to let me do my own thing, so really I can't see any change that it's had on my life. But I think that if it'll help the women with better jobs and better salary and with getting the recognition that they deserve, well, I think it's terrific. I think it's been really good in a lot of ways, helping women to realize that they didn't have to stay home all day taking care of the kids. That they could get out and do what they want. But I can't see where it's affected me personally.

Really it's not been that big a thing in our area. Most of our neighbors around here, the wives don't work. Especially the ones with small children. The husbands are coal miners, truck drivers, steelworkers, construction workers, carpenters, just a real variety of employment. But most of my friends are a lot like me and they do what they want to do. They consider their families and then make their decision and their husbands usually go along with it. Some work, some part time and some work full time, and so that really doesn't give them a lot of time to do a lot else. They might work in their church, and some have a few special-interest projects like the Business and Professional Women here in Sumiton. But I think a woman can do anything she sets her mind to and I don't think there should be any limitations on that.

I would like to see more women in statewide politics. They know more of the problems firsthand because they deal with them every day. And I think they look more toward the future and what their children and grandchildren are going to have to live with. It seems like women would have more patience and more drive to stick with it over a longer period of time to see good and hard-wrought results. They use a common sense approach that will work for three years from now, not just for today. I think a lot of men just spin their wheels while they're in office and they like to see results day after tomorrow.

Johnny ran for the House of Representatives right about the same time as the District 20 elections were ending. I helped when I could, but he did most of it himself. I thought it was the wrong time for him to get into a race like that, so I really didn't get that involved and I guess it was wrong, him being my husband. But he'd just come out of one campaign and he still had a lot of bad feelings from that and I was afraid he'd carry it over into this campaign. Well, he lost, you know, but maybe next time we'll both feel like he ought to run. He says he might run again and I kind of hope he does. But you can't ever tell about Johnny. He's unpredictable, isn't he?

Right now our biggest concern is Jenny. I just hope that there might be some way that she could live a normal life without medications and have a family of her own if she wanted to. That's what's most important right now. But also I worry about Johnny. He'll be twenty-seven in December and he's been in the mines since he was twenty-two, and younger miners than that have had black lung disease, or it's shown up on their tests. I don't know, but you always worry about it.

He's a young man now, but my granddaddy's got black lung, and Johnny's got uncles that have it. It's pretty hard to see them. My granddaddy stays in and out of the doctor's office and the hospital all the time. It's constant. And when he coughs, he just wracks all over with it, it's so painful. A lot of the miners have been in the mines since they've been thirteen or fourteen years old. And, you know, the younger you are when you go in, the better your chances of getting it. Johnny doesn't think about it that much because he's young, but you worry.

People have always been aware of it, it's just gotten so much more publicity in the last few years. And they're getting benefits now, supposedly. You have to go before a doctor and be certified that it's black lung and not from cigarette smoking or something, first. And there's a lot of papers to be filled out and doctors to be seen, X rays to be taken and all before you can even start getting your benefits. Sometimes it takes a year, two years. Sometimes you have to have a hearing, go before a judge. In the meantime, your health is deteriorating, but you're not getting any benefits from it.

Really a coal miner gets paid for the danger of going underground, chances of getting black lung, cave-ins or explosions or something like that. The work's not that hard in the mines, with all the new equipment and all that they have. If they had to do the same kind of work outside, they probably wouldn't draw as much money. And in spite of the danger, that's their job, you know, and you have to live. With Johnny, mining has been in his family for so long now. And you know, when you're brought up with it and living with it, that's a way of life.

The good thing about being a miner is you're sure of things. You've got regular hours. You know that you're going to work at either seven or three or eleven o'clock, whatever shift you're working, and you know what time you're getting off, what holidays and what vacation you get. And you can just about figure your payday every week. When he was selling, he'd leave early and come home real late and he did all that driving. And he wouldn't make the money that you make in a coal mine, and he wouldn't have benefits like the hospital card. A man that has a family to support and all, unless he has a partner in a business or he's a supervisor or something, it's hard to make a living.

I don't ever regret getting married, but I wish I had put it off and I'm sure Johnny does at times. When we graduated from school, the "in" thing was to get married and have your family. But my parents had wanted me to go on to nursing school and Johnny could have got a baseball scholarship. His daddy regrets that, and I guess he always will, and kind of holds it against me because he didn't go. But of course I told Johnny when we got married that he could have gone on to school and I would've worked and supported us, but he didn't want to at the time. Now you look back some, and you realize where he might have been now if he had gone on.

I want my girls to have a wider choice of what they can do when they get older and not be rushed into things. I'd like them to go to college and do some traveling and then to realize there'll be plenty of time for whatever else they want after that. But not to feel that this is what my parents or so-and-so thinks I ought to do, so I'm going to do it. I want them to please themselves first and make up their own mind and then go from there. That's really what my mother wanted for me, to have some more experiences before I settled down, but I was young and wouldn't listen.

Sherry's six now and she picks up things real quick, so I think anything she wanted to do she could do real well. She loves to learn and she's got an inquisitive mind. She likes taking care of Jenny when she's sick, so she said one time she wants to be a nurse, and then a kindergarten teacher because she likes teaching little kids like Jenny. She's at the stage where she wants to be and do everything that she comes in contact with. I just want her to be happy doing whatever it is that she does do.

One of the worst problems we have here is education, and now Sherry is in school I'm getting more concerned about it. I don't know what it is in other states, but in Alabama it's terrible. Especially at the high school level, but elementary too. It seems much worse than when I was a kid. For several years things pretty much stayed the same and then suddenly it started on a downhill fall, and it certainly isn't getting any better.

Then there's the drug problem that worries me. It's getting bigger every day, and when you know your children are going to grow up into this mess, you're kind of afraid and you don't know which way to go. And now the hard drugs are beginning to come in and they're getting more and more into the schools.

Also now it seems that there's more need for sex education than ever, and the parents still don't want it taught in the schools. They say they can do a better job of teaching it at home, but very few homes do I know of that sex has been talked about. And the age level is dropping all the time about where girls start learning about sex. A lot of ten- and eleven-year-olds are learning a lot of things through other ways than their parents. And a lot of times now, pregnancy is causing marriages, especially when girls are still in school. When I went to school, there wasn't a lot of "have to" marriages. There were some, but most of them didn't get pregnant until they graduated or dropped out of school.

I hope when Sherry and Jenny get old enough that Johnny and I will have enough sense to sit down and discuss it with them and answer their questions and not be embarrassed about it. I'd rather them learn it from us or from some qualified teacher than off the streets or in a dirty book. I want them aware of the problems and that there's nothing to be ashamed of about it. It's life. And I want them to experience it when they're ready for it in the right way.

In Alabama now they are having good results with birth control clinics and there's so many methods of birth control that there's not much sense to abortion. But they do have places where you can go that I've read about and have an abortion and pay according to how much you can. A lot of them give them free if they're indigent patients. I didn't believe in abortion until Jenny was born and then hospitalized at Children's. You see a lot of kids over there that their parents just leave them. They might not come and visit for a long time or they might never come back. So I can't see bringing a child into the world that's not wanted and you can't provide for it. I think if you can settle it with your conscience, you ought to be able to go out and have an abortion.

There's just so many problems down here and the campaign and all made me more aware of things that do need to be changed. And that it takes a long time to make changes but it's well worth it. It helps to know that there's somebody else fighting too. But I think more and more people are beginning to open their eyes and realize what's going on around them and be more involved in getting some changes made themselves, instead of sitting back and watching. I think before people always thought that somebody else would do it, but now they're realizing that maybe it's going to be up to them.

You know you keep thinking things'll get better, but they just keep getting messier and stickier. I think Watergate has affected most everybody. People are more aware. They know what can happen. And Alabama has had a bit of dirty politics in our state department and all, so it's all just pushed in our face and you have to open your eyes. You're still going to have these people that'd rather sit back and let somebody else do the work and then just criticize. But I feel like you're not entitled to a criticism unless you're going to go out and do something about it.

Politics is really a mess right here in Walker County. The county is sort of divided into two parts—one side of the river and then the other side. Well, we're on the other side in our area and we don't get hardly any representation at all. Our little town of Sumiton and the whole area suffers from this. When Johnny ran just recently, we tried to get new politicians in office, but we didn't succeed this time.

Statewide things are really pretty bad too. If we'd had a candidate running against Wallace for governor this time that a lot of people could identify with, Wallace probably wouldn't have won by the margin he did. But a lot of voters didn't even turn out to vote for their own governor, which is pathetic. But it happened. So I don't know if he is really that popular or that we just didn't have any other candidates that Democrats in Alabama could really go with. I do think most people see Wallace's governorship as a stepping-stone to the presidency.

He's a fighter, we can see that from his accident, you know.

He's going to hang in there. But I can't see that he's done Alabama any good. I wouldn't vote for him for President. But he's an Alabama political figure that's known nationwide and there's a little bit of pride in that because most Alabamans aren't well-known. I have a little sympathy too. But not enough for a vote.

We know there's corruption in Alabama politics, but I don't know to what extent. We've had some investigations and trials about a couple of different departmer̲s, and Wallace's brother was messed up in some things too. But at the time there was this other trial going on in the highway department, and I think that kind of got swept under the rug. So that was real handy. But a lot of Alabamans voted for him and they like him. His wife really knows how to meet the public. She's a good campaigner and a good vote-getter, so that helps too.

I suppose I tend to give people with a lot of status the benefit of the doubt about whether they're being truthful or not. I think that's only natural. But still you never know if they're telling you an honest opinion or if they're just giving you something to cover up their honest opinion. With most people I know, you either know that they're shooting you a big line or that's the way they really feel. And I don't like to be talked over.

Like with Nixon, he tells us all this stuff and I don't know if he thinks we really believe it or if he's just fooling himself. You realize that he knew what was going on, and here he's saying, "I didn't know a thing about it." And so you know deep down that he's really lying and he has been all along. But you don't know if he thinks you're a big enough fool to believe it or what. I just don't know what to think about things like that, and I'll just stay away.

It's the same with people with a lot of education. Where we live in the South you don't see a lot of highly educated people every day, in our walk of life. And well . . . you're kind of afraid of them. Sometimes I really don't know what they're thinking when they're talking to me. I can't see through what they're telling me. I don't know if it's what they really feel or not, so usually I just withhold, because I'm not sure.

I guess I feel that I'm not as well-informed as maybe I should be on a lot of different things. I haven't maybe had the experiences that a woman who has attended college and trav-

eled and all might have. So you know you feel kind of . . .
you're hesitant about joining in a discussion about some things.
You think maybe what you have to say might not be as interesting to them as somebody else, or I might not get it across to
them as well as maybe somebody else who's had a similar experience could do. And you're kind of afraid that something
you say might be taken the wrong way.

I think probably if I could get involved in a lot more things,
and feel that I had done all I could do in different areas that I
like, and knew that I had accomplished something that would
make me a better person and give me a little bit more interesting background, it probably would help me overcome some of
these things. I like to talk to people that have traveled and
done things, gone places. I'd like to do that too, and if I did,
that would kind of break the barrier down a little. It's not the
book learning, it's just the experience, and I feel like I haven't
done that much myself.

Even with Chris I was that way at first. She had done a lot
of things and been a lot of places and worked with a lot of different kinds of people. But when you get down to it, she's just
as basic as anybody else. She may have a little more education,
but Chris is able to laugh at herself and that helps. It helps if
they've got a good sense of humor and can talk about different
things on maybe say a different level. But basically I feel kind
of ill at ease a lot of the time.

I do have faith in my common sense and I know what I believe in, and I know my feelings on everything. In things that
I have experienced or I have done, I'm fairly well at ease talking with you about them. If I feel that I can discuss it with a
reasonable amount of intelligence, I'll hold my ground. But if
it comes to things I've never done and if I'm not sure, instead
of being made to look like an idiot, I'll back off.

Anyway, I think a lot of us have learned that you can't take
things at face value anymore. I think probably now people are
going to begin to open a lot of doors that have always been
shut, because now they know that they can be opened—if not
voluntarily, the courts can open them. I think now there'll be a
lot of revising of the old attitudes that a lot of politicians always had. Because you can't pull the wool over the public's

eyes forever. They're going to wake up one day and come knocking at your door.

And I think probably a lot of voters, like me and a lot of women and men, are going to realize that if we don't get out and vote and do a lot of homework on each candidate that this thing can happen again. With each new campaign, we're probably going to be more aware of it. I know I've been guilty of not really studying the issues or knowing what the candidates really stood for and all.

But I think now you're going to be looking and studying instead of just voting. We've learned that a lot of things are rotten, and they've got to be changed, and that our system needs some revamping. Maybe people will think about what they're doing before they jump on the bandwagon. I don't know, but something does need to be done.

● POSTSCRIPT

During the past year, Anita Cupps became the "official" bookkeeper for two new family business ventures. By December of 1975, she said she was beginning to feel like she was going "slightly haywire," keeping up with her regular family and community responsibilities as well as keeping two companies running on a daily basis. "But we're doing real well," she said. "We're keeping our head above water."

One of the new businesses is a small strip-mining company that Johnny Cupps and two of his brothers started. The second is a trucking company that Anita, her uncle and husband took on jointly. At the same time, to assure a steady income and to protect the union hospital card so vital to Jenny's life, Johnny is working in the strip pits for another company.

In terms of mining politics, things have been fairly quiet in District 20 over the past year. One of the more controversial officials from the district was killed (some say assassinated) at a United Mine Workers contract negotiations meeting in Washington, D.C., late in 1974. Evidently, his death cooled the local political climate, at least for the present.

Campaigning for the next district elections (to be held in 1977) will begin early in 1976. While there is still some residual bitterness about the outcome of the last elections, Anita is not ruling out the possibility that she may become involved again. "We're waiting to see what will happen. It seems like Frank [Clements] and [Arnold] Miller are having some trouble now. If someone good comes up as a candidate against Frank and has a chance to win, I'm ready to go. If there's someone we think will really do a better job, we'll get out there and work for him."

Anita has become even more deeply involved in church activities, claiming, "They're working us to death, but I really enjoy it." Some new programs were started this year, including a children's church. In addition to working with the youngsters in weekly Bible programs, her most time-consuming project late this year was helping them prepare for a special Christmas play.

Alabama Women for Human Rights became relatively inactive in the second half of 1975, primarily because Chris Hintz, who had organized the group and served as coordinator, had to devote her energies elsewhere. The Selma Project was unable to raise sufficient funds to stay afloat. Chris and her husband, who had worked there for several years, both had to find other jobs. The result is that AWHR is currently without a full-time statewide organizer.

A considerable amount of Anita's time is devoted to her family, in part because of its enormous size. Births, birthdays, funerals and illnesses keep her "going and coming." One of her sisters-in-law had twins this year, which Anita described as "a special thrill for the whole family. They're the greatest thing in the world." Much of her "free" time has been spent with the twins, whose birth brought the current total of Cupps grandchildren to twenty-one.

Jenny still requires intensive medical care but was ill less frequently this past year and is, all told, "doing fine." Sherry entered first grade and evidently "loves it and is doing real well." Aside from these developments, Anita said, "It seems like everything is just day-old down here."

Listening to Each Other Across Class Lines

Ann Winans

Terry Dezso

Ann Winans in her former office at the University of Minnesota's College of Engineering.

Paul and Ann Winans, outside their home in Minneapolis.

Ann Winans

GHETTO TO GHETTO IN MINNEAPOLIS

I was born in Fargo, North Dakota, on May 5, 1928. My mother was warned not to travel, but my father had gone there to find work. They were hard times in those days. He was a painter and decorator and they had this big job in Fargo, so he wanted her to come and join him there. She had one child that was almost two then, my older sister, and she was pregnant with me.

The doctor told her, "It'll be hard. Take a pair of scissors with you on the train and be prepared to deliver your own baby on the way." My mother's very brave and courageous, so she went, but luckily she got there before I was born. She was only about seven and a half months pregnant though, and I weighed three and a half pounds when I was born. She was very ill from it and they hired an Indian nurse to take care of my mother and me. The nurse was a little rough because she was on the juice a lot, so my mother had to get out of bed and take care of me herself. Somehow she managed.

She nursed me for quite a while but then she got pregnant again with my sister, so I was cut off at an earlier age than the other four kids. And in those days there just was no giving a bottle to a baby. It just wasn't believed in if it was at all possible to nurse a baby. She said I had a very slow start and they didn't expect me to live. So that was my beginning. We didn't live in Fargo very long. After my father was through with this big job, they came back to Minneapolis.

My father was born in Norway. He joined the Merchant Marines when he was sixteen and he sailed the seas for four years. He saw a lot of the world and finally settled in America. He had a rough time, coming to America, especially out east, because he couldn't speak the language. Some of the fellows he'd meet would make fun of it by telling him bad words. I think the first word he learned was "son of a bitch." So he'd go around saying "son of a bitch" and shaking people's hands until he darn near got hit for it.

It must have been terribly hard on him, twenty years old, trying to find his way around in a new country. He did find his way west to where the Scandinavian settlement was in Minnesota. He stayed here for a short time and then went on up to North Dakota. He found there were more Norwegians up there and then he felt at home with his own people. They could talk his language. He found there were so many Rasmussens, a typically Norwegian name, that the mail was getting all mixed up. So he changed his name in court to the name of his little village in Norway, Hoyland. That was my maiden name.

My mother came from Greenwich Village, New York. Her mother was French and she died of the black smallpox at forty-six. The plague, I guess they called it. Her father was English and he was a descendant of President Harrison. I lost Grandfather when I was four years old. He was already retired and sickly, but I remember him sneaking candy to me behind the shed out in back. He was wonderful to me.

Anyway, my mother's parents moved west when she was probably around twenty, and then she went to the Northwestern Bible Institute here in Minneapolis. It's like a college, only it's religion. They teach the ministry. The way she met my father was she went down to the mission on Washington Avenue and she was helping the very poor people that'd come there. They had soup lines and all. And my father stopped in one time just out of curiosity. That's as much as I know of how they met. They had five girls.

My father taught us some of the Norwegian Christmas songs as little kids, and he had an accent, but outside of that I think we were very, very typically American, other than they were extremely religious. But then if you stop and figure that many of the people in Depression days turned to religion as something to hold on to, I guess maybe it wasn't unusual. Much like people today are searching for something, too. Some are what they call the "Jesus freaks," but I think they're just looking for themselves and I think that's what held for my parents.

My father wasn't very strong in religion till after he met my mother. He drank very heavy when he was a young man in the Merchant Marines. I think it was more the wine. He liked wine. Then the doctor said he had a very bad heart and he wouldn't live very long if he didn't quit drinking. So he cut it off completely and that's when he started getting back to his church and living a better life.

My mother was Baptist and he was Lutheran. Lutheran is probably closer to Catholic, where Baptist is closer to the Pentecost, when you go from one extreme to another. But when we were growing up, we all went to the Full Gospel Church, which is what you call Pentecostal. That's what my mother still is today.

We were raised going to church—Sunday school and morning worship and evening worship on Sundays, and then we went to church prayer meetings on Wednesdays and Friday nights. As children we had gold buttons given to us for perfect attendance. It never meant that much to me, although I think the religion stays with you a great deal through your life. At least I feel it has. But then after you grow up, you know, you kind of change your ideas. And that church was too extreme.

I guess I was more or less active in the church when I was young. But as I came close to my teens, I didn't want to be tied down to all these things. All my friends were doing different things and I wanted to be like them. But we weren't allowed to go to movies or go dancing or roller-skating, all the fun things that you want to do when you're young. I was deprived of all that and they were so important to me. See, they believed that anything worldly, is the way they put it, was a sin because you were supposed to dedicate your whole life to the church.

I remember when I went to my first movie. It was just something I had to find out, what a movie was like. So I made a stab at it. It wasn't very far away and I figured I could sneak down and be back home before they noticed me. Well, I don't like doing things alone, so I got my little sister, Pearl. I was fifteen and she must've been no more than about eight. To her it wasn't terribly important, but she liked going with me.

So we went and we saw *Crossroads*, which was the most beautiful picture, with Hedy Lamarr. I saw love and this was the first time I'd ever seen love displayed between a man and a woman. She was beautiful and I wanted to be like her. And suddenly I started wondering about love and kissing, because I never saw my mother and father kiss and I never thought anything about it.

Well, of course, when I walked in the door it was half an hour past curfew and my father was waiting for me with his fists all doubled up. He hit me one good hard hit that knocked me clear across the room and my head hit the cedar chest and I was knocked out. When I came to, my mother was bending over me and saying, "You shouldn't do this, you shouldn't do this. This is not what God wants you to do." She felt bad, but she didn't really fight him, you know?

I remember I even asked her, "Why don't you and Dad ever kiss?" I wanted to know all about this love, this beautiful thing. I guess I just felt an emotion I never had felt before when I was watching that movie. I started wondering about life and I just could hardly sleep, even though my head was pretty sore.

Then when I was about fifteen or sixteen, I had gotten some valentines. I got this one that was real cute. It said, "For crying out loud, will you be my valentine?" Well, my father heard me reading it and he hauled off and hit me right across the face. He said it was a bad word—"for crying out loud." It was really something how far out he was. We didn't even say "gee" because that was part of Jesus. "Gosh" was slang for God, so we didn't say that, either.

Because of being a little bit on the weak side and having a bad start in life, my parents said that I shouldn't play as hard as other children. My sister Millie, who's a year younger than me, was a ten-pound baby. She'd climb trees and she was as tomboy as you could be. She had perfect attendance in school and she could ice-skate like a whiz and she just did everything.

The only thing I could do is maybe I'd get a piece of dough from my mother when she was baking bread and I'd play with it till it turned black, my little dirty patties. Then I started drawing pictures of comics, something on the order of Moon Mullins, a comic character in the old days. I'd make up stories and put on puppet shows for all the little kids. Sometimes I'd end up with a few pennies from the kids and I'd buy candy at the penny candy store. That was quite a treat because money just wasn't given to children those days.

My mother first went to work when my father broke his leg with a compound fracture. I was twelve years old at the time. She always did dry-cleaning and laundry work. The pressing is what she was real good at. She had typing and shorthand in school, and why she never went into that is beyond me, though maybe she did when she was younger. She was older when she got married. She was in her thirties. Both of them were.

I don't think she really planned on being married. It was related to her religion and she's still the same way now. She thinks that her reason for living right now on earth is to do things for other people, to help people. She thinks everybody has a purpose and this is her purpose. She's eighty-one now and she's doing volunteer work with elderly people and she's older than most of them! She's going out to dinner with friends and she's going to the church and she's visiting the sick. She's always on the go. I wish I had her health. Mine has never been that terrific since I was a child.

My father was always a painter and decorator, but he was a seasonal worker in construction. He'd get real big jobs sometimes like one of the big Catholic churches here. He was a contractor for himself, and when he could afford it he'd hire a man or two. But usually he only worked during the summer or late in the wintertime. He never did join the union, I think because it cost about a hundred dollars and that was a lot of money. He never got his second set of citizenship papers either, because he never could afford it.

I remember the big trucks coming to our homes, so much of my childhood life, and bringing a crate of apples and a crate of oranges. And the church brought us all a basket for Christmas, so we always had food on the table at Christmas. There were times when we might be down to something like oatmeal or just plain rice, but Mom and Dad would always go without to make sure that we had food, and they'd drink their coffee. They were hard times.

My father was a gypsy. I think he'd get tired of a place, or the house, or he didn't like the neighborhood or the neighbors. He just wanted to move all the time. I went to so many schools it's hard to remember all of them. Every place we moved into my father would wallpaper it and clean it real nice. And Mother was meticulous. She would fumigate completely and use kerosene on the springs. She wouldn't put up with those conditions that you have in your tenement homes. I remember bedbug bites when we moved in. They'd bite in a row, a big long line, and right away she'd see the evidence and she'd work so hard, cleaning and sanitizing everything. She just had a lot of guts. And she always believed that cleanliness was next to godliness, you know, and she really lived the part. She still does.

We usually lived in that row housing where the houses are no more than just a foot apart. There were no yards, and even at that time we were told to stay on the front porch. All the kids were poor. Most of us were on welfare, or their fathers only worked once in a while, at least until the forties, when things started looking better. We lived in an area that was almost all black and still is.

My mother had good friends in church that were black people and Orientals. My father was very prejudiced, though. He was prejudiced against the Catholic religion. He was prejudiced against Jewish people, the Irish and the French. He didn't like my husband because he found out that he was part French. And my mother had to lie and say that she was English and Norwegian because otherwise he wouldn't even consider her. And she really looks French!

The French were the dirty French. The only thing I could figure was, I heard him tell my mother stories about what he saw on the seas. And he'd seen some bad displays of sex in France, in the lower districts evidently, where they had prostitution and sodomy, with animals and people. At the time it didn't mean anything to me because they never even used the word "sex."

I was sixteen when I had my first date and it was the thrill of my lifetime. The guy said to me, "Is this the first time you've ever been kissed?" and I blushed and said, "Yeah." I know I puckered up awful tight. I guess he didn't realize that I was really as naive as I was. Then I started going out, but if I got home late, my father was usually waiting for me with his fists.

I remember one time that I had a terrible beating. Sometimes he'd use a strap, and that hard metal edge on the strap that would draw blood. I remember trying to run from my father's hands, his terribly big hands. I was trying to get up the stairs and he'd keep hitting me all the way up so I'd fall down and pick myself up and he'd hit me again, all the way up the stairs.

After that I went to my corner drugstore where I knew the clerks and the people who owned the store and I showed the woman behind the counter my bruise marks and she said, "You know, you should report that to the police." And I remember saying, "I can't turn my father in. I mean you just can't do that." She said, "That's against the law." So I said, "Yeah, but he'd go to jail and I don't want my father to go to jail."

I guess what got him angry was just that I was growing up. He'd insinuate things like I was becoming a whore. I didn't even know what the word was. I must have been about seventeen when I met two young women that were a couple of years older than me at the drugstore and I found out they were prostitutes and then I learned a little about what a whore was. They talked very openly about sex and they tried to explain a little bit about the facts of life to me.

I didn't even understand my menstrual time, because that wasn't even explained to me. My mother had told my older sister and expected—because it's so embarrassing—for her to tell the younger ones. Lilly did tell me that you have to wear a rag once in a while. It seemed so dirty to me and I couldn't figure out why my body was functioning this way. I didn't like to go to school because it was an embarrassing situation. I thought there was something wrong and I wished it would hurry up and stop. And I couldn't understand why this happened to girls and not to boys.

I'm so happy that they've got sex education in the schools now. I know parents should try to teach their children, but I know that's real hard sometimes. In raising my son, I found it a little bit difficult to try to talk, I guess, because he's the opposite sex and because of my being a little bit shy. But now if he were just coming up as a teen-ager it would be easier, because I too have grown up so much more.

As a kid, I think the only times my father praised me was when I did the grocery shopping, because I was very budget-minded. And I'd be so very happy because I got so little praise from him. Except for my smile. He might be sitting at the head of this big, long table and he'd suddenly say something about my big smile that's going to make me make it in the world all right. I did want approval from him very badly and it was, oh, so very difficult. He just had his ways, the old country ways, you know? The father, the head of the family, and we were just all inferior.

In my teen-age days, I guess between about sixteen and eighteen, my father used to say to me, "You aren't worth a shit in a tin can." I hated that, but it probably helped push me and push me. It's been with me all these years and even today with some of my employers I'm thinking to myself, "I'm going to show you I'll make it, even if you don't think much of me." Or, "He thinks I'm not as good as him. I'll show him. I'll learn more than he knows." So he really influenced me that way, as far as trying to prove something or fight back.

My father always wanted a son and he blamed my mother a lot for not giving him one. All she gave him was five girls so he was surrounded by women, and for him that was really the end. Girls just weren't as good as boys. But he did respect my mother and he leaned on her an awful lot. As much as he beat the children, he never touched her. She was very strong and she made most of the decisions. I think I learned that part from her.

As far as education, my father said, "I had an eighth-grade education and it was a good education and that's all you need." My mother thought it was really important, but she wanted us all to continue on in the religious area. I did think of going to college but there was no opportunity to go. We had no money. It would have been in the arts because that was all I wanted. I wanted to be a fashion artist, and I know that would have been fun, although that's a hard place to break into.

I won some art competitions in grade school and I had the opportunity to get one of my paintings into the Minneapolis Art Institute. The whole family was very proud of that. I never did see the painting again though. I don't know if the teacher kept it or what. But it's an area I'm still very much interested in. I've thought about taking some art classes at the university, doing some sketching. I really like just sketching faces and facial expressions. Maybe I'll get into it after retiring.

I was brought up totally to believe that I had to know how to cook, take care of a house, and I'd have children someday.

And that was it. There was no consideration of a career whatsoever. You just got married, because otherwise you were an old maid. And I had planned on having three children because that was the ideal family. I went to work, but that didn't mean anything.

As far as money goes, I was ambitious. I mean, I wanted money since I never had any. When I first went to work, I worked evenings as a bookkeeper, when I was still in high school. I didn't mind because I was getting paid for it and I could buy some clothes. I always felt kind of inferior in school . . . well, not when I went to typical city schools where everybody had hand-me-downs or relief clothes. But when I changed schools and went to West, there were some rich kids there and I really felt jealous because they had beautiful clothes. They had everything. There were a few that even had cars. Maybe that's why I have that terrible strong feeling about clothes now. I love clothes.

After high school I worked for a big law firm in Minneapolis. I would relieve on reception and also work in the library, just odds and ends type of work. It was when I was working at Honeywell that I met Paul. I changed to factory work, assembly lines. I really didn't like it much, but the money was better. I stayed in factory work for a few years and during that time I got married.

MARRIED WOMAN, WORKING MOTHER

When I met Paul, he was on recuperation leave from the Navy. His ship sank and he'd been in the water for quite a while. He had some bad times in the war. I guess all wars are bad, but there was a purpose to World War II, more than something like Vietnam. Anyhow, he wasn't injured. I guess you'd call it battle fatigue. It's like all your nerves are shot. He was very shaky. So they sent him home rather than put him in the hospital. I met him when he came through Minneapolis on his way home.

My sister was a USO hostess. I was just sixteen going on seventeen and I wasn't supposed to be there, but I wanted to hang around with my big sister so much. So I met Paul there and we talked and he walked me home. We sat on the porch until about three o'clock in the morning and I decided I'd write to him. He was stationed in San Francisco.

The next time he came home on leave, he came looking for me. He was impressed with this little innocent girl, and that's what I was. So tiny and so innocent, yet very outgoing and happy-go-lucky. I was just full of life and had so much living to do and hadn't enough time to do it. It seemed like I'd lost so much. I'd just turned eighteen then.

So he came looking for me and I didn't even know him. We lived out in Richfield then, which was nothing but farmlands with a few scattered houses. I looked out the window that day and there's my father talking to a black man. I couldn't figure out if he was Spanish or black. Then my father hollered, "Anna, come out here!" And I walked out and I put out my hand to shake hands and he smiled and said, "Don't you remember me?" He was in the South Pacific and his skin was so black and he's got dark eyes and hair, and here he was in this white uniform. So he said, "I'm Paul."

Well, I really laughed, and he came in the house and we talked for a while. Then he said, "Let's go someplace." He had to be moving. He still does. He's restless, which is typical of an Aries person. And so we walked over to the only place out there where you could sit and talk and dance and stuff. Then we took a bus downtown and went to a bar. We got to talking quite a bit and we started talking about getting married.

Actually, I proposed the marriage! The next day he went out and got me an engagement ring, and we were supposed to meet the next morning to go out and get our license. I waited on Tenth and Hennepin for about an hour and a half and he never showed up. I felt really bad, quite rejected. But I was engaged and I wore that ring. I was being true.

Then, finally, I heard from him. He had gone down home and changed his mind. He'd chickened out. So I wrote him a "Dear John" letter and told him I didn't want to be engaged to him anymore. He was very upset and he wrote back and said, "Well, can we be friends?" So I said okay, I would write to him, but I was dating.

Well, then it was my birthday and my older sister was taking me to a movie and to see Gene Krupa, who was in town at the

Orpheum. We happened to be going down a street downtown and I saw Paul standing on the corner waiting for a bus. So I said, "Lilly, that's Paul." So she said, "Ring the bell." We got off the bus and I crossed the street and ran down to where he was waiting and he was real happy. He was going out to find me and I had no idea he was coming to town. Then Lilly said, "I suppose you two want to be together," so she left us and he and I went out to dinner.

I think we spent quite a few hours in there just talking and sipping on a drink. Then we roamed around town and went to a movie and then he finally said, "Well, I think maybe we can get married now." He was afraid of losing me, I think. So the next day we picked out a pretty ring that matched real close and then we went to the courthouse. The elevator man said, "Third floor, marriage licenses. Fourth floor, baby booties." Both of us turned beet-red. He could just spot us holding hands, looking very typically in love. When we got the license, we went to my parents' new house. They were in the process of moving again, and nobody was there. So I just left a note and said, "I'm getting married. I have my license and I'm going to Paul's home town."

Of course my father didn't like him, being French. Actually, Paul's name is Dutch. His father was Dutch and a bit of French and a bit American Indian and Scotch. His mother is French and German. Her father came from France and her mother came from borderline Germany. It's funny in that family, nobody will say they're German, because they say the Germans are mean. So it's "borderline." But Paul's proud of the name and our son Larry, too. Larry looked it up and found there was a great Captain Winans in the Civil War, and a lot of people with the name came over shortly after the Mayflower.

Anyhow, we took a bus down to Paul's home town in southeastern Minnesota and we went to the Presbyterian church there. We asked the minister if he would marry us and he said he could, but he had a funeral at one o'clock, so he'd have to hurry. We called Paul's sister to stand up for us but she was too busy with the chores on the farm and all, so the minister got his wife and mother to be witnesses.

Then Paul was afraid they'd have a shivaree, like they had in small towns. All the people from the town come out with their beer and their booze and they clang bells and make a big noise and sometimes steal the wife, hide her out away from her husband. I think it would've been fun to have the celebration, but his family's kind of shy and they didn't want any big noise.

When we told his mother we had just gotten married, her only response was, "Well you made your bed and now you have to sleep in it." I think she thought we were young, though she was even younger when she got married, and at that time she had ten children between the ages of fifteen and thirty-seven—five boys and five girls.

Paul was very affectionate and I just craved affection. But he said I was very bashful about sex. I just didn't know anything about it. He had to teach me all sorts of things like about hygiene and everything. But I went from a very full-of-life teen-age life into a marriage of nothing but passivity. I was very quiet, sweet, and I let him dominate me. I thought this is the way it was supposed to be.

We were married exactly seven days when he had to leave to go back to San Francisco. We were apart about five months, and I think I spent most of my fifty-dollar-a-month allotment checks on buses going back and forth between Paul's home town and Minneapolis, his family and mine. Then I just sent him a telegram and said, "I'm coming out there." And he sent one back that said, "I have no place for you to stay." But I said, "I'm coming anyway."

The train ticket out there was around fifty or fifty-five dollars. I had that much, but I borrowed five dollars from my brother-in-law and five dollars from my mother-in-law and I knew I had to make it stretch for food. The trip was three nights and two days. This was in '47, when they protected the women by having a car for women only, so I sat with a young woman that had a five-year-old daughter, and we talked all the way. We slept on the seats, so there was no sleep really and I smoked a lot. I got so broke that when we had a short layover in Omaha, I went into the depot and bought a whole quart of soup and made it last until I got to California.

Paul met me in Oakland and we took the ferryboat across, but he didn't seem to be happy to see me. I guess the problem was that I created an extra burden for him, having to rush out, find an apartment and put out forty-five dollars. I think he only got twenty-seven dollars a month then. But we cut ourselves down to two meals a day, and I got my fifty dollar allotment and we didn't spend too much money. It was like a honeymoon for us. We did get around but we went places that didn't cost money. We went to Fisherman's Wharf and the Cliff House and looked out at Alcatraz rock and to Chinatown.

We got along well then but he was very jealous if another man even looked at me. Insanely jealous and close to violent. And I was young then and nicely built. I must've weighed about a hundred pounds and I had long hair, a real round face. But in those days, you know, you belonged to your husband. You were his possession. Anybody looked at another man's wife, it just wasn't done. And Paul had his Aries temper.

I got pregnant just a couple of days after we got there, it turned out. I knew exactly when my baby would be born and I was right. I was so happy, so excited. It was like having my first doll, you know? I never thought about the pain or the agony that a woman can go through for pregnancy. I just thought about my baby. This was something special. Paul was real happy about it, too.

We stayed in San Francisco for about two months and then we went back to Paul's home town and he signed up for the 52–20 Club. That was the same thing as unemployment compensation, only the veterans could have twenty dollars a week for fifty-two weeks. That was supposed to give them a chance to get started and look for a job. Only jobs were scarce in '47 and I couldn't see him hanging around this small town, playing pinochle and talking with the old guys and drinking a little beer.

So I talked Paul into going to the city and we moved in with my folks. Paul got a job. He went to work on the docks in a warehouse. It's hard work but Paul's strong. He's always worked hard, like in rock quarry mines and things that are really tough. But he didn't stay there long because he would have had to join the union and he didn't have the money. I guess it was Teamsters, where you had to pay quite a bit of money.

Then he tried a construction job, but his temper got the best of him there. Something happened and he blew up and quit that one, too. Then he found a job out in Hopkins and worked there maybe fifteen, sixteen months and was laid off. And then he went on a good drunk. I mean, he was drunk and so hung over. That's when I found this ad in the paper and I said, "You've got to go out and try for it because they want several production workers."

I went with him and he went out, so hung over and head-achy. With his G.I. bonus, we had picked up an old '37 Chevy with a rumble seat for $385, which was a lot of money then. So he applied for the job and they offered him the day shift be-cause he was married, but he said, "I'll take the night shift be-cause it pays a dime more an hour." It was $1.20 instead of $1.10. And that's where he still is now, the Minnesota Rubber Company. He worked in just about every department in the company. Just recently they presented him with his gold watch with his name inscribed for his twenty-five years of service.

The job Paul has now is called a "mill man." He works on a mill making rubber. It's a two-story machine. He adds all of the compounds and the black that makes the rubber on the up-per part of the machine, and takes the rubber off the machine on the lower floor. That means he's got to walk up and down the stairs of the machine probably thirty-two, thirty-four times a day and he has to sometimes lift up to two hundred pounds in weight. He just recently got a raise, so he makes $5.65 an hour now.

For sixteen years Paul worked on the night shift, from 4:30 until 12:30. And I've got to say he was terrific. He always cleaned up the kitchen and it was nice to come home to. But when I started to go to work, it was hard on Larry. Paul had the job of trying to toilet train him. Having a person that's very impatient to begin with and a man to top it off, Larry had two strikes against him right off the bat. And if he'd cry at night, Paul would shake him because he'd be so irritable, just getting home from work. In those days, I think those were the only times I really stood up to him. I wouldn't let him touch my baby like that.

I went to work when Paul was laid off after his first year at Minnesota Rubber, so that was over twenty-five years ago. I felt bad at the time having to work. I loved my baby dearly and I just felt kind of left out that I couldn't be with him all the time. He was the most important thing in my whole life.

Just having him was an experience, since I was supposed to have a Caesarean because I'm so little. But I found a real good Catholic doctor who said, "We're going to try a normal birth for you." I had seventeen and a half hours in labor, but Paul sat with me all night long and I delivered him all right. He was a seven-pound baby and that was big for me. But that meant he had a good chance, a good start. He was like a delicate little doll. I thought he might break. Just so beautiful, with a little turned-up nose, the darkest eyes and so bouncy and happy, the most beautiful smile.

He was just full of life and a lot of fun to raise. There were just the two of us in the evening, when I'd come home from work. We'd spend time with books and reading and things. Everything was Larry. I was wrapped up in him and I could hardly wait to get home from work to be with him. We'd go to the drugstore for dinner, and we'd go shopping and to the park, and he was always so good.

He really never had other children to play with before school, so the first day of kindergarten I thought it would be tough for him, but he was one of the better ones. He looked around and sized up everything, and when I said, "Well, Mommy has to go now, I'll come back and pick you up," he just looked at me and said, "Okay." Now I don't think he'll ever quit school. It looks like he's going to be a permanent student. He's now planning to go to law school.

As I said, I went to work when Paul was laid off. By then he had a little seniority, so they did call him back again. But the layoff was still . . . well, it doesn't give you a feeling of security when you always have the feeling that you're going to get laid off. And so I kept on working. It's hard to remember all the places I worked at.

First, I worked as an artist with Fanny Farmer's. You know, in their stores they have all these real pretty decorative things in the windows? That's what I worked on. And that was right up my alley. I just loved it. There were mostly women there and we had a wonderful elderly woman to work for. There were only three of us at this job and we had a special place all by ourselves, away from everything. Our boss would tell us how she wanted certain things and then she just kind of left us on our own. It was a real relaxed atmosphere, and we could eat all the nuts and candy that we wanted! I think I stayed there about a year and then they had a cutback.

Then I worked at Brown and Bigelow. I worked on punch presses and all kinds of different machines and I didn't mind that. I kind of enjoyed it. They made leather products and ball-point pens and things like calendars for advertising. They finally laid me off there due to lack of work, but they said they'd like to call me back and they said, too, that if I would be willing to do office work they'd keep me on. They said I was really "office material." To me that doesn't really mean anything, but I've had it said to me several times. The only thing is, the pay was so poor for office work in those days. Even now I have a lot of friends who work in factories and make a lot more money than I do.

When I finally came back to office work, I went back to receptionist. Even though the money was not all that great, there was a certain amount of respect that people seemed to show to women that worked in offices that you didn't get in factory work. Sure, we had to wait on men and we had to run after their coffee. We had to do a lot of things that we didn't like to do, but still we were given some respect. In those days it was, "Oh, you're a secretary! How nice." Now it's, "Oh, you're just a secretary." It's like some kind of a lowly job. So times have changed.

I worked for Control Data for over five years. I have my five-year bracelet with the ruby and everything. I started there during the recession, so I was lucky. I just walked into the job. It just happened that they needed a clerk-typist and they hadn't even had time to advertise. I wasn't too sure how my typing was. I'd taken business practice and typing and short-hand in high school, but so much hadn't been used and it was pretty bad by then. I was in my late twenties.

I was to relieve on the switchboard and work in purchasing. That was my beginning—purchasing. My boss didn't take to me too much at first, but the man in personnel had, and as I worked my typing picked up faster and faster and I remember the day that Mr. Telford came in and he said, "Louie, I told ya so. Just look at her go." And I felt really proud because I had gotten his approval.

So I thought, well, I'd master this and reach out for more. They had just one buyer at that time and one purchasing agent, Charlie. So I'd go to Charlie and he'd always back me up in just about every way. I started taking on some of his responsibilities. And I was gaining more confidence, I guess, developing my personality, growing a little bit.

Little by little I started learning more and more about the purchasing end. We'd devise new ideas and I'd pick them up so fast. Then I discovered I had a knack for remembering numbers. I got so I knew all the numbers of the parts and I could rattle them off and tell them it was shipped on such and such a date. It just stayed in my mind like that, and I found out I had an excellent memory because I had to use it.

You know we let our brain go kind of lax, because we don't use it all. I find in my job now that I really don't have to use my own thinking, because everything is being created by the professors and I just follow what they want done. That's what a secretary usually does. But I like thinking for myself, thinking of new ways and new ideas.

So I'd started as a clerk-typist and I worked my way up to a secretary and was doing very well. And I did work hard. So hard that some of the secretaries would make remarks like they thought it was something degrading to work that hard. You know, like, "What are you doing that for?" And they'd stand around and talk.

It was a real heavy job, but I did feel that I wanted to learn everything there was to know. I was going somewhere with myself and I knew that I really hadn't reached all that I was capable of doing. I'd learned how to handle people through the reception part, so that helped me in handling people in the purchasing area. I did have a different way of handling customers, too. Where the men would cuss and swear and demand, I had a completely different way. And I didn't use sex either. They used to say, "It must be your sex."

I think it was just a matter of understanding what kind of situation the suppliers were in. Having worked in production a little I knew that there were such things as production shutdowns. These other buyers, they thought they were being put on and held off deliberately. But I'd say, "Yes, I can understand that. What is the best you can do, and when will your supplies be in so you can finish the product for our company?" Well, they knew they were talking to someone that understood that they too were under pressure. This is the way I got action. And I got good action.

Well, finally I went to my immediate superior, the purchasing agent, for a promotion. He said, "I'll try to do what I can for you. You're doing an excellent job, and I'll see." But I waited and he didn't do anything. So one day I was thinking about it very hard. I was thinking there's something wrong here. These men are making a lot more money than I am, and I'm doing what they are, and besides they've got the prestige in their jobs and I really don't have anything. And there was no union. They tried to keep the unions out by giving people raises or getting rid of the so-called troublemakers.

We had an open door policy there, so I walked into our manager's office and I said, "I'd like to talk to you, Doug." And he said, "All right, sit down." And I said, "Well, first of all I'm going to stand." I had to stand up because if I sat down I might relax! So I told him how I felt, that I was doing the same job as the men, and he laughed at me. It was terrible. He ended up laughing and telling me that was a man's job. And I said, "Yeah, but I'm doing the job, I just don't have the money or the title. I just don't think it's fair." But he just kept making fun of me. I was hurt and mad and I stormed out of there and made up my mind I was going to do something.

I really had put everything into my job, and that was a lot. I'm a Taurus and I may do things a little differently, but I'm very deliberate about it and I do a good job. Something else I did was I had set up the purchasing library from scratch. I set up all the catalogue files and I had a card system that gave a cross reference for where to find everything by parts. And this is in electronics, so there's lots of parts.

Well anyway, I'd never really been accepted too much by the secretaries because I worked so hard. I guess they thought there was something wrong with you if you really put everything into a job. And maybe on the one hand there was, too, when I think about it now, how hard I worked. I had so much energy in those days and still managed to keep up with my work at home. I couldn't do it now.

I had several good friends there in different departments and on different levels. I always got along well with most people. But I did seem to run up against the wall with some women in the office—in particular, the division manager's secretary. She was a leader-type person, very dominating, and she could draw the group to her because she was the number one girl in the office. They were really kind of cliquish and they didn't accept my good friend Dorothy too well, either. She was on the unattractive side and kind of businesslike, but she was such a warm, genuine person underneath her businesslike appearance. I didn't like them for that and they kind of ignored me, too, so I withdrew. And it was about this time that I began to feel this terrible depressed feeling.

A CYCLE OF MISERY ON AND OFF THE JOB

At this time I was going to school nights too. I went back to brush up on shorthand, so I was studying and trying to keep up the house. And I was worried about my son. He was at a moody age, thirteen or fourteen, and I was afraid he was too studious and wasn't developing as a normal kid. And he was rebelling quite a bit against his father. He was all right with me, but he would often just go off up to his room and stay there and wouldn't have anything to do with Paul. Paul would try to get him to do things like go fishing, but Larry would never put down his books long enough to do anything, and Paul felt really rejected.

So my work problems were eating at me—being looked down upon as inferior, being laughed at and ridiculed. Then Paul started drinking quite a bit on weekends. He was still working nights. And it just seemed like my whole life was falling apart. I went to see my parents in California then. Paul thought it would be nice for me to fly out there because they were getting old. But even while I was there, things were still building up.

I was thinking and thinking, really too much. I was trying to put things together, but nothing seemed to be in the right place. I was very, very deeply depressed. I should have enjoyed myself more with my parents, but I had so much on my mind, and I was tired from the schooling and worried about Paul's drinking and his attitude when he'd come home drunk and I'd be sound asleep, the demands he'd make on me. If I could have gotten some satisfaction from my job, I think I could have come through, but that too was bad.

Then about two months after I came back from California, Paul had gotten very drunk one night and I'd said something that set him off in the wrong way and he stayed mad. The next morning he gave me a bunch of orders and he kind of threatened me. He had slapped me around a couple of times when he was drunk and I knew he was still hung over, but after he left for work that day I was really frightened.

I called a friend who's divorced herself and I said, "I'm leaving." I said, "Larry says it's fine. He's fourteen years old and we'll make it all right." We packed our bags but we didn't know where to go, since we had no car to drive. So I got a cab and we went to a motel near where we lived and near the bank. I had been saving money because of the trouble between Paul and me. I was putting away $100 a month so I had saved $2,400.

Well, I went to this motel, but the next day the manager made me get out. Maybe he was suspicious of me being a runaway wife or something. You know men protect the man, not the woman, even when they don't know the circumstances. So then I called a good friend and he came to pick me up and I found a hotel room right downtown that was a lot cheaper than the motel. Then I contacted the Bar Association and they gave me a recommendation of a good lawyer for a seven dollar fee, and I went ahead to start filing for the divorce. I told my story to the lawyer and he was going to make out the papers. But he did say that he would like to talk to Paul, to see if there's any chance of saving the marriage.

Well the public library was right across the street from our hotel, so Larry used to always spend time there. And Paul knows Larry's habits and mine pretty good. I went to pick up Larry one day after leaving the lawyer's office, and there's Paul. He just figured that's where Larry would be. Larry wouldn't tell him where I was, but Paul just waited and waited till I came to pick him up.

Then it was a matter of pleading and asking me to come back. "How's Larry going to get a college education like he deserves?" And, "We can do it together." And that got to me. It really did. He knew that I wanted the very best for the only child I'd had, you know. I'd had several miscarriages. So that started me thinking a little more seriously and I thought he was right. He promised he'd change and he went on trying to convince me that he was going to be a completely different person. I didn't understand so much of it—why he would be like his father so much and why men in my life were always treating me so bad. I couldn't really see that I was so bad. But I told him, "Well, let me think about it."

I finally decided to go back, but I still wasn't sure I'd done the right thing. I was very confused. I went back to work and I'd missed about three days so I had to tell them. The division manager came in and he said, "Are you getting a divorce?" And I said, "No. I'm trying to straighten it out." And he said, "That was a terrible thing for you to do." And I said, "Well, you don't know the circumstances." And he kept telling me how terrible it was, the way I behaved. Nobody seemed to understand. I guess it's hard for people to understand unless you actually live in the situation.

So I worked a couple of days with this heavy criticism and this lack of feeling that I was doing what was right in accepting things the way they were, and I was so confused and depressed. Then this good friend of mine in the office said, "I think maybe you better go see a doctor about it." He said, "I can't help you."

So then I went to the doctor and I was just a wreck. I tried to tell him the whole story and he said, "Do you feel like committing suicide? Do you wish you were dead?" I said, "Right at this moment, if it was a way out of all these problems, yeah." But he took it that I was going to actually literally go out and do the thing. Well, I'm one of these people that don't have the guts to do anything like that. And practically everybody in this world, I've read this many times, has at one time or another in their life thought of suicide. Everybody has a real hard time at some time or another—whether it's illness that causes it, a death in the family, a problem at work, you lose someone you love, or what.

So it was just a reaction to a depression, but he got shook and he said, "I know a real good doctor." He called this psychiatrist, and suddenly I'm labeled, I want you to know, as mentally ill. I never lost my mental capacity at any moment. You know, I was really very upset about what happened to Senator Eagleton.* I just think it was terrible and Paul felt the same way. You've got to have been there to know how it feels. The rest of your life you've got a label on you. You can be a leading, outstanding citizen and be an alcoholic, but you can't have emotional problems.

Well, after the doctor called the psychiatrist, he gave me a shot. He said, lay there until you're relaxed and then go out and tell your husband you're to go right to the hospital. So Paul said, "You're not going to have a psychiatrist. You're perfectly all right. All you need is a little rest." So I said, "I think I need the help and I'm going to sign myself in. I'm very upset and depressed." But he just couldn't see it. He said, "There's nothing wrong with you. Everything's been real hard on you now, but I'll try to make it up to you and things will be fine."

Well, I felt that this was probably the best way. It would give me a chance to be away from things, think it out and try to look at things in a better light. So eventually we went home, I got all my clothes and I signed into the hospital. It was kind of strange. It wasn't like a regular hospital. You wear your own clothes, you make your own bed and take care of yourself. You go to a nice dining room where you all sit around the tables and have your meals together.

My psychiatrist was the chief psychiatrist, so he was very good. It was a private hospital and it was good that I never had to experience a real bad state hospital. I guess they're bad, from what I know. Because it was no different than just living in a rooming house, except that the nurses were there and we had sisters there.

At first it was hard, because I wouldn't follow orders. I didn't want to do things like go to occupational therapy, I just wanted time to think. The nurse really yelled at me one day

---

* Thomas F. Eagleton, U.S. Senator from Missouri since 1969, served as George McGovern's vice presidential running mate briefly during the 1972 elections, until his history of hospitalization for emotional problems was publicly disclosed.

and she said, "You've got to snap out of this. You've got everything going for you. You're a secretary, you've got a wonderful son, you've got this and that," and she really laid it on me heavy. It was probably good. I finally yelled back at her, "Well, okay, I'll go. I'm sure good at following orders. That's all anyone asks you to do anyway, is follow orders." She got a real rise out of me. Before that I had been real quiet and withdrawn, but then I started to go to occupational therapy and look forward to doing things.

Altogether I was there a little over a month. During that time my sister Lilly died in a fire in her home in California, and that was pretty rough, but I took it fairly well, as well as anyone would take something like that. But the psychiatrist said the shock of it was a setback so I stayed a little longer than I thought I would at first. Actually, I kind of got used to the place and kind of liked it there.

I did have some rough times at night, like when I'd want to call Larry. Even though he was fourteen and I knew that he could feed himself and get by with Paul working, I still worried about him and I'd try to get to the phone, but it was always busy with everybody calling home. I'd get so frustrated about that.

One time the nurse had spotted my fuming, you know, just holding it all in. She came into the room and she said, "What do you want to do, scream?" So I laughed and I said, "Yeah, I'd love to, but if I did that I'd end up in the other ward." She kind of agreed with me, but she said, "It really is good to be mad sometimes."

That nurse was evidently very sharp in just observing and telling the psychiatrist things so he could work with you. I saw him about twice a week and it was twenty-five dollars a visit in those days. I was lucky that I had part coverage under medical insurance. Even today, not many insurances allow for emotional or mental illness, and the costs for treatment have more than doubled.

That's something I think is so important. We've got to have more help for people who are emotionally disturbed. That's all I was, and being depressed is almost as common as having a bad cold. There've got to be doctors that aren't out there looking for that much money. Sure, they've got their expenses, but they ought to be able to charge a price that people can pay. Anyhow, Paul helped me pay some of it. He helped me a lot.

I think it was a good experience for me because I saw and heard so many stories that were much worse than mine. I kind of began to feel that I really wasn't so bad off at all. The psychiatrist did help. He seemed to tend to steer me away from the divorce idea and back to the wife and mother and secretary bit. But I did accept it.

I became quite a fireball when I came out. I had my old spirit back and I wasn't depressed in any way. Things were going better at home. Larry seemed to be in a fairly good mood and Paul was being really good. I wasn't going to school and I wasn't working any extra hours, even though I was working real hard. I'd made a lot of adjustments and I still was doing beautifully at my job.

After a while I went in again to the manager to ask for a little raise and a promotion, but I got nowhere. The same old routine. "It's a man's job. You just forget it, and go back to your secretarial job." He knew that I was really fired up and he didn't like a woman being aggressive. He didn't like that one bit. So they fixed me with some dirty politics and made the records show that I had been absent when I hadn't been.

I knew I was being accused of something that was false, so that did it. Paul said, "Just quit." But I said, "I've got a record there. I've been there over five years. I've got to give my notice." So I gave two weeks' notice and finally my friend Dorothy found proof—records in our long-distance log—that I had been there on the days they said I hadn't. She showed it to my boss and he said, "Too late now. We can't do anything about it." It was really a very rotten deal.

One thing I found out was it doesn't really pay to be honest. I had made a stab at finding a job and telling the truth about being in the hospital, but no one wanted to hire me. They would be interested until they'd ask about that little period of not working, and I thought I'd have to tell them the truth. I said I'd had a nervous condition, is the way I put it, and then they said, "Well, you can't take any pressure then." So if a woman goes out into the working world now, I would advise,

"Don't tell the truth." The less they know about you the better off you are. And that's from learning the hard way.

Well after Control Data, my husband said, "You've got a little bit of savings, why don't you just take the summer off?" So I just relaxed and then in the fall I started looking for another job. I wanted to stay in purchasing because I knew I was good at it. It was hard finding a job in that area, because it is a man's job, but that's what I wanted to do—either expediting or buying, but in that area. Finally I found a buying job, but it was away from my electronics line, so it meant I'd have to learn a new product with 24,000 fasteners—screws, nuts and bolts. And that's a lot.

This was a distributing house and sales was their business, so a good part of it was keeping the customer happy. My boss was so impressed with how well I was doing that he let me be a middleman between the hard-to-handle customers that really needed special attention. So I would see what I could do both ways to keep everybody happy. I was on the phone constantly and it was very difficult for me not being able to smoke. Women couldn't smoke there. Only men could, even though I had a private office. Then I couldn't take a break because I would be paged for long-distance constantly. So it was really hard.

I made exactly half of what the men made, except I was doing more because I also had to type. The men had their own secretaries. My boss was very nice and when I did ask for more money, he even said I was doing fifty percent of his work. We divided everything down equally, only I had the hard-to-get-along-with customers. Then the director of our department . . . well, for one thing, he was an alcoholic and he was never around. He'd come in about 9:30 and leave at 11 and wouldn't get back until 3:30 or 4 and he'd be in a stupor. Everybody said, "Well, he was entertaining customers as part of his job," you know.

Then he asked me to do shorthand for him, and evidently he liked my looks or something. But I told him I was too busy and he didn't like that. He called me a "high-priced assistant." Actually, I knew that some of the secretaries were making more than me. I'd talk with other women in the office and they'd shrug their shoulders and say, "Well, that's the way it is around here. We can't smoke and things, and it's not fair, but you just put up with it."

"You can always quit," is the way they usually put it. And secretaries seemed to move around a lot because there's nothing they could do about a situation. So they'd just quit. It's that way today, too. They have something interesting for a while, then they go out and find something else. And I don't think it'll ever change unless somehow there are some real big changes in things.

I do think the Women's Movement has helped some. Men are more cautious now, I find, at the university anyhow. They don't refer to us as "girls," although we do sometimes ourselves. We've gotten so used to it and we haven't erased it from our language yet. But men are more careful of what and how they say things to us. Although every now and then we'll be referred to as civil "servants," which I don't like. Or like I heard one of the professors say, "Oh, that's just my secretary."

That's one thing the organization I belong to—the Council of University Women for Progress—is trying to fight, this inferior status with the civil service people. We're not servants in that sense of the word. You think of a servant as a person who ought to do nothing but wait on people, like a maid. We're civil service personnel and that takes in a lot of people, the professors too. They work for the state and for the people.

Well, my next job, they hired me as a one-girl office. That was a good deal, but the company was always going broke at the beginning and I found my checks were always bouncing on me. My two bosses were both Shriners, so they were never there. They were in the Circus and they were always out running around on their motorcycles or something. So a lot of the work started falling my way and gradually I started doing expediting in the sales area. They were in precision investment castings.

The company started going better after a while. They had a lot of work from the Vietnam war. But the vice president was crooked as could be. He threw bad parts in with the good parts and they would go into the helicopters that go to Vietnam. Coincidentally, a friend of mine from Control Data also happened to be a government inspector, and then there was this young company inspector who'd tell me ahead of time, "Ann, there's going to be a bunch of bad parts." Then I would call Bill and tell him, "Look, I want you to have a hundred percent check today."

So Bill would come out. Normally, he would only make what they called a ten percent check to see if the parts were right. When I called, he would reject the whole thing. But Ed, the vice president, would save his rejected parts and try to sneak them through another time and get rid of them. John, the president, was glad that I'd do these things because he had a boy over there who had been shot down. Ed only thought of money. I just wonder how many more businessmen in this country are like that. Here this part goes into a helicopter, which is behind the lines picking up wounded in Vietnam.

I stayed there over three years and I liked it. By this time I was more just the president's secretary plus the sales coordinator, working with customers. But then the vice president brought in a CPA and they were stealing money out of the company and I wanted out. Eventually they did go under.

I really liked sales. I liked working with people. So I hunted and finally got a job with a sales rep. This was an electrical business where they warehoused a lot of items. It was a brand new office for a major multinational corporation. Actually they helped my boss Stan get started and he was selling their parts. He used to be a general manager for them, so he was big time, at least at one time.

When I came there were no files, no nothing. They had a list of potential customers and that's all I had to go on. So it meant digging from the very bottom and building something. They called my job "city desk and office manager." Well, I was the only person, so that's not much of a management job. But I had to do all the buying, arrange for printing, set up the files and type them up. No typist, just me.

Anyway, they had no place to park and the second day he started griping about the parking tickets him and his partner were getting. So his partner said, "Why don't we just give Ann a bunch of nickels and we'll have her just run down every hour and put nickels in both machines." So every hour I had to run down with my nickels. And it didn't matter if I was on the phone with a customer or what. The business started pouring in real fast from people who found out about the office and needed one of our products. Actually it threw me into the job and I had to learn a little fast, but I liked it.

Besides running out every hour to the meters, he expected me to do things like make coffee for them, but I was so determined that I was going to prove to him that I could really do it. He swore a blue streak. He'd holler at me and yell, "Get on the telex and tell that goddamned so-and-so this or that," "Get on this, do that, I don't care, make him answer right away." So there I sit, following his orders right to a tee, but hating every bit of it inside.

I didn't think I could stand to work there for too long, but I still felt, well, I've got to learn this job. And the pay wasn't too bad—at least it was the most that I had ever made, around five hundred dollars a month. Then finally they hired a young woman to help me, even though Betty did end up working for Stan. And then they found parking places.

I was getting to the point where I knew the job well and Stan didn't know what was going on. And he was starting to go out and stir up trouble with the customers. He'd try to demand that they buy from him and you can't do that. So I knew he wasn't going to make it. And he had been living at a beautiful hotel downtown for months, living it up big off the company. His partner kept bugging him to get an apartment, but he said, "I'll wait till my wife sells the house and gets out here."

Then he was chasing around with a little nineteen-year-old girl. The girl would call all the time and ask for him and he'd yell, "Say I'm not there." Then finally she showed up in the office and I felt so sorry for her because he had really put her on. She came right to me and asked if she could talk to me in private and she said, "You know, Stan's my boyfriend and we're going to get married." And I said to myself, "Oh God, what did he do?" Then she says, "Is he really rich? He told me he was." Well, I just couldn't bear to tell her that he's married and got a teen-aged daughter and a son almost a teen-ager.

Anyway, she started calling me and calling me and calling me. She was starting to get more and more depressed because he wasn't seeing her. His wife was coming out and evidently he wanted to get rid of this young woman and he didn't know how, so he left the dirty job for me. Then one day she called and said she wanted to commit suicide. I couldn't leave the place because there was no one there, so I kept talking and I said things like, "Stan isn't worth it, really, he's rotten, and I'm going to quit pretty soon," and finally I talked her into going to the hospital.

Then Stan went back east on business and his partner was away, so for about three days I was all alone handling things. I was doing pretty good. Then he called in from the airport when he arrived and he wanted to know what was going on. So I told him that our principals were pretty mad about him trying to fix prices on copper. The companies found out about it and they made accusations to me, but I put it right where it belonged, on his shoulders. So he started screaming on the telephone, calling me dirty names.

By the time he got back to the office, I had already cleaned out my desk drawers. I'd never been much of a person for swearing, but I tore into his office and I stuttered over it trying to find words that would describe just what I thought of him. His face turned from red to pure white and he sat there with his mouth drooping. He'd been way up there, you know, and I guess nobody talks that way to him. So I grabbed my bag and out I walked.

They weren't paying their bills and eventually they were forced to fold up, but I went back there before they folded and Betty told me that the young girl ended up in an asylum, completely out of it. The parents got to him later. It turns out he had really abused her sexually and everything, too. He was really an awful man. In the end, he lost everything—his home, his business and his wife. So if you want to say, "Sin does not pay," that's about it.

After that, there was another job I had where they hired me because of my background, but they had me typing all day. Then I went to Tolamatic and I stayed there for two years, '70 and '71. I was hired in there as an engineering secretary. I had been asked there through a grapevine, like for other jobs that I had, to come and set up their engineering department. So I got the files organized and got a cataloguing system devised.

Also I had to run the blueprint machine, but they had no exhaust system on it, for the fumes to get out. Instead they were coming at me and I was breathing all that ammonia and stuff.

The smell was really making me sick, nauseated. So I went to my boss and told him, and he said, "I'll see what I can do." But he was turned down about getting an exhaust system and he wanted to save his job, so he said, "There's nothing I can do, Ann. I agree with you, but it's not going to change."

So I kept putting up with the situation and finally it got real bad. My stomach was swelling up and I was getting nervous too. I didn't know what it was, so the doctor said, "I think you've got ulcers." I didn't really agree with him, but he said, "I'm going to put you on an ulcer diet." But that only made me worse. Then he gave me tranquilizers and I was taking sleeping pills. I was really sick but I kept going to work.

In the medical books it explains colitis and I thought maybe it sounds like that, you know? Then the doctor said, "I think maybe you better go in for X rays." I went into the hospital, and I didn't have any ulcers. They said the only thing they could figure would be colitis and that was due to emotions.

When I got out of the hospital, I called up and said, "I'll be able to come back to work. I'm going to be all right." My boss said, "Good, very good." Then he called me back later in the day and said, "I'm sorry to have to tell you this, Annie, but Burt says he just can't have anyone that's got stomach problems." He said, "Burt had just about all of his stomach taken out and he just can't put up with that here, so he doesn't want you back." Well, that was a real blow. I was really upset. Fired on the phone for having stomach problems. They called it "laid off." So I went and signed up for unemployment because I was willing and able to work. I do try to stick to jobs real hard, it's just that things don't always work out for me.

Well, one time I said to my doctor, "How long do you want me to stay on these iron pills?" I'd been taking them for two years. And he said, "Oh my God, are you still taking those?" He had told me to take them indefinitely. See, at menstrual time, I was losing too much blood and my iron was dropping down, so he wanted to build me up. But even when my blood was okay, he completely forgot that I was still on these pills.

So he said, "Don't take any more." So I told my husband about it and I said, "There must be some connection because he was too excited when I told him about the iron pills." Well I looked it up in the medical book and I found that if you get too much iron, it can cause stomach troubles. Then I put it all together and I tried to tell the doctor about it and he said, "You're just a very emotional person. You're really sick."

Well Tolamatic paid me a whole month's salary. I don't know if it was to keep me quiet or what. And I was on unemployment, so I thought I'll take it easy and get feeling better. So I stayed home and started sewing up a storm and I love to sew. I was really enjoying myself, being home. I kept my house spotless, which I don't do too well now, and it was just fun being here.

Then I started getting rambunctious and ready to go back to work again and I found that jobs were real hard to get. I couldn't figure out what it was, so I began thinking, well, maybe it's my age, you know? So I was downtown, really working hard trying to get a job and, doggone it, I went back to Control Data. I thought, I've got stock in the company, so I can always get a job there and right now I can't get a job anywhere else.

There was a clerk-typist job that they needed someone for at another plant, so I went over and saw the personnel man. He said, "I'm sorry, Ann, you're overqualified." So I said, "That's saying that I am qualified, so I'd like to have the job." So finally he said, "I guess you're hired then, as far as I'm concerned." So I said, "Okay, tell me where the job is located and I'll go out there."

So I had my lunch and when I came out it was just pouring out and the wind was whipping it around in balls down the street. The cars were stopped dead still. The rain was so bad they couldn't move. Not a soul on the streets. It was really spooky. But here I am, determined to get that job. Talk about Taurus and their being determined. I was wringing wet and shivering cold and I had to wait for the bus, but I had an appointment at one o'clock and I had to make it to the northeast part of the city.

I met the boss and he also told me that I was overqualified and everything, but I said, "That's okay, I'm a hard worker and you won't be sorry." So he says, "Well, good. We're way behind in our work." That meant doing real production typing in the drafting department. All the technical data had to be typed on the prints and the typewriter carriages were enormous. And I really did work hard.

Monday, the first day of work, I passed my physical, but already I had a pain in my head and I didn't know what was wrong with me, except that I had gotten a cold from the storm. I just thought it was a bad headache, so I didn't pay any attention. But by Friday night I was pretty bad, so I called a doctor at the clinic. The pain was spreading and he didn't know what to make of it, but he called it a neuritis. I later found that it was called Bell's palsy and I could have become blind from it.

So he said, "You've got an inner ear infection and it looks pretty bad." He gave me some medication, but I just got worse. Already it had spread so bad. A few days later he said, "I think maybe you better go to the hospital." My mouth was really hanging low, kind of numb, and it was affecting my eyesight and everything. And the pain was terrible. But then my regular doctor came in and looked at me and he gave me a prescription just for the pain. He told me to go back to work and stay on the medicine.

The next day I went back to work, but the pain was very severe and the pain pills were not giving me any relief. And oh, I had tranquilizers and sleeping pills. I thought I'd go out of my mind with the pain, but I went to work thinking, well, at least maybe it'll help me keep my mind off myself. And I was brand new on the job, trying to prove myself so that I could hang on to it.

The pain was still undiagnosed and every time I'd go back to the doctor I'd say, "Do something for me, please. Find out what it is." Well, he never said anything like, "You're sick in the head," but I think that's what he was thinking, that it was psychological or something. He said, "Your ear has healed up beautifully. There doesn't seem to be anything wrong with you. I'll give you another prescription for the pain and you continue taking your drugs."

So I went on this way for two months, and finally I decided that I'd better get some more help. I got the name of a doctor who specialized in neurology. On my first visit he gave me a brain wave and he took X rays of my skull to see if I had a tumor developing. To be honest with you, the pain was so great

I was beginning to wonder if I didn't have a tumor on the brain.

He examined me and he said, "I can't say for sure yet, but my diagnosis now is temporal arteritis." He said, "You're very young to have that. That's usually a degenerative disease." He told me a little bit about it and he said, "I can treat it, but I'm going to have to dose you up with cortisone." And he gave me more Percodan for the pain, but he said, "I want to warn you that that is an addicting drug, so be careful in how you use it." I hadn't been warned about this by my regular doctor.

I kept on working up to the holiday, when I reached the point where I no longer cared to eat. If I got up, I passed out. My right eye locked shut and I couldn't open it. So the disease had spread through the cranial nerves and moved into the optical nerves. Finally, the day before New Year's, my son came over and he told Paul he thought he should get me to a hospital.

With all this pain and everything, I hadn't slept for fifty-seven hours and I started hallucinating. I'd be wide awake and be aware of where I was, but I could see this weird, wild flash of colors through my eyes that was like a vision and it was frightening. So my doctor said, "Your medicine's not reacting right." This was my regular doctor and I never could figure out what he was doing there at the hospital. He said, "I'm going to cut you down on the cortisone and give you some new medication." Then he put me on some kind of a pill that speeded me up, and I started to stutter like mad. I felt like I was kind of floating.

Finally I got some Valium from one of the nurses and I slept five hours after not having slept for fifty-seven hours and I really felt so much better. The next morning he came in to tell me that he was going to change my medicine again. I tried to tell him that the mild tranquilizer was helping me more than all this other junk. After I slept I was feeling so much better that I thought I'd be getting up soon. But no, I had another setback because they gave me this other drug, Mellaril, that slowed me down so bad and I started having severe chest pains. So they made me stay in bed for two more days.

I had just short of a month in the hospital. I was lucky that I had started working at Control Data again, because they had

real good coverage. I went right back to work afterward and
the pain was gone. It finally healed up, even though the neu-
rologist said it could come back at another time in my life. He
didn't know how I had stood it for two months.

I stayed at that job for one year to the day and then I quit
and started looking again. As you get older, you have more
and more difficulty. Finally I found a job at Western Union
through the state employment agency. My requirements were
shorthand, typing, filing, telephones, very normal kinds of secretarial duties. The money was good and the hours were beautiful 8:30 to 4:15, with forty-five minutes for lunch. I'd get to
work about an hour early because of the bus schedules, so I'd
have coffee, relax, read my book and maybe jot down notes
from a book if something really was impressing me. So it
seemed real nice.

Then one day I was standing on a file stool that was shaped
like a four-leaf clover and my heel slipped and I wrenched my
back. There were five-drawer files, and since I'm only four feet
ten, it was way above my reach. The other girl in administration that had the same level job as me was young and much
taller, but she dumped all the dirty work on me because she
had some seniority there.

She was a tall, thin, attractive blonde and she'd go on up to
the eighth floor and fool around in the sales department. There
was a lot of good-looking men up there. She once explained to
me how important sex was in that organization, how you can
make it up to management if you go to bed with the vice president or something. Some of the women that had done this had
disappeared for a few months at a time. I don't know if they
went away and had babies or abortions or what, but they'd
come back and land a management job. They'd be out of the
union.

I really thought that was kind of different, being so open
about it. I'd seen some flirtations in offices, and I myself, you
know, had kind of been attracted to men, but I really strongly
believe in the old vows and all that stuff and so does my husband. Get a divorce if you want to fool around.

Well, when my heel slipped over the edge, I was able to
grab a hold of the drawer, but that pulled my back. That happened twice. So I missed one day because my back was really

hurting me bad. The next day the supervisor—he had made it up the hard way, from a machine operator on up, and he was kind of the typical old-fashioned crack-the-whip kind of person—he came over to my desk and he said, "You go on into the mail room." He said, "The girl's leaving the country and we're going to have to train you in."

I said, "Well, you know my back is bothering me," and I said, "I'm not even dressed for it." That's a dirty job and I had high heels on and there's a lot of walking around. This was the central office for a seven-state area and it meant going around to all the floors, picking up the mail from all the departments and sorting it out.

So I went in there and I did the best I could, but by the end of the day my arm was getting so that I could hardly move it up above my waist and my neck was starting to hurt. I told my husband, "Looks like I'm going to get stuck with that job. Jobs are scarce now and here I can't get hired anymore because of my age. What am I going to do?" So he said, "Let's get you some jeans for one thing." Then I thought if I got a good rest that night maybe I'd feel better in the morning.

But I was pretty bad in the morning. I couldn't lift up the coffee pot to fill it with water and then I just broke into tears. My God, I thought, what happened to me? The pain was just terrific. My husband was pretty nervous, too, and he said, "You'd better stay home today and we better get you to a doctor."

The doctor never even examined my back. This was my old doctor again. He took some X rays and told me they were negative. I had two large lumps where the neck and head are connected together and he wouldn't lay a hand on it. Then he sent me down to a hospital for testing to see if there was any nerve damage and finally he says, "Your X rays are negative, your EMG* is negative, there's absolutely nothing wrong with you." I said, "Then why have I got this pain?" He says, "It's all psychological. You're sick in the head and I won't treat you till you see a counselor."

Finally, he said, "Ann, would you go see a psychiatrist?" And I said, "Okay, and I'll prove that I'm right." So I contacted this

* Electromyogram, a measurement of electric waves, used to diagnose neuromuscular disorders.

psychiatrist that I had for my depression. He was very soft-spoken and nice, and I gave him a complete rundown of my medical history. He had me take some psychological tests and then he says, "You tell that doctor that there is a real injury and it's not your fault." "Negligence" is what he called it. So I said, "You mean I'm not sick in the head?" He said, "Yeah, you're just as sick in your head as all the rest of us who have to live in this crazy world." That's just the way he put it, too.

So I went back to my doctor and he wouldn't believe me and he said, "Well, I'm not going to treat you." Paul picked me up from there and I said, "I guess I'm going to have to keep this here Sopor habit to sleep nights and I'm going to have to try to find another doctor." But when I tried calling other doctors, they said, "There isn't a doctor in town that would touch you with a ten-foot pole," because of the claim against Western Union.

Well, finally I got in to see an orthopedist. And I told him everything, the psychiatrists, even about the doctors not touching me with a ten-foot pole. So he put his hand on my knee and he said, "I touched you." He says, "Now you listen to me and you follow my advice because it's going to get you back on your feet." He treated me for sixteen weeks and he was really good.

Then finally I broke from the old doctor and flushed all my pills from him down the toilet. Paul and I did it together. I said, "You're going to have to help me. I've got a lot to get through, and it won't be easy, so I hope you're going to be patient with me till I get through this." Well, it was a matter of staying awake at night, it seemed like all night long, but then I was home so I could rest during the day. I guess the worst part was a queasiness in my stomach and irritability. Other than that, I was okay. See I think part of the reason I kept going to that doctor was that I did get hooked on the sleeping pill. So I called him and I left word that I wasn't going to report to him any longer. And that was it.

The orthopedist had found a permanent injury in my spine, in the vertebrae, and once in a while the pain comes back, but the upper arm healed up pretty good and the injury really doesn't interfere with my work at all now. I don't know how I had the strength to keep going, though. At times I said to Paul,

"How much can you take?" Being turned down at the doctors and not being able to know where to go. But Paul helped me a lot, you know, standing by me. Until I found this orthopedist, he was the only person I could turn to.

A UNIVERSITY ENVIRONMENT, THE WOMEN'S MOVEMENT: NEW OPTIONS

I started working at the University of Minnesota first of November '73. I tried real hard to get in there. It took me about five tries before I did and I had to take a clerk-typist job in order to break in. But I wanted to get away from business and their politics and into something better. And my son Larry had told me about all the interesting things going on around the university. I really do like the atmosphere over there.

It's been terrific working in the Engineering College. I've had a lot of increases in pay and levels in less than a year. I jumped up two levels right away in the area where I started and then they moved me into senior secretary. Now I've just had another review and moved up another level in the senior secretary area, so I've done well. With the new increase, I'll be making about $625, and figuring that I started at $500 a month just a few months ago, that's not bad.

I'm working in a special program for minority and low-income students to get into college. Since I was an inner city girl myself once, I have a special feeling for them. The program is called Project Technology Power. Part of it is peer teaching, where the older kids help teach the ones one or two levels below their age group in math and sciences. Then there's another area called Recruitment and Retention Program, and this is where they try to help with scholarships. It gives kids an opportunity and hopefully it will create more interest in the aerospace area.

Another area I work in is a special math course designed by the professor I work for, for pre-calculus. It's to help kids make the adjustment from high school because most of them really don't have enough preparation in that area to come right into college and it's mostly supported by foundations. My boss also has a new special program called Math and Science on the

Job, where the students and the teachers will go out and actually work on a problem in a company. The students earn two dollars an hour that way. It's really terrific.

One really nice thing about the university is that I can take the Regent's Scholarship, which you can start after you've been there six months. I'm signing up for English Comp and I can take one class every quarter during my working hours. It's with pay and also it's completely paid for. You have to get good grades, though, to hang on to the scholarship, so I'm really going to have to work on that. I'd really like to do some writing eventually, but I still feel a little inadequate in my grammar, like am I using the right punctuation? Am I saying this just right?

This is about the only way I guess I can get some education. I'll never get a degree, although many have gotten degrees this way, by working years at the university. But they have to start young. Since I'm forty-six, I'd be pretty old by the time I got it. We've talked about getting a degree, my husband and I. My husband is really . . . he doesn't have enough education and he wishes everybody could get more.

My son won what they call full scholarship for two years at Macalester, a private school, after his first two years at a local community college. He really liked it up there and was so active in the government of the school, student council, president of the class, writing in the paper. He was just always involved.

Then when he was twenty-one, in his senior year, he ran for mayor. He had gone to a lot of council meetings and really got interested in the area here. We were very proud of him and I think we probably walked more miles to campaign than he did. Actually, I kind of grew with him in politics. When Larry gets interested in politics, he really gets high on it, you know? So you can't help but become involved. Paul keeps real close contact with the happenings of the world, too. He's a very thorough reader of the papers.

Anyway, we all knew that he was too young and that this would be a factor. But people were interested in him. They played him up big in the Minneapolis papers, especially the *Tribune,* the morning paper where a lot of the younger and more liberal reporters are. Besides Larry, there were four businessmen running and one was the incumbent. Also, this would be the first mayor after it became a city. We used this same election to vote for Brooklyn Park to become a city from a village. So Larry really didn't have too great a chance, but it was interesting and fun and I hope someday that he can make it in politics.

In my job now, I think I have to tone myself down a little to get along with my boss. He likes me to take initiative, but not be too aggressive. He wants a line drawn. When we had my review, he thought I wanted to become more active in the program and, well . . . it's his baby and he takes a great deal of pride in it. So I told him, "No, I don't want to be a co-part of your program. I'm not qualified. I'm only in the background." To a certain degree I think he is a chauvinist in his beliefs. He's liberal in some ways, but when it comes to women, he's different. People are funny.

I always welcomed the Women's Movement, right from the start. It was something I was waiting for. I mean I was for anything that would just start making people aware, "Hey, we don't have to be like this. We're not slaves anymore." Somebody was starting to say something and do something. So I was always rooting for the movement to come through. And whatever measures they have to take to get some action, it's okay with me. I'll march right along with them if they want to march. Without it, I would still be on that treadmill, still fighting the whole system by myself. But even before it, I was kind of a libber all by myself, I guess, since the days I started rebelling against my father.

I guess I've gone into a lot of so-called men's jobs, and it always gave me kind of a scary feeling at first. But I just went ahead and pushed on regardless of the fear that I had built up inside of me, and within a few days I'd feel pretty much at home. I think that's what holds back a lot of women, the fear of, well, can I make it? A man did this before. Can I handle it? Because we've been held back so many years. Even right now there are feelings of inferiority, in terms of how I'm treated, mainly.

One of the reasons I wanted to work at the university was because I thought, well, there's where I can get active, I can get involved. I just felt I had to open up, talk to somebody, and I had contacted a couple of women's organizations but I couldn't get them by phone. So I thought even if it's mainly students, there's got to be some people my own age, too.

Then I was taking a business procedures class after I started there. They have courses for people that work there to help you with your job, and it also builds up your record. So in one of our discussions, the teacher said, "I should probably tell all of you women that there's a new organization on campus called the Council of University Women for Progress. It consists of civil service workers and faculty and students." She said, "We try to improve conditions on the campus and we're mainly concerned with women and also minority workers."

Well, that really interested me. Here was my opportunity. I was going to get involved. So right away I contacted the organization and attended my first meeting and I liked what they stood for. They were talking about a faculty member that had been eliminated in the cutbacks, and of course it happened to be a woman. They were trying to fight for her.

They also talked about getting together statistics so that we can know better what's going on at the university, how many women have an opportunity to get these management jobs, professional jobs, and how men, of course, seem to have all the better jobs. It sounded like really what I wanted to get involved in. At least an opportunity to start something, so I was real enthusiastic.

Then I read in the *Daily*, the university's paper put out by students, that there was a thing coming up soon called "Woman Power." It was an all-day workshop. So I thought, well, here's something else opening up for me and I've got to go to that too. I was really getting excited about the way things were turning out. So I spent a Saturday, from eight o'clock in the morning till four in the afternoon, really enjoying every minute of it, the workshops and seminars.

I would say the majority of them were young women, but some of the women who were doing their doctorates were kind of the leaders, and one was thirty-five years old. They had sessions on things like assertiveness. And I just wished all women could do this. I thought, Gee, wouldn't it be great if we could have this—I don't know if you'd call it consciousness-raising or what—if you could just get women together, because they can really enjoy each other's company.

It seems like too many women are always fighting one another. In business you see it probably more. Sometimes I've found that it's much easier to work with men than with women, because women are trying so hard that they put one another down. I think they're trying to please the men, so if you can make one look bad, then it makes you look better, or something like that. I don't know.

Anyway, at this day-long meeting there was such a togetherness and a feel for each other. We talked about day care centers and working on that. We talked about forming our own groups. They had a lot of things to hand out. People came from all over the state and we learned at that time about International Women's Year in 1975 and I was really just thrilled over that. I thought, well, Gee, now next year, even though it was given to us by men, we still could do something. At least we could sit up and be noticed. So I called people all over the campus about getting involved.

We have a special committee for civil service in CUWP, and one thing we want is representation on campus. There's the student senate, and the faculty has their senate, but the civil service has nothing. I've been a participant in the meetings that I've gone to and I guess they feel that I have good ideas. They nominated me for that committee. So I'm starting, but I'm not quite sure where to start, you know? I would like to organize things to get more membership so we can have more of a voice on the campus.

There's more and more changes for women, but I think the hardest thing still is, when you go to apply for a job, the first thing they ask is can you type? They made a test recently at the university. They took a man and a woman and gave them the same qualifications, and he got a completely different picture as far as the job opportunities than the woman did. And this is your employment agencies, where you have to pay for a job! I think it's the groups at the universities that are doing so much to change things.

My niece is twenty-one and she's taken women's studies and she's really getting interested in the movement. She's going to be a nurse and she doesn't want to get married, at least she isn't thinking about it for now. She wants to be able to support herself and have a career. I tried to encourage her mother to go take at least one course in women's studies because my sister Millie has never been able to get out of the house to do anything. She's pretty well tied down at home.

I'd like to think there'll be a time when women become recognized as human beings, not inferior to men, and not having always to be by men's side, but actually as another person on their own instead of just belonging to a man. I think working as long as I have has helped me feel more independent, even though sometimes it was really rough. We'll never be rich, but we've raised our standard of living because we both do work. My salary goes in the same checking account with my husband and *we* pay the bills and *we* buy the furniture or whatever. It isn't Ann bought this or Paul bought that. If we do anything we both decide because we are working together. It takes me, too, to be able to afford special things.

What I'd really like is to retire in a few years and not have to worry about money and become more active in the community. I've been interested in the Democratic Party. I've gone to some local meetings and I did some volunteer work and I really want to get more involved. Maybe in the Minnesota Women's Political Caucus. I found out about it at the women's center on campus and I'm kind of interested in that. But I feel that education might be a barrier there. Most of these women are quite well educated and I wonder, how can I do something useful? You know, am I going to feel out of it? Can I fit in with these people?

At the workshop I went to I was feeling a little that way, too. I thought, oh my gosh, here's all these women with doctorate degrees. I'd love to have that education. It would be terrific. But I really do feel nobody's higher than you or lower than you. Like I couldn't look down on someone that dropped out of high school and I don't look up to a professor either. Or I don't look up to a person that's got a lot of money. They're all just people. And that goes for races too.

But when I see a black person who has a very powerful job, I really admire them. We have a woman here that has a powerful job and she is really what you call woman power. She's got it. If she's got a problem, she goes right to the Regents and she tells them. I just really admire her and I wish I could have the education so I could have some woman power too.

Some of the women in my neighborhood that I meet on the bus going to work have tried to encourage me to run for the City Council. They said that everybody's disgusted with the councilman we have and they think I'd win real easy. My husband wants me to run, too, but I'm not sure about it. Not that I'm not willing or capable of handling some of the problems of our city. I think I could. And I do think people would accept a woman, though we did have a woman mayor at one time and she ruined it a little for women. Instead of sitting down and trying to work out problems she would scream at the men and make a lot of emotional scenes.

I remember the mayor saying that he learned a great deal when he came into office and he left the office being a wiser man. He came in as an engineer and he knew absolutely nothing about running a city, but he learned it on the job. I think you've got to be able to compromise. And you've got to respect other people's ideas and opinions because we all have them and we're all different. There's no one way to look at anything.

One of the things the women worry about in our neighborhood is some facilities for the young people, to keep them from mischievous kinds of offenses—little things, like setting grass fires, dumping garbage cans, ripping down signs. These are young teen-agers not able to drive yet and too old to be sitting around watching TV or to be kept at home. They have no place whatsoever to go, really, so they go into the park and maybe they end up smoking pot.

So we need a youth center of some sort, where they could go and dance, let off a little steam. I'd like to see that in every area where there are lots of homes. Sort of a community center. I know it would cost the taxpayer a lot of money, but it would sure cost a lot less in property damage and there's a lot of that in our area.

Well, getting on the council means a lot of extra hard work after you come home from work. And then people can dig up information on you and you can get a label so quickly. I really wish the American Medical Association would come out and finally do something to educate the people about emotional problems. It's funny about people. They're sympathetic with the man who has become an alcoholic. His friends, his boss, everybody'll try to help him back. But the person who has an emotional problem of any kind, regardless of why, right away you're unstable and you have that black mark against you.

Paul has really been encouraging to me. He encouraged me to go to the all-day workshop for women at the university. He encouraged me to go ahead and get involved in the groups and organizations I was interested in. He encourages me to get involved with politics if this is what I want to do. He feels that everybody should be happy with their life. He says, "You don't really have anything with just your little going to work, coming home, routine life. You've got to have something else." He's been searching, too, for something. He's making changes. But he too feels a certain amount of discrimination toward men in the lower . . . status, I guess you'd call it.

They're discriminated against by management in so many ways. Like the profit sharing goes only to the salary people at his plant. And the ones that really do produce the product, they're really the ones that should share in these big profits. Then when it comes to sick leave, they're terrible at his company about that. He has seven days a year but, if you stay out even one day, you have to have a doctor's statement. Well you might have the flu and you don't want to go to a doctor for ten bucks, you just want to stay in bed and get a good day's rest, but to get your pay you have to go to a doctor.

That's just for blue-collar workers, not for the salaried people. And the salaried people can go get their haircuts on company time, because they say it grows on company time! The blue-collar workers have got to do it in their spare time, of course. They really have to take a stand and see that they get things like profit sharing and better working conditions.

Paul was a shop steward in his union, the International Association of Machinists, for about four or five years and the men wanted him to run for president. He did a lot within his own company and I think the men look up to him for that. And I think he showed me a lot about how you can fight back legally, without doing anything wrong. Like if there was a noise pollution problem in the plant, he'd take care of it by threatening to bring in the Occupational Health and Safety Board. He'd really stand up to people.

A lot of the problems of blue-collar workers are a question of respect and the same kind of thing happens at the university. Once my professor came back from a meeting where his proposal for a special project he wanted was rejected, and he started jumping all over me about typing mistakes. He had pushed me so hard with the deadline that I didn't have time to proofread it and make corrections if there were any errors. At that point I would just as soon have stayed in the job where I was, no promotion or anything, just a clerk-typist's job with no responsibility. Just type and do what I'm told. But I'm not going to be yelled at.

One of the girls in my office has told me how she's gone home at the end of the day in tears. When she's trying her darnedest to get it out fast, to have someone yell at you for really small things like typing a comma in place of an apostrophe, instead of just saying, "Well, I guess you didn't notice here, but I think that should be an apostrophe." It's the way a person comes and tells you. Because we all make mistakes. Our bosses too. Sometimes when they're writing something down, their thoughts run faster than their hand and they skip a word or misspell a word and it's up to the secretary to try to make the corrections.

I guess what I'd like to see most is to have levels erased and to have everyone accepted as an equal human being. I don't want this high class, low class, superior, inferior. I want people to know that I'm equal and not to think of me as dumb because I hadn't noticed that I'd reversed a letter in my typing or something. And I want them to know that they too are capable of mistakes.

If people would only stop and realize what they're doing to the next person and how it hurts to be considered lower. It hurts inside. It's the kind of hurt that you can't really talk too much about, but you feel it right inside your chest. It just tightens up and you can't let tears come, so there's no way of letting it all out. Sure you can explode and lose your job. Or quit.

So I'd like to see that kind of change in work situations, but not only that. Husbands too. They've got to quit belittling their wives if they want to stay home and be a mother and a housewife. I think they're just as important as the husband who goes off to work. He probably thinks she sits home and doesn't do anything all day, and she's probably thinking he has an exciting life at the office. Well neither is what you'd call an exciting life. The man has his problems and frustrations at work, and the woman has hers at home too.

Then a mother's expected to train her child to do right and the father comes home and just kind of enjoys the pleasures of playing with him. And this is all wrong too. I think a father should take a much more active part in the discipine. I don't mean harsh discipline, because I don't believe in that, but in the upbringing of the child.

As a whole, I just think that all women should have a complete change. No matter what your career is—housewife, secretary, doctor, professor or what. Men have got to see that all of us are just as good as they are. We know we are. It's just that *they* don't.

● POSTSCRIPT

Ann Winans's job at the University of Minnesota's Institute of Technology ended in early 1975. Despite the program's success and an impressive increase in the enrollment of minority students the previous fall, private funding sources dried up. Ann wrote, "All of us—the kids, university coaches, teachers, staff and myself—felt like our whole world was crumbling with the ending of this program. Why large foundations invest their money in a worthwhile cause and then drop their oars in the middle of the stream is something I'll never understand."

The university's personnel department found Ann a job with a female professor in another department. At first, she was enthusiastic at the idea of working for a woman. It developed, however, that this woman made greater and more demeaning demands than most of her previous male employers. Still, Ann received an excellent performance rating. After a short time in that department, however, she entered the hospital for diagnosis of recurring pains. While she was still there, the professor informed her that she was being replaced. Ann's reading of the situation was that the professor contrived a "phony story" about her job performance, in her impatience to have a secretary.

Starting from her hospital bed, Ann became engaged in a lengthy bureaucratic battle, both to preserve her good standing at the university and to assure the continuation of her medical coverage. Although several people at the university took Ann's side, "Few people," she wrote, "will challenge the word of a professor. It's almost impossible for the average person to come out ahead, but I'm going to keep on trying." In the end, her persistence paid off.

She began interviewing for other jobs at the university shortly after she left the hospital. She felt that she had found "her place in the world" there and was looking forward to going back and "working for a better world for future generations through women's organizations and political groups." Over the course of several months, however, she became crippled by severe rheumatoid arthritis, which attacked most joints in her body. The swelling and pain restricted her movement to the point where she could barely type or grasp a pen.

The past few months have been filled with both emotional and physical pain. Ann spent much of it looking for responsive doctors and reading medical literature at the public library in order to learn more about the disease and what to anticipate for her future. She recently found some excellent job possibilities and wrote, "Good days are ahead for me and hopefully I'll be pounding the typewriter again for a salary," but she feels unsure about returning to work until a suitable medical treatment is developed for her. So far, "it's been a program of trial and error." Her arthritis is complicated by lupus (a blood disease) and ulcers, making medical treatment all the more difficult.

In a moment of desperation this fall, Ann called the Minnesota Chapter of the Arthritis Foundation to find someone to talk to about her condition. Within hours, she received a call from a woman, a member of a new group called Arthritics Supporting Arthritics, who invited Ann to attend a meeting. She has since attended several monthly meetings and met some "wonderful people" who try to help each other cope with the life-long disease by sharing experiences and offering support. Family members are also invited to attend, to better understand the effects of the disease and to be better prepared to offer emotional support. In a moving letter to the executive director of the Arthritis Foundation, Ann wrote, "I merely wish to convey that our attitude towards this disease depends heavily on the general attitudes of others around us—be they family, friends or our medical teams."

Much of Ann's time has been devoted to writing over the past few months and she is gaining greater confidence in her talent in this area. "If I could take a college course (something I'd really like to do now that I have time to study) and merely write about my new learning, I'm sure I would have a degree in short order. As for my first article, I have many notes and off-and-on diaries—a new one on arthritis—that need to be worked on to be made into stories worth reading. I'm glad I've kept a diary of my struggles with arthritis because this is another area where the public is not told what to expect. This is a disease that hits millions each year and the media continue to falsify the seriousness of it."

Her arthritis and lupus are both temporarily under control now, but Ann faces another unrelenting problem. She wrote, "I feel that my letters are quite depressing at times to healthy people on the go. But one thing I hope is that they will show others how not to end up like me. Working too hard to attain an unattainable goal, trying too hard to please others to the extent of forgetting myself, fighting for rights that society says I should have but won't let me have, accepting oppression which too often ends with a lump in my throat. All this boils down to one thing: stress. Stress is the number one killer in our nation.

"It's interesting that even when it's the man who creates the problem in a particular situation, it's always the woman who desperately looks for help. I believe that means that women are stronger than men, because they recognize a problem and feel they must do something about it. Men often won't even recognize the problem." The closing of her letter read, "Still in there fighting, and I'll never give up."

Terry Dezso at home in Willimantic, Connecticut.

The Dezso family in the kitchen of their new home. *Back row, left to right:* Henry, Tina, Pal, Terry, David and Mark. *Front row, left to right:* Rita (Henry's wife) with first grandchild, Ernie, on her lap, Teresa, Chris, Michelle and Jonny.

BOTH PHOTOS BY JOAN ROTH

Terry Dezso

GROWING UP FRENCH AND CATHOLIC
IN WOONSOCKET, RHODE ISLAND

I was born in Woonsocket, Rhode Island, on August 23, 1931. My mother and father were both from France and sometimes, when I think about what I've been able to cope with in my life, I think there's some of that strong peasant in me. You know, the real plowsharing kind of thing! I can see that it's partly heredity. Our name was Salembier and they named me Marie-Thérèse, a typical French name. I was the oldest of three. My sister is four years younger than I am and my brother is eleven years younger.

My father came here as a young boy and then went back and met my mother, married her and came back here. His father was a cabinetmaker, and I guess my grandparents just decided to come here to make a living. I've still got a night table that my grandfather made, but I never met my grandparents on my father's side. They'd all gone back to France before I was old enough to know them.

I never met my mother's parents or any of her relatives either. Her mother died in childbirth with her eighth or ninth child, when my mother was about eight. When I had my eighth and my ninth, you can imagine what my mother went through. She was frightened that the same thing would happen to me, and it almost did. I hemorrhaged a lot when my ninth was born and I almost died. It was so strange, the similarity with my grandmother. And my mother lived through it all but didn't tell me any of this till afterward.

My mother was a special kind of person. Proud, very shrewd, but she'd been really hurt as a child. When her mother died, her father sent her away to live with an aunt who was a midwife, and all the rest of her seven brothers and sisters stayed home. I guess they could take care of themselves and help out with the new baby, and my mother was one of the youngest. Then the baby died. My mother said they had a funeral, a baptism and another funeral all within a few days. But it was like she had been given away, so I think it was a real blow to her pride and maybe sometimes she kind of had to prove herself a little more. She had it rough, but being hurt like that strengthened her, too, in some ways.

She told us that she wanted to be a nurse and the day the Germans occupied her town in World War I she was supposed to leave on the train to go to nursing school. So she never got into the career she wanted. Her father had a vegetable farm, a dairy farm, an inn and a restaurant which was part of the inn, a dry goods store where they made their own clothing. So my mother worked on the farm, in the store, at the inn, whatever, and she learned a lot of different things.

In those days, the French in Rhode Island thought they should go back to get a wife or a husband. A lot of them did, like my father, when he was twenty or twenty-one. I know when he was seventeen or so he had lied about his age to join the U.S. Navy and he went after that. Then the funny thing was, he stayed in France too long and got drafted there! There was a law that if you were born in France, left the country, came back and stayed more than three months, you were drafted. So he went into the French Army, which he always talked about being real tough—a bottle of wine and hard bread, that kind of thing. After that he met my mother in the small town where she was living in northern France, near Calais.

When they got married they came back to the U.S. and I was born here. It was really difficult for my mother because she didn't know any English at all. She learned it purely from talking to people, listening to the radio, reading the newspapers. And she was a great one for keeping up with political things and world issues. When I was young she spoke French and my father spoke English to us. Then later on she spoke mostly English, but always with a French accent, which I really liked. When I hear that accent now, it really brings back memories.

My mother was emotional a lot, because she had a rough life. And my father had a hot temper. But I think my parents really deeply loved each other, and there was that deep feeling that they really cared about us. They did a lot for us. I don't mean materially, I mean they cared. There were times when I had it rough with my first marriage and I think that's the kind of thing that really gave me strength.

I was born in the Depression, so my father was lucky to work a couple of days a week in the worsted mills. He was an electrician. He had worked himself through electronics school by working at a candy shop and different things. So at least he had some money, which was better than some people who never had any at all. But my mother was very proud and very thrifty. I guess that's where I get some of that. She knew how to economize, stretch things out. And she never wanted to take any of the things that were being given out during the Depression. At the very end somebody gave her a dress or something, and I remember she just stuck it in the drawer. She made all our clothes and she wore the same dress, I think, for about ten years.

Woonsocket was a real mill town. There might have been ten or fifteen woolen mills and worsted mills. U.S. Rubber came in the forties, but the textile mills started moving down south or to Canada. Then the town went down, down, down. In the fifties, the main street had already gotten to be like a ghost town. The businesses were all empty. It was really frightening.

I guess most of the men in our neighborhood worked in the mills, and a lot of the women too. On one side of the street there were a lot of houses that were like one-family Cape Cod houses. On the other side there were a few of those, but mainly big blocks with six-family houses, three stories, that were like apartments. I think most of the people in those were mill workers.

It was kind of a mixture of a community. I remember I had a few friends who were Jewish and some that were Protestant. But most of the neighborhood was Irish Catholic. Catholic, but Irish Catholic, and here I was French. I was kind of put down a little. Like they'd call me "French frog" to tease me. So I kind of felt like a little minority group of one, you know?

One incident really sticks out in my mind about that. I think I was in the sixth grade and a nice young Irish priest came to our school—a public school, imagine that! He asked if any of the girls in our class wanted to join the Girl Scouts. Well, all the other girls raised their hands except me and he asked me why. So I said, "Well, I don't belong to your church." Our church was a little ways away and it was all French, actually mostly French-Canadian, and his church was mostly Irish. I just felt . . . well, I wouldn't dare. So he said, "Well, of course you can come." So I joined, even though I had a really funny feeling about it. I ended up enjoying it.

I started off in a Catholic school, in nursery school, but by the second grade my father discovered that I wasn't reading and he was very unhappy about it. He would work with me and could see that I wasn't really making any progress, so he took me out and put me in public school.

I'm not sure what the problem really was at the Catholic school, but I think at the time there was too much concentration on French and religion. And they used this sight-reading method and I just wasn't learning. Everybody learns reading in different ways. Also, this was during the Depression and there were a lot of children who were very, very poor. It was very sad as I look back. Some of them were probably not clothed very well and some had lice in their hair. My mother was so afraid I'd get it in my hair, and I had these long banana curls down to here.

Sometimes I've wondered if the sisters kind of . . . I don't know if it's just a thing you pick up as a child, and probably at least part of it is my imagining, but I think the sisters kind of looked at me as being more fortunate than some of the others and maybe thought I looked kind of like a spoiled brat, with the long curls and the clean dresses. So they weren't that nice to me. Maybe I was just unlucky to get a few who were kind of frustrated and unhappy. But I had this friend, whose father used to pick us up sometimes, and I remember her saying, "It seemed like every day he'd pick us up you'd be crying." I do remember being very unhappy and I guess I just blotted the rest out of my mind.

There were a lot of French-Canadian people in Woonsocket, but my parents didn't like me to play with the Canadian kids too much. They didn't want me to talk with some of the Canadian words that were slangish and they talked very guttural. The French people kind of disdained the French-Canadians. I saw it even in my early twenties there. Looking back now it's sad, but I guess that's where America was at that stage. It was all these groups, everybody conflicting with everybody else.

I guess a lot of my mother's prejudice came from what she saw when she came to Woonsocket. A lot of the Canadians lived in tenements, quite a few to a building, and according to her standards, their homes weren't properly cleaned or whatever. Then, very often the woman would work in the mill and she didn't take the time to prepare a proper meal. She'd just pick up something or the kids would go to the store and buy something—that was before McDonald's—just pastries or something to fill up.

Well, to my mother that was disgusting. The most important thing to her was to take care of your family and to see that they were properly fed. Matter of fact, in terms of money she placed more importance on proper diet than anything else. Then she saw these people spending money on frivolities like fancy clothing or big cars or something for show, and she thought that whole system of values was wrong.

I remember there were all these clubs in Woonsocket—a Belgian club for all the people that had come over from Belgium, a French club. They were mostly social things. The people got together and had old-fashioned parties and had a good time. My parents went once in a while, but they didn't socialize very much. Our life was very quiet. No relatives and few friends.

But my father was active with the Disabled American Veterans. I think he was state secretary for a while. He worked very hard to help others get the allotments and whatever benefits they were entitled to. His wasn't a wartime injury—he'd fallen off a submarine in dry dock—but he was really banged up so that they didn't think he'd walk again. One leg hurt him all his life and he had a limp and was kind of round-shouldered, but he kept on going just the same.

After his job at the mills, he worked at a machine shop as an inspector. That was during the war and he made pretty good money, but it was too much of a drag because he was traveling all the time. So then he went to work for a big electric company and stayed there until he became really ill. It was a kind of creeping paralysis that started in his toe and grew until it reached most of his body. My father wasn't a man of great ego. He was a mild man, very generous and sensitive, but it was humiliating for him to have to just sit there and not even be able to hold himself up in the wheelchair. It was really hard for him.

My mother always worked very hard, but she never had a regular job and I think she was kind of proud of that. She worked for political organizations and for the church and she did things at home and all. But here again I think you've got this French versus Canadian kind of thing, this friction. When she came to Woonsocket, an awful lot of women were working in the mills and she thought that was very dirty work. She thought it was degrading and she'd rather scrimp and save than do that.

During the war we moved out to the country a few miles from Woonsocket. My parents had a garden there and they were raising chickens and rabbits and goats to have enough food, since it was hard to buy meat during the war. Also my brother had developed an acid condition when he was real young and he needed to take goat's milk. I remember my mother with a big stack of chickens on the table in the kitchen. She'd kill them and clean them all out, and then she and my father would go out and sell the chickens and eggs to people. They did that for a long time. It was hard work, but then she made good money. She was very shrewd and she liked anything enterprising. I guess that's where I got my feeling for enterprise.

She played the stock market too. She started that when she was eighteen years old in France! That she loved. She didn't tell us much about it, but she must have made a little money, judging by the inheritance she left. Even though she was very thrifty and saved some of my father's income too, I couldn't imagine that they could have saved that much. It was something like ten thousand dollars. She had drive and she had savoir faire. She had the guts to do the things she wanted to. I remember she used to take us to Providence sometimes to that tall building where the stock market was. I'll never forget that. It was really fun to see the ticker tape.

Lately I've realized that my mother's and father's roles were not like the old stereotypes at all. They both crossed the boundaries and they worked well together. My father was not at all chauvinistic. My mother was a strong-willed person and in a lot of areas, like finances, she probably had a lot to say. I think my father respected this almost like a talent that she had, with the stock market and the ways she found to save money.

I guess probably he just was happy enough to do his own thing. He liked to read and he did all the baking and loved that—cake and cookies, pies, cream puffs. And he liked working around the house and gardening. He had his own way of stretching things, like building a shed for the animals out of just scraps of wood. He'd get up at 4:30 in the morning to feed the animals before he went to work at 7:30. They were not afraid of working, which is another thing that I think helped me with all my children. The work involved didn't overwhelm me because I didn't grow up pampered.

Once I learned to read, I was really a big reader. My father always gave me a lot of books and encouraged me. Once I started, I wouldn't stop. My mother'd be worried that I'd ruin my eyes or I wouldn't get enough sunshine. When my brother was born, she was forty-two and she wanted me to start to help her. I remember I started to bake when I was eleven and she sewed a lot and showed us how. Of course she'd brag about how in France everybody sewed. And she'd say the big designers stole their designs from the young women walking around in the streets because they were really original!

She liked to make her own clothes and when I was in high school I made quite a bit of my own too. They were kind of tight for money because we'd moved out of the city and we weren't able to sell our old house for a while. I guess I can't ever remember really being comfortable. It was always being careful. So, anyway, I saved by making my own clothes too. And we'd all pitch in with the animals or if there was haying to be done and things like that. But she didn't force a lot of things on us.

I think I felt closer to my father than my mother. Being the oldest child, I was kind of the apple of his eye. He would do things, like he bought electric trains for me and made me a desk out of his drawing board. He just liked doing things for people and he did a lot for me. My mother, as I said, was very emotional and I really hated to let her down. I remember when I was in high school, if I went to a dance or something, I always told her I had a great time, no matter what. I couldn't confide in her about problems. I must have sensed that it would be upsetting to her.

She never wanted me to marry my first husband. She was really unhappy about it for several years, she disliked him so much. I got separated in November of '69 and she died the April after, just at the point that I was beginning to feel much better and happier. I didn't realize it until much later, but I think her last few years she spent an awful lot of time worrying about me.

I think my parents were deeply religious with a strong moral sense of right and wrong and respect for hard work, but they were not completely convinced of the infallibility of the Church. They felt there should be a little more freedom and flexibility. My mother didn't always go to church, but she would say to me, "It's much more important to really practice what you believe than to go to church every weekend like a hypocrite and then do everything else six days a week." That was her philosophy. It was more important to live a decent life and do the right thing, help people if they needed help. And she did that.

My mother always wanted us to retain some of that French feeling. I think she did want to give us a sense of pride in our heritage and there is a certain amount of that that you can't avoid. Also she felt that some American ways were maybe too fast or something. And she didn't like the coldness in some people. She liked to have a closer family relationship than some of what she saw here.

It was my father who always encouraged me to try new things. Like the Girl Scouts. And I loved painting, oil painting, but anything to do with art. And like in high school I was a drum major for a couple of years and he got a big kick out of that. That was a lot of fun. I remember the uniforms the school had were so old they were yellowing and we were disgusted so we got together about how we wanted them, and I designed about six or seven different kinds for the principal to pick one.

We told him we'd pay somebody to make them up if he didn't mind, and that's how we got new uniforms.

The town I lived in didn't have a high school, so they would pay the high school of my choice for my being able to go there. I went to Burrillville High in Harrisville, Rhode Island, right near the Connecticut border. It was small, only about four hundred pupils, and out in the sticks you might say, but I thought the people were nicer and it was a pretty place. The school in Providence was right smack in the city with no lawn, hot, crowded, smoky, the whole bit. I guess I'm just the kind of a person who likes small towns.

I'd been thinking of going to college, so I took a college prep course. But I was a lazy kind of student. Just worked when I had to and I'd get by by the skin of my teeth. But it's a funny thing. If there was a physics problem that was really tough, I'd really work at it and solve it. I guess I respond to the challenge in things. I can remember those problems and I did okay in physics. But if it was something easy, like French—which I should know, right?—well, I just got by.

I don't know why I was like that, because I always wanted to go to college. I was about ten when I started to think about it. I used to play teacher with my sister and the kids in the neighborhood on the porch. Somehow I always wanted to be a teacher. There's a respect for education that my father instilled in me, like a feeling of awe. He had it himself. Even now, I'm still determined to get that degree and my sister who has four children went back to school a few years ago and is going to graduate soon.

By the time I got into high school I stopped thinking about teaching so much and started thinking more about psychology. We touched on it in this biology course my second or third year and I discovered it then and always liked it. There's just something about it that's intriguing. I guess because I like people and I wonder about why they do what they do. As far as I can remember that's always been a natural interest with me.

Anyway, I thought if I could get through college, take the four years and become a teacher, I'd try to work it out through a fifth year, take more courses, and I'd be a psychologist! But by the time I was in my last year of high school, I'd already decided I wasn't going to college. I guess by then I had resigned myself to the fact that I was just going to get married and have children and a happy home and that was all.

Now I know my whole life would have been different if I had gone on to school. My mother was very disappointed when I didn't. I probably would not have married my ex-husband. I would have gotten away from him and had a chance to kind of catch my breath and grow up a little, and have time to think of what I really wanted to do.

I met my ex-husband when I was sixteen and I remember we had a class meeting not too long after that where the teacher asked who was interested in getting a scholarship. There was no one who encouraged me personally, but still I thought about trying to work toward getting one and I mentioned it to him the next time I saw him. He was angry about it and said he didn't want me to go. He was really unhappy about the idea.

MARRIAGE, NINE CHILDREN, DIVORCE

I met my first husband swimming one day. We were just playing around in the water and his brother was there with his future wife, who I had gone to that Catholic school with. And my sister was there. She must have been eleven or twelve and she just yelled out my phone number. She always felt bad about that.

My mother was impressed by his veneer at first and she kind of liked him, even though he was French-Canadian. But it didn't take long until she saw that she didn't like his way of domineering. And as I look back, that and his jealousy were evident then. If I had had a little more maturity, I would've seen this. But the way my mother handled it was, she didn't talk to me about it, she yelled at me about it. She got so emotional about it that she pushed me right into it.

I graduated in June of 1949, when I was seventeen. He gave me an engagement ring for a graduation present and we married the June after. I was working in the Lerner Shops that year, doing everything. I was a saleswoman and bookkeeper, even modeled a couple of times. Then they had an assistant manager's job open and I applied for it and they said, "Well you're only nineteen." I said, "I've had a lot of experience here and I'm married." They said they were sorry but that was it. Then a few months later I got pregnant and I quit.

After that I worked with my husband. When we got married, he was working in the mill as a spinner, spinning the thread onto a spool. He was two years older than me. He had quit school and, as far as mill jobs are concerned, that was a fairly good one. You had to have a certain dexterity, a kind of skill. So it was more difficult than a lot of jobs. But when the mills closed down he went into selling and that's when I started working with him. He was afraid to do anything on his own, like go out selling.

I didn't want to have a large family. I was thinking of two or three kids. I never thought of having nine! It was more a matter that I'd be lucky if I had the two or three. And then my mother never talked to us very much about sex or even contraception. I don't think I knew what the word was. So it just never occurred to me to have that many children. But the children were the all-important thing in my life.

After the first two or three, my initial reaction to being pregnant was, oh gosh, I'm not ready right now. I'm just tired, you know? And then, well, after two weeks or so, I'd talk myself into accepting it and then I'd just adjust to it and then we'd look forward to it. You kind of hoped it wouldn't happen but then you would accept what you got. I guess it was the Catholic teaching. I just couldn't practice birth control. Now I look back on it and I really think about it very differently. In fact my son and his wife are using birth control and I'm all for it. They have one child and right now that's all they can afford and take care of.

With my own, the only time I got upset, really, was with the last. At that time I'd already been considering divorce, and I already had eight and I was getting very tired physically. Things were really bad then. In 1959 my "ex" had his first nervous breakdown and he'd been put in the hospital for shock treatment and everything. He'd gotten pretty violent with me and the kids, so it was difficult emotionally and physically and then financially too. As of the beginning of the sixties, he never really earned a great deal.

I don't think he planned on having that many children

either, but I think he was very proud each time because that male ego was really happy. But as time went on, maybe after the third, he knew he didn't want any more and said that. In fact, the last time I found out I was pregnant, he mentioned an abortion. To me at that time, that was just unheard of, and I remember I cried at the thought of it. Even now, I may have changed my thoughts on a lot of the Church's teaching, but as far as abortion goes, I don't think I've reached the point where I could see that. I'm not sure I ever will.

Well, it was only maybe three months after we were married that I realized what I'd gotten myself into. Every Sunday we used to go to his mother's house, and his three brothers would be there, I think all of them married by that time. The men would play cards and we would just talk, you know, the male-female thing. There was a time when I would go over there and I just felt so sad, so low. I remember my mother-in-law noticed I was depressed, but of course I couldn't tell her how I felt.

But again, just like everything else, like after learning about each pregnancy, it took me a certain amount of time to adjust to it. Then I just realized that I was in that situation and could not, first for religious reasons, get a divorce. And it was about that time that I got pregnant. The way I feel now, I think I should have left right then and there. But with the thinking we all had at that time that was just impossible.

Then there was another thing. I really felt my mother kind of shut the door on me. I kind of always expected her there, right behind the door, saying, "I told you so." As I mentioned, she was very emotional and would say things in anger, screaming sometimes, so she kind of shut me off. Whereas I think if she had sat down with me calmly and said, "Look, don't you see this or don't you realize that?" I probably would have.

Anyway, then it became almost a contest to prove that I could do it. I decided that I would do everything I possibly could to make the relationship as successful as possible. So I tried to become the perfect wife and mother, which was just about all I could think of to do at that time.

So when the mill was shutting down, my husband answered an ad in the paper for party-planning work. It was called the

White Cross Party Plan and we started to do it as a team. It was putting on demonstrations in homes, you know, selling brushes and cleaning things, and then eventually we got into plastics too. Then they were beginning to have lots of deals and he always had great ideas of being big, you know.

His boss was a great salesman. You know the kind of sales pitch, the whole bit, and he hinted that maybe someday my "ex" could expand into another area. But he was always in a hurry, always wanted to do things fast, so we moved really before we were ready. We moved to West Warwick and lived there for a year to kind of get the territory started. But I guess the grass is always greener or something, so then he decided that he wanted to come to Connecticut. That's when we came to Willimantic and got an apartment in 1953.

Altogether we were in that business for about ten years, from 1951 till '60 or '61. He had people working for him and he had a lot of drive. He was an intelligent man with talent, and if it hadn't been for his neuroses, he could have maybe made it. But also this business was very much of a drive thing, pushing him constantly. So for both of us it was difficult.

Sometimes he worked days setting up parties or something and sometimes he didn't work at all. I remember there were times when we were both putting on parties the same night and I'd be angry and frustrated because he would often schedule them so we'd both work Thursday, Friday and Saturday night. And he wasn't one to help out in the kitchen or anything, so it was very difficult physically, with more and more children.

Even when I came home from the hospital after having a baby, there were times when I really needed his help and I didn't get it. As a result, maybe it was better in some ways for my older children, because I tried to get them to learn to do things. Most of my older boys will prepare a meal, they can bake, they know how to do the wash and their ironing and stuff like that. It was a necessity.

Well in '59 when he had his nervous breakdown, he was so afraid he wouldn't go anywhere. He wouldn't do anything at all, so then the business petered out. I took care of the last parts of that from home and finished it up. I remember him being in Hartford Hospital when I was putting on one of the last parties. It was a crazy time! Eventually the whole company went under, I think in 1964. They went bankrupt.

After that he worked part time for a while with a man in a kind of a hardware store that also had appliances and flooring and things for household repairs. Then finally he met this other man and they went into a janitor-supply business. I did the bookkeeping for that and for about a year or two I worked in the office with him. Because again, he was so afraid to do this thing that he just needed to be picked up and held up all the time. I wondered just how much I might have contributed to it though, because I did help him. If I hadn't, it would've been sink or swim.

So he started with that in '62 or '63, and that business lasted three or four years and then he had another nervous breakdown in '67, a complete collapse. He was drinking all the time and getting wild and smashing things. It was scary for me and for the kids too. By that time I really saw no way out of it. Not only the religious reasons, but by then it was physically difficult because I had so many children and I would have had to be the one to leave at that point. He still didn't recognize that we had problems.

Anyhow, we finally moved that last business to the basement of our home, a little ranch house. I remember signing the paper putting it under in about '68. That's a funny thing, looking back. It's always that I was the one who had to make the decisions on these things. He would just kind of run away to the state hospital.

I finally got him to arrange to see a psychiatrist. Every time we went it was sheer torture because he didn't want to go in. He was so obviously sick, and seeing this is where the responsibility I felt toward him began. After that psychiatrist we tried another one at a mental health clinic, we went to priests, we went to Catholic Charities, we tried every kind of help. There were so many I'd really have to sit down and count them. It was the same old story with everyone. They'd tell me, "You're the strong one, so you've got to keep being strong because you can take it."

The TV was always on because that was practically the only thing he did after work—drink beer and watch TV. So you'd just go in and, out of sheer exhaustion, just sit down, because

I didn't really like the TV. But if I'd just sigh because I was tired, he'd assume that was a sigh of disgust toward him and he'd start ranting and raving. He was really paranoid.

It was a kind of mental torture. Constant. He would ridicule me and put me down in front of people, but it was even worse when people were not around. Toward the end he'd get home from work, he'd have his beer, and then he'd sit around and pick at me or nag at me. In some ways it was worse than any kind of interrogation because this was a person that knows your weaknesses and knows you the way no other person could. And he knew how to hurt me.

There were only a few times when he got really violent and started smashing things, but that gave me a great kind of training, not to want to have property or material things. Anything I cared about he would smash. It was like this day after day, and all of us, the whole family, dreaded the nights. He'd wake the boys up in the middle of the night and shake them and say, "Why were you sassy to me this afternoon?" or something like that, and he'd whack them. Or smash a guitar or something else they really cared about. Life was really impossible.

Finally I reached the limit and I went to a lawyer. Then I went to our priest, Father Liberty, to tell him and he said, "It's too bad you've done that already because maybe we could really solve the thing." You know, the old beautiful story, we're going to take care of everything. He said, "Now wait a while. I promise we'll work on it and if I really believe that there's no hope," he says, "I won't make you wait a day longer."

So it went on and on until about a year later I just felt I'd had it. Physically I was really down, not only the children, but I'd had fibroid tumors. And emotionally, well I was getting to the point where I thought I was going to crack up. Nineteen years, I figured, enough. So I went to Father Liberty and I told him, "Look, I really believe that I'm deteriorating physically and emotionally and I can't take it anymore. I've decided I'm going to get a divorce." By that point we'd been through a lot of sessions and he'd seen there was no way to make him come around, so he agreed.

The week before my last child was born there was a time when he could have really killed me. He threw a very heavy leather hassock at me, with heavy wooden legs on it, and it hit me in the head. The blood just gushed all over me, so I was really lucky that I was alive. I still have the scars there. It was so awful I was embarrassed to go into the hospital, but I had a public health nurse, Mrs. Abbey, who was helping me a great deal then. She'd come sometimes twice a week just to talk and have coffee with me, because she knew I was going through a very difficult period. So I called her and she told me how to take care of it.

Mrs. Abbey came over the next day and another friend of mine had seen me another time when I had a black eye and a cut lip, the night he left, so that's all I needed to get the divorce in this state at that time—two witnesses to say that they had seen signs of physical violence. By that time he knew that was the end of it, so he just left and he didn't contest the divorce. He didn't even go to the court. He knew he didn't have a chance.

Toward the end, we weren't really getting by and we started getting surplus foods, like flour. I'd bake and bake and bake and stretch the dollar as much as possible. But most of it was starch so I was really worrying about trying to get the kids enough vitamins. There were times when you didn't have meat. Sometimes we got five pounds of cheese with the surplus foods, and sometimes there'd be things like dried raisins, dried prunes and a few times we got grapefruit juice, which was oh, just terrific. The times we got butter, we'd go around eating it on everything! There was something so luxurious about it.

There were times when there was very little money and if he wanted two or three dollars for beer, and he could spend at least that much in one night for beer, there was always a conflict between us. I'd try to keep the checkbook because it was the only way we had any money. Depending on what job he had, when he got a check we put it in the checking account and usually we were overdrawn. Then, very quickly if I could, I'd take care of the most important bills—the mortgage payment, the telephone, electricity. You'd never be sure you could pay those bills and sometimes the telephone was disconnected. Then, when the businesses went under, we had other people

454 · NOBODY SPEAKS FOR ME!

chasing us for money which was owed to them. The pressure was nightmarish. People calling you, collection agencies dunning you.

You can imagine how happy I was when he left. I remember the first weekend. All of us, the older children and me, we just sat down in the living room and relaxed. It was such a quiet, peaceful, comforting feeling to know that we wouldn't have him ranting and raving and screaming and fighting and smashing. I just started to take it easy a little bit, take care of my family, and then I started to figure out what I wanted to do. I wasn't thinking at all about getting married again.

If you went exactly by the Church, I could only get a legal separation. But it didn't take me long to figure out that the legal separation wouldn't solve everything. I wanted him to have to give a certain amount of money to help take care of the children and I wanted to be completely free of him. So I figured the only thing I could do would be to get a divorce.

I think I began to change more of my thinking about the Church when I was facing the world on my own all of a sudden. Before, I had tried to rethink the divorce question when I was in my early twenties. I tried to understand the Church, and kind of talk myself into agreeing with it. You know, if two people were married in God's sight, then they were married forever. That's the biggest reason why I didn't get divorced sooner. I guess you cannot ever really deny this religious feeling. If you get it early in your life, you've got it forever.

During the last ten years of my marriage, I went on six different weekend retreats that the Church has. They were very often, I think, what gave me the strength to pull through. There were discussion groups on popular questions to help you think out things, but most of the ones I went to were silent, where you didn't talk. You would eat and sleep there, and it gave you a chance to get away from everything, get a little more perspective, and also just to relax or physically collapse. Often I came out really keyed up emotionally because I'd made decisions.

After the last one is when I went back to Father Liberty. I just realized I had to get the divorce. When I went and told him, I think that was the beginning of my changing. I told him, but in a way I think deep down I was still asking him, you know? Anyway I was really relieved when I came out. I knew what I was going to do and I did it, and from then it was just a matter of time.

By this time I was finding out a little more. Mrs. Abbey would find out things for me about my legal rights. Then if he did leave and I had all these kids to feed, here I had no training and I was afraid I wouldn't be able to find a job, and I had a baby who was just a year old then. She told me what I should do if I had to get on welfare, which I did for a while.

I think public health nurses are the greatest thing. They're a way of getting all kinds of services to people who need them. What they did is, when they saw the birth of a baby in the paper, they'd call on the parents and offer to help. That's how I met Mrs. Abbey. She'd come right before the baby was born to help and advise you about certain health matters, and then about once a month after the baby was born. They're really depended on here.

This town has expanded so much that now they have a social worker, but he doesn't have that same angle to walk into a home, like with a new baby. And so many times people have really great problems—emotional, financial, physical illness or whatever—and they may tend to feel they don't want charity, so they don't want a social worker.

Anyhow, I think Mrs. Abbey deserves a medal. She's one of the most special people. At first when she came it was more like just a physical health kind of thing. Then as she saw that things were worsening, she would just help by sitting and talking with me or letting me talk to her, which was very therapeutic. Just by expressing these things to her, by voicing them and thinking about them, she helped me to clarify my thinking. She acted almost like a psychologist.

It was through her that I found out about people like Trudy* at WACAP, which is the community action program

---

* Trudy Coolbeth, a former OEO (Office of Economic Opportunity) outreach worker for WACAP (Willimantic Community Action Program). Was a welfare recipient; raised eight children by herself for the past sixteen years; now has twelve grandchildren. Together with Betty Heiss—the wife of a faculty member at the University of Connecticut in Storrs who volunteered her services to WACAP—helped form the Mothers' Group in 1967, visiting poor women in the rural areas, delivering surplus foods, and finding out what their needs were.

in Willimantic. They work in cooperation with the public health nurses. And then Trudy would acquaint us with things like Title 19, which is medical aid, and tell us how to apply for it. And then once a week there was a really nice woman, a home economist married to a teacher at the University of Connecticut, who would pick me up and take me to the place where they would give out the surplus foods—the town hall or the church, wherever. This area is very fortunate that way, because we have a lot of faculty wives who are aware of things and care about people enough to want to go and help.

Sometimes it's hard for middle class people to understand why low-income people live the way they do. Like if a house needs paint or repairs, they'll say, "Well, why don't they just paint?" It looks so simple, but it isn't so simple. I mean if someone said to me at one point, "Here's ten dollars, go out and buy a gallon of paint," I'd probably rather have bought a nice steak, or just some meat. Sometimes you're just in a down and out place, just struggling to keep your head above water and not sink completely. You may have some money come in, but you don't put it to the wisest use. You kind of do emotional buying, just to make you feel better momentarily.

When you're in that position, you really can't just stand back and look at the situation and say, "Well, this is what should be done." You're so involved in other problems. It's like being in a rut that you just can't get out of. It's a vicious cycle. One problem leads to another. If you've never been there, I think it's pretty hard to understand.

A lot of good things that have happened to me in the last few years kind of just happened. Things would come along and I'd say, "Gee, that really seems like something I'd like to do," and I'd just jump into it. Some things I thought about for a long time, like going back to school. I'd reason it out that that was the thing I had to do, and if other people could do it, I could too. I was very apprehensive and insecure about certain things, but I kind of took one step at a time. That makes it a lot easier.

The thing I was most fortunate about was in having met so many beautiful people like Mrs. Abbey, and then Nancy Chance, who I met through the Mothers' Group. I really seriously think that if I hadn't had people like that to help me

through . . . well, I know there was at least one time there
where I was really wishing just to stop living.

HELP FROM THE MOTHERS' GROUP:
REMINISCING WITH NANCY CHANCE

TERRY: I first met Nancy when she came to pick me up and
give me a ride, the first time I went to a meeting of the Mothers' Group. That was in '68. My family was living in a condemned convent for a few months, because our house had
been gutted by fire. Nancy's husband is at the university and
her family had just moved into the area. I went to the Mothers'
Group from then up until some time in '71, when it got to be
too difficult with studying and then I was working afternoons.
But it was really important to me for those years.

NANCY: The group actually started the year before I came
to Storrs in some homes in Eagleville where a lot of low-
income people are concentrated. Betty Heiss and Betty Jane
Bennett, whose husbands are also on the faculty at the University of Connecticut, were really responsible for getting it
started. Then other middle-income women got involved, and
more and more low-income women from other parts of town
and the trailer parks.

TERRY: I hate to think how my life might have been without
the Mothers' Group. It was like an oasis because it was a place
to go and get some kind of relief, and some kind of enjoyment
and knowledge. It was something that directed me to the
things I needed and helped me to find things I didn't even
know about. Also I hate to think what would have happened
if I'd have gone on feeling completely friendless, because at
that point I don't think I had a friend, except for the public
health nurse. She couldn't have been a greater help, but it was
almost like a therapy session and I needed something relaxing,
too. So both kind of complemented each other.

NANCY: That was one of the things that was important to
many of us about the group—the possibilities it had for individuals. The first thing was trying to break down the kind of
isolation women live in when they have small children, no day
care centers, no transportation and no money. Every solution

you find has to be your own personal solution. In general, it was a way to help people find ways to kind of come back in control of their own lives, rather than feeling like victims in life. I don't know that we succeeded in that very well in a group sense, but I think that has happened for some individuals. And now there's a network of people who can be called on for emergencies and things like that.

TERRY: The feeling of being alone and not being able to handle a situation is almost defeating itself. I think everybody who went to the Mothers' Group really needed each other. The whole week started to focus around that Tuesday. I remember so many times when we had to end the meeting because the kids were coming home from school, but we just couldn't end it. Sometimes you had something worrying you and it took a longer time to get it out. But if you were able to talk about it, you just felt that much better and you'd go home really lifted.

With my divorce, the personal contact there gave me a great deal of support. I was beginning to give up on ever having any kind of peaceful relationship by that time, but I didn't know how to go about certain things, and I needed help in just thinking it out. People like Nancy, especially Nancy, would act like a sounding board for me a lot of times. And she didn't only say things to make me feel I was right and I should just leave. She was really good at seeing both sides of it and helping me understand what was going on. I think that was one of the big reasons why I came through it and could function from then on. I finally felt I'd done everything I possibly could, so I was able to just shut the door on the past.

NANCY: Besides helping each other personally and developing really rewarding relationships, we tried to do things that were useful in a concrete way too.

TERRY: I think the first year was the community garden and then we started a kind of nursery school in the church where we met, and then dieting.

NANCY: There were several women who wanted to lose weight, which was pretty impossible on the diets their budgets forced them on. We also talked about how to get the most out of surplus foods, and we had cooking and baking demonstrations.

TERRY: It was about then we started the buying club too.

We went to visit other people who had them in nearby areas and we wrote and got literature from different places around the country. Then we set it up the way we wanted. We decided to keep it simple, just a few items we could really get a good buy on, and not get into complicated bookkeeping. We decided we really wanted meat, that was the biggest thing, but we also have produce. On some items you save maybe 5 or 10 percent, but it varies a lot. Sometimes it's much more. It just means that you have to put a little time away and plan ahead, but if you're on welfare, it really makes a difference.

NANCY: Almost every week we had speakers. One was an insurance man, a professor, and that was really important. I think what made us most sharply aware of it was that one of the mother's sons had been killed while he was delivering newspapers. He was struck by a car. When they went to the funeral director, the first thing he said was, "Well, where's your money?" Here they were, just wiped out with grief, and he was saying, "I want my money first and then you can bury your son." Always the same kind of problem for poor people, which the middle class almost never has.

Well, that made people who were poor feel it was almost imperative to carry that many more kinds of insurance, just in case. And there's quite a difference in types of insurance policies and what you pay, what kind of rights you have within that. I didn't know you could really shop around for insurance like that either. So this man came, and we tried to have other speakers who would have some kind of input into what were really concrete problems for people.

TERRY: We had marriage counselors, too, and a psychologist who talked about sex education for kids. I think everybody was trying to figure out where they were at. It was the kind of thing where you wanted to do right by your kids and you were worrying about all kinds of things.

NANCY: I think that really helped people to open up a lot. Maybe it's because a number of us had teen-aged kids at the time, but that was an area we really wanted to talk about and rarely do with anybody else, especially not in a whole room full of people. There was a lot of worry about young girls—are they going to get pregnant, what's the relationship between young men and women? And adults, too, some real feelings of defensiveness about it, that it was men who made the decisions about sex. And maybe women felt powerless, not knowing how to cope with it, but worried about it. So the sex education and marriage counseling were very helpful.

TERRY: One of the biggest things that happened to me in the Mothers' Group was getting involved with the Montessori School. I remember Edie Carey had just come back from England and she was setting up her nursery school again, and someone mentioned that anybody with a three-year-old child who was interested should talk to her about getting a scholarship. That's how the whole thing really started. Michelle, my second youngest, went to the nursery school there and then I read in the paper about there being a Montessori course, and it seemed like the kind of teaching I would like. But there again, I needed a little encouragement.

That was the transition year, when my husband left. I went to the Montessori School the last day to pick up Michelle. They were cleaning up, trying to pack up to move to another church, and I thought I really should try to help with the kids, especially since Michelle had gotten this scholarship. While I was there I talked with some of the teachers about the school and then, about two weeks later, Edie called me and asked if I wanted to work there in the fall.

In the meantime, the Mothers' Group was starting on developing a day care center too. It took about a year or more to get it going, and I had applied for a teacher's aide job. I thought I could work there as a start and then eventually maybe go to school. But it all happened much faster. Things have a way of happening to me, bang, bang, bang! So when Edie offered me the job, I said I really didn't know because I'd already put in an application to the day care center and I was really involved with it at that point. That was my first love. I was on the board for a few years, and I was the first secretary of the board. But I decided to take the job at the Montessori School and gradually I kind of broke away from the day care center. Then I took the Montessori course in the summer of '70, my first course since high school, and I really got into it.

NANCY: We spent a lot of our energies getting that day care center started. We also started looking at a lot of other problems—like housing, for instance—which we never got very far

on. There's a big housing debate going on in town now because low-income people have been consistently squeezed out.
The university controls land prices here and we've seen the
pressure and what it does to people.

Then health care in general is still . . . people get to the
doctor when it's an emergency and there just aren't enough
doctors to go around. The same is true with dentists. We found
out there was only one dentist in town who was kind of known
as the welfare dentist. He wouldn't take a child under eight
and I guess he's a real butcher. But the dentists felt they had
made a reasonable solution by saying, "Well, everybody who's
poor can go there."

The dentists claimed there were too many problems with
the welfare office, too many forms, and that welfare patients
were unreliable. Well, we began to put pressure on them and
finally we did get them to agree to take people who were on
welfare. But you still have to really be willing to fight for your
rights if you're poor, and if you have any feelings of insecurity,
that's really difficult.

TERRY: I was only on welfare for a year and a half all together. My family helped me a little, and then what I did was
I started a nursery school in my home so I could get off of it.
This is where a lot of people in the Mothers' Group and with
the Montessori School were really great, especially one woman
who was a teacher there. She called people she knew at the
university who had small children, and I gather she got the
people to donate to a fund for scholarships for low-income
children to come to my school. I thought that was really
incredible.

When I got off welfare, I got off clean. I just told them I
didn't want anything to do with it anymore. But the way we
got by that year was part of the divorce agreement. It was very
interesting how the state welfare representative, who I don't
think ever said "hello" to me, was very concerned about talking with the judge. He spent an awful lot of time in his quarters. He knew I had nine children and, according to him, I'd
probably be on welfare forever. My attorney made the same
kind of comments. They love to say sarcastic things to you,
look down at you. They don't imagine you'd ever try to get off.

So this guy talked to the judge and he was really trying to

get everything he could for the State of Connecticut. They had it written out that my "ex" would pay six dollars per child each week to the state for as long as there was still one child left, and as long as I was on welfare they would then give me what I needed to live on. Then they also insisted that he get full medical coverage on all the children. The state was really protecting their own interests. But we were lucky in that way and that's how I was able to get by.

The first year I worked at Montessori I was getting forty dollars a month, because welfare wouldn't allow me to get any more. Talk about incentives. It's such a discouragement, constantly putting you down. But by the second year I had gotten off welfare and I was working as assistant teacher, which meant I got about a hundred eighty dollars a month, which again wasn't enough to support myself and the children. So I did the housework at the school too, and I got three dollars an hour—a little more than they normally paid—for that. With that and the money I got for support, we just about got by.

A WHOLE NEW LIFE:
TEACHER, COLLEGE STUDENT, NEW MARRIAGE

Being Catholic, I was really accustomed to the idea that you can't get married again. I figured I would just raise my children, and I had pleasure in the work I was doing, and that was a satisfying enough life for me. It's a funny thing, but what turned the point was that some friends wanted to have a New Year's Eve party in connection with a winter recreation program they were having. I wanted to go, but it was all couples and who's going to go stag on New Year's Eve!

Well that was the one and only time in my life I asked a man for a date. I didn't really know any single men, but one of the two foster sons I had for a while had a friend who came to the house once. He was a man who had had a summer camp and he was up at the university working on his doctorate. So I called him and I stumbled and faltered and it was awful, but finally I got it out and said, "Will you be my escort?" Oh, wow, I almost died. But he said, "Fine, just so long as you don't ask me to dance!" It was a quiet party and we went home early, but it started me thinking. It was kind of fun, you know?

The next day, New Year's Day, I took the kids to church as usual. We had gotten there early and there was a book stand and I picked up a magazine to look through it for a few minutes. I opened it up and there was this article about Catholic people who had remarried. Either they were divorced or widowed, but they remarried, believing they were doing the right thing by themselves and their children. They felt the Church should modernize its thinking on a lot of these things. And this was in the *Catholic Digest*!

So that got me thinking, too. Maybe this wasn't so queer, you know? So I began to think about the possibility of dating. Then a friend of mine said to me one day, "What would you do if you ever found somebody you wanted to marry?" And I said, "Are you crazy? Who in the heck would marry a woman with nine kids?" She says, "Well, you never know." But I really thought that was impossible.

Well, at that time I had a friend who was the head teacher at the Montessori School. She was more or less my boss. She was breaking up with her husband and one of the things she was afraid of was that she wouldn't have any social life and she really liked to have fun. So she asked me did I know of any groups or anything. So I said, "I just happened to talk to somebody who's connected with Parents Without Partners about one of her children. I'll give you her number and you can call her up."

She joined, and one Friday night she called and asked if I could give her a ride to the PWP dance, and she said, "Why don't you join?" She said, "You should really be going yourself." Well, I wasn't looking for that really. I felt sad in some ways, because I thought that part of my life, the romantic part, was over. There were times I saw happy couples and things and then I felt kind of sad. But then I was able to put that aside.

I remember I was tired that night and I didn't really feel like going, but I kind of hated to disappoint her, so I said I'd go. And that's the night I met Don. We danced a couple of times and he seemed like a nice guy, a really considerate kind of guy.

That was a Friday night and on Saturday he called me to go to a PWP coffee hour. They have a lot of things for the parents and children too. That wasn't really a date—it was kind of a little get-together with other people.

Then he called me for what turned out to be our first real date. It was dinner and dancing at a little restaurant and we danced till about one in the morning. That was the first time we really got to know each other and found that we liked a lot of the same things. We like the same food, we both love the ocean and fresh air, fresh vegetables, freedom. Natural things. And dancing!

When I was going out with him, I was really noticing the differences between him and my first husband—the lack of drinking, smoking, differences in language. And there was a kind of respect and thoughtfulness. Just a lot of differences in manner and personality. But then I asked him what he did and he told me that he was an electrician and I was really surprised. It hit me that there was a similarity to my father, a lot of personality traits.

Well, that date we had was in the spring of '72. We dated all through the summer and in about October we were talking about getting married maybe in the next spring. Then we said, maybe we should start looking for a house, because mine was crowded, to put it lightly, although I had plans to renovate it. We were just talking about it and decided to look through the newspaper and there was this little picture. We went out to see the house and the price was reasonable and the more we looked at it, the more we liked it. And that was it. We grew so attached to the house we realized we were going to have to get married and not wait till the spring!

So we got married within about two weeks by a justice of the peace. Don's father's Hungarian and his mother's Danish and he had been raised a Protestant. But his first wife was Catholic and he'd taken the instructions in Catholic liturgy and, as a result of the problems they had, I think, if anything, religion kind of turned him off. But he's not one of these people who shows his emotions a lot.

It's interesting though. He's really into the whole Catholic Marriage Encounter movement. Maybe it's because he's that kind of a sensitive person who really sees so much in it, you know? We went for a weekend last year and it was great. But with the dialoguing and all that, I feel like I've been the one who's been dragging my feet. Again it's the Catholic upbringing, but in some ways I felt almost like an outcast. Because actually, if you go by the book today, being a Catholic and being divorced just doesn't go together. And I haven't run across any other couples in the movement who are remarried.

Don knew about me before I met him, so he knew how many children I had. For a long time while we were dating, I never stopped to think that it might be serious, but several times he'd say, "Nine kids. Wow!" I think it made it harder for him to make a decision on whether we'd get married or what we'd do. It was kind of scary for him, but it's worked out. I think the kids respect him. He's very quiet but now he's beginning to get more and more into it—you know, the mob!

Anyway, I was just floating. I was really swept off my feet. It was crazy. No matter what age you are, it's still the same thing. It's painful, like being a teen-ager, and it's beautiful at the same time. And this was really more than I dreamed of. So after the ceremony, I wanted my friends to have a good time, to kind of have a taste of how I felt. We were barely moved in and it was really chaos with eight kids at the time and a collection of sixteen years of junk, but we had a big open house and a reception and it was really fun.

I kept going along just kind of pinching myself, saying, "Now, this is impossible." It really didn't seem the kind of thing that would ever happen in my life. Imagine a house big enough so there were no more than two kids to a room! It took me close to a year to believe this is really my home. There are four bedrooms upstairs and the living room is so large that at the end of it Don made another bedroom and he just finished off a room in the attic. He's so terrific at making things like the breakfast bar in the kitchen and the woodwork in the dining room, all kinds of things around the house.

I think my kids miss their old friends and they're a little nostalgic about certain things in our old neighborhood, but I think they're beginning to appreciate that they do have more—a better house and better food, more clothing, not all hand-me-downs. Occasionally I can buy them something nice for an outfit. And they can go places. They'd never been on vacations before. My older boys were lucky if they went swimming once a summer, where these kids have been on camping trips for a few days.

Sometimes I worry about how my kids have come through all this. They do have certain hang ups. I feel it. Maybe, like Don says, the younger ones still have a chance to see what a fairly normal kind of life can be. But the older ones . . . well, like Pal told me once, "I don't know if I'll ever get married. Maybe I'll wait till I'm forty." Which isn't that bad either. I think it's great when you grow up a little first, like I should've done. But, in other words, there's a question about it in his mind. He's a little bit afraid.

Johnny, I think, was one of the ones who had the most difficult time when I got married. He was so used to seeing his older brothers get beat on by his father, he was afraid Don would do the same to him. He voiced this to one of his counselors at school. See, when I began to date Don, we went camping with Parents Without Partners and took the younger children. We had a great time and the kids got to know Don, but Johnny never did. He stayed away most of the summer and the next thing he knew, I was getting married and moving out.

I think they're forming a comfortable relationship with him now, but they're still puzzled a little by certain characteristics that he has that are so different from the usual male characteristics they've seen. Maybe with time they'll see that not everybody's like their father. I sure hope they will and that they'll come through it okay.

My kids range in age from six to twenty-three. Henry's the oldest and he's the only one who's married and has a child. He was in the seminary for two years after high school but he quit that and decided he wanted to do something technical. He studied airplane mechanics for a while and then he started an apprenticeship program at Pratt-Whitney for tool and dye machine work. But he quit that because he was offered a good job by a man who has an auto parts business. He told Henry he'd set him up with his own machine shop, which he did. That's what Henry's always wanted to do and he's making pretty good money. In fact he bought our old house from me.

Some of my kids are thinking about college. I've always told them I thought it was good background to have, no matter what you did, and I would be able to help them to some extent, but I wouldn't give it to them. I always felt that the way to get the most out of college was to work at least part of it your own way. Of course, I realized I'd never be able to afford to give it to all of them.

I think I see in most of my children a trend toward mechanical things, working with their hands. They've always loved building things since they were young. They love machinery and speed. When Henry was at the seminary, he helped one of the brothers build a bus out of an old body and a motor they found somewhere, so the choir could get around. David, the second oldest, used to have a motorcycle, a big one, and he'd ride that thing along on the back wheel for a good mile. He's a real daredevil kind. And Tina, who's eleven, is an engineer in the radio club they have at school! So that's the kind of leaning they have, like the sciences in my family, rather than English or writing or something.

David is different from Henry. He's much more happy-go-lucky, more of a playboy. He went to community college for a while but then he got involved in a chef's job, which took all his time. He's been debating going away to school with his friends. One day he thinks he's going to go to Florida, next day he's going to go to Vermont so he can ski. He's a real nut for skiing. I think he'll probably go to college. He's different from Henry in that. He's got expensive tastes.

Martin, who we call Pal, is the one in the hospital bed in the living room with half his body in a cast! He finished high school and was looking at jobs with some kind of training or an apprenticeship program at the university dealing with machinery repairs, and then he had his motorcycle accident. He's lucky that he's alive.

So, all together, there's Henry, David, Pal, Johnny, Mark, Tina, Chris, who's nine, Michelle, who's eight, and Teresa, who's six. Six boys and three girls. Don has five kids, four boys and a girl. The oldest is twenty-six and the youngest sixteen. Most of them live pretty far away from here.

Going back to school myself was in the back of my mind for a long time, but I really thought it would be so expensive and so hard and so difficult to study. I thought I could never do it. But then I was so happy with that one Montessori course. I knew that I was getting a lot out of it, that I was really being stimulated and raised up by it, you know? I talked to some women there who were going to school nights and I asked a lot of questions about how they managed and they really tried to encourage me. So then it began to seem feasible.

Then I went to talk to the man who's the head of extension, the evening courses at Eastern Connecticut State College. He said, "Why do you want to go?" So I said, "I've always wanted to go to school and I really need it now." I said, "I'm alone and I look around and I want to get a better job someday so I can do more for my kids and myself." So he said, "Do you think you've got the gray stuff to do it?" And I said, "I think I can." He kind of challenged me a little and I was really scared, but then he said, "All right."

I was so scared when I started. I think it took me about three years to begin to feel comfortable. With each course it took almost the whole term before I'd begin to feel comfortable. I hardly ever spoke or asked a question because I thought I'd make a fool of myself. Like if they were discussing something in sociology or psychology, I might have something to say or to ask but I'd die before I would say anything. I'd just kind of listen and I always enjoyed the discussions, but I was afraid to join them. I still don't feel very comfortable unless it's a small group or they're discussing something I know a little about, like children and reading and so on.

I was kind of fortunate to be able to take some of the courses I wanted to take, after the regular intro courses. Like the "kiddy lit" course, which really helped me to learn more about reading and books and children and understanding them. That helped me in my job immediately. Then this last year I took the developmental reading course with a really special teacher, a great older woman. That helped me right away, too, in working with children, and one of the things I learned that was maybe most important to me was that I do know something. I've always had this feeling that I didn't know enough or I didn't know anything or I don't know what I'm doing and I can't do it. Then I began to watch these kids, the things that they were presenting and what they didn't know and I began to think, hmmmm, I'm not so dumb after all!

I'll never forget the first exam I took. It was crazy. I kept saying to myself, "What in the heck are you doing? You can't really do this!" Oh, I had butterflies in my stomach and I was a nervous wreck. And those first couple of years you had all those intro courses with regular exams. I was terrible to live with. I was really grouchy and I'd shut myself in my room and, of course, the minute I'd shut my door, you'd hear, "Mommmmm?" It was so frustrating. I think they kind of understood but kids still have a tendency to think, oh yeah, that's true, sure, but Mommmmm? And you can't just overlook it, you know?

When I got a B in that psychology course, the first time I saw that card come in with a B, I let out a whoop and a howl. I told the kids and wow! We were still on welfare then, but we were getting by and maybe I had a few bucks in my bag once in a while. But if we were going to splurge, we'd go out and have pizza pies. For nine kids, that takes a lot of pizza. But it was so great. And this was the kind of thing that kept me going at that time. My life to some people was maybe boring. Maybe a lot of work. And there's no doubt that I had a lot to do to keep going. But it kept me from thinking too much about my problems, and by then I was beginning to see my way clear of them and straighten things out.

I've been at Montessori now for five years, but I really feel that I know very little about it. It's like so many things, I guess. The more you learn about it, the more you want to learn and the more you realize you need to learn. I guess I really do have a thirst for knowledge in general. But with the Montessori method, I've got practical knowledge in working with children now, and I want to go more into her theories and some of the materials that deal with more advanced things.

Doing this kind of thing keeps you young. And it's interesting, taking courses. There've been times—like between semesters when I had nothing to do and especially when I was single—I found life to be dull and boring. I needed something else, that challenge, to really stimulate me. And, at the same time, it gave me an awful lot of satisfaction. I think that's one of the biggest reasons that anybody would want to do it, whether you get a degree or not. It's the kind of thing where you can take pride in yourself and feel like a decent human being. And so many people today just really feel so put down.

So I think it gives you a lift. And I think in some ways I can be a better mother, because I feel better about myself.

I feel that I'm just on the way to becoming a good teacher. I really want to get there and I think being a good Montessori teacher is trying to help children to be themselves, be happy with themselves. But to know themselves first of all, even before the math or the English or the reading or whatever. I think that's where the psychology comes in. Then a lot of it is trying to help children work on their own, to have self-discipline, and that's one thing I have a healthy respect for.

There's still times I really feel so insecure and so inferior for some reason. The first year it was really hard for me to say I was a teacher. I just felt it's dishonest, because I'm not a teacher. This one friend at Montessori is a great one for telling me off. Oh, she'd get angry about that. The second year it was a little easier to say I was a teacher. Now, this is my fifth year teaching and my third as head teacher for the afternoon. There's also a head teacher in the morning. It's just lately now that I'm beginning to feel I can do it.

We've seen things happen to children that are really beautiful. It's really exciting. Our dream is for some kind of foundation or something to give us any old building. With everybody's labor, the parents and all of us, we could just repair it, repaint it, rebuild it if necessary and have our own school. Now we just have nursery school, but we'd like to have a kindergarten, maybe a first grade and someday a day care center.

I think I was divorced before I really got into all these changes in thinking about women's roles. With me it became more of an awareness growing out of the things that happened to me. Like the feeling when you're on your own that you're kind of a second class citizen because you're female. Especially with all the financial things. I was lucky because I had my own home already, but I had to establish my credit and things like that and I could see there was a difference.

Then my friends at school who I work with, some of them are great women's libbers. I just began to talk to these people and read magazines and think about things. Probably a lot of what happened to me wouldn't have been as easy for me to think out if I hadn't had friends who were so really up on things, like around the university. At school, only one other teacher besides me is not a faculty wife. And then there are all the faculty wives in the Mothers' Group. So that has definitely been a big influence on me. I've been learning a lot of things just being with these people. They've traveled a lot and they know a lot. It's just a rich, rich environment for me. And the friendships—at times when I really needed support, that was the kind of support I got.

I guess I've always been a little strong-minded about doing things, and yet I was always put down for it by marriage counselors and people like that. I think what the movement did is it made me realize that there's nothing unusual or wrong about having a strong feeling about wanting to do something and going ahead and doing it, without being aggressive in the bad sense. I think the marriage counselors and the psychiatrists, the social workers, these people all have to be brought up to date, you know, raised up. I think a lot of them still have those old criteria of a woman and a man. They really go back to Freud.

Sometimes I think the Women's Movement could be like civil rights, where you reach a certain point and then you step kind of backward again. Like with civil rights, there was an initial impetus and we were equipped for a while and then it slowed down in certain areas. And in some areas it still isn't very good. In a way I think the Women's Movement is similar, but I also think it's one of these evolutionary things that has just got to come about. Maybe it will take longer in some areas. There's an awful lot of people now who have bad feelings about it, probably mostly because they don't understand it.

It's funny, but I see two worlds. Around the university here, I see great improvement and really exciting things happening. And then when I visit some relatives in the city, or like some of the women here in the rural area, it's depressing to see that they're just so unaware. They say, "Women's lib, ugh." They're kind of afraid of it. They're a little puzzled and confused and they don't have the opportunities or the thought-provoking things that you might have in some places, like consciousness-raising groups or something along those lines. But I think there's a certain amount of change even without some people being aware of it.

I'm hoping my daughters' environment when they grow up will be a little more enlightened. I'd like them to have college or training, like for all my children. But if they prefer some kind of manual trade, fine, if that's what they really want. It doesn't make any difference. But I want my girls to know that they should do something, try to find out what they like to do and get some training for it.

I don't really feel that everybody has to go to college, but I'd like to see the girls at least have an equal chance. The way I put it across them is I say, "Suppose you do get married and suppose something happens and you're alone? You should really have what you'd like to do to stand by on." But I think at this age you can't really stress the satisfaction part of it too much. I think they're a little too young to understand that yet.

Looking back on the Mothers' Group, I think one of the best things was that it was a chance for low-income women and middle class women just to know about each other. I think it's good for the low-income people to know that there's something better and most of all to know that there's somebody who cares and wants to help them. And I think it's good for all people to be aware of the fact that there are people who have less, because it's so easy to forget. Maybe it's because we've got some really special people who started the thing going and created such a good atmosphere, but a lot of good came from it.

It's funny, though, I still feel closer to the poor women in the group who I became friends with. I still feel like I'm one of them. With the others, I don't know if it's the clothes and the travels, or their thinking or their knowledge and the experience they've had, the way they know how to handle things or whatever. But they've got something that . . . even if I've got brand new clothes on, the latest style, or I live in a nice big house, I don't think I could ever have. Deep down in my heart I still feel more a part of the lower income group. There's something there that I'm more sympathetic to, that's more me.

There've been times in the last year or two where we've been invited to people's homes, beautiful homes and wonderful people. Everything was great. But I kind of feel like a fish out of water. I don't feel completely uncomfortable, but if I stop and think about it I feel I really don't belong there. So I guess you don't ever really deny that background. Maybe if you were young and you went away to college it might be different. But at the same time, I really feel lucky. If I've been able to buy myself a new leather bag or something like that, I feel part of the fortunate group, the ones who have a lot, and it's great to enjoy and indulge yourself.

There are still times when I'll go into a middle class group like that and I feel like I don't want to say a thing. I really feel out of it. Part of it is you don't feel you know as much. Then sometimes, like at school, I'll use a larger word and I feel uncomfortable with it because I'm not sure I'm pronouncing it right. Part of feeling that I wasn't a teacher was that I didn't have the lingo. Like if people said something like, "The child is hyperkinetic," I'd say to myself, "What does that mean?"

It's like when you look at a person, you see a picture and maybe you can change the picture, but it's pretty difficult to change the way they talk. You could take any poor person to a store and have their hair done and get them brand new clothes and everything, but when they open their mouths, that's when the truth comes out. Then you really get to see what they are. And this is why I guess they're often afraid to speak up. Because if they say something, they're proving that they know less and then they feel like they *are* less.

I think it's an American thing, too. In other countries it seems people with a trade are looked up to more. We put so much of an accent on college, even though a plumber can make more than most teachers probably. Maybe with all this change and the new technology where trades people can make more than some people with college degrees, maybe someday the scales will balance and people will have respect for a technician as well as a college graduate.

Yesterday was the first day that I ever had a day off from work when the kids weren't home, because Teresa, my youngest, just started to go to school all day. It's really a strange feeling when the house is quiet and I can hear nobody but myself. It's almost never happened in my life. There have been one or two days when Don was home and the kids were with their father and maybe we had a little time alone. Sometimes I just dream of being able to say, "Today I can stay home, lie in bed all day if I want to, read, or just clean the house from top to bottom." I'd just love to have one or two days to do all the cleaning and fixing I wanted to do. And maybe flower arranging. Who knows? Most of all, the quiet. There's always been so much noise.

Someday we'd like to retire to Jamestown in Newport Bay, where my mother had a lot that she left us. Then again, twenty years from now who knows what that place will be like? Maybe there'll be big buildings all along the coast there. Who knows? I'd like to think that there'll be at least some land where it'll be quiet and peaceful with just trees and ocean. Just you and the ocean.

I guess I'm an eternal optimist. There's a lot of things I worry about but I'm not hopeless about them. All these new problems that we keep learning about like the gas from spray bottles that supposedly goes up in the atmosphere and is going to destroy our protective screening. All the pollution and the energy problems and the food additives you always have to be looking out for, that's all pretty scary. On the other hand—this goes back to my religious training again—I just don't think that God created all this beauty on this earth to just let it destroy itself.

My faith is still important to me. I think it's a basic part of a human being that you need to have a faith or belief in something. If you don't, when something happens to you you're more apt to fall apart because you don't have that structure inside of you. I think there were a lot of times in my life that my faith really helped me pull through. Maybe it was blind faith then, but I still have faith in my Church and that God will show us the way to perfect the Church. The impurities, the things that are wrong with it are man-made. It's not what Jesus Christ said or what the Bible said that is wrong. It's what the popes did and what we did. What man did.

Anyway, there must be a solution to inflation and pollution and energy, all these things. The government should do more, but I think we have to be aware of what it is in human nature that kind of makes people look the other way and pretend it's not there. I'd really like to see more people get involved in things and get out and vote in the elections. In my own small way I've been active in politics locally for years and I always felt strongly that every vote counts, but a lot of people still don't. Maybe the Women's Movement will help, because it's making women more aware that they can exercise their own vote; they don't have to vote as their husband does.

Television could maybe help in making people more aware too. There's an awful lot of things on TV that are just a waste of time. And there's an awful lot of indoctrinating of young children to the old sexist roles too. But TV is where you reach most of the people. And for women, well, there are some women who really like soap operas. So why couldn't they lift up soap operas to the point where they might be almost educational and put across good ideas? I imagine that some of these writers in the TV studios may be enlightened. That would be a great way to reach more people.

Another thing that could happen to get people involved locally is a community school kind of thing. People are going to have more and more leisure time, so if you were to take the schools—and they're beginning to do this—and use them year-round and nightly, you could try and get people involved in education and recreation and fun things related to the community.

If you put a political thing on TV, people often aren't in the mood for it. They're tired, they want something relaxing, and they're going to shut it off. You can't approach it by throwing it at them; you've got to have them come together for something they need, like education or recreation. When people start talking together and saying how they feel, maybe you'll have people becoming more interested and learning more and being more aware, and maybe they can get together and start electing the kind of candidates they want. I think we'll find the answers as we go along, if we try.

● POSTSCRIPT

Last spring, the Montessori School was asked to look for other quarters. The premises of the Lutheran Church in Storrs, which had housed the school, were becoming overcrowded. At that time, the school's director was in England on a sabbatical, one teacher was moving away and two others were ill. The job of finding a new home for the school fell to Terry Dezso. "I was determined," she said, "not to let the school go down the drain. It had been in existence for fourteen years and was doing such a great job."

Her search began. Many of the town's other churches were already housing day care centers. Terry embarked on what she calls "an incredible education." She first had to learn the intricacies of state licensing requirements, and of health and fire codes, which automatically eliminated most buildings. She eventually found a house that would have been suitable for the school but "the neighbors were up in arms and fought us at an emotional public hearing. We did get some publicity for our cause, but I feel that in at least two neighborhoods in town my name has become notorious."

When finding a building to lease seemed like a dead end, Terry met with a mortgage banker, learned about the investment field and proposed a plan to the parents involving the construction of their own building. The parents felt that was too large an undertaking. "I came home from meetings so frustrated, almost in tears once, because I just wanted to get us a place to continue our school, and they didn't seem to see the immediacy of the problem."

Finally, Terry found a home, a new "raised ranch," which met the state requirements. Again the neighbors protested. A zoning permit was needed and Terry was frequently attacked at zoning board meetings as "that woman." In the meantime, she persisted in looking for workable compromises. For example, she sought advice from a landscape architect at the university on what kinds of shrubs to plant for hedges and how far apart they should be so that the school would be out of the neighbors' view.

By a vote of five to four, the zoning board finally awarded the school a permit to locate in that residential area. But several neighbors brought suit against the school, putting a halt to the move for now. Among other complaints, they claim that their property values will decrease and that the school will create a traffic problem. "In reality," Terry said, "the house sits right on a main thoroughfare, less than a half-mile from a public school, and almost directly across the road from a town dump. I think the people who are suing are just a few, slightly fanatic individuals out for a cause."

The town council is still defending the zoning board's decision, but the board of the Montessori School is now debating the need to hire an attorney. In the meantime, the school is still operating in the Lutheran Church and has a new and innovative all-day program for the benefit of working parents. And if this plan falls through, there are now other possibilities. One board member whose child had attended the school offered to invest $25,000 in a new building.

In addition to being a learning experience, the struggle of the past six months and the expertise she acquired will earn Terry college credits through a new program called SWEAT—Students Work Experience with Applied Theory. The "stacks" of newspaper clippings she has saved will be put to use when she writes about the experience for her course. "Who knows, it may be long enough to be a book."

While teaching and "SWEATing," Terry is also taking several college courses. Last spring she finally was able to attend college as a full-time student. Although she felt somewhat strange having recent high school graduates as classmates, she found the experience rewarding. She plans to graduate in 1976 and is already thinking about taking additional courses, perhaps toward a master's degree.

Anticipating her graduation Terry said, "I'm wondering what it would be like to have nothing to do!" She is not only still a head teacher, but has also become director of the Montessori School and chairwoman of the board. "Everyone was so busy during all of this," she remarked, "that the whole thing just kind of got dumped in my lap."

Two of Terry's older and more adventuresome sons have moved out west to work—one "who's a ski nut" to Aspen, the other to Tucson. Talking about the younger children, she said, "For the first year since our drastic move and my remarriage they seem settled and more secure, and as a result they're doing much better in school." Don has been extremely supportive, accompanying Terry to the more heated hearings and, in general, helping her to "keep on going."